SALVATION HISTORY

SALVATION HISTORY

A BIBLICAL INTERPRETATION

Eric C. Rust

JOHN KNOX PRESS
RICHMOND, VIRGINIA

Library of Congress Catalog Card Number: 62-19459

BT
751.2
R8

Second printing 1964

© M. E. Bratcher 1962
Printed in the United States of America
9814 (20) 6505

To the memory of
H. Wheeler Robinson and T. W. Manson
Inspiring teachers and profound biblical scholars

PREFACE

This book is concerned with the biblical understanding of history and analyzes the biblical testimony. In our time the problem of a Christian theology of history has become critical for our understanding of the Christian faith. Christians are bound to the particularity of history and to a historical revelation. They are realists in the sense that they take time and this world seriously.

Historical experience is the realm within which God is pleased to encounter and redeem man. There is no mystical escape from the world but rather a positive affirmation of it as the realm within which man's redemption is wrought out by a gracious God. The center of the Christian faith is the incarnation, the affirmation that God has lifted up history into his own life, and in so doing has redeemed all history. The relevance to this of the biblical testimony is the major theme of this book.

In the course of the discussion, matters such as biblical criticism and the nature of biblical language and imagery are discussed. The major concern, however, is how such issues enable us to understand the eschatological import of the revelation in Jesus Christ. For evidently the biblical understanding of history is eschatological, and the relation of biblical eschatology to the incarnation, the cross, and the resurrection occupies the central place in this biblical study.

Portions of this book have previously appeared in articles in several journals: *Theology Today*, October 1953, "Time and Eternity in Biblical Thought"; *Journal of Bible and Religion*, January 1959, "Possible Lines of Development of Demythologizing," and January 1961, "Interpreting the Resurrection"; *Review and Expositor*, April 1959, "The Apologetic Task in the Modern Scene," and January 1960, "The Authority of the Scripture—The Word of God and the Bible."

In writing this book I am indebted to my friends Dr. Raymond Brown and Dr. Glenn Hinson, members of the faculty of the Southern Baptist Theological Seminary, and to my son-in-law, Mr. J. M. Smith, a student at the Seminary, for generously reading and criticizing the full manuscript. To other friends who have read portions of it and suffered from its contents in the give and take of discussion, I express my thanks. Mrs. Glenn Hinson has proved herself, as ever, a competent secretary. The typing of this manuscript and her patience with the vagaries of its author place him more firmly in her debt. My wife and family have patiently borne with an absentee husband and father while this book was being written. Their love and fellowship have for many years made the life of teaching and study a joy to me. And I would express appreciation to the editors of John Knox Press for their insight and co-operation as this manuscript has been prepared for publication.

The dedication of this book to the late Professor T. W. Manson and the late Principal H. Wheeler Robinson is a very inadequate tribute to two men who shaped my understanding of the biblical revelation, whose scholarship has provided a continuing challenge to my own academic life, and whose devotion to the Christ has inspired me often in the sometimes arid wastes of critical biblical scholarship.

Eric C. Rust

CONTENTS

PAGE

CHAPTER I   HISTORY AND REVELATION   11

1. The Nature of the Historical in Biblical Thought   12
2. Special Revelation and the Meaning of History   17
3. The Word and the Testimony—The Modes of God's Approach to Man in Salvation History   25
4. The Background of General Revelation—Salvation History in Secular History   28
5. The Nature of Religious Thinking and Its Relation to Salvation History   33
6. Demythologizing and the Validity of the Biblical Imagery   38

CHAPTER II   THE HISTORICITY OF SALVATION HISTORY   49

1. Salvation History and Historical Criticism   50
2. The Failure of Historical Explanation in the Old Testament   57
3. Historical Explanation and the Historical Jesus   67
4. The Historicity and Uniqueness of the Resurrection   75
5. The Certainty of Faith and Historical Knowledge   84

CHAPTER III   THE ESCHATOLOGICAL STRUCTURE OF SALVATION HISTORY UNDER THE OLD COVENANT   91

1. The Covenant and the Promises   91
2. Judgment and Promise in the Vicissitudes of History   102
3. Prophetic Eschatology—The Remnant and the Messiah   108
4. Postexilic Eschatology—The Son of Man and the Age-to-Come   125
5. The Emergence of Legalism   130

CHAPTER IV   SALVATION HISTORY—THE FULLNESS OF TIME AND THE KINGDOM OF GOD   134

1. The Graeco-Roman World and the Fullness of Time   135
2. The Apostolic Kerygma and the Fullness of Time   142

3. *The Nature of Fulfillment*   149
4. *Jesus and the Kingdom of God*   157

CHAPTER V   SALVATION HISTORY—INCARNATION
                     AND REDEMPTION   171

1. *The Kingdom and the Incarnation*   171
2. *The Background of Secular History—Sin and the
   Flesh*   182
3. *The Kingdom in Secular History—Judgment and the
   Christ*   186
4. *The Demonic Bondage of Historical Man*   194
5. *The Cross and the Kingdom*   199
6. *The Sacrifice of the Son of Man*   208
7. *The Triumph of the Son of God*   213
8. *The Resurrection and Exaltation of the Crucified
   Lord*   219

CHAPTER VI   SALVATION HISTORY—THE CHURCH
                     AND ITS ESCHATOLOGICAL
                         FRAMEWORK   229

1. *The Christian Eschatological Framework*   230
2. *The Gift of the Spirit and the New Humanity*   244
3. *The Church and the Reign of Christ*   249
4. *The Church in the World—The Mission to the
   Nations*   258
5. *The Church in the World—The State and the Cosmic
   Powers*   267

CHAPTER VII   SALVATION HISTORY—THE PAROUSIA
                     AND THE CONSUMMATION   277

1. *Jesus and Apocalypticism*   277
2. *Jesus and the Parousia*   284
3. *The Parousia in the Apostolic Witness*   293
4. *The General Resurrection and the Age-to-Come*   305

Index of Authors   313

Index of Passages Cited   316

CHAPTER I

HISTORY AND REVELATION

The Christian faith is intimately bound up with history. It does not spring from rational speculation or from mystical identification with the Spirit of the universe. A rational faith depends upon man's ability to arrive at a knowledge of the divine power behind the universe by discursive argument, no matter where in space or time man chooses to begin his logical development. No moment of human history is distinctive, and the experience of man at any time or in any place has no necessary priority over human experience elsewhere.

Mystical faith leaves all outward phenomena and concentrates on man's inward and subjective experience. No matter where man is located in space or time, his mystical absorption in the one Spirit is open to him, and the ineffable experience of identification with the mystery behind the universe is possible.

But the Christian does not begin with rational argument or mystical experience. He begins with a confrontation by God in human history. God has chosen to disclose himself not as the end point of a rational argument or in a mystical identification available in man's subjective deeps. He has chosen to disclose himself in and through certain particular historical events—through an exodus of a slave people from Egypt, through the vicissitudes of Israel's history as interpreted in the prophetic consciousness, through the mystery of the incarnation, through the death and resurrection of a humble carpenter.

Faith is man's commitment to this disclosure, a saving response which, to use contemporary jargon, is existential. It is a decision which is expressed in a man's life and produces a definite form of existence. Faith also involves an understanding of the divine, an awareness of God which is expressed in certain images and symbols.

Such a faith does not make history the ultimate reality. History is not identified with God, and its process is not regarded as the development of the divine life. God is immanently active in history, but he is also other than and beyond history. This implies that history has meaning for God. It is the scene for the actualization of his purpose. Yet even his creation of the realms of nature and history is an act of grace. God is not compelled to express himself in this way. He suffers no inner deficiency, for he is a perfection of love in his own triune nature.

The biblical faith affirms that God's creation of the world and his government of history have resulted from the gracious intention to share his own innermost bliss as love with creatures who can freely respond to it. So, in his grace, God sustains nature and history alike over the brink of nothingness, and actualizes his intention within them. His creatures may freely make the universe into the theater of his glory.

1. The Nature of the Historical in Biblical Thought

What, then, is history? We might define it as the totality of events in time in which man is actively involved. In this sense, we should not speak of nature as having a history, and the story of evolution prior to the advent of man would not be history in this specific sense. History is concerned with past human activity in all its diversity, the expression of human freedom as man responds to and struggles with his environment, as man lives in relationship with his fellow men, and as man encounters the ultimate mystery behind the universe. Yet history, in this sense, would be a bare chronicle of the past, a haphazard heaping together of a multiplicity of apparently unrelated and atomized happenings. This is just what history, in the deeper sense, is not.

The historian is not just concerned with chronicling and recording the past—with *Historie*, as the Germans call it. He is concerned with recovering some meaningful pattern out of the past which reveals the true significance of events. History has its inner meaning, which we must comprehend in order to grasp its secret. For this meaningful record of history—history as a remembered and significant past—the German language fortunately has a second word, *Geschichte.* It is with this understanding of history that we are concerned.

Every historian is concerned with doing two things. The first is recovering what actually happened in the past. The second is gathering past events into a significant pattern of meaning. In the case of the first concern, sources and records have to be weighed and analyzed; artifacts and historical remains have to be examined; an attempt has to be made to arrive at some objective judgment. But no historical judgment is free of the subjective element, and there is no such thing as a bare historical fact. The human factor has to be reckoned with in the end.

Eyewitness and chronicler record from their own points of view, and always the historian is left with some uncertainty. He never has the dogmatic assurance about his historical facts in all their details that the scientist has in his laboratory when he is investigating some natural phenomenon. The historian's fact is shut up in the past and not directly open to his observation. It is bound up with the irreversible flow of time and cannot be repeated. He knows it only through the records and eyewitness accounts that come to him. He may be able to reconstruct the atmosphere of the time, but he always must reckon with the human factor. This is especially evident in our approach to the biblical record, and it is the basis of the science of biblical criticism, the higher criticism as it is called. The biblical critic endeavors to arrive at the bare historical actuality, always knowing that he has to reckon with the attitude of the witnesses by whom the event is recorded.

The second concern of the historian is that of meaning. Historical actualities are of interest to a historian only insofar as they have meaning. He endeavors to gather events into a meaningful pattern. The pattern is woven around some continuing event, such as the biography of some historical figure, the development of some branch of culture, the movement of a war or revolution, the persistence of a national group. The historian will select events and evaluate them as he judges them significant for the pattern he is weaving. At this point the attitude of the historian himself comes into play, for he will have his own point of view on the subject.

It is true that a good historian will form a point of view on the basis of the evidence at hand. Yet it is not rational argument, but imaginative sympathy with past events, accompanied by an intuitive insight, which leads him to the key of the pattern he is seeking to weave. However, this pattern must always be true to the historical actuality with which he is concerned. Here is his objective standard. He has to begin with the pursuit of the historical actuality and, as he handles this, his intuitive insight may come and his sympathetic imagination can function.

This concern with meaningful history that also seeks for a true objectivity is largely a product of the modern era, yet its roots go back to the Greeks and the Hebrews. The Greek did not believe that anything significant was accomplished in history; nevertheless, he did attempt to record faithfully the events of his time. Herodotus and Thucydides manifest the roots of historical science, insofar as this was possible in those days.

The Hebrews attempted to grasp meaning and to write history as a meaningful pattern of events. The Hebrew was able to do this, more than the Greek, because of his understanding of God as a living, personal reality who acted in history. Yet he lacked the objectivity partially manifested in the more scientific approach of the Greeks to historical actuality.

In consequence, the Hebrew tended to place several traditions from the historical past side by side in his finished document, rather than to attempt a historical appraisal and arrive at some final judgment as to the exact nature of an actual historical happening or situation. Hence the biblical student faces the problem of duplicate traditions and parallel sources. Further, the Hebrew was more concerned with the meaning than with the bare actuality; thus the original event is often hidden by successive attempts to expose its inner meaning.

On the issue of an all-embracing world view, the modern historian works from a different perspective than the metahistorian.

As a critical historian, the former is concerned with evaluating a limited area of world history and drawing out its inner meaning. Here a judicious and critical examination of the evidence is enlightened by intuitive insight and sympathetic imagination. The Greek historian, at a comparatively low level, belongs to this category.

The metahistorical thinker, on the other hand, seeks for an all-embracing meaning in world history—a metaphysics of history. Hegel, Croce, Marx, Spengler, and Toynbee are outstanding examples of this attempt to investigate history in its entirety as possessing an integrating meaning—positive or negative, idealistic or materialistic. Here the Hebrews were pioneers. This faith found its expression from the very beginning in confessions which identified the activity of the living God with certain events in history.[1] It was grounded in the Exodus event and involved the promise of an inheritance in Canaan. This faith seems to have become the interpretative key on the basis of which they sought to understand their own history and the history of the world.

Several strands of historical interpretation can be distinguished in the Old Testament. The oldest appears to be the Yahwistic or J tradition, which viewed the history of Israel from the times of the patriarchs to the entrance into Canaan in the light of the Exodus faith. By adding the stories of creation in Genesis 2—the expulsion from the Garden into the wilderness and one version of the flood—the Yahwistic school showed that they understood their own history as the center of a world history. Behind God the Deliverer from Egypt they saw God the Creator of the world. Behind the chosen people of God they saw man created by God, fallen from his high estate, wandering in the wilderness, and subject to divine judgment. In intention, if not in developed understanding, this J school belongs to that prophetic stream which gave a rich flowering in the oracles of the eighth-century prophets.

---

[1] Gerhard von Rad has found such confessions buried in Deuteronomy (26:5-9) and Joshua (24:17-18). See his *Theologie des Alten Testaments*, Vol. I (München: Chr. Kaiser Verlag, 1958). Cf. G. E. Wright, *God Who Acts* (London: SCM Press, 1952), pp. 70 ff.

The Deuteronomic tradition sought to interpret the history of Israel in the light of this prophetic message, as it was expressed in the doctrine of retribution contained in the Deuteronomic Code.[2] The Code in its present form is the first of a series of Deuteronomic writings continued through Joshua, Judges, 1 and 2 Samuel, and 1 and 2 Kings. In these writings, the recurrent theme of judgment and repentance provides the underlying motif. History is seen in the light of God's dealing with his people in judgment and mercy.

The Priestly school of history writers, who flourished during the Exile and after, were responsible for the final form of the first four books of the Pentateuch. This school included the J tradition, adding other versions of the creation and the flood, thus providing their own version of Israel's history within a setting of world history. To this story of beginnings is added, in the same tradition or in a parallel one from the Levitical singers, the rewriting of later history in 1 and 2 Chronicles, Ezra, and Nehemiah.

This setting of Israel's history within world history indicates that the Hebrew believed quite early that his own history provided the key to all history. The God who had disclosed himself to the people of Israel in historical events was the God of the world, its Creator and Sustainer. What he had done for Israel disclosed both his own nature and his purpose, not for Israel only, but for all mankind. The monotheism implicit in the prophetic work of Moses and explicit in the oracles of the eighth-century canonical prophets also found expression in the traditions and writings of the J school of historians and their successors. We notice that this point of view is no result of speculative thought and discursive reasoning, but of an encounter with the living God in history.

History thus became for the Hebrew a realm in which three factors were significant. First, man was made in God's image, free

---

[2] This Code undoubtedly preserves early covenant traditions and may well go back to Shechem. Cf. Gerhard von Rad, *Studies in Deuteronomy* (London: SCM Press, 1953); A. C. Welch, *The Code of Deuteronomy* (London: James Clarke and Co., 1924).

to live responsibly with his fellows in social relationship, and free to be obedient to God's command and serve his purpose. Second, man was given superiority over nature, which he was to subdue for God's glory. The third and most important factor was the all-embracing reality of a personal God who encountered man in history and laid upon him his demands. History was a realm of free persons in whose social relationships the inner love of God could be reflected. The order of nature was to provide a setting so that all creation might become a theater of God's glory.

2. Special Revelation and the Meaning of History

The Judaeo-Christian tradition is itself a special stream of events, beginning with the call of Abraham and the deliverance of a slave people from Egypt, and consummating in the life, death, and resurrection of Jesus of Nazareth and the creation of a new people of God, the Christian church. The Christian claims that the hidden meaning of history is bound up with the purpose of the living God and that it is here disclosed. Yet this meaning is by no means self-evident. It is not arrived at by argument or reason. What is called the wisdom or learning of this world Paul regards as foolishness (1 Cor. 1:20). Dealing with a Graeco-Roman world in which the Greek emphasis on philosophical reasoning was predominant, the Apostle had to remind his readers that this wisdom was not the correct approach to the inner meaning of the universe and thus of human destiny.

The way of reasoning requires that the starting point not be limited by particularization in space or time. So Greek reason sought that which was universally true and rejected, as has modern reason, the scandal of particularity. To be told that the universal meaning of all things, or the ground of all becoming and existence, was to be discovered in a particular event or events, meant demanding the sacrifice of reason. For reason was concerned with universals—those laws or ideas which suffered no change, thus providing a constant background for the moving images of time.

To find truth man must seek for the unchanging reality behind the changing. No matter where he began his investigation in this realm of space and time, reason should lead him to the same unchanging principles. Like a spectator upon a balcony, he could view the flux of change and move from the particular to the universal, from the concrete to the abstract. He was left with an objective realm of ideas which required of him no commitment and in which he was not actively involved. With pride in his own rational powers, man was able to understand the secret of the universe and thus determine his own destiny. The way of knowledge and salvation was thus a rational achievement, reserved for the aristocrats of the intellect. One is tempted to draw a parallel to the modern cult of scientific knowledge, with its search for universal relations or laws and its belief in the powers of man to control his universe and order his own salvation.

The Judaeo-Christian tradition holds that God is not to be discovered by human reason and that man does not find the secret of his historical destiny written across the face of the universe. Indeed, by his own rational powers, man cannot arrive at the secret of history. God chooses to make himself known in and through a particular stream of historical events. In this stream of events the divine purpose, which is the meaning of all history, becomes dynamically and redemptively active in history. This places the emphasis upon God and not upon man.

God is no static, unchanging substratum of being, discoverable by human reason and expressed in abstract concepts. He is no object of man's thought, with whom man need not become actively involved. He is the living God, a dynamic personal being. He is known only where he chooses to make himself known. He himself takes the initiative and discloses himself to man in such a way that man has to become personally involved with him. God encounters man within the movement of history and through historical particularity. Man cannot evade God; and when God encounters man redeemingly, man becomes involved with and committed to him.

This failure of reason to comprehend God is caused by sin, as portrayed throughout the biblical revelation. The story of the Garden which the Yahwistic historians placed at the beginning of their history holds the key to the human story. The cross of our Lord, which provides the key to the whole pattern of these historical events, is a revelation of man's sinful state. Man is in rebellion against God. The Hebrew emphasis is not upon the reason but upon the will, not upon the intellect but upon man's freedom. The Hebrew sees man as made in God's image, with a capacity to respond to God and live in fellowship with him, and finds the key to man's nature in the freedom and moral responsibility which mark him off from all other creatures. But man's tragedy is that in his arrogance he chooses to set himself up against God and to determine his own destiny. He is in alienation from the ground of being, a creature in contradiction with his own true destiny. He is a being who derives his existence from God, and yet determines his existence as if there were no God. This is the state of historical man.

The story of the Garden presents this truth in symbolism. The story was doubtless once used to explain certain phenomena of human life and of nature. The wearing of clothes, the toilsomeness of labor, the pains of childbirth, the slithering movement of the serpent on its belly—all these issues lie in the background. To emphasize these details is to miss the point, for the story is really concerned with a very profound analysis of sin. Man's sin is rooted in his pride and in a fear for his own security. These lead man to seek security in himself and not in God. Man would thus determine his own existence, for he is certain of his own powers. So, in his arrogance, he sets himself up to be like God. The result is his tragedy. He finds himself outside the Garden, cut off from fellowship with God, and condemned to wander in the wilderness.

In biblical thought, the desert symbolized frustration and meaningless existence. It is the place of chaos and the demonic. Man's life becomes emptied of meaning and without direction. Further, man becomes subject to a demonic bondage from which he cannot escape. For, once man has mishandled his freedom and chosen himself, he must go on making the same kind of choice. His sinful rebellion determines the set of his being, and by no amount of his own planning and devising can he return to the

Garden. The angel with the flaming sword and the barred gate stand as irrevocable symbols for man's tragic bondage. He is a creature of bondage and must remain so, unless God in his mercy comes to his rescue.

This picture explains Paul's despair of human reason and human morality. Neither argumentation nor good works, neither discursive logic nor moral righteousness, can deliver man from sinful pride. His pride in his own powers pursues him on every side. Sin is not just bound up with his sensuous nature. It penetrates the inner sanctuary of his spirit. He cannot escape his love of self and finds himself a prisoner of his own egocentrism.

It is significant that the most important word for sin in the Old Testament, *pesha'*, means rebellion. When Paul speaks of sin in his epistles he uses the word *hamartia* in the singular only to describe a demonic power that holds man in thrall. In this bondage man's mind and reason are as subject as his passions. He is a bond slave of sin, living in the prison house of death.

Hence God's revelation must also be redemption. His self-disclosure must also be an act of deliverance. Apart from such an act of reconciliation and grace, history will continue to be the story of sin and death. It will be life in the wilderness, a realm of alienation in which man alternates between arrogance and hopelessness, pride at his own powers and despair at his demonic bondage. God's revelation must be an act in history which restores man to the divine fellowship and makes possible the actualization of the divine purpose. The meaning of history has to be wrought out in history in a special stream of events in which God acts. The self-disclosure of God is, at the same time, the re-creation of history. History recovers its meaning. To be true to himself God must both condemn sinful man and yet reconcile man with himself, meet the demands of his righteous will and yet show his innermost nature as love.

So the process of revelation in history is consummated in the incarnation. God in the person of his Son enters history as man, and does for man what man cannot do for himself. The scandal of particularity is brought to a focus in Jesus of Nazareth, in whom the whole fullness of the Godhead dwells bodily. This Jesus, being in the form of God, yet takes the form of a slave. God enters history and becomes a part of his own created order, a part in whom the whole meaning of that order is gathered up and actualized. The stream of events in which God discloses himself is therefore called "salvation history."

Yet God's redemptive self-disclosure must be consonant with his purpose. God will never give himself so completely to man that the creature may possess the Creator. That is, indeed, impossible. How can the finite possess the infinite? Man must learn to walk by faith and not by sight, by trust and not by self-confident reason. Furthermore, it is the mystery even of finite personality and love that there must always be an element of hiddenness at its heart. One can never give himself completely to another person, never be completely possessed by the other. Personality always retains mystery at its heart. Even as one discloses himself in communication, he still remains mystery. The other person may increasingly love and trust and have confidence in him, but such love and trust are never of the order of mathematical and rational certainty. The knowledge of love involves mystery. We cannot solve the mystery of personality as we solve a scientific problem. The mystery remains mystery even when some of its heart is disclosed.

Human fellowship and personal love and trust are central in God's plan, and they owe their very richness and infinite possibilities of creative existence to that aspect of mystery which lies at the heart of human personality. How much more must this be true of the personal infinite God! (1 Cor. 2:1.) If we are to love God for his own sake, to trust ourselves to him in final commitment, we must be cleansed of pride in our own powers—intellectual, moral, and spiritual. Yet certainty about God would beget in us the very pride that would spell our ruin. So God hides himself as he gives himself, and we can know him only by faith and not by sight. Ours is the assurance of love and not the certitude of reason, the knowledge that we are held as we hold on in faith.

At the center of the biblical revelation we find an emphasis on God's holiness, his transcendent otherness. He is the Holy One who inhabits eternity, who hides himself even as he discloses himself. He is Israel's God and Saviour, and yet in the very reality of his saviourhood, he is a God who hides himself. Even revelation has its aspect of hiddenness. God comes to us in historical dress, clothing himself in the garb of historical events, and finally in the form of a man. The Apostle Paul speaks of the revelation in Jesus Christ as the opening up of the divine mystery (1 Cor. 2:1-9). For Paul mystery denotes God's hidden or secret purpose, a purpose now disclosed in Jesus Christ.

In Ephesians 1:9-10 Paul speaks of God's having made known the mystery of his will, and declares that this is so to order history that in the fullness of the times all things shall be united in Christ. Jesus Christ gives significance to both human history and the whole cosmos. In him God's secret purpose has been disclosed.

Again, in the Letter to the Colossians, the Apostle speaks of the mystery which was hidden from all ages but now has been manifested to the saints, and defines it as "Christ in you, the hope of glory." History has a hidden meaning, made plain to the saints in Jesus Christ, and actualized in their lives as Christ dwells in them (Col. 1:26-27). As that indwelling takes place, a process of sanctification occurs, culminating in the ultimate glorification of God's Kingdom.

Paul is careful to indicate, however, that the unveiling of God's nature and purpose, the disclosure of the mystery, owes nothing to man's syllogisms or sophisms. To those whose eyes are not opened, it remains hidden. Even as God gives himself in Jesus, he hides himself. The unbeliever, lacking the insight of faith, sees, at best, a good man and a martyr. The believer cries, "My Lord and my God." Hence the Apostle continually emphasizes the function of the Spirit. He is careful to state that the mystery is not disclosed by words of learning and human wit; it is proved by the activity of the Spirit in the believer (1 Cor. 2:4, 10). So a man's faith does not stand in the logic and wit of man, but in the power of God (1 Cor. 2:5). To men who operate solely by their own mental powers, the mystery of God remains mystery. The eternal Word remains veiled in the flesh. God hides himself as he gives himself.

Men grasp the reality of the divine mystery by faith, which itself is awakened by activity of the divine Spirit. That Spirit sets them free from sin. They yield themselves in total commitment to the Christ, as he discloses to them the redemptive grace of God. The whole man is involved here. This is not simply an activity of the human wisdom. It is a total act of the personality. A man becomes aware of the divine grace as that grace becomes operative in his life and begins the actualization of the divine mystery in his own living. So the purpose of God becomes actualized in history and Christ becomes a potent indwelling presence in the believer. This process moves toward that final actualization which is the glorification of personality in the fellowship of God's consummated Kingdom.

The revelation of the hidden meaning of history is thus, for the biblical testimony, a mediated revelation. It comes through history itself. In the movement of salvation history the hidden purpose of God is disclosed as it is actualized. It can be grasped only as it becomes operative in a man's own personality, as demonstrated by the power of the Spirit. John (7:17) records the declaration that he who does God's will shall know. The knowledge of revelation is no result of discursive argument and human wit, but is grounded in the will, in that commitment of the total personality to God in Christ which the Bible calls faith.

God approaches men through the medium of his creatures in the biblical understanding of revelation. The creatures may thus veil God and the mystery of God's nature and purpose remain hidden, unless our blind eyes are open to the glory of his presence. In the events of salvation history, God comes always veiled in flesh. It is through the humanity of the prophets and the "flesh" of Israel's history that God chooses to confront Israel. It is through the human life of his Son that God in the fullness of time savingly encounters man. The principle of incarnation holds not only of the central redemptive act in Jesus of Nazareth but throughout salvation history. To understand God's revelation we must find him veiled in flesh.

Despite the mediated nature of the revelation, it is immediate encounter. The biblical testimony is clear that through the historical events man is directly addressed by God. John can declare: "That which was from the beginning, which we have heard, which we have seen with our eyes, which we have looked upon and touched with our hands, concerning the word of life" (1 John 1:1). Just as through the bodily words and gestures of human beings one has direct encounter with the other person even though the presence be mediated, so God directly encounters his creatures, while at the same time using the creaturely orders of nature and history to mediate his presence. Thus the biblical faith avoids any danger of pantheism or mysticism. Nature and history are not divine, transient modifications of the divine substance. They exist by their own right under God. He has granted to them freedom and yet dependence upon his own sustaining power. Their space and time have been given them that, in his creatures with their measure of freedom and dependence, his purpose may be fulfilled.

Creatures are not one with God, and man's spirit is not the divine Spirit. Yet man's spirit provides the point of contact between God and his creature. Man is made in God's image, capable of being addressed. And when God addresses him, there is no mystic escape from this world, no flight from the alone to the alone. God directly encounters man through the medium of his created order. And because the presence is mediated, God hides himself as he gives himself. Sinful man cannot arrogantly claim a mystical oneness with the divine or assert that he has a nature which belongs to God alone. His knowledge is the knowledge of faith and commitment, the certainty that trembles on the brink of rational uncertainty, the trust that stands poised on the razor edge of doubt. Man knows himself to be addressed by God, to be loved by God. But always God hides himself as he gives himself, so that man's certainty rests in no human capacity but in the divine grace, in the illumination of the Holy Spirit. In faith man lays hold of God by whom he is first addressed and knows himself to be held.

3. The Word and the Testimony—The Modes of God's Approach to Man in Salvation History

The biblical record preserves the transcendence and immanence of God in historical revelation by the symbol the "Word of God." This is the distinctive way in which God's relation to and action within the historical order is understood. In this connection, "Word" must not be limited to verbal expression. The Hebrew equivalent, *dabar,* can stand for "deed" or "event," as well as "utterance," and as such it must be understood when used of the living God. It covers the whole gamut of the divine activity in creating, sustaining, and redeeming the creaturely order. Thus the Word is the characteristic mode of creation and revelation.

The Word of God both discloses God and transforms the human situation. In Hebrew thought, even at the human level, the word was thought of concretely. When a man uttered a word, especially in the case of blessing or curse, something of himself went into his utterance. Once the word had been uttered, it carried within itself the personal intention of the one who had uttered it, became an extension of his personality, and accomplished his purpose. This meaning is even more present in the image of the "Word of God."

God's Word is a concrete extension of the divine presence into the created order. At the moment of creation, it is the dynamic, creative principle by which the chaos is transformed into cosmos, and the formless and void deep becomes the world of which the Creator can say that it is good, very good.[3] When the Word of God comes to the prophets and they speak to the situation in which they are involved, the Word becomes a creative element in that situation, for God's Word shall not return empty to him but it shall accomplish his intention (Isa. 55:10-11).

Such a Word may come to the prophets through visions presented to the eye as well as through auditions. Always it is bound up with the divine activity in history. God shows himself through the concrete situations of historical existence, and the history of

---

[3] Genesis 1; Psalm 147:15-18.

Israel centers in his mighty acts. Such historic deeds become the
turning points of Israel's history, and, as such, are revelatory of
the nature and purpose of God himself. Yet they are so only because in and through them God's Word comes to his prophets
and they testify to what they have seen and heard, conveying
God's Word to their hearers.

The crossing of the Red Sea and the divine manifestation on
Sinai in the thunder and the lightning were meaningful and creative in the life of Israel because in and through them the Word
came to Moses, who transmitted it to the people. Again, the successive imperial activities of Assyria and Babylon became spiritually formative in the history of the Hebrew people because they
were also divine acts in the history of that people. In them God
spoke his Word to Isaiah and Jeremiah respectively, so that they
bore their testimony to his presence in judgment and in promise.
God's Word also came through Cyrus the Persian to a people in
exile, because even through this historical upheaval, the Second
Isaiah saw that God was still the Holy One of Israel, its Redeemer, whose historical intervention commanded the activity of
the Persian hosts.

In the New Testament the central conviction is that God has
intervened in history in a unique way by clothing himself fully
in our humanity. Once more the divine activity in described in
terms of the Word—the Word become flesh. Jesus is not a prophet
through whose human testimony the Word of God reaches man.
The prophet found his authority in the Word of God which was
given to him, but Jesus carried his authority in himself—he *is* the
Word. The prophet in his testimony called on men to repent and
believe in God, but Jesus demanded faith in himself. The words of
the prophet pointed beyond himself to God who had spoken the
Word to him, but the words of Jesus pointed to himself. His words
were thus identical with the Word, in a way that the words of the
prophet could not be. They were Spirit and they were life (John
6:63). If men abode in his words, they abode in him (John 8:31).
The Word of God is not given to Jesus as something distinct from
him; it is Jesus himself. Here the divine action in history becomes
identical with the words Jesus utters and the deeds he performs,

because it is identical with his person. God becomes personally present in history, even though still veiled by the humanity of Jesus of Nazareth.

The evangelists and apostles of the New Testament are those to whom this incarnate Word came with compelling and re-creating power. Their witness, like that of the prophets before them, points to the Word of God which they have received, but the Word they utter is not what Jesus taught but Jesus himself. Their proclamation, *kerygma,* is Jesus Christ, manifest in their verbal witness and in the testimony of their lives, individual and corporate.

Another biblical word which should be noted is "testimony" or "witness." The Word of God which comes to the prophets is proclaimed by them in their testimony. They interpret to men the divine meaning of the historical situation in which the Word has come to them. Thus the situation embraces the historical actuality and its interpretation, and as such it constitutes a revelatory event. The witness of the prophets points to such events, declaring the Word of God, the divine self-disclosure, in them. As such this witness, although it is the word of man, becomes the bearer of the Word of God. In Lutheran language, the Word of God is in, with, and under the testimony of the prophets. The prophetic witness is God testifying concerning himself through a man's inspired testimony of what he has seen and heard.[4]

Such witnessing is at one and the same time a proclamation and a confession. It proclaims what God has said in the concrete confrontation of history, and it confesses the faith of the witness in the living God, his own recognition of and commitment to the God who has spoken. Such witnessing is inspired, for only God can open men's eyes to his presence, lift the veil in the historical mediating event, and only God can direct aright their testimony to what they have seen and heard. The human response to revelation is faith.

In the New Testament also, the witnesses are those who have

---

[4] Cf. Sigmund Mowinckel, *The Old Testament as Word of God* (Nashville: Abingdon Press, 1959), p. 129.

seen in Jesus of Nazareth the One whom God has sent, the Word incarnate. Although one important element in such testimony is the eyewitness relationship to the incarnate Lord, to his life, passion, and resurrection, yet even this is not a necessary requirement. Such a requirement did not exclude Paul. The significant factor was that the evangelists and apostles had received grace to acknowledge Christ as the risen Saviour and Lord, and to testify to this. It is the coming of the Word in the flesh conjoined to their inspired insight, confession, and testimony that constitutes the revelatory situation.

The Word of God is thus a description of the divine self-disclosure in and through history which at the same time re-creates history. If the history of sinful and fallen man is generally one of frustration and meaninglessness, the events of salvation history, while occurring within it, also transform and redirect it. The divine meaning of history is both disclosed and made effective in history through the special stream of events in which God has chosen to visit and redeem his people. Salvation history is redemptive and re-creative. The incarnation of the Word in Jesus of Nazareth constitutes the center point of a stream of events in which history is being redirected toward the divine purpose and in which man's misuse of his God-given freedom is being corrected. This is the meaning contained in the Hebrew understanding of the Word as both disclosure and creation. God shows himself to be a Saviour, and he shows himself as he dynamically intervenes in history to redeem his fallen creation. This is not something that can be attained by speculative reason, but something that comes in the saving encounter in history, in which God awakens faith and commitment in man.

4. The Background of General Revelation— Salvation History in Secular History

When the tradition preserved in Genesis 1 describes man as created in the image of God, it represents man as capable of being addressed by God. More than replica or copy is conveyed here. It implies that there is a personal approach of God to man outside the realm of special revelation or salvation history. The earlier J tradition of Genesis 2 and 3 describes man as able to walk and converse with God, and we do not understand the full implication of the biblical language unless we interpret it dynamically. Man is a creature capable of fellowship with God, of being addressed by and responding to God, of living in responsible relationship with God. Although the word "image" is not repeated outside the Genesis P tradition as a description of man's unique creaturely status, the whole burden of the biblical testimony, with its emphasis on covenant relationship with God, emphasizes this element of responsibility. And if responsible, man must be free.

On this understanding, the religious consciousness is a manifestation of man's capacity to live responsibly before God. If this be so, there is a general approach of God to man. Furthermore, it is a personal approach in which God lays his claim on man. It takes the form of a personal encounter, and in all human history this approach of God to his creatures is basically involved. History is thus the realm in which man encounters the living God.

The story of the Garden implies that man has rejected this approach of God. Yet life in the wilderness, which is the biblical description of the life of historical man, must not be dismissed as a realm where the living God is not active. It is a realm in which God still approaches man, and in which man still carries a sense of moral responsibility and some capacity for religious response to the universe. This is still God's world, the work of his creation. It still bears the marks of the divine creative activity. Further, it is conserved by God's providential activity, so that his sustaining will is present at every point. Man's capacity to respond is not totally destroyed. Rather, his sinful rebellion has perverted and misdirected it. He remains religious. He still has a conscience, a consciousness of duty, an awareness of moral responsibility.

The religions of the world and the ethical systems of human society testify to the fact that man still retains something of the divine image. The biblical testimony makes no attempt to define this more closely, and theologians of the church have never arrived at unanimity as to what is involved. Their positions range from a complete denial of the presence of the image in sinful man to an almost Pelagian assertion of man's competence to respond to the divine presence.

A phrase that is often on the lips, "total depravity," is so frequently misinterpreted that we need to remind ourselves, from the biblical standpoint, that it does not mean absolute corruption of human nature. Fundamentally it implies that there is no aspect of man's life that is not vitiated by his sinful arrogance and creaturely pride. His religious and moral consciousness is involved here as much as is every other part of his personal being. His response turns upon himself and his pride on his own powers. Religion becomes a religion of works bound up with moral obedience, or a religion of mysticism in which sinful man arrogantly asserts his own divine nature, or a religion of idolatry in which man the sinner elevates some aspect of the created order into the place of the Creator. Morality becomes man's attempt to control and determine his own life, in accord with a moral law which he apprehends and obeys solely by his own powers. It is the morality of duty and not of grace, of works and not of faith. Yet in these aspects of his life, man attains a measure of response which would forbid our arguing that the realm of secular history contains no vision of God and his will, however perverted that vision may be by human egotism and sinful pride.

This is the verdict of the New Testament testimony. Paul, in Acts 14:16-17, declares that God has not left himself without a witness in the regular routine and providence of nature. On Mars Hill the Apostle identifies the unknown God to whom the superstitious have raised an altar with the living God, implying that man's religious response has its ground in the approach of God to him, however veiled and dimmed by man's sin and weakness that approach may be (Acts 17:22-34).

The Letter to the Romans asserts that God's nature can be discerned through his created order (1:18-21), and that the natural law in man's heart is indicative of God's claim on him (2:14-15). This must not be taken to mean that God has left some original mark, some innate knowledge, in man's nature at creation. The Stoic idea of an inherent natural knowledge of God may have contributed here, but fundamentally the emphasis falls on the active and dynamic understanding of God which characterizes the Hebrew tradition. Even in Romans 1, Paul states that the heathen knowledge of God has been made manifest to men by God himself. Whether through the external created order or the inner voice of conscience, there is no emphasis on recollection of innate natural knowledge but the sense of confrontation with a personal being. Paul Tillich states that "an inner revelation must reveal something which is not yet a part of the inner man. Otherwise it would not be revelation but recollection; something potentially present would become actual and conscious."[5]

The dynamic nature of such encounter with God may be indicated by the covenant structure of the Old Testament revelation. Prior to the Sinai covenant in which God chose Israel and shaped it in a succession of mighty acts is the covenant with Noah which embraces all mankind (Gen. 9:8-17). The rabbis later regarded Noah's covenant as the one which made the demands of God binding upon all men. Since, in the biblical testimony, all revelation takes place within a covenant structure, man's rudimentary knowledge of God must spring from an initial approach of God to him and not from an innate endowment. Such an approach of God lies behind man's moral consciousness at its various levels of development and his religious response to the world in its manifold forms.

The Hebrew had no appreciation for causal sequence or for an order of law interposed between God and man. Largely a product of the Greek way of thinking and encouraged by the developing study of scientific law and natural order, this point of view has tended to interpose between God and his creatures an impersonal order. What regularity and order the Hebrew found in nature was an expression of God's direct personal covenant relationship with his creation. As such, it was the immediate personal manifestation of his creative and sustaining will, of his habitual activity. The law of Moses and moral law in general were not given some intermediate and impersonal status governing man's life. They expressed the direct demand of God upon man. Thus

---

[5] Paul Tillich, *Systematic Theology,* Vol. I (Chicago: University of Chicago Press, 1951), p. 125.

what the Greek and medieval thinkers termed secondary causes had a minor place in Hebrew thinking. The biblical testimony is much more aware of the vertical dimension than the horizontal. The horizontal causal sequence in the created order was itself upheld by a vertical causation. At every point it leaned back upon the creative and sustaining will of God, whose presence it manifested and who expressed his sovereign will through it.

Thus all history expresses the personal meeting of God with sinful man. It is true that man in his sin fails or refuses to apprehend the divine presence in its reality. Yet whatever is religiously and morally significant in human nature must be understood in the active sense of God's dealing with that human soul across the long process of history. In absolute demand and final succor God presses in upon man within the process of time.

Sin does not deprive man of moral aspiration or religious response, but it does misdirect him. Paul is quite clear about this (Rom. 1:21 ff.). In the biblical view sin is no mere deficiency but a positive act of will. In religion it is manifested as a rebellious elevation of the created into the place of the Creator. Man's sin leads him to concentrate upon the media of revelation and thus to blind his eyes to the revelation itself. Hence he turns the media into idols, and makes gods out of the order of nature, out of individual men, or out of human societies. He even deifies himself. Naturalistic pantheism, naturalism, polytheism, idolatry, spiritualistic pantheism, mysticism—all provide him with a way by which he can reconcile his religious needs, the movement of God in his soul, with his pride, his sinful egotism. Man perverts the mystery of God by making God in his own image or in the image of the creaturely media of revelation. He misrepresents the revelation and transforms it into idolatry.

Secular history becomes the scene of judgment rather than redemption. Hence, the biblical emphasis on the wrath of God. God gives men over to the sin of their hearts. Yet his wrath is also the reaction of love, for its object is to turn men to repentance, as the Old Testament prophets make abundantly clear. Furthermore, the biblical witness does not reject the thought that some truth about God may be disclosed outside the specific revelation of salvation history. The claim to uniqueness of the latter is very evident. The prophets claim to speak in the name of the living God and deride the pagan deities as either nonentities or subordinated to Jehovah of Israel. The Christian church affirms that there is no other name under heaven whereby men shall be saved except the name of Jesus Christ. But, at the same time, the biblical revelation absorbs into its thought stream ideas and symbols, images and myths, from its religious environment. It is true that these are transformed and filled with new content, but biblical research is revealing that the biblical understanding of God was indebted not only to Greek and Roman but to Babylonian and Egyptian, Canaanite and Persian.

The background of general revelation must not be viewed negatively. Man in his sin did grasp in his religious consciousness some significant aspects of the divine nature and purpose. His religious imagination did weave some images and patterns of the invisible reality which foreshadowed the truth that was to come. Even though he experienced the living God more as wrath than as grace, even though his religious consciousness was strangely perverted by his sin, we cannot see secular history wholly in a negative way. Something of God was breaking through. God's mercy was being faintly recognized, and the light that lightens every man by coming into the world was dispelling man's darkness.

5. The Nature of Religious Thinking and Its Relation to Salvation History

The religious response to reality is intimately bound up with the human imagination. Its language is the language of symbol and myth, metaphor and parable,[6] poetry and drama. The spiritual intimations, emotive experiences, and intuitive insights of the religious consciousness find expression through symbol and

---

[6] There are full discussions of this issue in Ernst Cassirer, *The Philosophy of Symbolic Forms*, 3 volumes (New Haven: Yale University Press, 1953-1957), and W. M. Urban, *Language and Reality* (New York: The Macmillan Co., 1951).

dramatic image. In the general religious consciousness we thus find a preponderance of symbols and myths. Primitive man was very aware of the numinous overtones which surrounded his religious images, and he would never have made the mistake of treating them as fables or legends. They were designed to convey and to evoke the intimations and emotive experiences which were central in his own religious response to reality.

All the religions of the world have myths in which significant images are borrowed from the natural and human realms to describe the life, activity, and nature of the invisible order. The phenomena of the religious life and its significant experiences find expression in a story which uses the processes of the natural order metaphorically and symbolically to describe the life of the gods and their relation with man and the world. Such myths have diverse origins and include those of creation, eschatology, the death and resurrection of a god, and the origins of man's customs. Buried in the obscurity of man's primordial past, these myths embody much of man's prescientific thought about the world and mark the stage before abstract ideas took over.

It is an interesting fact that even in these days of generalized and abstract thought, we still retain concepts which originated in the concrete imagery and metaphorical thinking of myth. One example is the idea of causation. Another is the recent revival by cosmologists (like Fred Hoyle) of the idea of creation, freed from religious associations. In the myth we have, indeed, a strange blending of a prescientific apprehension of nature and a symbolic insight into the heart of reality, the invisible ground of being. In the myth, religious thinking is done in the form of history and narrative.

The fact that all over the world certain primordial images and symbolically dramatic patterns recur is an indication that this is not all purely human fabrication. Man's creative imagination has been at work, but it has been in response to ultimate reality. Because God is the living God, active and dynamic, approaching men everywhere in absolute demand and final succor, we may believe that these images and symbols disclose some insight into the nature and intention of the divine being. So often the religion portrayed is some form of naturalistic pantheism, and the true God is not grasped. Yet the recurrent patterns, such as that of death and resurrection, the Prometheus theme, and the like, re- mind us that there is some insight present, distorted though it may be. Thus general revelation remains revelation, but it lacks its norm.

We must not, therefore, be surprised if salvation history itself sometimes uses the dramatic patterns and symbolic religious images that are found in the surrounding religions of the ancient Near East and the Graeco-Roman world. If the living God is dis- closing himself everywhere, something of the truth will be grasped, however distorted and perverted, in the religious con- sciousness of man. Only in salvation history does God disclose himself redemptively so that man's eyes are opened to the full truth. Hence salvation history is the norm by which the truth in all other religions may be evaluated and the religious conscious- ness of humanity interpreted.

Even in salvation history the understanding of God is still figurative and symbolic. God is envisaged in images borrowed from the visible at the natural and historical level. The images of "father," "husband," "king," "warrior-god," and "judge" are em- ployed again and again. The images of "covenant," "marriage," and "creation" are employed to describe the various relations of God to his creation. Jesus is pictured as the "suffering servant," the "Son of Man" or "heavenly man," the "Son of God." Man is described as in the "image of God." The figures of atonement and redemption occur. The ascension, enthronement, and second ad- vent of our Lord are evidently dramatic symbolism. The stories at the beginning of Genesis describe the history of creation and of man's rebellion and judgment in a figurative pattern, bear- ing some superficial resemblance to pagan myths and yet utterly distinctive.

The language of salvation history which conveys its inner and revelatory meaning is, therefore, dramatic, poetical, and sym- bolic. Yet there is a significant difference, for these images are bound up with historical actuality as those of the pagan religions are not. They give the inner meaning of actual historical events and convey their revelatory significance. Indeed, they are now a significant part of the revelation, for without them there would be no apprehension of the divine and redemptive meaning of salvation. Thus we may say that, in salvation history, the dramatic images and symbols present in the general religious consciousness have been purified and actualized in history. Transfigured by the true and new content they bear, they are now bound up with a historical revelation.

It is unfortunate that, since the time of Voltaire and the Enlightenment, the word "myth" has carried the misleading connotation of the incredible and untrue. Actually, in our analysis, it is a highly imaginative way of describing the life of the invisible order and its relation to the visible. It offers, despite its frequent association with naturalistic forms of the religious consciousness, insight into a realm to which the normal use of language does not apply, for language is molded to the visible. Myth and symbol make an emotive use of language possible, but they are also paths to the understanding of the ultimate mystery. The fact that salvation history still retains the imagery and symbolic patterns evident elsewhere warns us against dismissing the significance of such imagery. The significant point is that in salvation history the imagery is used to describe the inner meaning of that historical actuality whereby the living God discloses himself to his creatures. Furthermore, by being bound up with history, it is freed from the cyclic naturalistic associations in which myth is grounded in the general religious consciousness. Thus the word "myth" is not so applicable to the biblical images.

Some of the images in salvation history are peculiar to the revelation itself. Others seem to be borrowed from neighboring cultures and religious faiths. Thus the kingship ideology of the ancient Near East undoubtedly made its contribution to the understanding of both the Hebrew kingship and messianic hope.[7]

---

[7] Vide A. R. Johnson, Sacral Kingship in Ancient Israel (Cardiff: University of Wales Press, 1955); the essays contributed to Myth, Ritual and Kingship, ed. by S. H. Hooke (Oxford: The Clarendon Press, 1958); Sigmund Mowinckel, He That Cometh (Nashville: Abingdon Press, 1956); Ivan Engnell, Studies in Divine Kingship in the Ancient Near East (Uppsala:

The creation myths of neighboring peoples provide a background for the creation stories of Genesis 1 and 2. The similarities between the P creation saga of Genesis 1 and the *Enuma-elis* myths of the Babylonians are such that we find it difficult to deny interdependence.[8] The myth of a struggle between two great superhuman personalities takes the form of the struggle between Yahweh and the serpent in the Garden story and God and Satan in Job. The myth of a first man or a heavenly man must not be dismissed from the thought of the seer of Daniel or the New Testament image of the Son of Man.[9] Yet, if there were borrowing, the imagery has been re-created or transfigured in the inspired consciousness of prophets and apostles so that it may convey the revelatory meaning contained in those events which culminate in the incarnation, death, and resurrection of Jesus of Nazareth.

We must not overemphasize direct borrowing or influence, however. There are two considerations at this point. One is that if the symbolizing consciousness does embody a response to reality, we might expect similar patterns and images to arise independently. This is certainly true of the creation myths of many widely separated cultures. Further, if our contention of the uniqueness of salvation history be sustained, we might expect that the partial visions of truth grasped elsewhere would be fully displayed in it, and that the movement of the Holy Spirit in the minds of prophets and apostles would make possible a fuller vision of what men have grasped elsewhere, and would do so independently of the background of the general revelation. Where direct influence and borrowing are evident, these do not invalidate our thesis, for the God who approaches men in salvation history approaches men everywhere.

Almquist and Wiksells, 1943). Often these studies are extreme. Johnson's is the most balanced.

[8] Cf. my book, *Nature and Man in Biblical Thought* (London: Lutterworth Press, 1953), pp. 20 ff.

[9] *Vide* the sometimes fanciful work of Aage Bentzen, *King and Messiah* (London: Lutterworth Press, 1955). There is an excellent appendix on the *Urmensch* myth in Eduard Schweizer, *Lordship and Discipleship* (Naperville: Alec R. Allenson, Inc., 1960), pp. 117 ff.; cf. also Mowinckel, *He That Cometh*, pp. 346 ff.

We may to some degree regard the symbolizing consciousness of man as a *praeparatio evangelica,* which is gathered up, purified, and given its true significance when the truth becomes incarnate. The real inspiration comes when a witness is made to see the image in purified and transfigured form as the inner meaning of a historical event. The meaning of inspiration at least must be that the Holy Spirit inspired the imagination of those to whom the revelation was given. Here the divine and human elements are inextricably mingled, and the prescientific cosmology may yet supply elements which are of permanent significance. The latter is, of course, present. God's creative inspiration has worked in and with the contents of the human consciousness. To some extent the imagery represents the way in which the contemporary thought-world was shaped. The three-tier universe and current cosmology often provide the basic material from which the imagery is molded. But God is also creatively present through his Spirit, and the imagery is lifted above contemporary thought-patterns to become contemporary with every time.

6. Demythologizing and the Validity of the Biblical Imagery

We must now consider Bultmann's challenge to demythologize the New Testament message. He points to the obvious fact that the biblical view of the world is completely different from our infinite, expanding universe. It is a "three-storied" structure. It shows no knowledge of our scientific outlook, but speaks instead of angels and demons, heaven and hell, and believes that men and their world are subject to supernatural forces. In the place of modern psychology, it talks of demon possession, while modern man cannot comprehend the sacramental idea, the belief that spirit works through matter. Some of these strictures, such as the existence of created beings higher than man, the possibility of miracles, and the sacramental principle, we cannot accept, for it is by no means clear that here modern science with its positivistic form has any clear view. Bultmann needs to pay heed—before becoming so dogmatic—to another great German theologian, Karl Heim, who is an apologist with a keen understanding of science.

Along with these prescientific ideas, Bultmann also dismisses the *parousia,* the pre-existence of the Son of God, the idea of atonement through the vicarious bearing of the sin of the world on the cross (which he declares to be abhorrent to modern man!), and the resurrection as a historical reality that vindicates the triumph on the cross. He thus can offer no Christology and can find no cosmic significance in the biblical imagery.

Bultmann's use of myth for the biblical viewpoint has increasingly raised questions. He evidently uses myth with a certain flavor of its modern meaning as incredible and untrue, and thus has made it difficult to retain the word to describe the inner meaning of the revelation. Myth in the religious consciousness can be an imaginative vehicle for conveying truth, and this word has merit over the words "symbol" and "image" in that it implies activity. It is a dynamic symbol and it involves a story which is akin to history. Hence the word could have real meaning for conveying the inner significance of a historical revelation. The word is now so discredited, however, that many theologians are endeavoring to find an adequate substitute.

Actually, the word "myth" in association with salvation history would have to carry a connotation different from that which it carries in the general religious consciousness, where it is bound up often with a pantheistic naturalism. The cyclic and recurrent aspect of myth is replaced by the association of the biblical imagery with the linear and historical nature of salvation history. Because of such considerations, we propose to employ the term "historical image" to describe the transcendent and revealed meaning of salvation history. Barth uses "saga" to denote the stories in the first chapters of Genesis, thereby seeking to retain the historical reference, for these stories describe history. But these stories also fall under the category of "historical image," so the word "saga," which is still unsatisfactory, will not be employed here.

Even though Bultmann is concerned specifically with the biblical revelation and not with the general religious consciousness, a confusion can immediately be noted in his use of the word "myth" itself. Fundamentally he agrees with the definition given in this book when he writes that "myth is an expression of man's conviction that the origin and purpose of the world in which he lives are to be sought not within it but beyond it," and that "the real purpose of myth is to speak of a transcendent power which controls the world and man."[10] Within every myth, even at the level of the general religious consciousness, there is a blending of symbolic insight into spiritual reality and prescientific thinking. Hence, we cannot agree with him when he dismisses all mythical thinking as prescientific and subrational. Nor can we accept his view that the biblical imagery is not ontological but anthropological, not cosmic but existential.

Bultmann fails to differentiate between the primitive world-structure and the world-view which is expressed within that structure. The German words *Welt-bilt* and *Welt-anschauung* convey this distinction quite adequately. Now it is true that the world-structure, arising out of prescientific thinking, is outmoded. This does not mean, however, that the world-view, the revelatory insight, spelled out in the alphabet of this structure, is obsolete. Bultmann tends to identify all biblical imagery with a prescientific way of thinking about the world, to dismiss it as myth in the currently accepted meaning of that word, and to leave room for little revelatory insight except an existential encounter with a Christ-event.

It may be agreed that the historical imagery of the Bible does embody a prescientific world-structure, and here demythologizing will, to some degree, be in order. Obviously we cannot take literally the structure of a three-tier universe. What Bultmann has failed to see is made plain in Reinhold Niebuhr's differentiation between prescientific and permanent myths: "Pre-scientific myths disregard what may have always been known, or have now become known, about the ordered course of events in the world. Permanent myths . . . are those which describe some meaning or

---

[10] Essay in *Kerygma and Myth*, ed. by H. W. Bartsch (London: S.P.C.K., 1953), pp. 10 f.

reality, which is not subject to exact analysis but can nevertheless be verified in experience."[11] Thus permanent myth is concerned with man's orientation to the absolute or ultimate. It is such permanent myths, in the best and nonskeptical sense of that word, which constitute the significant historical images of the biblical revelation. Some such images are grounded in particular historical events, and others make use of prescientific views of world-structure.

The story of creation in Genesis 1 provides an illuminating example of this combination of the prescientific and the permanent, of world-structure and world-view. We can no longer take literally, as the biblical writers did, the picture of the three-tier universe. In our expanding universe we have, in such a spatial picture of heaven, a housing problem with regard to God. Yet insofar as the prescientific element is concerned with the portrayal of God as Creator and with man's relation to God, it takes on permanent significance and conveys revelatory meaning. The "above" and the "beyond," God's creative Word and the divine image in man, take on a symbolic and abiding meaning. They become revelatory historical imagery.

Bultmann also dismisses as myth that which for many is historical actuality. Salvation history is grounded in historical actuality. Miracles are historically attested occurrences. The Virgin Birth is not myth, however difficult it may appear to modern man. The resurrection cannot be dismissed as the creation of faith. Rather it is the historical actuality that vindicates the cross and creates faith. Historical actuality as such must not be confused with pure symbolism even though the interpretation of it may involve us in historical imagery.

In salvation history, the true insights in the myths of the religious consciousness have been bound up with the inner meaning of historical actuality. Thus the images of the Old Testament prophetic and postexilic eschatology have become reality in Jesus of Nazareth. When men sought for the inner meaning of this

---

[11] Reinhold Niebuhr, *The Self and the Dramas of History* (New York: Charles Scribner's Sons, 1955), p. 97.

climactic event of the life, death, and resurrection of a historical figure, they expressed it in terms of the images taken from this background of promise, and immediately had to use symbolic language. The heavenly-man myth and the Son-of-Man figure of Daniel became history in Jesus, to describe whose meaning the early Christian witnesses retained the historical imagery.

When John declares that "the Word became flesh" and that "God ... gave his only Son," again he is using symbolic language which has abiding significance. So, the New Testament witnesses also speak variously of the pre-existent Son, of the throne of God, and of the heavenly ascension of our Lord at the right hand of the Father. Bultmann would reject the term "ascension" because it is bound up with the three-tier universe. But this is permanent historical imagery. It is deeply true and conveys symbolically and dynamically, in the form of a dynamic image, that the exalted Christ is a spiritual reality and a potent force in history. How better can we express this? Throughout the New Testament, in varying degrees of emphasis, we find the hope of the *parousia*. Here are analogical and symbolic pictures—dramatic images, in which the relation of eternity to the historical actuality of the man Christ Jesus, the inner redemptive meaning of the Christ-event, is made plain.

Now these images are not arbitrary, or bound to the time and place in which they emerge, as Bultmann contends. This brings into view the association of divine inspiration with the imagination of the prophets and witnesses. In various ways, contemporary thinkers have argued that the religious symbols and images arise by the activity of God's Spirit within the religious consciousness in a revelatory situation. Thus Austin Farrer[12] would both liken biblical inspiration to and differentiate it from the inspiration of poets and musicians. He holds that, in the latter, the element of free human creativity is to the fore, whereas, in the case of the prophets and the apostles, the imagination is so creatively controlled by the divine Spirit that the images and symbols have

---

[12] Austin Farrer, *The Glass of Vision* (Westminster: Dacre Press, 1948), pp. 35 ff.

divine authority. The events and images are concomitant elements in the revelation, and without either there would be no revelation. Tillich argues that religious images are not arbitrarily chosen. They arise out of the ontological structure of being as an expression of the divine life, so that they convey an *immediate* awareness of the presence of God and have a compelling authority over the life and historical existence of a person.[13]

The central imagery of the Bible has a numinous quality about it. It participates in and is molded by the revelatory situation. Such imagery is a treasure house of dynamic import. It does not just convey information about God but brings immediate encounter with God.

Reinhold Niebuhr takes up a parallel position when he argues that the Genesis stories come from beyond the frontier of human knowledge. These do not originate in man. Man knows that, of himself and by reason alone, he could not arrive at what they convey about his own nature and destiny and about God's judgment and redemptive activity. These biblical historical images are concerned with the vertical aspects of relationship and not with the horizontal aspects with which science deals. The biblical writers use images that transcend human rationality and that express more adequately than abstract philosophical categories God's organic relation to the world and his distinction from it.[14] Thus biblical historical images point to the transcendent realm of being, to the transhistorical, and yet they are firmly grounded in the historical, for the relations and purpose they seek to describe have become actualized in history. Events in history have their inner meaning expressed in the divinely given images and symbols. As Niebuhr puts it: "there is a significant distinction be-

---

[13] Tillich, *op. cit.*, Vol. I, p. 126. Farrer makes over-absolutist claims for the central biblical images and, because of his Thomistic background, rejects all thought of direct encounter with God. For him God is known only in terms of the images and not personally through them. Tillich corrects him at this point, but adopts an eventually similar attitude to the nature of divine inspiration and the authority of the images themselves, although he would be freer in his definition of what constitutes revelation.

[14] Reinhold Niebuhr, *An Interpretation of Christian Ethics* (London: SCM Press, 1936), p. 24.

tween the 'myths' with which a pre-scientific world describes natural phenomena and the symbol which is central to the structure of Christian faith, namely, the assertion that a Jesus of Nazareth was the 'Son of the living God.'"[15]

The determination of what is permanent historical imagery turns upon its relation to Jesus Christ himself. If he is the midpoint of salvation history in whom the final meaning of historical existence is made plain, we may expect that the images which express that meaning and thus are bound up with his person are of abiding significance. Farrer distinguishes between the master images of the biblical revelation and the secondary images.[16] The former are those which are integral to the revelation, and for which there are no equivalents or substitutes. The subordinate images are not basic to the revelation, and other equivalent images may be substituted for them without destroying their content. They serve to illustrate the meaning of the Christ-event, the gospel which contains the meaning of history, but they may disappear in the process of time to be replaced by others.

The most significant images are those which speak of God, man, and the world in a cohesive unity which centers in Christ. They are images which are brought to a focus in the life and self-revelation of our Lord and are quite often used by him in his own self-communication.[17] They are not images concerned with the aspects of nature and cosmology with which science deals or concerned with man as modern psychology treats him. They relate man and the cosmos to the transcendent ground of all existence which is brought to a focus in Jesus Christ. They are concerned with those ultimate spiritual and ontological relations which underlie man's historical existence. What comes clear in our Lord and his cross is man's radical estrangement and God's gracious reconciliation. The insights offered by the images of the fall, atonement, sacrifice, redemption, people of God, and the like

---

[15] Niebuhr, *The Self and the Dramas of History*, p. 98.

[16] Farrer, *op. cit.*, pp. 42 ff.

[17] Here we reject extreme form-critical analysis which ascribes the Gospel picture to the church and treats the historical Jesus agnostically. We shall justify our position later.

are thus central to the understanding of history and to the gospel. They may not be dismissed in deference to the "adultness" of the modern mind. The central imagery of the revelation has permanent significance.

Because of his demythologizing process and his rejection of any ontological and cosmic significance in biblical historical imagery, Bultmann moves toward a distinctive interpretation of history.[18] It has the virtue, at least, of being existential, and it takes note of the eschatological import of the New Testament testimony. Bultmann rightly holds that the real offense of Christianity is that of a transcendent God present and active in history. He is anxious to retain Jesus Christ as a concrete historical figure who is also the eschatological emissary of God. He declares that the redemption of the New Testament was not a miraculous event, but a historical event wrought out in time, and that this is an eschatological event in the sense of final and absolute. The eschatological is, however, demythologized totally and reduced to the existential. Eschatology becomes purely personal and all cosmic and social elements are stripped from it. The New Testament vision of a new heaven and a new earth disappears, and we are told that the present is the moment of decision in which past and future may be gathered up and transformed. Man becomes truly historical as he makes his decision about existence in encounter with the Christ-event. This supreme event challenges all relativism. The anthropology implicit in it uncovers the deeps of man's historicity, giving it a transcendent ground.

Bultmann is quite clear that the offense of the Christian faith lies in the basic paradox that the absolute and unconditioned ground of all existence has chosen to disclose himself in one particular event within historical existence, and that the meaning of all history is fully and perfectly contained in one particular event in history. He will not move from this *skandalon,* and he condemns efforts to demythologize the gospel story by finding in it some universal truth which it exemplifies. He finds his own interpretation in the historical actuality and particularity of the Christ-

[18] *Vide* Rudolf Bultmann, *The Presence of Eternity* (New York: Harper & Brothers, 1957), *passim.*

event. Bultmann contends that *"Jesus Christ is the eschatological event,* the action of God by which God has set an end to the old world. In the preaching of the Christian church the eschatological event will ever again become present and does become present ever and again in faith."[19] Thus, as men are confronted by the Word of God in preaching, they are driven into a situation which brings them face to face with an eschatological question about their existence and involves them in history. A transient occasion may, under this impact, become an event. Jesus Christ is the revealer in this event, and here we concur, but what does he reveal? This is not redemptive revelation in the New Testament sense, but rather revelation of the latent possibility in the events that beset man's life whereby they may become truly eschatological. The revelation is not concerned with God but with man's existence.

Bultmann's weakness lies in his demythologizing. The Christ-event is reduced to the existential and anthropological level from the cosmic and the ontological. Hence, Bultmann empties revelation of its true content and provides no adequate Christology to justify his claim that the Christ-event is eschatological. All the dynamic images by which our Lord is described in the New Testament have no Christological and ontological import for Bultmann. When salvation history is thus reduced to the existential level, we are left with an understanding of it strangely at variance with the Old Testament social concern and the New Testament cosmic hope.

The biblical historical images are intimately related sets of symbols which carry their own authority because they are grounded in and give the meaning of revelatory historical events. They must not be dismissed, and demythologization only too often robs them of their true content, just as taking them literally does. It is probably true that, at the time of the biblical revelation, some of the insights of the biblical imagery were taken literally. But if we believe in the dynamic nature of revelation and the mystery of God's hiddenness in his unveiling, we are not

---

[19] *Ibid.,* p. 151

forced to take the historical images literally simply because those who formulated them did so—although the latter would be a highly disputable judgment. In any case, modern science has helped to liberate us from the literal interpretation and enabled us to grasp the permanent within the prescientific.

The *Mündigkeit* (adultness) of the modern mind can be challenged to grasp this symbolic meaning rather than to regard the dramatic imagery of the Bible as an absolute cosmology and chronology. The biblical world-view taken symbolically can then be a serious challenge to the contemporary rationalistic, naturalistic, and scientific mythologies.[20] The biblical elemental images are not just dogmatic propositions, but dramatic images of the existential situation of historical man. The symbols of creation, the divine image, the barred gate, the desert, and the serpent have a profound meaning for historical existence.

In the succeeding chapters we shall be concerned with both *Historie* and *Geschichte*. Employing the methods of biblical criticism, we shall endeavor to assess and lay bare the historical actuality in which the revelation is mediated to us. To arrive at bare *Historie* is an impossibility; rather the task is to begin by establishing the historical foundation of the *Geschichte*. This is the reason that the category "*historical* image" is suggested. The images are grounded in historical actuality and offer an insight into its basic revelatory meaning. It does matter whether the events which the images describe actually occurred. God has given himself in history, and that historical actuality may not be dissolved in the interest of presuppositions which are not bound up with the revelation, but with the contemporary secularism, positivism, naturalism, and scientism of our time.

The first task, therefore, will be to investigate the historical actuality of the events in which the revelation is grounded and their distinctive nature, their uniqueness. Only when such a task

---

[20] We agree with G. V. Jones: "A Christianity which jettisons the so-called mythological element in the New Testament Christology instead of retaining it *in the knowledge that it is mythological* not only impoverishes itself but weakens its own historical-biblical roots." *Christology and Myth in the New Testament* (New York: Harper & Brothers, 1956), p. 281.

has been performed, can we move on to consider their revelatory meaning. The revelation can never be detached from its historical base. The historicity of the resurrection, in particular, is crucial for an understanding of the revelation. Historical minutiae and detailed chronological frameworks do not belong essentially to the revelation, but the climacteric events do, and it is the historical actuality of the latter with which this book is concerned.

CHAPTER II

THE HISTORICITY OF SALVATION HISTORY

In emphasizing the uniqueness of Jesus Christ and the events of salvation history, of which he is the center, we have yet to consider the historical authenticity of those events and their inner nature and structure. History is the significant past, the record of events which carry meaning. Hence the events of history can never be dissociated from the value judgments of the group in whose traditions they are perpetuated and who have singled out these events because of the meaning they bear for that group. This applies, in particular, to salvation history, for this is a record of historical events regarded as significant by the Jewish nation and the Christian community.

The bare historical happenings are seen through the eyes of faith. No part of the biblical record can be divorced from this insight of faith—an insight by which the facts of history were seen in the light of the divine purpose and became media of a divine revelation. The events of salvation history belong to the ordinary continuum of historical occurrences, from one point of view, but they also belong to a meaningful series which faith singles out as the bearer of revelation. They are given special significance as events in which the meaning of all history is disclosed by a series of divine acts of judgment and redemption, of wrath and grace.

The Bible records the mighty acts of God. We have explained them in terms of "historical images" because they are historical actuality, and yet have a dimension of eternity so hidden within them that only symbolic and imaginative language conveys their inner meaning. This means that the events cannot be explained in the horizontal dimension of historical existence alone. They cannot be explained in terms of history, even though they are history, for they belong to the eternal order as well. In these events the continuity of secular history is broken. Behind them there is a mysterious hinterland. They mark the points of intersection of eternity and time, and they cannot be reduced to the level of historical causality or placed in the categories of the analogy which historical science so readily employs at the positivistic level.

1. Salvation History and Historical Criticism

The events of salvation history are historical facts, therefore legitimate subjects of historical investigation and critical inquiry. But their inner and eternal content is not disclosed to such observation. On the purely historical plane, the events of salvation history may be regarded as normal occurrences—the wanderings of nomad tribes, their settlement in Palestine and the development of their religious ideas, the imperialistic aggression of their more powerful neighbors and their own deliverances, their internal discord and experience of captivity, their prophets and their cultus, the life and death of a young and enthusiastic religious teacher and the rise of the community of his followers. Yet, like every other historical event, the events of salvation history cannot even then be dissociated from the meaning which is discovered in them and which determines their retention in the historical consciousness. The critical historian does violence to these events if he strips them of that meaning and gives it no place in his analysis of history. A historical happening changes history and becomes a potent factor in the life of a group according to the meaning discovered in it. It is this meaning which constitutes it as an event.

Thus the deliverance of Israel at the Red Sea might have been "explained" on purely natural grounds as the result of a wind sweeping across the desert and piling up the waters of the Red Sea before it. This is actually suggested in Exodus 14:21. Then historical contingency and natural forces might be drawn on as explanation. But the deliverance became an event in the life and destiny of Israel and changed the course of history, because the prophet Moses saw its deeper significance for faith. For Moses it constituted a revelatory situation. It was God's Word to him and to Israel, not to be explained in terms of historical and natural categories, but numinous with the presence of God. The dimension of eternity was disclosed in the historical actuality, and the event was interpreted as a divine intervention in history, an act of God, whereby the people were delivered from their enemies. The historical critic may strip the event of this meaning and "explain" it as a natural phenomenon, but he has yet to explain its significance for Israel and he may not do this by explaining away the divine presence. If he ignores the psychical and spiritual factors involved, he distorts the subsequent history of the Jewish people for whom the deliverance at the Red Sea set a seal upon their religious faith.

Similarly, our Lord's cross might be regarded as one martyr's death among many, one more exhibition of the nobility of the human spirit, to be explained within the continuity of history and on the basis of analogy with the deaths of men like Socrates. The historian has at least to give this much meaning because the death has been singled out in the consciousness of the Christian community. It has become a significant event and the historian must take account of it. The Talmud presents us with a perverted example of such explanation when it states that "they hanged Jesus on the eve of the Passover . . . because he practiced sorcery and led Israel astray."[1] The true historian may have his own private interpretation, but he cannot leave it there. He must, when considering the cross in its historical actuality, take into account the faith of the early Christians which grasped the dimension of eternity in the event, saw it as a divine act of salvation, and transformed the actuality into *the* event in the Christian consciousness and *the* turning point of world history.

Historical investigation may be divided roughly into two parts. The first is concerned with the investigation of the records, the documents and the traditions, and the establishment of the

---

[1] *The Babylonian Talmud, Sanhedrin*, f. 43a.

historical datum itself. The second is concerned with the "explanation" of the event on the historical level. In the case of biblical criticism, this second aspect sometimes results in the explaining away of the numinous presence, the eternal dimension.

Of the first aspect of critical historical investigation, faith has no criticism to offer. A fair and scientific investigation of the sources should help us to put biblical events in their proper setting and to understand the movement of revelation in history. A good example here is the postulation of Deutero-Isaiah (Isa. 40-55) as a separate source, dating from the latter period of the Exile in Babylon. This throws light on the development of the Hebrew understanding of God's purpose, as the unknown exilic prophet catches a vision of the Suffering Servant and helps us to see the relation of the prophetic consciousness to historical events like the advent of Cyrus, the Persian conqueror.

Other good examples are provided by the analyses of the sources of the Pentateuch and the Gospels, fluid though they may be at the present juncture. The increasing understanding of the importance of oral tradition and of the place of this in a worshiping and confessing community is seen in the work of scholars like Von Rad[2] in the Old Testament and of form critics like Martin Dibelius[3] and Vincent Taylor[4] in the New Testament.

Since A.D. 1439, when Laurentius Valla demonstrated that the Donation of Constantine was spurious, historians have grown increasingly conscious of the need for sifting the literary material from which our present knowledge of a historical event is derived. Hence there has grown up the vast structure of literary criticism in its many forms. Lower criticism seeks to eliminate copyists' errors and to reach the original form of the record itself. Higher criticism critically sifts the structure of the record, en-

---

[2] Von Rad, *Theologie des Alten Testaments,* Vol. I, *passim; Das erste Buch Mose, Das Alte Testament Deutsch* (Göttingen: Vanderhoeck and Ruprecht, 1953).

[3] Martin Dibelius, *From Tradition to Gospel* (New York: Charles Scribner's Sons, 1935).

[4] Vincent Taylor, *The Formation of the Gospel Tradition* (London: Macmillan & Co., Ltd., 1933); cf. E. F. Scott, *The Validity of the Gospel Record* (London: Nicholson & Watson, 1938).

deavors to trace the sources and traditions behind it, and attempts to determine the dependability of these various literary and oral elements. Here the personal factor has to be taken into account—the situation in which the writer lived, the availability to him of correct information, the purpose which guided his record of historical fact, and how far he has distorted the latter, consciously and unconsciously, in order to fit it into his preconceived notions or to influence posterity. Related elements and references have to be carefully examined. The results of archaeological investigation have to be brought into relation with the literary records. Often the words and images used may help us to discover the background, the *Sitz im Leben,* of the writer. When we are dealing with a tradition rather than an individual writer, we become concerned with a continuing community. We have to take into account much of the above, but we have to look also for early elements which do not manifestly belong to the period when the tradition became a fixed part of a written source. A tradition grows as the historical experience of the community moves forward, and thus later elements may tend to obscure the original purity of the tradition. Using such a structure of critical apparatus, the historian may hope to come nearer to the event itself, to its historical actuality.

The second aspect is that all documents and sources in the New Testament, even the Synoptic Gospels, are colored with the faith of the writers. This is also true of the Old Testament, even in its early traditions. Thus when source criticism and form criticism have done their work, we are still left with an event as it is seen through the eyes of faith, and not with bare fact.

This becomes evident in the attempt to write a life of our Lord. The quest for the historical Jesus seemed to end with the critique of Albert Schweitzer,[5] but it is now being renewed by those who belong to the post-Bultmann group of New Testament scholars.[6] The form critics have raised serious issues. Their thesis

---

[5] Albert Schweitzer, *The Quest of the Historical Jesus* (New York: The Macmillan Company, 1948).

[6] There is an able treatment of this in J. M. Robinson, *A New Quest of the Historical Jesus* (Naperville: Alec R. Allenson, Inc., 1959).

that the material in the written sources of the Synoptic Gospels
circulated originally as detached oral units is now well established. There can be little doubt that such units were preserved
orally and separately within the life of the community of faith.
Hence it is necessary to separate these units from the frameworks
imposed on them by the evangelists. By this means we are able
to clear out some of the secondary meanings imposed later by
the church, and approach a little nearer to the true significance
of the sayings and events recorded.

There seems little doubt that the form critics are right when
they see the central *Sitz im Leben* of the detached oral units to
be the preaching and worship of the early Christian community.
This means *ipso facto* that a sifting process has been at work,
whereby only the traditions of the life and sayings of our Lord
that had importance for the preaching, worship, and witness of
the primitive church have been preserved. Events and sayings
were important because they pointed to the saving significance
of Jesus. Others were preserved because of their place in the
worship and ritual of the early community. There is yet another
motive for preserving the traditions and memories. Would not
love for and devotion to the Lord prove a potent factor in preserving many incidents in the early days?

Some extreme critics, like Bultmann,[7] would go beyond this
and hold that most of the traditions were *created* by the early
community, the product and expression of its *kerygma*, and that
we are still far removed from the historical Founder of the faith.
At this point we may interject two comments: The first is that a
community is not creative, as are individuals. The second is that
this believing community included many eyewitnesses who had
lived with and loved the historical Jesus. It is difficult to believe
that, quite early and near the primary events, individuals could
foist spurious material on their fellows and create a faith. This

---

[7] Cf. Bultmann, *Jesus and the Word* (New York: Charles Scribner's
Sons, 1934). He writes: "I do indeed think that we can know almost nothing concerning the life and personality of Jesus, since the early Christian
sources show no interest in either, are moreover fragmentary and often legendary; and other sources about Jesus do not exist," p. 8.

argument has special value with reference to the resurrection.

Form criticism provides a picture of the early worshiping community and a series of detached sayings and incidents from the life of the historical Jesus. It usually dismisses from the picture of Jesus the Synoptic frameworks and thus chronological order and historical movement. This too is very radical. After all, memories in people like Peter, whom tradition at least puts behind the Gospel of Mark, cannot be so easily dismissed. Even the Fourth Gospel, often considered as unreliable history, is finding its way back into the favor of historians, providing supplementary chronological information. We are left then with a broad sweeping chronological framework of the life of Jesus. The evangelists did, however, exercise great liberty in the way in which they inserted their detached material into the framework. For example, the Sermon on the Mount in Matthew becomes the Sermon on the Plain in Luke, and the two versions are inserted at different places in the framework. Hence, we can never approach the historical actuality in detail and provide ourselves with material for writing an accurate life of Jesus of Nazareth.

All the Synoptic material and traditions provide us with a picture of Jesus as faith sees him. When form criticism has finished its task, it leaves us with a historical understanding of Jesus from the standpoint of the believing church. If what we have said be true, the church sifted its materials and memories, preserving what carried the true meaning of Jesus as faith saw it.

Now, if we dismiss the viewpoint that the tradition was the creation rather than the foundation of the *kerygma*, we must believe that we are touching historical actuality here.[8] It is true that occasionally in the Synoptic traditions the historical actuality seems to be overlaid by its inner meaning. The Christ of faith is so emphasized that it is difficult to determine some of the details of the historical event that veiled him. The vertical dimension of eternity is so significant that the horizontal plane of history is laid

---

[8] This is the viewpoint of many mediating New Testament scholars like Vincent Taylor, O. Cullmann, J. Jeremias, T. W. Manson, R. H. Fuller, W. G. Kümmel, A. M. Hunter.

open to make clear in the testimony of the church what history veiled in actuality. This may have happened in some miracle stories.

Perhaps the Fourth Gospel, finished literary product and not oral tradition though it be, illustrates what is meant. In it the historical and the eternal dimensions are so woven together that the eternal dimension is laid bare. Often the historical actuality fades into the background as the inner meaning is made the center of attention. The Fourth Gospel is, in this sense, the spiritual Gospel, the record of Jesus in the light of postresurrection faith. But then this is true also of even the earliest traditions. They also point to Jesus as Saviour and Lord. They are all part of the witness and worship of the community, and yet they are also treasured in the love and devotion of believing hearts. Many of us would say, indeed, that this is the true Jesus, and that the traditions are here grounded in historical actuality, drawing out its inner meaning, rather than being fabrications of the believing community. Belief would surely otherwise be a misnomer!

The conclusion would be that it is difficult to paint a detailed life of Jesus. There is only a broad-sweeping framework of his ministry. We can see the tensions that formed between him and his contemporaries, so the cross becomes understandable. The early formation of a continuous passion narrative has generally been acknowledged by critical scholars, and we can see the course of events which led up to Calvary.[9] But it is not easy to ascertain where individual sayings and incidents may belong. This need not be a stumbling block, however. For if the Jesus of history is the Christ whom the faith of the church has preserved in its traditions, and preserved lovingly, there is a sufficient picture of the historical Jesus for the task of witnessing. Would a detailed and accurate life have more saving significance? The important thing is the dimension of eternity in our Lord's coming to us in, with,

---

[9] Cf. the judgment of T. W. Manson in *Expository Times*, liii, 251. He comments, "as we apply our best scholarship and insight, sympathy, and sincerity to these various tasks, we may hope that the portrait of Jesus will emerge with some sufficient clearness." Manson has attempted to fulfill this hope in *The Servant-Messiah* (Cambridge: University Press, 1953).

and under his own historical life. But the crucial turning point of his cross and resurrection and his own testimony to these must, at least, be available. If we dismiss traditions at this point, as Bultmann does, we are left, like him, with an existential encounter which the Christ-event makes possible, but with no Christology and no real understanding of Christian salvation.

2. The Failure of Historical Explanation in the Old Testament

The second task of the historian is that of "'meaning'"—discovering the significance of the events he is investigating and weaving them into a coherent patterned whole. Now in the normal movements of secular history, various possibilities of interpretation are possible, and different approaches are open to the historical thinker. Thus we have the attempt to explain history in terms of the natural order, and to omit as far as possible any supernatural or unique element.

This viewpoint is concerned with causes, believing that every event is sufficiently explained if it can be accounted for on a causal basis. Hence we have the development of historical geography, the attempts to show the effect of geographical environment upon the story of a people. We have, too, an increasing recognition, since the time of Karl Marx, of the large part which economics plays in history and of the element of truth in Feuerbach's dictum that "man is what he eats." Sociological and psychological investigations of the past decades have meant that the search for cause has been carried into the deeps of the human consciousness and into the laws which govern social action and communal life. Religion becomes one of many phenomena studied in this way, and it is reduced by such historians to the same level of causation.

This hunt for causes is based on the belief that a fact is explained when its cause is found. The truth is that the claim of historical causation only serves to veil the deeper and more potent presence of human freedom and decision and divine encounter and purposiveness. To explain by finding genetic causes and drawing analogies from other human situations does not mean that we have understood an event.

Most of all is this true of salvation history in all its uniqueness. Such historical explanations of salvation history are not sufficient. If salvation history is revelation there may be continuity and yet discontinuity. God discloses himself and man's historical destiny within the stream of history and puts himself in it. There is continuity. But his revelation is the act of his absolute freedom. The events that are its media are unique and radically discontinuous also with all other history. In the succeeding sections we shall consider the failure of historical explanations and the uniqueness of the inner meaning of salvation history, of its *Geschichte* as opposed to its *Historie*.

Many attempts have been made to bring the events of salvation history into the sphere of historical causation and make them intelligible as part of the general stream of history. Parallels and analogies from other historical periods are employed to show the continuity of this series with the rest and to rob it of its uniqueness. The psychology of primitive tribes is harnessed to explain the Hebrew cultus and sacrificial rites; the prophets are explained psychologically until their deep consciousness of a divine compulsion and of an objective word coming to them is lost in a maze of subjectivism; parallels from the history of religion are brought in to explain the New Testament interpretation of Christ. The theology of Paul is set in antithesis to the religion of Jesus, and the former is explained as due to the infiltration of the ideas of Hellenistic mysticism and mystery religions.

Years ago Vico pointed out in his *New Science* that one source of error in historical investigation is the "scholastic succession of nations."[10] He means by this the idea that because two nations have a similar idea or institution, one must have derived it from the other. He held that this implied a denial of the creative capacity of the human mind. Man should be able creatively to rediscover ideas for himself. It is by no means certain that we al-

---

[10] *Vide* R. G. Collingwood, *The Idea of History* (Oxford: The Clarendon Press, 1946), p. 69.

ways have direct borrowing in the history of Israel, particularly where historians like to find it. Furthermore, even where patterns of thought are borrowed or where institutions are derived from elsewhere, the use to which such are put and the basic meaning they are then made to convey may indicate a radical mutation and support the uniqueness of salvation history.

In the history of the Old Testament revelation, two instances among many rise to the mind. The first has already been dealt with in part—the creation stories and their relation to the myths current in the ancient Near East. The similarity of structure and cosmology between Genesis 1[11] and the Babylonian *Enuma-elis* myth might indicate a relationship of some kind. The chaotic deep in which the created cosmos floats and out of the division of which it is created forms a striking parallel to the chaos monster Tiamat, floating in the deep and cut in halves by her rebellious brood to form the heavens and the earth. The three-tier universe implied in all this primitive imagery belongs to the common atmosphere of thought of the time. Yet there is a radical difference. The pattern of thought has been so filled with new content that the pattern itself is also transformed.

The Babylonian myth is a primitive form of naturalistic pantheism. The goddess Tiamat bears Marduk and the other gods who slay her, and the cosmos is formed out of her body. Man is made that he may supply the gods with sacrificial nourishment, implying that there was a divine necessity behind the appearance of man, of Babylon and its priests, on the earthly plane.

This viewpoint stands in direct contrast to the absolute Creator of Genesis 1, whose transcendence and beyondness are safeguarded by the symbolism of the creative Word which he hurls into the chaos, who creates man not out of necessity but out of freedom, and who graciously makes man responsible, a social being, granting him a capacity for fellowship with his Creator and for responsible stewardship over the natural resources of his world. The pattern may be roughly the same but the whole is

---

[11] For a lengthy discussion of this, *vide* Rust, *Nature and Man in Biblical Thought,* pp. 20 ff.

transfigured by the revelatory content that is presented in it. It
has been lifted up into salvation history and illuminated with a
new light.

The second instance is the relation of the Hebrew prophetic
consciousness to similar phenomena elsewhere in the ancient
Near East. The milieu of the biblical revelation gives evidence
that the prophet, as far as this pattern of behavior was concerned,
was not peculiar to Israel.

In the Sumerian and Akkadian region, there were *baru* priests
who performed a divinatory and oracular function.[12] They see
a vision (as their name implies etymologically), decide a decision, judge a judgment. The *baru* is "one who observes the secret
of the great gods," and we might call him a seer who employs
divination and dreams. Alongside these were the *mahhu* priests
who also served an oracular purpose, but who delivered their
oracles in a state of ecstatic frenzy in which they seemed to be
regarded as identified with the god. The name *mahhu* may mean
that the man's mind has been replaced by the breath of the god.
This is naturalistic pantheism. His ecstatic states seem also to
have been associated with the seeing of visions.

Similar and more pronounced phenomena are manifested
among the Phoenicians and Canaanites. An Egyptian story, dating from the 11th century B.C., tells how at Byblos during a religious festival "the god seized one of [the] youths and made
him possessed,"[13] an evident reference to the ecstatic state. The
frenzied behavior of the priests of Baal on Mount Carmel indicates that this phenomenon persisted centuries later (1 Kings
18:25-29). Haldar[14] cites evidence from Ugarit that such phenomena were present in the Canaanite religion and associated
with the giving of oracles.

In the Mari texts we have evidence of the nonecstatic type of
oracular official. Instances can be cited in which such an official

---

[12] A. Haldar, *Associations of Cult Prophets Among the Ancient Semites*
(Uppsala, 1945).

[13] *Vide* James B. Pritchard, ed., *Ancient Near Eastern Texts Relating to
the Old Testament* (Princeton: University Press, 1950), pp. 25-29.

[14] Haldar, *op. cit.*

comes before the king, declaring that the god has sent him to convey a message. This suggests the canonical prophets of the Old Testament and their great predecessors. Noth contends that such agreement cannot be accidental and that we have here more than a parallel.[15] Because nothing really comparable has been found yet anywhere in the whole Hebrew milieu, he believes that the "messenger of the god" in the Mari texts belongs to the prehistory of Hebrew prophecy and that there is historical connection.

The relation of this background to the Hebrew prophetic consciousness is noteworthy. The latter seems to have had a somewhat varied vocabulary, probably originally describing different prophetic types. *Nabi,* now commonly translated "prophet," may originally have described the ecstatic type, whereas *ro'eh,* "seer," and *chozeh,* also translated "seer," may have represented the divinatory oracular type, which was not dependent upon ecstatic frenzy but upon visions and auditions and was more stable psychologically.[16] By the time the Old Testament records were formulated, all three descriptions were almost coterminous, and *nabi* had become an all-embracing term for prophet (1 Sam. 9:9). It seems that by this time Israel was beginning to produce her own distinctive type of prophetic consciousness, although we find many examples of the purely ecstatic prophet at least to the time of Ahab.[17]

Scholars disagree as to the relation of the Hebrew canonical prophet to the ecstatic type and thus to the general background of religious ecstasy and frenzied utterance in the ancient Near

---

[15] Cf. M. Noth, "History and the Word of God in the Old Testament," *Bulletin of the John Rylands Library,* xxxii, 1959-1960, pp. 194-206.

[16] There is a discussion of this differentation in A. R. Johnson, *The Cultic Prophet in Ancient Israel* (Cardiff: University of Wales Press, 1944), pp. 1-28; A. Lods, *Israel* (New York: Alfred A. Knopf, 1932), pp. 442 ff. There are also valuable summings up of the present position in H. H. Rowley, *The Servant of the Lord* (London: Lutterworth Press, 1952), pp. 89-128, and the essay by A. Eissfeldt on "The Prophetic Literature" in *The Old Testament and Modern Study,* ed. by H. H. Rowley (Oxford: The Clarendon Press,, 1951), pp. 115 ff.

[17] See the story of Micaiah, 1 Kings 22:1-28; cf. 1 Sam. 10:5, 10; 19:18; 2 Kings 2:3, 5; 4:38.

East. Some, like T. H. Robinson,[18] take the extreme view that all
Hebrew prophecy was of the ecstatic type. They describe the
prophet as caught up into an ecstatic trance and as speaking, if
at all, in unintelligible and ecstatic language. Later when nor-
malcy had returned, the prophet translated into intelligible speech
the message he had seen and heard. This extreme position has
found little support. Superficial resemblances do not necessarily
indicate the same psychology, and scholars should beware of
pressing them too far.

The fact that abnormal elements are present, however, warns
against the opposite extreme, advocated by Jepsen,[19] that there
is no relation between the canonical prophets and the ecstatic
ones. Jepsen claims that the canonical prophets made no claim to
spirit-possession and never called themselves *nebi'im*. He holds
that they differentiated themselves on the ground of possessing
the Word, and that the possessors of the spirit, the ecstatic
nebi'im, became increasingly the false prophets whom the canonical prophets attacked.

Scholars like H. W. Robinson[20] stand between these positions.
They hold that a pattern of ecstatic behavior may be present but
that it is pushed out to the periphery of the prophetic consciousness. The center is now occupied by rational reflection and moral
judgment. Abnormal elements remain—the inward sense of com-
pulsory visions and auditions, unusual symbolic acts. But the
word "ecstasy" is inappropriate. Actually it is bound up with naturalistic pantheism and mysticism. It implies that the soul is
temporarily able to leave its bodily prison house and enter more
ethereal spheres.

The Hebrew, however, understood man as a psychosomatic
whole, and could have no sympathy with such a view. Robinson
suggests that a better description would be "possession." Lind-

---

[18] T. H. Robinson, *Prophecy and the Prophets in Ancient Israel* (London: Duckworth, 1936).

[19] Jepsen is supported in part by Mowinckel, *Journal of Biblical Literature*, lvi, 1937, pp. 261-265; *Acta Orientalia*, xiii, 1935, pp. 264-291; xii,
1936, p. 319.

[20] H. W. Robinson, *Inspiration and Revelation in the Old Testament*
(Oxford: The Clarendon Press, 1946), pp. 173-186.

blom[21] rejects the idea of absorption ecstasy with its pantheistic associations, and would use the description "concentration ecstasy." By this he means that there is a concentration upon a specific feeling or idea, such that the normal consciousness is blotted out and even sense experience may cease. The theistic distance between God and man is preserved in such an experience. The prophet is possessed by an overmastering emotion accompanied by obsession with one idea or by abnormal stimulation of some bodily sense. So exclusive and channeled is the experience that other bodily functions cease. The instances of aphasia in the life of Ezekiel illustrate this. A distinctive type of experience thus emerges, even though outwardly it manifests behavior similar to that of prophets elsewhere.

The essential experience needs to be disentangled from the psychology in which it is expressed. The Hebrew had no understanding of secondary causes. He related every happening directly to the divine activity. Hence, the normal processes of rational reflection and moral judgment might be described in the language of miracle and the unusual. Mowinckel has sought to emphasize the rational and moral element by contending, like Jepsen, that the essential category for the canonical prophets was "Word" and not "spirit." He agrees that abnormal ecstatic elements were present, but holds that the prophetic message was characterized by spiritual clarity and reasoned judgment. It was not a wild, stammering, involuntary glossolalia, but a moral and rational presentation of deep spiritual apprehensions. These arose in the depths of the consciousness, but they attained lucidity through the moral and rational judgment of the prophetic personality.[22] Jeremiah especially exhibits his share of enduring fel-

---

[21] J. Lindblom, essay on "Einige Grundfagen der alttestamentlichen Wissenschaft" in the *Bertholet Festschrift* (Tübingen: J. C. B. Mohr, 1950), pp. 325 ff.

[22] Mowinckel, article in *Journal of Biblical Literature*, liii, 1935, pp. 207 f. Mowinckel and Jepsen are supported at this point in Oskar Grether, *Name und Wort Gottes im Alten Testament* (Giessen: Verlag von Alfred Töpelmann, 1934). Grether contends that the "Word of Yahweh" is a separate category of revelation, and holds that dream, vision, audition, and ecstasy in general conveyed the revelation only insofar as they were asso-

lowship with God at the fully conscious and rational level.

It would seem that the word "intuition" best describes the inner appprehension of the Word. The prophet sees into the nature and purpose of God by sympathetic insight. There is a sympathetic feeling with cognitive content, in which the prophet participates in the rhythm of the divine pathos. God became overpoweringly real as the agony of the prophet entered into the agony of God, and the prophet was constrained to deliver the message which became articulated in his consciousness.[23] The meaning of vision and audition, of mysterious inward promptings to speech and action, passes into the prophet's thinking and is given articulate expressions.[24] There is the awareness that the prophet is being addressed by God and that he must patiently seek to understand and communicate the Word which comes to him. The Spirit is no longer an irrational force that takes possession of a man but a power which operates in his conscious moral and rational life, standing him on his feet.

In the outward behavior that accompanied their utterances, the false prophets were not easily distinguishable from the true prophets. The former used traditional methods. They palmed off lying dreams for real prophetic visions (Jer. 23:22) and mimicked the prophetic form of utterance (Jer. 23:30). The differentiation

ciated with the "Word of God." Furthermore the Word does not come in audition or ecstasy but involves conscious reflection, rational understanding and interpretation. While much could be made of the fact that, until Ezekiel, the canonical prophets did not claim the spirit, we must not press this too far, as Mowinckel and Jepsen would. It is probably true that the way in which the category had become associated with the frenzied *nebi'im* and the claims of false prophets may have driven the canonical and reform prophets to avoid its usage. This does not mean, however, that they were not tying it in with the Word of Jehovah. It may well be that with Ezekiel we have a return to proper usage. Ezekiel alternates between the two categories; indeed, the "word," the "spirit," and the "hand" of Jehovah all serve to describe the same type of experience. If this be so for Ezekiel, can we accept a different position for his predecessors? It is more probable that the rational center of the prophetic consciousness was as much describable in terms of the Spirit as in terms of the Word.

[23] Cf. A. Heschel, *Die Prophetie* (1936), pp. 127 ff.; H. H. Rowley, *The Servant of the Lord*, pp. 123 f.

[24] Cf. John Skinner, *Prophecy and Religion* (New York: Cambridge University Press, 1922), p. 220.

is not psychologically based but turns upon the content of what is uttered. The false prophet promises peace and prophesies smooth things,[25] whereas the true prophet has stood in the council of Jehovah and knows his will.[26] The message of the false prophet is condemned by its moral and spiritual content. In addition, the prophet's own moral life testifies to the authentic nature of his utterance (Jer. 23:13 ff.; 29:21 ff.).

Finally, however, it is the inner conviction of his own soul that gives Jeremiah assurance in the face of opposition and persecution. No outward pattern of behavior or psychological test can differentiate a true message from a false. Yet it is also true to say that the content of the true prophetic consciousness even radically transforms the pattern of psychological behavior, and this Old Testament phenomenon cannot be explained on the basis of surrounding cultures.

Again we have both a continuity between salvation history and secular history, and a discontinuity. The prophetic consciousness of the great prophets of Israel is continuous in some sense with similar phenomena elsewhere in the ancient Near East. But there is also a radical difference, for the content is the Word of God. Theistic communion has replaced pantheistic naturalism and absorption, with the result that rational reflection and moral judgment dominate and control the ecstatic and abnormal elements.

This fits in with what we have noted already about the veiling of revelation and the mediated immediacy of God. Such explanations as we have rejected are possible because God does not come in blinding theophany but is disclosed on the ground of faith. In salvation history men are not blinded with an unveiling of the divine glory. What is true of our Lord himself is true also of the whole course of events centering in him—the Godhead is veiled in flesh. Hence this special series of historical events is history like all history. The prophets were men and they had similar counterparts elsewhere, yet through them God spoke to men in a unique saving way.

[25] Jeremiah 23:17; cf. Micah 3:5, 11.
[26] Jeremiah 14:14; 21:8; 23:18, 21, 22, 32.

The human life of Jesus of Nazareth stood out by its sinless purity, yet it veiled even then the reality of the incarnate Son. The communication of human destiny and the self-disclosure of the divine nature are mediated through the order of nature and the channels of historical life. The revelation employs, even though it transcends, the regular processes of nature and of human thought and action. Sometimes, in the biblical testimony, miracle is the breaking up of the normal by the manifestation of the abnormal. More often the veiling of the dimension of eternity within certain events can be explained without the insight of faith on the purely human level.

There is always in salvation history an enigmatic element to which the historian does violence when he pursues the method of historical explanation. He comes up against the unique and the unusual, something that makes a break between the history of Israel and the history of the rest of humanity. Here we have a people who lived in existential encounter with a God who came to them in wrath and mercy, as a just God and a Saviour, the avenger of sin and yet the redeemer of men. The whole life of this people revolved around its covenant relationship with this God.

Kings and priests were, at their best, servants of this covenant, and the prophets were the mouthpieces of the divine claims and promises which the living God made within it. This covenant relationship did not result from the action of Israel. It was God himself who took the initiative and created a people for himself in the deliverance from Egypt. It was he who chose Israel. The bond between him and them was a deeply moral one—he had chosen them and delivered them; in the shadow of a great deliverance they had acknowledged him and accepted his claims. There is nothing like this in secular history. The Hittites may have known something of covenants, but Israel gave covenant a unique meaning by lifting it to the center of her history. Here a lofty ethical monotheism is grounded in historical encounter. Here a people claim as their God a Being who is Creator of all men and Lord of the nations. Even at the level of history this stream of history is unique, and no attempt to explain it historically succeeds without doing violence to its unique element.

The prophetic message is characterized by its ethical quality, its spiritual insight, its hope and promise. The last-named is the central element in the old covenant. Israel's faith was focused in her hope. There was an anticipation among her prophetic spirits and great saints, a gazing to the far horizon for the inbreak of the heavenly kingdom. There is nothing like this eschatological vision anywhere in history. Zoroastrianism comes nearest, but lacks the deep faith and earnestness of Israel.

The sacrificial system superficially resembled the ritual patterns of the Canaanites but had a far deeper content. There seems to be no true analogy. The inner content is ethical, not merely ritualistic. It points to the moral demands of a covenant God while using practices similar to pagan rites. On every hand the patterns that might give continuity with the rest of history have so been filled with new content that often they themselves have been transfigured. A unique faith in the living God has profoundly transformed the life of a people. The unusual and the unexpected in their life sprang from a divine presence in their midst.

3. Historical Explanation and the Historical Jesus

The next task at hand is to examine various attempts to understand Jesus, not in terms of his own testimony and that of the church, but in terms of historical explanations based on presuppositions taken from the modern historical setting and from the milieu of the historical Jesus himself. An important motive in these attempts is to present Jesus in a way acceptable to the modern mind.

One issue is the eschatological framework in which the traditions unanimously present the Lord and his teaching. Was this inherent in the message of Jesus or incidental to it? Did he actually use such terminology himself or is it the creation of the *kerygma* of the early church? If the latter is the case, what remains as a picture of the historical Christ? In this consideration we shall cover the situation before and after form criticism.

Wellhausen[27] believed that the background of Jewish expectation must be severed from the outlook of Jesus. Jesus must be stripped of the Christian conception of messiahship in which he had been clothed by the early church. We should then find a prophetic leader who sought to teach man a better and higher form of righteousness.

Wellhausen was completely skeptical and held that we could not know this Jesus of history. Wrede[28] also taught that the messiahship of Jesus was a theological formulation of the primitive Christian community. Hence there arose the idea of a messianic secret having been developed in the Gospel of Mark. Jesus himself was actually a prophetic figure with an intensely spiritual message. Here we have attempts to "de-eschatologize" the tradition and to reduce Jesus to the level of an ethical religious teacher. This historical explanation is based on the presupposition of the ethical theism at the turn of this century.

The basic assumption in these viewpoints is that the Christ of the church is not the Jesus of history. The skepticism inherent in them was not shared by Adolf von Harnack[29] who, however, started from the same premises. There was a "fall" in which the first Christian community turned the gospel of Jesus into the gospel about Jesus. However, Harnack did accept the eschatological framework, holding that the church had failed to grasp the deep spiritual content veiled within it. Instead of de-eschatologizing the teaching of Jesus, he sought to ethicize the eschatology. He sought for a permanent ethical element in the contemporary garb of apocalyptic imagery. Hence he eliminated all Christological references.

The message of Jesus had not to do with himself as Son, but with God as Father. Christ came to found a spiritual Kingdom on earth in which men should live together as brothers in the family

---

[27] Julius Wellhausen, *Israelitsche und jüdische Geschichte*, 4th edition (Berlin: Georg Reimer, 1907); *Einleitung in die drei ersten Evangelien* (Berlin: Georg Reimer, 1905).

[28] William Wrede, *Das Messiasgeheimnis in den Evangelien* (Göttingen, Vandenhoeck und Ruprecht, 1901).

[29] Adolf von Harnack, *What Is Christianity?* (New York: Harper & Brothers, 1957).

of God. This Kingdom works inwardly and grows steadily like a seed, bearing fruit.[30] Man attains sonship when he becomes united with God as Father.[31] The timeless core of Jesus' message was a deeply moral and spiritual religion. Harnack made Jesus a modern man, an ethical teacher who fitted the humanistic nineteenth century and who spoke of the Fatherhood of God and the brotherhood of man. The Kingdom of God became a spiritual community of those who followed this teaching and sought to actualize it in history. The death of Jesus gave to his teaching ministry a final consecration. As Schweitzer contends: "He is a figure designed by rationalism, endowed with life by liberalism, and clothed by modern theology in an historical garb."[32]

Schweitzer likewise accepted the eschatological framework of the Gospels as authentic but believed it to be all-important and determinative. He made Jesus a thoroughgoing apocalyptist who accepted wholeheartedly the Jewish outlook of his time. Liberals like Harnack held to a this-world conception of the Kingdom as a spiritual community and contended that Jesus was using the contemporary framework to express this new understanding. Schweitzer followed Johannes Weiss, declaring that Jesus retained not only the framework but also its contemporary content. Our Lord gave the Kingdom of God a supernatural and future reference. Even his moral teaching was mere interim-ethic. Once more the principle of analogy is at work, robbing Jesus of his uniqueness. He becomes a thoroughgoing eschatologist, whom Schweitzer leaves crucified, hanging on the wheel of world history in the supreme effort to turn it and bring in the coming Age. It is significant that Schweitzer has to turn from this historical Jesus to the living Christ of faith at the end of his book. Thereby he tacitly betrays his own dissatisfaction with the picture he has painted. "He comes to us as One unknown, without a name, as of old, by the lake-side, He came to those men who knew Him not. He speaks to us the same word: 'Follow thou me!' and sets us to

---

[30] Cf. *ibid.*, pp. 60, 61.
[31] Cf. Adolf von Harnack, *The Mission and Expansion of Christianity in the First Three Centuries* (London: Williams and Norgate, 1908), p. 42.
[32] Schweitzer, *op. cit.*, p. 396.

the tasks which He has to fulfil for our time. He commands. And to those who obey Him, whether they be wise or simple, He will reveal Himself in the toils, the conflicts, the sufferings which they shall pass through in His fellowship, and, as an ineffable mystery, they shall learn in their own experience Who He is."[33] Thus, Schweitzer finishes with a position quite near Harnack, in which Jesus is the guardian and propagator of a reverence for life.

Skepticism with regard to knowledge of the historical Jesus increased with the advent of form criticism. Bultmann denies the possibility of such knowledge and leaves only the *kerygma* of the early church. The Gospels are simply extended samples of this testimony of the faith of the primitive community and offer us only the Christ of faith, a gospel about Jesus. We cannot obtain a clear picture of the Jesus of Nazareth. This *kerygma* is itself clothed in apocalyptic imagery and dependent on the three-tier universe. Hence the eschatology of the *kerygma* must be demythologized, and we are left with a Christ-event in which man comes into existential encounter with the true meaning of human existence. Even the ethical teacher has gone and there remains only an enigmatic event.

Bultmann's attempt to re-express the gospel in terms of Heidegger's existentialism and his denial that its imagery has cosmological and ontological significance must not be undervalued. He does endeavor to preserve the eschatological emphasis of the *kerygma* by existentializing it. He would even keep the historical event, while being skeptical as to its content. The Christ-event is still for him a *skandalon,* and he is anxious to retain Jesus Christ as a historical figure who is also the eschatological emissary of God. New Testament redemption is a historical event, and the *skandalon* is the basic paradox that the absolute and unconditioned ground of all existence has chosen to disclose himself perfectly in one particular event within existence. The meaning of all history is fully and perfectly contained within one particular event in history. Hence, philosophers tend to deny the salvation history in which such a *skandalon* arises and to demy-

[33] *Ibid.,* p. 401.

thologize the gospel story by finding some universal truth which it exemplifies. Bultmann will have none of this. The *skandalon* must remain, but it must be demythologized to the degree that its mythical framework will not offend modern man. Such a framework must not prevent man from facing the true offense, the existential challenge.

In describing the Christ-event as eschatological, Bultmann is not ascribing cosmological significance to it. Its eschatological uniqueness is given only anthropological reference. It conveys the ultimate knowledge about human existence. Actually the historical factors connected with the event are irrelevant once its existential truth has entered history.

Thielicke interprets Bultmann as holding that "this act of Christ conveys a new understanding of man's being which it is beyond his own capacity to achieve."[34] This is no climacteric event in which all history is redeemed. In orthodox Christianity the truth of Christianity remains historical truth. Redemption is bound up with the life, death, and resurrection of the historical Jesus. To know Christian reconciliation we must be involved in this *skandalon,* this once-for-all divine act in history.

But Bultmann is not concerned with sin and guilt in the deep Christian sense. He is applying the existential philosophy of Heidegger to the Christ-event and is concerned with estrangement of existence. Thus, the change is an existential change whereby a man can come really to exist. Such a change is not self-originating, but "it needs an event to bring it to birth. It must as it were be 'cranked up' like the universe in deism."[35] Once this event has happened, the truth has entered history, and like all knowledge it is independent of the contingencies of history. In this sense, to participate in Christ means to participate in the knowledge that he brings. The cross and the resurrection, instead of being divine acts of redemption and reconciliation, become moments in present experience whereby in order to achieve existence myself I learn to die and rise again with Christ. The Christ-event points the way to existence and makes it possible for

---

[34] Essay in *Kerygma and Myth,* ed. by E. W. Bartsch, p. 151.
[35] *Ibid.,* p. 148.

men by disclosing the true nature of existence. It is difficult to discover here more than an *imitatio Christi*.

The post-Bultmann group of scholars are now endeavoring to resuscitate a quest for the historical Jesus. A study by J. M. Robinson[36] indicates that this has received some support from Bultmann himself, who is moving from his position of extreme skepticism.[37] Robinson also points out that scholars like Hermann Diem of the Barthian group are moving in a parallel direction. It is now clearly recognized that a theological faith must have a ground in some knowledge of the historical Jesus, if it is to be retained as the expression of a historical revelation. The new quest is thus a theological one. There must be a basic continuity between the *kerygma* of the early church and the proclamation of the historical Jesus. Diem holds that the history of the proclamation is a central object of New Testament research and that the church proclaims a Jesus who proclaims himself.

We must search behind the church's *kerygma* for the proclamation of the actual incarnate Word himself.[38] We have already contended that the Synoptic Gospels, theological as they are and reflecting the *kerygma* of the early church as they do, are yet basically one with the teachings of the earthly Jesus. For us the

---

[36] J. M. Robinson, *op. cit.* The leading exponents of this viewpoint are Ernst Käsemann, G. Bornkamm, Ernst Fuchs. Cf. the article on "The Historical Jesus" by Hugh Anderson in the *Scottish Journal of Theology*, June 1960, pp. 113 ff.

[37] Schubert Ogden, in an introductory essay to Rudolf Bultmann, *Existence and Faith* (New York: Meridian Books, Inc., 1960), pp. 11 f., contends that Bultmann has always supported the objective of the new quest and implied it in some of his writings. Thus he quotes Bultmann from an essay included in this book: "If Paul, like the earliest community, saw in Jesus the Messiah he did nothing other than affirm Jesus' own claim that man's destiny is decided with reference to his person," *ibid.*, p. 196. Ogden concludes that "it still remains a fair question whether the extent of the alleged 'newness' may not depend entirely too much upon seeing it against the background of a highly over-simplified and even false impression of Bultmann's own position," *ibid.*, p. 12. In the light of Bultmann's essay quoted above, it would seem that Robinson's reference to the quest as "new" is specious.

[38] Cf. "Der irdische Jesus und der Christus des Glaubens," *Sammlung gemeinverständlicher Vortrage*, 215, 1957, pp. 9-12. Quoted in J. M. Robinson, *op. cit.*, p. 23.

Christ of faith is the Jesus of history, although we should accept the critical analysis of many peripheral utterances. The Gospels do present us with authentic history within the limits we have already outlined. The historical Jesus is seen through the *kerygma*.

The post-Bultmann approach to the historical Jesus is based upon a definite methodological procedure, in which the determining factor is still the lingering skepticism about the relation of the *kerygma* of the early church to the earthly teacher. The basic premise is that those sayings of Jesus which bear a resemblance to the *kerygma* must be set on one side indefinitely, and that only those which reflect his Jewish background in all its forms and which do not show the characteristic viewpoint of the early church must be regarded as historical. Thus the investigation is made on the basis of the nonkerygmatic material.

It is argued that when this investigation is undertaken, we do find an eschatological Jesus. We may not have any details of his *Historie*, his chronological life, but we do find ourselves confronted in the Gospels by Jesus' own understanding of his meaning, his existence. We find him saying the same thing about his inner history, his *Geschichte*, as does the *kerygma*. His historicity turns upon his own understanding of his selfhood, and the material available supplies this understanding. He understood himself eschatologically, and the Gospels confront us with his true selfhood, identical with that expressed in different language in the *kerygma* of the early church.

Bornkamm, in his *Jesus of Nazareth*,[39] employing this methodology, recognizes Jesus as messianic. He holds that the church recognized his messiahship because it so encountered him in the inward meaning of his words and acts. Bornkamm does not believe that our Lord himself used any of the accepted messianic titles, including "Son of Man." He contends, however, that Jesus was completely eschatological, believing that the Kingdom was present in himself, that he had introduced the *eschaton*, and that in his person men were confronted by the divine claim for decision.

---

[39] Günther Bornkamm, *Jesus of Nazareth* (New York: Harper & Brothers, 1960).

The fact that Jesus called men to decision implies his recognition of eschatological selfhood and carries implicitly the Christological understanding of his person present in the early Christian
kerygma. Indeed, Jesus called for an existential decision completely in line with that demanded in the primitive *kerygma,* so
that the message of Jesus is of one piece with that of the early
church. Hence, though Jesus did not, in this view, offer an explicit Christology, yet the Christology of the early *kerygma* is
implicit in his nonkerygmatic teaching. The conclusion of this
line of study is that, quite apart from whether or not Jesus used
the messianic titles applied to him in the *kerygma,* the secret of
his innermost being is still disclosed in the nonkerygmatic parts
of the Gospel records.

The disturbing element about this approach is the inherent
skepticism that still persists, partially burying the historical Jesus
under the covering of *Gemeindetheologie.* It is true that elements
in the Gospels may be due to the influence of the *kerygma*[40] and
that always we see Jesus through the eyes of postresurrection
faith and commitment. Yet the kerygmatic elements in the Synoptic Gospels, such as the messianic titles, also give us a picture of
the earthly Jesus and must not be waived as evidence indefinitely.
What is significant in the new approach is the recognition that
without some emphasis on the historicity of Jesus, our faith lapses
into docetism, and the gospel becomes an abstract form of universal truth. Even though we can form less of a picture of the historical life of Jesus than was once hoped, and some measure of
conjecture remains as to chronological sequence, we are brought
face to face with a historical person whose transcendent selfhood
is disclosed in his words and works, who claimed decision from
men and regarded his selfhood eschatologically. We cannot say
that men were not immediately aware of his innermost nature as
eschatological self during his earthly ministry. This shone at times
through his words and deeds. He was veiled in flesh, but through
it his Godhead, his transcendent selfhood, shined. A Christology

---

[40] Here critical methodology applies, e.g., the debate over the "Son of
Man" sayings, which the author would accept as authentic.

is implicit in our Lord's eschatological claims as well as in the messianic titles he employed.

This Christology must not and cannot be severed from the resurrection faith. It is faith in Christ as Lord which provides the framework for the Synoptic tradition. The early Christians believed themselves to have encountered a personal risen Christ, but we forget that this Christ could only be understood and responded to because he was continuous with the historical figure whom they had known on earth. The resurrection and the historical Jesus belong together. In the resurrection, disciples who lovingly cherished the words and deeds of the historical Jesus and sadly remembered his death now saw the inner meaning of his life in its totality. This does not mean that our salvation will be any the richer if we know more details about Jesus' earthly life. After all, the resurrection faith springs from encounter with a person, a transcendent self who lays claims on us.

This person is meaningful only because he is continuous with the person who walked the hills of Galilee in the days of his flesh and died on a cross. The exalted Christ is meaningful because he is also the humiliated Jesus, despised and rejected of men. We are called as Christians to participate by faith in the life and selfhood of one who unveiled that selfhood in historical words and works as well as in the glory of the resurrection morn. Hence we welcome all efforts to show that the person whom the early church encountered postresurrection was the transcendent self who laid his eschatological claims on men in the days of his flesh, and that the latter is no product of the *kerygma* about the risen Lord.

This brings us to an issue that comes up often in current debate, and a crucial point in our own position—the historicity of the resurrection itself.

4. *The Historicity and Uniqueness of the Resurrection*

Was the resurrection the creation of faith or the creator of faith? This question has become central in the contemporary debate on demythologization, although it has been a live issue since the liberalizing movement of the last century. Across the past fifty years, a critical approach to the New Testament has made us increasingly aware of the issues involved in the evidence for the resurrection provided by the New Testament documents.

Sometimes we have tended to overemphasize minor divergences among the different streams of tradition, and often we have bent the knee to what we have mistakenly believed to be the regnant scientific world-view. The latter is particularly evidenced in the case of Bultmann who, as we have already indicated, accepts a view of science and scientific law which would be subscribed to by few contemporary scientists. It can safely be said that the positivistic outlook of modern science, with its concern for description and prediction rather than explanation, gives us no ground for denying the possibility of miracle, unless we link to it a deistic metaphysic, which has no more justification in science itself than a theistic or a pantheistic presupposition. In addition we have to decide whether the *kerygma* of the early church is grounded in events to which its traditions point or whether these events are to a large extent created by the *kerygma*. We must look then at the New Testament evidence, bearing in mind that the faith of the witnesses is central and that the resurrection in some historical form is the presupposition of this faith.

The New Testament evidence indicates that the apostolic testimony clearly regarded the resurrection as historical event and differentiated certain elements within it. One of the earliest testimonies comes from 1 Corinthians 15. It would appear to be prior to Paul himself and to possess a creedal form. In 1 Corinthians 15:4 it is quite clear that the Apostle, and the confession of faith that he used, regarded the resurrection of our Lord as historical event, a particular moment in *Heilsgeschichte*. Hence the affirmation that Christ "was buried" and that he was raised "on the third day."

Insofar as the apostolic preaching represents the primitive Christian *kerygma*, it is evident that, from the beginning, the church affirmed the resurrection as a fundamental element in its faith. The very term "apostle" carried with it usually the stipulation that these "called men" were eyewitnesses to the resurrection.

They were, of course, not necessarily the sole eyewitnesses (1 Cor. 15:6). Yet the apostolate was limited historically to those who had seen the Risen One, with the added condition that upon them was laid the commission to bear their witness to what they had seen (Matt. 28:19).

We find two elements in the resurrection faith—the fact of the empty tomb and the visible appearances of the risen Lord. To these two elements each Gospel tradition bears witness in its own distinctive way. The very divergences in the accounts support rather than discredit the testimony, since, as many have pointed out, they indicate what might be expected of the vagaries and failings of human testimony and memory and prove that we have in these traditions no common and engineered story.

What we may call the public element in the records is constituted by the fact of the empty tomb. Mark and John alike affirm that the women found the tomb empty, John limiting the experience to Mary Magdalene alone and preserving a separate tradition. Kirsopp Lake and others believe that this element was a late addition to the resurrection faith, and it is true that the Gospel traditions are late in their final form. Yet Paul's silence about the empty tomb in 1 Corinthians 15 must not be interpreted negatively, for he states that he has already convinced his readers and is now only reminding them of this.[41] Furthermore, we have already noted the way in which Paul's confession sets "was raised" over against "was buried" (1 Cor. 15:4). It is significant that even the polemic of the Jews was not able to dispute the emptiness of the tomb but rather had to attribute it to the disciples' theft of the body (Matt. 28:13-15). Klausner, the Jewish scholar, finds such an accusation incredible, and can write that "the nineteen hundred years' faith is not founded on deception." [42]

If we allow that the empty tomb is historical actuality, we have to consider next the private element in the resurrection faith —the appearance of the risen Lord to the disciples. It is note-

---

[41] Cf. Kirsopp Lake, *Historical Evidence for the Resurrection of Jesus Christ*, p. 194.

[42] Joseph Klausner, *Jesus of Nazareth* (New York: The Macmillan Company, 1925), p. 359.

worthy that canonical traditions record appearances only to believers, whereas the later and apocryphal Gospels endeavor to support their case by recording appearances to nonbelievers also —the Gospel to the Hebrews makes Jesus appear to the servants of the high priest, and the Gospel of Peter tells how the risen Lord appears to both the Roman soldiers at the tomb and representatives of the Jewish Sanhedrin. Evidently the church soon desired some kind of public demonstration in which nonbelievers were included, whereas the earliest records from Paul through the Gospels indicate that the risen Lord showed himself only to believers.

It seems clear that, judging by the earliest traditions, the evidence for the resurrection was confined to the faithful. Matthew 28:2-15 may be the beginning of an attempt to introduce a more public element, although in this passage the Roman guards do not see the Christ but are awestruck at the mysterious happenings. We shall return later to this element of the incognito of the resurrection in relation to the world. At this point we must note our dependence upon the testimony of believing eyewitnesses.

What was the nature of the resurrection appearance? It needs to be emphasized again that the critic can never be purely objective. Often historical criticism has approached the records of the resurrection event with certain presuppositions on the ground of which it seeks to explain the appearance. It is almost axiomatic that a historical critic who is true to his scientific principles will regard all evidence with suspicion when it comes to an issue like the resurrection, just because such an event seems to be denied by the normal course of historical events. He will therefore be sympathetic to explanations which reduce the resurrection appearances to the level of psychological or psychical phenomena.

On the other hand, as O. C. Quick[43] points out, the Christian believer will be predisposed to accept the New Testament evidence. He will not demand any proof that science or the law courts would regard as cogent. If he finds the evidence sufficient, he accepts it, not because like evidences would establish any

---

[43] Vide O. C. Quick, The Doctrines of the Creed (London: Nisbet and Co., Ltd., 1938), p. 150.

other resurrection, but because the uniqueness of Jesus makes it credible. In actual fact, the radical and decisive factor in the treatment of the New Testament evidence would appear to be in the presuppositions with which it is approached.

A. M. Ramsey[44] points to three such presuppositions which appear in various forms behind modern criticism of the records of the resurrection: (1) the body has no place in man's future life; (2) the human race is destined for spiritual immortality by survival of the soul after death; (3) the resurrection of Jesus is not the unique spring and source of our resurrection, but is an exemplary, edifying symbol of our survival, so that the movement is from us to Jesus rather than from Jesus to us, and humanity supplies the norm. We may sum these up by suggesting that they belong to a world-view alien to that of the biblical revelation and more akin to the thought of the Greek world and to contemporary religious humanism.

The truth is that historical criticism as such is at best a tool that may be used constructively or destructively, dependent upon the way in which the critic approaches his evidence. The claim for objectivity in this area cannot be validated. Only as we approach the evidence sympathetically—participating in the faith and attitude of the eyewitnesses—shall we understand the meaning and significance of the resurrection event as God's Word to men. We have already shut our ears to that Word, if we approach the testimony with presuppositions that are alien to the biblical faith or that are supported by happenings in the natural order.

The two most familiar explanations of this type are those which may be categorized respectively as the subjective vision theory and the objective vision theory. The first suggests that the resurrection appearances resulted from the imaginative activity of the minds of the disciples under emotional stress and expectation. This viewpoint runs counter to the evidence, which indicates that it was the disciples themselves who at first found it difficult to believe in the resurrection of Jesus. It is furthermore difficult to understand how such self-hallucination and projection of wish-

---

[44] *Vide* Arthur Michael Ramsey, *The Resurrection of Christ* (Philadelphia: The Westminster Press, 1946), p. 55.

ful thinking could lead to the tremendous insights of the New Testament, insights which the proponents of this view are often ready to acknowledge.

The second viewpoint suggests that the resurrection appearances of Jesus were objective visions imparted to the disciples by God himself in order to assure them that the Christ survived death. As offered by B. H. Streeter,[45] this was combined with the acceptance of the empty tomb. But other scholars, dismissing the empty tomb as a later addition to the tradition and wishing to avoid the difficulty of explaining the disappearance of the physical body of our Lord, have rested upon the theory of a purely spiritual resurrection. This is the position apparently adopted by Emil Brunner.[46]   If, however, we accept the evidence for the empty tomb, we must seek elsewhere for an understanding of the resurrection appearances. Even Kirsopp Lake, who advocates the idea of a purely spiritual resurrection, is prepared to admit that "the story of the empty tomb must be fought out on doctrinal, not on historical or critical grounds." [47] Ramsey points out that the real issue is how we really understand the nature of the Christian faith and gospel. If we adopt an evolutionary and developmental approach, we shall be content to discredit the evidence for the empty tomb and postulate some form of spiritual resurrection. The resurrection of Jesus would then be regarded as an example of how the righteous may survive death. If, on the other hand, we believe that the evidence for the empty tomb must be accepted and that the resurrection was a divine creative intervention in this order of sin and death which inaugurated a new humanity, then the bodily resurrection will not be incredible and the empty tomb will not appear crude and unnecessary.

While the evidence of the Gospels patently indicates a bodily resurrection, this is also implied in the testimony of Paul. First Corinthians 15 indicates that Paul believed in a bodily resurrection

[45] Essay in *Foundations,* by seven Oxford men (London: Macmillan & Co., 1912). He believes that the empty tomb served to confirm the disciples' belief in the resurrection.

[46] Emil Brunner, *The Christian Doctrine of Creation and Redemption* (Philadelphia: The Westminster Press, 1952), pp. 365 ff.

[47] Lake, *op. cit.,* p. 253.

of which the resurrection of our Lord was the prototype as well as the creative center. The acceptance of such evidence and the refusal to dismiss it in terms of some purely pneumatic survival and to explain it in the light of evidence supplied by psychical research leave us with two possibilities.

The first is that our Lord was raised in his physical body. At first sight, this might seem to be supported by the traditions preserved in Luke and Acts, and we may note that Luke surmounts the problem of disposing of such a physical body by translating it to heaven in what appears to be a literal acceptance of the three-tier universe. Yet even Luke preserves the tradition of the journey to Emmaus in which the risen Lord disappears from sight as soon as he is recognized by the disciples.

The truth in this viewpoint is that there had to be physical recognition of the Lord and continuity of the risen appearance with the historical Jesus before there could be a cognition of his true significance and the meaning of his mission. The historical event is a necessary precondition for the inspired insight of faith. R. R. Niebuhr has made this point effectively in a book which has many brilliant insights. He cogently dismisses the views of mere spiritual resurrection or psychical appearance. The resurrection is bound up with the individuality of Jesus of Nazareth, and it cannot be understood as a manifestation of some general law of psychical behavior.[48] He points out that there is an emphasis in the tradition on the signs by which Jesus' identity is disclosed, and that these signs are bound up with the historical life of Jesus as this was preserved in the living memory of the disciples. We would add "loving" memory, too. Thus there is an element of flesh involved, and Niebuhr rightly points out that what is stressed is not so much the corporeal appearance of Jesus as the recognition of him.[49] At this point theologians cannot abandon the realm of ordinary history, and the historical signs remind us that the revelation is still through the medium of history. Niebuhr writes:

---

[48] *Vide* Richard R. Niebuhr, *The Resurrection and Historical Reason* (New York: Charles Scribner's Sons, 1957), p. 164.

[49] Cf. Matthew 28:16 ff.; Luke 24:30 ff.; John 20:20 ff.; 21:12 ff.

> . . . insofar as historical signs effect the dramatic moment of rec-
> ognition (and recognition is an indispensable element in all
> cognition), no meaning can be attached to the event if that to
> which the witnesses respond is not the historically recognizable
> Jesus.[50]

There could be no insight of faith without an anchorage in historical actuality and the recognition that accompanies it. Barth
can point out that

> Self-manifestation means . . . that the meaning and purpose of
> these encounters consist simply and exhaustively in the fact
> that the risen Christ declares himself to them in his identity
> with the One whom they had previously followed and who
> had died on the Cross and been buried.[51]

The second view of the resurrection body preserves this important element but, at the same time, recognizes the universal
elements recorded of the appearances in the traditions. This view
is that our Lord was mysteriously and miraculously raised in a
transfigured and transformed body. Paul quite clearly believes
this and speaks of the resurrection body as a pneumatic body or a
body of glory. Stauffer suggests "a spiritual body, which is as
different from a purely physical body as it is from a purely pneumatic existence." [52] This body was continuous in some mysterious
way with the physical body that was buried. The New Testament
testimony thus emphasizes the identity of the One who suffered
with the One who was raised.

Here, let it be noted, we have so little scientific knowledge of
the true nature of physical energy that we may not affirm dog-
matically such continuity and transformation to be impossible. In
any case, this may not even be subsumed under normal scientific
phenomena. It is miracle, divine inbreak. The apostles did not
attempt to psychologize about it or to explain it. They simply proclaimed it. The resurrection occurs within the natural order, but

---

[50] Niebuhr, *op. cit.*, p. 174.

[51] Karl Barth, *Church Dogmatics*, IV, 2 (Edinburgh: T. & T. Clark,
1958), p. 144.

[52] Ethelbert Stauffer, *New Testament Theology* (New York: The Macmillan Company, 1956), p. 135.

not at the normal level of behavior. We agree with Alan Richardson that "scientific explanations cannot be given for events in the eschatological order." [53]

This bodily form was not an impediment to spirit and was suited to the conditions of higher and risen life. It could take on its preresurrection physical appearance, but could also transcend our conditions of space and time, pass through closed doors, be transported from Jerusalem to Galilee in brevity of time. Even the New Testament witness in the Lucan tradition clearly regards a purely spiritual and disembodied appearance as repugnant even though it tends to be physical only (Luke 24:37). Further, we face the mysterious contradictions in the Johannine tradition that, while one witness is told not to touch the risen Lord (John 20:17), another is commanded to put his hand in the wounded side (John 20:27). We may agree with Karl Heim that

> God who has such abundant possibilities of materialization is not only capable of producing the kind of material existence, the substance of which is now being examined by nuclear physics. God's abundant power can also be materialized in a completely new form for which we have no analogy in the present world and which is therefore not available for scientific analysis. God can create a material existence which is no longer subject to the mortal law of mutual displacement, that is to say a substance which is tangible and is yet capable of passing through a locked door. [54]

As Heim puts it, the risen Jesus can move from our dimension into another, so that our spatial and temporal limitations no longer hold for the new corporeal form of his humanity. In this sense, we must still hold to a historical, a bodily, and even a physical resurrection, without being crudely material. By so doing, we shall be nearer the historical actuality in the early testimony, for such a view will conserve the unfathomable deeps in the mystery of the resurrection as God's act in history.

---

[53] Alan Richardson, *An Introduction to the Theology of the New Testament* (New York: Harper & Brothers, 1958), p. 197.

[54] Karl Heim, *Jesus the World's Perfecter* (Philadelphia: Muhlenberg Press, 1961), pp. 172 f.

5. The Certainty of Faith and Historical Knowledge

In the light of the foregoing, our contention is that the Christian faith cannot be detached from concrete historical actuality. At every point *Heilsgeschichte* is grounded in actual historical events. We cannot have the insight of faith which makes *Geschichte* possible without the happening in *Historie*. Günther Bornkamm, himself a student of Bultmann, has put it this way: "The task set to us is to seek history in the *kerygma* of the gospels, but also the *kerygma* in the history. If we are bidden to make the distinction between them, it is only that we should bring out more clearly their relationship and their mutual interpenetration.[55]

In this chapter we have endeavored to look at the historicity of salvation history in the light of the tools of historical criticism available to us, and we have attempted both to refute purely historical explanation and to establish the historical actuality of the events of that history. Historical knowledge at best can never be final. There is always an element of uncertainty about the judgment of the historian *qua* historian, and such judgments are liable to reversal in the light of subsequent knowledge. Historical judgments involve probability, and the historian as such can never be absolutely certain. Even in the matter of the central events in which the revelation of the living God has come to us, the historian can offer no certainty. His critical investigations will offer greater or lesser probability as to their authenticity and as to the authentic nature of the descriptions of them. We have seen how true this is of the resurrection and of the chronology and detailed events in the life of our Lord. Yet, at this point, faith takes the stand of certainty and affirms the absolute historicity of the crucial events of salvation history.

Further, the man of faith is not dependent upon the investigations of historical critics. He would say that the Holy Spirit testifies in his spirit that these things are true. The believer, who is also a historian, knows that historical science can never find this cer-

---

[55] Bornkamm, *op. cit.*, p. 21.

tainty within itself. It must continue to search for facts, to seek
for efficient historical causes, and to find their explanations. But
the believer knows also that historical research can never rest in
a denial of those historical facts which he knows by faith to be
real, and that no indisputable fact which it brings to light will
destroy the veracity of his faith.

It is necessary, first of all, that we remind ourselves of what
we mean by "faith." We have seen that faith is fundamentally a
commitment to the living God as he comes to us in revelation. Its
cognitive content is a very real aspect of it, but it is a cognition
which centers in the redemptive significance of Jesus Christ as the
crucified and risen Lord, in whose face we have seen God's glory.
Such faith is thus not propositional and creedal. When we speak
of its certainty, we do not mean certainty about the inerrancy of
propositional truths, but rather the certainty that is born of personal encounter with and commitment to God in Jesus Christ.
This assurance is born of a love and devotion awakened in our
hearts, as the Holy Spirit testifies within our spirits.

When the Christ of the *kerygma* becomes our living contemporary, confronting us here and now, and calling forth the
decision of faith, he grants a knowledge which is ultimate—that
in him we have stood face to face with the living God. Revelation
carries its own assurance, and saving faith has its own certainty.
The Holy Spirit bears witness with our spirit, and with certainty
we affirm that the portrait painted by faith cannot be upset or
marred by our feeble efforts to fit the historical Jesus into our
man-made categories and to explain him away as the illusive creation of the community of faith. The living Lord brings to life in
our hearts a certainty which affirms the historical judgment.

In the second place, we must never lose hold of the fact that
here a historical revelation is central but that such history does
not wear, as it were, its heart on its sleeve. We have seen enough
in our investigation to make it clear that, in the events of salvation history in general, and in the life, death, and resurrection of
Jesus of Nazareth in particular, we are face to face with the enigmatic and paradoxical.

We have noted that a good historian requires an understanding of human nature, a sympathetic imagination, and the gift of intuitive and creative insight. This latter brings us near, at the secular level, to what we mean by faith. It does mean that, in some sense, the historical past has to come alive again in the imagination of the historian, so that he encounters its inner meaning. To quote Paul Althaus: "Even the scholarly historian does not use these resources alone. He too requires 'intuition,' an imaginative 'encounter' with the past piece of life, and this intuition goes along with his inductive research and has a strong influence on his historical judgments as to what is genuine and what is false." [56] Thus, in the case of the resurrection, the believing historian will be predisposed to accept the authenticity of the records. Any true historian has, as Althaus points out, this prescient encounter with the living past, which does carry with it a degree of certainty beyond that offered by inductive research. Faith, in all its uniqueness, belongs to this order and yet goes beyond it.

Now it is true that there is always a tension between this encounter and the inductive research. The encounter partakes of the quality of faith in its subjective aspect, and this faith has to be held, as historical inquiry pursues its investigation into the details and the background of the past event. When the historian finds elements that might call his insight into question, he will still hold on to it until further investigation makes it untenable. Further, this encounter will not give him certainty about the details of the past, but only of its essential content. Intuitive insight will enable him to grasp the whole, and the inner meaning that pervades it. Patient historical investigation will fill in the details and also the historical relationships in which this particular corpus of the past is involved. It is here that the tensions arise. In the study of history, "an immediate encounter stands in an ineradicable tension with the essentially inconclusive character of scientific historical knowledge, and must be content to abide in that tension." [57]

---

[56] Paul Althaus, *Fact and Faith in the Kerygma of Today* (Philadelphia: Muhlenberg Press, 1959), p. 69.

[57] *Ibid.*, p. 71. In my former book, *The Christian Understanding of History*, I was feeling somewhat fumblingly for the same insight on pp. 79 ff., and I have used parts of this treatment above and in the following section.

Saving faith in its uniqueness stands removed from even the level we have been discussing. Such faith is evoked by encounter with the living Lord, as he lays his claim on us. Faith is sure that the testimony of the church's *kerygma* is true—the Christ of the church is continuous with the Jesus of history. God has disclosed himself in history, and the inner secret of Jesus is the nature and purpose of God himself. If the church has fabricated this, then there can be no saving faith, for such faith depends upon the assurance that sin has been dealt with in a historic act. To experience the salvation is to affirm the historicity of the act. Even on the historical level, it seems eminently more probable that such a powerful organization as the church and such a potent force as the faith it professes are the creation of a great and unique personality, than that Jesus is a historical figure who has been dressed up in a supernatural garb for the purposes of a primitive society of followers.

Althaus reminds us that every layer of the traditions preserves fundamentally the same picture of a Jesus characterized by humility, the claim to divine authority, dedication to the purposes of the Father, dedication to the service of his fellows, limitless and unconditional forgiveness of the guilty, a turning to the needy and the sinful, and eschatological certainty about the advent of the end. He adds: "It is these which make him everywhere recognizable. They are no wish-fulfilment created by the human longing for a Savior; the reports about them are too concrete and individual for that . . ." [58] Bultmann has, at least, recognized this in part by his acceptance of the historical *skandalon*. The virtue of post-Bultmann scholarship is that it is increasingly awaking to this, and anxious to demonstrate that the transcendent selfhood of the Christ of the *kerygma* is continuous with the transcendent selfhood disclosed in what is regarded as authentically historical—the nonkerygmatic elements in the Gospel traditions. In actual fact, it then needs only a short step to affirm what faith would assert, that in the Gospels we encounter the authentic Jesus. The faith of the church and the historical Jesus are bound

[58] *Ibid.*, pp. 73 f.

together in indissoluble unity. When historical critics attempt to break this unity they are doing violence to the witness of the church and the faith of the believer.

Now this does not mean the end of critical inquiry. Faith, as encounter with a historical but also risen and eschatological Jesus, cannot affirm with certainty the details of his life, death, and resurrection. If Jesus is God entering the realm of historical actuality, then there can be nothing sacrosanct about him so that we cannot undertake critical investigation. We shall not be dismayed if certain sayings are called in question or if the detailed chronology of his life is not available to us. So long as his personal glory shines through to us and confirms our faith, we must rest content.[59]

The fact that faith exists indicates that enough of the historical actuality is present in order for the transcendent Lord to manifest himself and lay his claim upon our lives. There the historian *qua* historian is not actually of much help to us. He cannot unlock the inner secret of Jesus. As historian he will not find the inner side of the life, death, and resurrection of the Lord, even though the enigmatic elements will disturb him. A painstaking historical investigation will not bring us nearer to the heart of *Heilsgeschichte*. It may help to clear out secondary elements, but even the secondary elements and the inauthentic parts of the Gospels are still colored by the same transcendent self—the post-Bultmannians have to confess this. Even those parts which critics dismiss still have the same authentic content—the living Lord and the same Lord meets us in them also. Here faith unlocks the door.

---

[59] Tillich asserts that "theologians need not be afraid of any historical conjecture, for revealed truth lies in a dimension where it can neither be confirmed nor negated by historiography. . . . Knowledge of revelation, though it is mediated primarily through historical events, does not imply factual assertions, and it is therefore not exposed to critical analysis by historical research" (*Systematic Theology*, Vol. I, p. 130). We stumble at the phrase "does not imply factual assertion," for surely faith is grounded in the historicity of the life, death, and resurrection of Jesus of Nazareth, granting that it is response to the total event and is thus not concerned with the details within the totality. Otherwise we believe that Tillich has stated our case. The phrase we have questioned points to the kind of docetism we have pointed to earlier.

The secret comes through history but is beyond historical investigation. It is opened up by revelation, and we receive it by the illumination of the Holy Spirit as we receive it in faith. Thus faith keeps its certainty while the questionings of the historical critic are at work. It knows, even under the tension of honest historical uncertainty. Faith is response to the personal Lord who comes to it through all the records.

It is true that in the New Testament, as we move from the Synoptic Gospels to the Fourth Gospel, we find an increasing emphasis on the transcendence of Jesus. This is not surprising. As the actual historical event receded into the past, it was natural that the eternal, and thus contemporaneous, dimension in Christ should come to the fore. Yet it is through the historical that the eternal is disclosed. John recognized this, although he saw also that faith does not spring from historical observation alone but from that action of the Holy Spirit which strips away the incognito and unveils the Son of God. In the living tension of faith, the Jesus of history and the divine Christ are held together in indissoluble unity. Our understanding of the divine saviourhood and lordship becomes deeper as we understand the historical person.

The mystery of the contemporaneity of Christ cannot be detached from the historical figure. As Kierkegaard saw, the Christ who is our contemporary is the Christ in his humility and rejection on earth, so that "His earthly life follows every generation in eternal history; His earthly life possesses eternal contemporaneousness." [60] This contemporaneousness does not rest solely at the level of historical thinking. It does not mean a mere kindling of the historical imagination. It means encounter with the eternal Lord, "the same yesterday, today and forever." Yet the Word he speaks is the Word which he has spoken in history through a life, a death, and an empty tomb. The Jesus of history and the Christ of faith, the temporal and the eternal, are held together in faith, for they constitute the ultimate paradox, the God-man, suggested in the very name, Jesus Christ. We are faced with the

---

[60] Søren Kierkegaard, *Training in Christianity* (Princeton: Princeton University Press, 1945), p. 68.

question: Is Jesus Christ merely a great personality of the past or is he the living Lord who can tell us with authority what we are to do about the burning questions of the present? He confronts us with an either/or—either we have to entrust our whole life to him or we passionately have to reject him. That committal of faith, that existential decision, alone discovers his secret and makes possible the realization of our historical destiny.

CHAPTER III

THE ESCHATOLOGICAL STRUCTURE OF SALVATION HISTORY UNDER THE OLD COVENANT

Having established the general historicity of the events of salvation history and justified the use of the tools provided by historical criticism, we turn now to this course of events. We shall be concerned here with its essential nature and structure, and with the purpose of God disclosed in it. The emphasis falls on the events as acts of God in which the purpose of all history is redemptively disclosed and made creatively effective in the historical scene.

1. The Covenant and the Promises

It is significant that both the Yahwistic history in the Pentateuch and the Priestly history in which it was later incorporated provide a symbolic framework of creation, fall, and judgment for the story of God's dealings with his people in history. This is no accident, for it provides the setting also for the whole biblical revelation. Salvation history loses its significance if we do not see it in a setting of creation, sin, and judgment. It is the key to all history because it comes to us in a universal history—which is the story of the sin and bankruptcy of sinful man. So the creation stories display man as the crown of the process, made in the image of God with the high destiny of fellowship with and response to God. However, man in the image of God is not on his own. He is man with woman, man in relationship.

It is man and woman together who are made in the image of God, as if to imply that God's purpose in historical existence is to create a community of fellowship in which creaturely beings shall live in personal fellowship with him and so with one another. The Garden story reveals fallen man for what he is. We have already discussed its profound analysis of sin as rebellion against God, as man's use of his God-given freedom to determine his existence apart from God. We have also indicated the significance of the images of the wilderness and of the barred gate and the angel with the flaming sword.

Secular history is the realm of frustration and meaningless existence. It is also the realm where God's pressure still persists. Man in his sin still dreams dreams and sees visions, but because of his sinful perversion he tries to realize his dreams and actualize his visions by his own strength of will. Bent on himself, his will directed on creaturely means and ends, man yet longs for the fellowship of the Garden. But to realize his longing, he continues to depend on himself and so bankruptcy dogs his path.

At this point the dramatic imagery of the Babel narrative and of the epic of Noah and the flood is employed to remind us that man's sinful frustration is also his judgment. The tower lifting its head to heaven is a symbol of man's pride. The reference to the confusion of tongues undoubtedly was initially etiological —an attempt to account for the diversity of languages. Yet it has a deeper and more symbolic meaning—it indicates that man's pride leads to a breach in his social relationships, a failure to communicate, to hold fellowship, to live with his fellows. Could a failure in a universally understandable medium of communication have a deeper significance?

The Bible understands God's wrath as also man's bankruptcy. God gives men over to the sin of their hearts, and the sinful existence in which they are involved becomes also their judgment. As it works itself out in social division and spiritual bankruptcy, the divine wrath becomes manifest. Their judgment is their failure to communicate, their divided community, the meaningless and frustrated existence in the wilderness. The floods of God's judgment overwhelm them, and out of the midst God redeems his chosen ones. Like the ark upon the waters, God's salvation history moves on its triumphant way in the flood waters of secular history which are so marked by judgment and bankruptcy.

The biblical writers undoubtedly had a much more literal interpretation of these stories, but this does not mean that they did not intentionally and under divine inspiration write them with these symbolic undertones. What, at their stage, was taken literally could, in God's good providence, veil a deeper and more symbolic meaning which has been made clearer to us as the literal element has receded into the background.

It is within this setting that we have to understand the series of historical divine acts to which the Bible bears testimony. They are bound up with the history of the Hebrew people and imply a divine choice of Israel. The theme of the election of Israel is basic to the biblical understanding of what happened in Israel's history. It is not our purpose here to go into the involved issue of the nature and veracity of the patriarchal traditions, or to discuss whether the election faith of Israel originated in the call of Abraham or in the Exodus from Egypt. This has been done in many excellent monographs.[1] Our task is to point out that the emphasis falls fundamentally on God's free choice of Israel. The election is not regarded as due to any merit on Israel's part. The best spirits of Israel recognize this. Thus the Deuteronomic tradition reminds the nation that they were not chosen because they were great in number (Deut. 7:7-8) or because they were more righteous than their neighbors and upright in heart (Deut. 9:4-5). The Deuteronomist has to confess that Israel's election is bound up with the mystery of God's unconditional love (Deut. 10:15).

We have the same picture in Ezekiel's portrayal of God seeking out Israel as a desert foundling (Ezek. 16:8). This is a picture of sheer grace, of unmerited love. The Hebrews are revealed in the Bible as no different on the human level from their fellows. They were prone to sin and to fall away to the worship of false gods; they corrupted their religion with all sorts of evil practices; many of their priests and religious leaders were blind leaders of

---

[1] H. H. Rowley, *The Biblical Doctrine of Election* (London: Lutterworth Press, 1950); H. W. Robinson, *Inspiration and Revelation in the Old Testament;* Kurt Galling, "Die Erwählungstraditionen Israels" in *Zeitschrift für die Alttestamentliche Wissenschaft und die Kunde des nachbiblischen Judentums* (Giessen: Verlag Von Alfred Töpelmann, 1928).

the blind. Yet, despite their spiritual blindness and their prone-
ness to fall into idolatrous practices, God chose them to be the
medium of his revelation.

This choice involves a new and unique relationship between
a god and his people. Other nations around Israel also had their
gods. The Moabites can be described as the sons of Chemosh
(Num. 21:29), just as the Israelites are sons of Jehovah (Deut.
14:1). The Moabite Stone and Jeremiah 48:7 indicate that, like
Jehovah, Chemosh gave oracles for the guidance of a military
campaign, apparently through oracular priests. On the surface
Jehovah was Israel's God and Israel was fulfilling his purpose,
much as other nations might fulfill the purpose of their gods.
But there was a fundamental difference, and this lay in a divine
act of redemptive choice.

The gods of the other nations were eponymous ancestors who
depended for their own well-being and existence upon the existence of their nations. The bond between god and people was a
purely naturalistic one. Hence we have the fertility rites and
orgiastic rituals which accompanied the religions of the surrounding peoples. But Israel was bound to Jehovah by no such bond.
There was no quasi-natural relationship such as we find in the
fertility cults, in which the god was the husband of the land and
the people were his children. The emphasis falls on choice. Again
and again this is emphasized. God has "chosen" Israel.[2] He has
"known" them as a man knows his wife.[3] He has "acquired" them.[4]
All three Hebrew words employed in these passages carry the
implication not of quasi-natural necessity but of moral choice.

The continued existence of Israel is not necessary for God's own
being, nor does he depend upon her exaltation for his own honor.
This was one of the deepest lessons that the prophets sought to
teach Israel. The people prided themselves that they were the
"chosen people" and therefore that God was bound to give them
victory, protect their interests, and exalt them among their neigh-

---

[2] Deuteronomy 7:6-7; Isaiah 43:10; 14:1.
[3] Amos 3:2; Hosea 5:3.
[4] Deuteronomy 32:6; Psalm 74:2; Exodus 15:15, 16.

bors. But the prophet declared that just because they were privileged their responsibility was the greater. God's hand might demand rather their punishment and their exile (Amos 3:2). Since all was of God's grace, they should be consumed with wonder at his gracious act rather than puffed up with conceit. Otherwise God would visit upon them all their iniquity.

This structure of moral choice is brought out in the image of covenant relationship. The election experience was given a formal expression and confirmed in the covenant. Indeed, the election of Israel reaches its fullest expression in this image, which belongs to the very earliest strata of our traditions. Although later traditions pushed the covenant back to the patriarchs, the early traditions place their emphasis on the covenant made at Sinai/Horeb.[5] The image itself rests back upon the idea of natural brotherhood. It appears where there is no blood kinship and takes the place of it. The two parties to a covenant are under mutual obligation to each other, laying upon each other responsibilities and respectively pledging their loyal obedience to them.

The word which characterizes the covenant bond is *chesed*, which may best be translated "steadfast love." It implies that those who have covenanted together will show steadfast and loyal love one to the other, performing their mutual obligations. At the human level we have the covenant of marriage and covenants of friendship, while nations and groups may be bound by a covenant. In the latter case, when one nation is the victor and the other the vanquished, the victor imposes the obligations and the vanquished accepts. This probably is our best way of approaching the covenant of Jehovah with Israel. Initiated by God in absolute freedom and out of love, its conditions are divinely imposed through the prophet Moses. Under the shadow of a great deliverance from Egypt, with the memory of the Red Sea crossing fresh in their memories, all the Israelites could do was to accept and pledge their loyal obedience, their *chesed*, to Jehovah whose

---

[5] Cf. H. H. Rowley: "What we can say with certainty is that the oldest documents dealing with the wilderness period which have come down to us speak of a covenant" (*op. cit.*, p. 46).

chesed would never fail. The obligations took the form which is expressed in the Decalogue and was communicated by Moses amid the thunder and the lightning on Sinai's height.[6]

We may now draw out more fully the relationship between election and covenant. Election is grounded in the divine grace and initiative. The choice of Israel is consummated in the "cutting" of a covenant with Israel, and such a covenant is the revelation of God's will. Revelation takes place within a covenant relationship and establishes it. God has chosen Israel and lays his claims to her. It is significant that the most covenantal book in the Old Testament, the book of Deuteronomy, stresses the grace and initiative of God in election. Further, this linking of the covenant with election implies that the covenant is not bilateral in the sense that obligations are laid upon both parties. Israel could lay no obligation on God. God had freely taken such obligations upon himself prior to establishing the covenant. In choosing Israel, he pledged his *chesed*, his steadfast love, to Israel. His obligations sprang from, and were the expressions of, his free grace. What the covenant did was to lay moral obligations upon Israel in response to God's gracious act of election.

This divine election and its consummation in the covenant were concerned with the creation of a people for God's own possession. If man in God's image is man in relation, symbolized in the relationship of man and woman, and if man outside the Garden and under judgment is man in division and without true power of communication and fellowship as the Babel story implies, then God's purpose is to re-create man in his image and thus to re-create man in a community of fellowship. Hence the biblical revelation sees God's purpose in history as social. The covenant of Sinai was made with a people. So the Exodus source (6:7) affirms: ". . . I will take you for my people, and I will be your God . . ." In actuality, it created them a people. At Sinai the refugees from the Egyptian bondage became a coherent group, the

---

[6] For a discussion of the Mosaic origin of the Decalogue see the essay by H. H. Rowley, "Moses and the Decalogue," *Bulletin of the John Rylands Library,* Vol. 34, Sept. 1951, pp. 81-118.

nucleus for a yet larger national group as kindred tribes joined them at Kadesh-barnea and in Canaan itself.[7]

That the covenant relationship with Jehovah was enlarged and renewed to embrace more of the tribal groups is demonstrated strikingly by the covenant ceremony at Shechem (Joshua 24). Here, after the entrance of the Exodus nucleus into Canaan and in the course of the conquest, a tribal amphictyony was formed around the renewal of the covenant relationship with the God of Israel.[8] Israel's history must be traced back to the patriarchs and the Exodus, but the full constitution of Israel as a nation was consummated in Canaan itself. Clearly the covenant rite at Shechem, as recorded in Joshua 24, did not institute relationships between Jehovah and the tribes. Israel did not at this time become the "people of God."

It is probably true that other tribal groups now came to share in the experience of the nucleus which had been delivered from Egypt, and to pledge their *chesed*—steadfast love and loyalty— to the delivering God. Here we have a renewal of the covenant made on Sinai. As Köhler points out, "The people is not a limited community; its size is variable and it grows. The number of Hebrews who gathered around Moses and the number of tribes to

---

[7] I here accept the conclusion of most Old Testament scholars that the Josephite tribes, Judah, Levi, and the remnant of Simeon, may have constituted the original nucleus from Egypt; that there may have been Kenite and Kenizzite additions at Kadesh-barnea, the Kenite center; that there were already kindred tribes such as Reuben, in Canaan, as the Tel-el-Amarna tablets seem to indicate; and that the so-called concubine tribes were groups in which Canaanite blood, also Semitic, predominated. For details of this, *vide* originally C. F. Burney, *Israel's Settlement in Canaan* (London: Oxford University Press, 1918). For the most recent and authoritative discussion, *vide* H. H. Rowley, *From Joseph to Joshua* (London: Oxford University Press, 1950). Cf. John Bright, *A History of Israel* (Philadelphia: The Westminster Press, 1959), pp. 124 ff. and pp. 142 ff.

[8] This tribal league is discussed authoritatively by Bright, *op. cit.*, pp. 142 ff. Noth refuses to admit a detailed prehistory to this Shechem covenant, and contends that the history of Israel begins here. Cf. Martin Noth, *The History of Israel* (New York: Harper & Brothers, 1958), pp. 1-7. His position, however, has been adequately criticized by John Bright, *Early Israel in Recent History Writing* (Naperville: Alec R. Allenson, Inc., 1956), *passim*.

which they belonged may have been ever so small; it was never-theless an unrestricted open number. That means they might annex as many more later, in the wilderness, at the occupation of the Promised Land or in the Palestinian period, and they could do it without prejudice." [9]

Bright's comment is relevant at this point: "Early Israel was neither a racial nor a national unity, but a confederation of clans united in covenant with Yahweh. This covenant both created his society and held it together." [10] Around its central shrine, first at Shechem and then at Shiloh, the amphictyony linked its life, re-citing its history as the record of the mighty acts of Jehovah and centering the presence of the living God in the ark of the cove-nant. We have here, in process of formation, a religious-centered national group. Over this ultimately a king became the divinely ordained representative, replacing the charismatic judges. But always Israel remained a covenanted theocracy, subject to Jeho-vah. Even its kings were never regarded as divine.[11] They too were subjected to God's Word through his prophets as the histori-cal and prophetic writings make clear. Covenant and faith were central.

God was creating a people for his own possession through the vicissitudes of history. The tradition of a divine covenant with the royal house of David is subsumed within this covenant with the people. In the covenant the gracious election of Israel, which had issued in the redemptive act of the Exodus, laid upon the corpo-rate solidarity of Israel the divine claim for steadfast love and obedience to the divine commands. All the communal rules and moral laws of the community were gathered around the divine

---

[9] Ludwig Köhler, *Old Testament Theology* (Philadelphia: The West-minster Press, 1957), p. 65.

[10] Bright, *A History of Israel*, p. 143.

[11] A. R. Johnson, in *Sacral Kingship in Ancient Israel*, has demonstrated this effectively against extreme exponents of the kingship ideology like Eng-nell. *Vide* for the extreme view Engnell, *Studies in Divine Kingship in the Ancient Near East;* Mowinckel, *He That Cometh*, should also be consulted. The British "myth and ritual school" has recently published a symposium edited by Hooke, *Myth, Ritual and Kingship.*

commands in the Decalogue. Right and wrong were judged in re-lationship to Jehovah. Even tribal mores and traditional morality became subsumed under the divine claims on Israel.

Concomitant with the divine commands was the divine prom-ise. The traditions show that embedded in the memory of the call of Abraham and the other patriarchs there was also a prom-ise.[12] The promise as formulated was not exclusive; it was inclu-sive. Abraham's seed was to become a powerful nation but it was also to bring blessing to all the nations of the earth. Only as the years came and went was Israel to learn the full significance of this high destiny. In the Exodus traditions the promise takes a new form. Israel is a people whom God has blessed and who has received a promise.[13] The promise seems at this point to be inter-preted more at the material level—a land to dwell in, material plenty, and victory over their enemies.[14] Yet we also have the echo of the form of the promise given to the patriarch—whosoever blesses Israel shall be blessed and whosoever curses it shall be cursed (Num. 24:9). It remained for the prophets to draw out the deep significance of the divine election and covenant and to elaborate the content of the promise at the spiritual level.

One last point needs to be noted. The covenant between God and Israel was unconditional on both sides. Neither party to it had the right to termination. On his side, God would never bring the covenant to an end. It sprang out of his electing grace, his free love, and he would remain faithful to his covenant. On the side of Israel, God could not compel the people to remain in the covenant, for loyalty cannot be compelled. Yet Israel was not free to withdraw at will without obligation. If it did bring the cove-nant to an end, it would not be because the covenant itself gave God's people a right to do so. If it ceased to honor the obligations Jehovah had laid on it, then it was guilty of treachery. Hence the characteristic word for sin in Old Testament Hebrew is *pesha'*,

---

[12] This memory of a promise is so embedded in the earliest strata that it cannot easily be attributed to any later accretion—Genesis 12:2 (J); 18:18 (J); 26:4 (J); 28:14 (J).

[13] Numbers 23:7-10, 18-24, especially vs. 19.

[14] Numbers 24:3-9; Deuteronomy 33:13-17, 25-29.

rebellion or transgression.[15] Any transgression of the covenant is an act of sinful rebellion. It is so morally reprehensible that it brings down the divine judgment and subjects Israel to the wrath of Jehovah.[16] Köhler comments: "To help Israel is Jahweh's business and duty. He helps the people whenever their position is endangered; that is why the writer of Deuteronomy can always say that the decision for or against Jahweh is a decision for life or death; 4:1, 9, 15; 5:33; 6:2; etc. *Israel is kept alive by adhering faithfully to the covenant with Jahweh.*" [17]

We need to emphasize the centrality of the Exodus. Prophet and psalmist, lawgiver and historian, alike in the biblical traditions and writings point to this event as the turning point in the life of Israel, its creative center. The prophets exercised such a profound influence upon Israel because they looked back to this divine act. They did not regard themselves as pioneers in a new conception of God but as the mouthpieces of an ancient faith. Their task was to act as mouthpieces and witnesses of the Word of the living God who had called Israel to become his people, who had delivered them out of the hands of the Egyptians, and who had made a covenant with them on Horeb/Sinai. The faith which they proclaimed was grounded not only in their contemporary crises but still more in the initial crisis by which Israel had been welded into a nation.

Thus it is to the pure religion of the wilderness that Amos, the first great canonical prophet, summons his hearers in the name of Jehovah. He emphasizes that a divine vocation means a heavier responsibility and that upon Israel in consequence a heavier condemnation must rest. "Hear this word that the LORD has spoken against you, O people of Israel, against the whole family which I brought up out of the land of Egypt: 'You only have I known of all the families of the earth; therefore I will punish you for all your iniquities'" (Amos 3:1-2). That the prophets were responsible for the movement from monolatry or an implicit

---

[15] Amos 2:4, 6; 4:4; 5:12; Isaiah 1:2; 43:25, 27; 44:22; 50:1; 53:5, 8; Jeremiah 2:29.

[16] Cf. Hosea 8:1-2 where a different Hebrew word is used.

[17] Köhler, *op. cit.*, pp. 68-69. Italics mine.

monotheism to an explicit monotheism is only incidental to their task. It is not monotheism alone that is important in the Hebrew faith but the general framework in which such an understanding of the divine nature is set. It must be regarded as part of a larger whole, to which the canonical prophets made their contribution but without which their mission would lose its deeper significance. That larger whole is the faith in a God who had already disclosed himself redemptively in the events of the Exodus and who had chosen the people of Israel to be his peculiar nation.

It is this divine vocation that gives true significance to the successive crises in the life of the people. So Hosea cried: "When Israel was a child, I loved him, and out of Egypt I called my son" (Hos. 11:1). The roots of all the future life of Israel and of its religious history must be found in those historic moments when the returning waters drowned an Egyptian army and when, in the rumbling of thunder and the flash of lightning, Jehovah spoke to Moses and made a covenant with his people.

The prophetic message can only be understood in this larger whole of a historical faith which they reinterpreted and of which they deepened the significance for their generation. He would be bold indeed who would assert that the nation could have faced the Babylonian Exile as it did, solely on the strength of what the great eighth- and seventh-century prophets uttered, without the background of Horeb and the Red Sea. The Exodus was the crisis of crises in the salvation history of the old covenant, the focal point from which all subsequent divine disclosures took their orientation. So Elijah, when his divinely given message was ignored and rejected, returned to Horeb, to the creative center of faith in Jehovah (1 Kings 19:8).

Towering in the midst of the early traditions is the figure of Moses. Noth[18] would dismiss him from the central tradition, but such radical treatment is not fair to the historical evidence.[19] As military leader and lawgiver, as prophet and seer, Moses dominates the Old Testament records. He must not be dismissed as

---

[18] *Vide* Noth, *op. cit.* See also his *Überlieferungsgeschichte des Pentateuch* (Stuttgart: W. Kohlhammer Verlag, 1948).

[19] Cf. Bright, *Early Israel in Recent History Writing.*

merely a national leader, organizing the revolt of a group of no-
mads. He cannot be accounted for solely by his origin or his environment. That he should emerge at such a moment to lead an
enslaved people is the first of the mighty acts by which Jehovah
redeemed his people. The significant fact in revelation is how,
time and again, man and hour, prophet and event, were matched
in the inscrutable purpose of God. Moses was the first of the
prophets—the one who had gathered the faith of the patriarchs
into a coherent expression and given the personal name "Jehovah"
to the mysterious power and presence of whom they had been
aware; the one who acted as the witness to God's Word in the deliverance of the people from Egypt. So we find the prophetic
note in his words: "Thus says the LORD, the God of the Hebrews,
'Let my people go, that they may serve me'" (Exod. 9:1).

2. Judgment and Promise in the Vicissitudes of History

The divine self-disclosure in the Old Testament period was
not a continuous process. It was a series of divine acts and was
connected with successive crises in which the human situation of
the people became climacteric. A divine call is given to Abraham,
then a falling away from the somewhat nebulous faith in a
familiar "El" who accompanied the patriarchs in their wanderings,
and the heartbreaking period of the Egyptian bondage. Then
comes a redeeming inbreak of God in which the deliverance at
the Exodus and the establishment of the covenant relationship
center in the divine Word given to Moses.

There follows another period of decline, a falling away from
the Mosaic faith in Jehovah, in which the people lapse into the
fertility practices of their Canaanite neighbors, only to come under the divine wrath as waves of Bedouins invade the Promised
Land. The book of Judges records the cycles, sometimes evidently
coterminous, of such invasions, out of which repentance comes
to Israel and God raises a judge, a charismatic leader, under whom
deliverance is effected.

The advent of the Philistines creates a fresh crisis, in which charismatic leadership does not suffice, so that a kingship is projected and finally becomes established in the family line of David. This crisis, too, centers in the prophetic personality of Samuel. A lapse into paganism and religious syncretism during Solomon's reign leads to the breakup of the United Kingdom into the divided states of Judah and Israel. A period of crisis and judgment once more comes upon the people, and more powerful neighbors and aggressive imperialisms surge into the historical arena.

In a series of divine disclosures God acts through the eighth-century prophets; thus the historical crisis conjoined to the prophetic testimony becomes the Word of God to Israel. It makes plain the true significance of what is happening, shows it to be judgment, and calls on the nation to repent. Judgment and mercy, disaster and redemption, are commingled in these prophetic utterances, and they inspire practical measures of reform under Hezekiah and Josiah. Yet these reforms, and the prophetic words behind them, find no permanent response, and so at last there comes the supreme crisis of the Exile, in which the divine word is uttered through Jeremiah, Ezekiel, and Second Isaiah.

Once more the Word of God consists in the prophets' testimony conjoined to the historical events in which they see God acting in judgment and mercy. Cyrus becomes, in very truth, as Second Isaiah sees, the chosen instrument of Jehovah. He returns the people to the land of Palestine. Under the pressure of the prophetic testimony of Haggai and Zechariah, they rebuild the Temple, organize and develop its worship and its sacrificial system, and then once more fall away into indifference and unconcern. The religious practices become ossified and the missionary spirit is replaced by a harsh nationalism. Again crisis descends on the Jews in the person of Antiochus Epiphanes. In that judgment, it is the apocalyptists who emerge as mouthpieces of the divine revelation to interpret the historical scene.

It will be seen that we have here a series of detached crises which become the turning points in Israel's religious and social life. The religious life and the social structure of the people are lifted to a new level as God's Word impinges upon the historical situation. This divine activity is central. Israel's history is "a chap-

ter in the life of God." It is God travailing in the historical life of
one people to fulfill the meaning of all history, his purpose of redemption for all humanity. In consequence, the Hebrew people
had to sacrifice many desires and ambitions which their neighbors
cherished. Neither in poetry nor in saga were the praises of the
nation sung. Even its literature was gathered around the living
God, who had called the people out from among the nations, and
who was concerned not to praise their achievements but to
scourge them for their disobedience.

The main concern of Israel was not with culture, civilization,
world conquest, political power, or commercial success. These
factors played their parts in its life, and often it was tempted to
follow them and reject its divine destiny. Yet, in crisis after crisis,
God brought the nation face to face with its true place in history.
Finally, one element predominated over the rest—obedience to
the declared will of Jehovah, as these crises made that will and
its obligations plain. The relationship of the nation to God determined the form of its social life, the nature of its economic order,
and the development of its literature, as well as the constitution
of its religious cultus and priestly orders. The relationship of
Israel to other nations depended not upon nationalistic ambitions
but upon its obedience to Jehovah and its fulfillment of his will.

On every side, the corporate life of Israel was related to God.
He was its sole heritage, and around him, as he revealed himself,
its historical life was built. The Deuteronomist saw this: ". . . the
LORD has taken you, and brought you forth out of the iron furnace, out of Egypt, to be a people of his own possession, as at this
day" (Deut. 4:20).

The activity of God in the shaping of Israel's life must be understood in terms of a dialectic of wrath and grace. The background is the sinful bondage of man as the Garden story depicts
him, unable to find his way home to God, and blinded to the
nature and purpose of God by his own sin. We might reverently
describe Israel as the divinely chosen "guinea pig" through which
man's sinful bankruptcy was to be brought home to the whole
race. Israel was God's people, but it was God's people under rejection. Confronted by the living God, Israel turned its back upon

his ways and refused to walk in his paths, demonstrating the stubborn sinfulness of the human heart. God showed himself through his prophets as absolute demand.

The obligations embodied in the Decalogue and constituting the divine demand through Moses became the center of a vast legal code. The various shrines preserved this code in differing forms, and thus we have the book of the Covenant, the book of Deuteronomy (thought by many to go back to the Shechem covenant of Joshua 24), and the Priestly Code (possibly the code preserved in the Jerusalem tradition). In these codes were preserved maxims that covered the whole of life—moral behavior, social relationships, civil practices, and ceremonial rules.[20] The corpus grew as the nation passed through successive crises, and the central figures in its development were undoubtedly the prophets. The priests were the guardians of the codes and contributed much of their ceremonial content; the judges and law procedures contributed many civil maxims; but the focal point was the prophets, who arose successively to interpret the crises in the national life and through whom the moral claims of God upon his people became more intensified and detailed.

We note a continuity in the prophetic demands and legal claims. The prophets claim to offer nothing new but rather to speak in the name of the covenant God of Sinai, looking back continually to the climacteric event of the Exodus from Egypt. The demands in the Decalogue are amplified and reinforced again and again, but the content is essentially the same. If Israel is to be God's people, it must walk in his way. The law codes brought the nature of man's sin to a sharp focus and preserved the memory of the prophetic demands. Repeatedly Israel showed its moral impotence and its inability to walk consistently in the divine statutes.

Side by side with this impotence there grew up a certain national arrogance and a preoccupation with attempts by man himself to be reconciled with God. So the movement of Israel's

---

[20] Some of these maxims reflect the legal system generally accepted in western Asia. Yet the codes were stamped with the covenant faith and the distinctive apodictic type of law appears.

history involves a revelation of the depth of man's sin under the
pressure of divine demand and judgment, a disclosure of its in-
wardness, a growing conviction in the most devout minds that it
cannot be put right by human efforts at obedience but only by a
divine act, by a new covenant written within and on man's heart,
the re-creating of his spirit.

This aspect of absolute demand bears with it a divine disclosure as wrath and judgment. It carries the marks of what
Luther calls God's "alien work." So often men see God's face in
wrath. Yet the wrath is the underside of God's love, and judgment is an aspect of redemption. We note how in the Old Testament history, wrath is—as Paul defined it later in Romans 1—God
shutting men up in their sin and leaving their sin to work in them
its inevitable consequences of doom and disaster.

As the biblical writers see it, the divine wrath is an activity of
rejection which is not wrought out in some abnormal inbreak but
in the very processes of human and social life and historical
existence itself. All history is under God, and he can make even
the sin and wrath of man to work for his glory. World conquerors
like Sennacherib, bent on pillage and imperial power, thus become, in the eyes of the prophet Isaiah, rods in God's hand,
agents of his judgment.

The wrath of God cannot be dismissed as an outmoded an-
thropomorphism, for any serious consideration of contemporary
history recognizes it as a very relevant category. What we must
be clear about is that it is not to be identified with vindictiveness
or caprice. It is the reaction of a holy God who increasingly
stands forth in the revelation as essentially grace. The human
understanding of him moves progressively to a deeper understanding of the divine wrath and moralizes it, but does not discard this category. Wrath is the divine attitude behind judgment
and is a reality at the highest level of moral and spiritual apprehension in the revelation. It is a grieving of the Holy Spirit of
God which makes him man's enemy (Isa. 63:10). But grace is
God's prevailing characteristic, and the prophets were convinced
that his wrath could be tempered by his mercy.

Undoubtedly there is a retributive aspect in the biblical understanding of judgment, and the prophetic witness would not allow us to soft-pedal this aspect. But the prophets were also convinced that judgment is remedial. It has an evangelizing aim. Cried Hosea: "I will return again to my place, until they acknowledge their guilt and seek my face, and in their distress they seek me . . ." (Hos. 5:15). It is this gracious center in the midst of wrath which leads Habakkuk to exclaim: ". . . thy work, O LORD . . . In the midst of the years renew it; in the midst of the years make it known; in wrath remember mercy" (Hab. 3:2). The prophets would see judgment, therefore, as a call to repentance. Their heirs, the Deuteronomic historians, wrote the historical books of Joshua, Judges, 1 and 2 Samuel, and 1 and 2 Kings from this point of view. They saw that judgment is retributive but that this is not its last word—it is also the opportunity to repent. In the midst of the darkness there is light, for even the darkness can be in the strategy of grace. Men have to be brought to a condition of bankruptcy before they can cease to trust in themselves and throw themselves on the mercy of God. Like the prodigal son of the parable, they have to come to themselves. This is the strategy of God's wrath. There is ever the call to repent and the promise that he will have mercy.

The tragedy of Israel, as with all men, was that it could not truly repent because it would not and could not face the deep reality of its sin. In one sense the Old Testament is the story of the unfolding of man's failure to justify himself by works, of man's realization that earned righteousness is no righteousness at all because it magnifies and ministers to his sinful pride. Righteousness before God had to be understood not as a status that sinful arrogant man earns but as a gift which God graciously confers upon penitent sinners. Such righteousness, as Paul saw, is the very nature of God himself. He is a just God and a Saviour. He is absolute demand, but he is also final succor.[21]

---

[21] Cf. Köhler, *op. cit.*, pp. 211 f. He writes: "Even punishment is grace with God."

3. Prophetic Eschatology—The Remnant and the Messiah

The prophetic insight into the pathos of God was expressed as a tension between his righteous claims and his mercy. Hosea (14:1, 4) could cry in the name of Jehovah:

> Return, O Israel, to the LORD your God,
>   for you have stumbled because of your iniquity.
>
> . . . .
>
> I will heal their faithlessness;
>   I will love them freely,
> for my anger has turned from them.

and again (11:8-9), out of the divine pathos:

> How can I give you up, O Ephraim!
>   How can I hand you over, O Israel!
> How can I make you like Admah!
>   How can I treat you like Zeboiim!
> My heart recoils within me,
>   my compassion grows warm and tender.
> I will not execute my fierce anger,
>   I will not again destroy Ephraim;
> for I am God and not man,
>   the Holy One in your midst,
>   and I will not come to destroy.

So we find a prophetic hope growing in and out of the midst of the prophetic message, and falling into a fragmentary pattern of wrath and grace. If Israel would not repent, its judgment was sure. Thus the emphasis is on the end-time, the consummation of judgment, the Day of Jehovah. With Amos this Day is darkness and not light. It is doom and judgment. There are indeed those who have tried to make the canonical prophets into prophets of doom, and who have contended that this was the characteristic element which differentiated them from the false prophets. Yet the actual biblical evidence militates against this, for through the darkness of judgment the light of redemption breaks.[22] Hence we can say that judgment is concerned ultimately with salvation. God's honor and holiness are "injured and diminished by the sin of man. The end judgment has in view is the full restoration of these two things, so that really the whole earth is full of His glory, Isa. 6:3, and the name of the great King is terrible among the Gentiles, Mal. 1:14."[23] The Day of Jehovah contains promise as well as judgment, hope as well as doom. The prophets, torn between their conviction of God's righteous claim in his covenant and his steadfast covenant love, shared in the divine pathos themselves, and dared to hope that the tension would be resolved in the ultimate divine act, which would be the restoration of all things.

As the Hebrew faith looked back to a beginning, so it looked forward to an end. This understanding of a final "Day of Jehovah" is not explicitly present in the early days. As John Bright has put it: "One can find no doctrine of 'last things' in early Israelite religion, nor even, indeed, the anticipation of some terminus of events within history that might qualify as eschatology in a limited sense. Nevertheless, the seeds of Israel's future hope, one day to issue in a fully developed eschatology, lie in the soil of her primitive covenant faith." [24] They lie in the promise. A fuller expression of the hope seems to have been widespread in the time of Amos, for he attacks the popular belief that the Day of Jehovah will be light, blessing for Israel (Amos 5:18, 20).

How the idea of this day originated is a matter of debate among Old Testament scholars. Undoubtedly some thought of a consummation must have been nascent in the Exodus experience, just as promise seems to have been implicit in the election/covenant relationship with Jehovah. Thus, if Israel was chosen to be God's people and God was to be King, men's eyes would look forward to some time when the election would be made sure and God's kingship made plain. When we come to consider the glori-

---

[22] Cf. Köhler, *op. cit.*, p. 219.
[23] *Ibid.*, p. 218.
[24] Bright, *A History of Israel*, p. 136.

ous Kingdom which the Day ushers in, we shall have occasion to note the many references to the Exodus period.

Hence, one root of the image of the future Day lay in the Hebrew view of time as filled time. Just as God had his times in the historical life of the people, when he intervened to demonstrate his sovereignty to the nations, so there would be a day which would be full of his kingship and in which Israel would be fully manifested as his people. It is noteworthy that the phrase "that Day" can refer both to the future Day of Jehovah and to the time of deliverance from Egypt (Jer. 31:33).

It is possible that the kingship ideology and the celebration of Yahweh's sovereignty at the New Year's festival also played their part in the formation of Hebrew eschatology, as Mowinckel and others suggest. Although this position is hypothetical, it seems to offer the best explanation of many of the Psalms and of various religious rites recorded in the traditions. Apparently Jehovah's kingship was celebrated every New Year's day in a ritual in which the king played his part as God's representative, in which the drama of Jehovah's victory over the primordial chaos at creation was enacted, and in which the ark was carried in royal procession into the Temple to celebrate Jehovah's kingship over and presence among his people.[25]

Mowinckel believes that the disciples of Isaiah borrowed ideas from this ritual in order to portray the future. Ultimately this became a formulated eschatology in the postexilic period. In the pre-exilic period it became the basis for a prophetic hope. We must immediately point out that it may be true that the New Year's day as the day of Jehovah's enthronement helped in the formation of the hopes. There would be a Day in the future when what the festival day never seemed to realize would become a

---

[25] *Vide* Johnson, *op. cit.* The balanced view of Johnson has been accepted here. Undoubtedly Babylonian and Canaanite influences were at work, but the unique faith of Israel would mean that the ritual practices would be given a distinctive turn. There would be no thought of the king as a divine or demi-divine person and no pattern of Jehovah's dying and rising again as in these pagan rituals. It is highly probable, however, that the king enacted his own going down to the pit and renewal by Jehovah to signify Jehovah's renewal of the national life.

reality. God would fully be disclosed as King, and Israel would truly be his people.

Yet having admitted some influence, we would dispute whether it was the central source of Israel's eschatology. Israel's eschatology was implicit in the faith and promise of the Exodus covenant. It was Israel's encounter with the saving God in history that made it sure of the ultimate act. Even when God's face was turned from Israel and the prophets attacked a superficial optimism with a message of judgment, they still centered their oracles in the covenant experience. Shining through these oracles are realism and certainty born not of some failure of cultic actuality but of the actual deliverance at the Exodus. The God who acts in the end-time still claims a people for himself.

Jeremiah (31:33) sees a new covenant, but he and Ezekiel (36:28) use the old formula: You shall be my people, and I will be your God. God would effect the completion of that work which he had begun at the Red Sea and on Sinai's height. It is difficult to see how the failure of the cult could make people more sure of God in the future. Most of all, it is difficult to understand the radical prophetic message of judgment in the light of cultic ineffectiveness; one would expect rather a futuristic optimism, not doom. The prophets called men back to a covenant faith, in which judgment and grace were alike implicit and in which the promise carried the seeds of eschatological faith and certainty. Writes Vriezen: "Eschatology is a religious certainty which springs directly from the Israelite faith in God as rooted in the history of its salvation."[26]

In whatever way the idea arose, what really matters is its final content and its place in the divine revelation. From Amos on, we find the prophets endeavoring to free the hope from the wrong and misconceived content of national success and prosperity,

---

[26] Th. C. Vriezen, *An Outline of Old Testament Theology* (Newton Centre: Charles T. Branford Co., 1950), p. 370. He also writes: "It was not national optimism or mythical thought that led to the hopes of salvation, but only the certainty of [the] reality of God, of that God who had from the beginning been proclaimed to the people as the holy God of the Covenant, of that God who carries His work into effect in spite of the sins of mankind," p. 370.

laying upon Israel the divine demands, reminding the nation that
privilege meant responsibility, and seeing the Day as judgment.
At the same time, the grace that shone in every historical crisis to
which the prophets spoke would be dominant at the end. The
just God would also be the Saviour. Absolute demand would be
matched by final succor, and the promise would find its fulfillment in the Day. While it was true that the Day would consummate, for faithless and rebellious Israel, the successive crises of
judgment to which it had been subjected, it was also the Day
when the promise, so vaguely grasped at the first, would find its
fulfillment. God, who in the first great crisis of the Exodus had
begun the creation of a people for himself, would finally accomplish his purpose. A rebellious people would somehow be truly
restored as the people of God. Judgment would be matched
by restoration.

Some confusion has arisen with regard to the understanding
of the description "eschatology." There are those who maintain
that "eschatology" should be employed to describe a transcendental end of history which makes a radical break with the normal
historical processes. Hence they believe eschatology to arise after
the Exile, and some prefer to speak simply of a prophetic hope.
Morgenstern attempts to explain away the pre-exilic references
to the Day of Jehovah as being connected with the next New
Year's festival and not with the last things.[27] Mowinckel[28] holds
that the pre-exilic prophets had only a future hope, which is this-
worldly, national, and political in character. According to this
Norwegian scholar, they looked for a historical restoration of
Israel. This would be ushered in by a divine act, and here the
prophets made use of religious and otherworldly elements. Mowinckel's thought is bound up with his thesis that the eschatological outlook originated after the collapse of the Southern Kingdom
and with the passing of the enthronement ceremony.

It is true that, for the pre-exilic prophets, the Day of Jehovah
was a climacteric act of God within the historical scene and in

---

[27] Julian Morgenstern, *Amos Studies* (Cincinnati: Hebrew Union Col-
lege Press, 1941), pp. 408 ff.
[28] Mowinckel, *He That Cometh*, pp. 130 ff.

some sense continuous with what had already taken place. They often saw the contemporary scene and its crises of judgment as a partial realization of the final judgment on that Day. Yet the imagery they used carried a transcendental dimension within it, and there is a cosmic aspect in the vision of the future. It would seem better to speak of a pre-exilic prophetic eschatology, which, to use Vriezen's description,[29] is an "awakening eschatology." National and historical elements contained cosmic and transcendent dimensions within them.

Let us look at this cosmic aspect. The judgment is described in terms of the return of the chaos from which God by his creative fiat called forth the world. This theme has been well-established.[30] Furthermore, the presence of the motif of light recalls the divine victory over chaos in which light triumphed over darkness. Just as the world was begun by a creative act, so history will be consummated in a new creative act in which light will finally triumph over the chaotic forces of darkness that sin has released in history.[31] But this final triumph is pictured as a divine intervention in the scene of history. God's final triumph will be a more complete victory than that which he accomplished for Israel in the day of Midian.[32] It will be a Day utterly filled with his personal presence, a final theophany which will consummate his successive interventions in the historical scene. As the Hebrew saw it, all history was open to God's activity, and the final event would thus be more of the same on the historical plane, the ultimate act of creation and restoration.

In actual fact, we might take Isaiah as an early instance of the tendency to move to a more transcendental frame of reference, even though he maintains continuity with the historical. His messianic prophecies have a cosmic reference, embracing the whole world (11:9) and the animal order (11:6 ff.), and the dramatic images that he employs seem to point to a salvation

---

[29] *Vide* Vriezen, *op. cit.*, pp. 354-369.

[30] *Vide* Hermann Gunkel, *Schöpfung und Chaos in Urzeit und Endzeit* (Göttingen, 1895)—the pioneer study of this idea.

[31] Isaiah 27:1; Amos 9:3; Isaiah 51:9.

[32] Isaiah 9:3; 10:26; cf. Judges 9:3.

that will transcend the historical. Vriezen goes so far as to suggest that "Isaiah no longer sees the restoration on the historical plane only, but in a supra-historical light." [33] He would indeed make Isaiah "the first preacher of the eschatological expectation." The cosmic setting certainly contained the future seeds of postexilic development. We can agree with Johannes Hempel that "through this scheme of prophecy, both fulfilled and still to be fulfilled, even the universalistic cosmological eschatology maintains a close connection with the actual contemporary prophesying of the ancient prophets, however much the two may differ in their literary character." [34] We shall therefore regard "eschatology" as a true description of the prophetic hope, contending that the latter already contained, in embryo, the finer elements of the later, and postexilic, eschatology.

Each prophet saw the Day of Jehovah, the crisis of crises, as imminent upon the horizon of history. So sure was he of God's ultimate intervention that he could foreshorten the time. Often he seems to have identified some contemporary situation with at least the ushering in of the climacteric event. Hence, for Isaiah, the Day seems associated with judgment at the hands of Assyria; for Jeremiah, Judah would be judged in that Day by the instrumentality of Babylon. The note changes from judgment to hope in the Exile, as Second Isaiah sees Cyrus the Persian as the herald of the coming Day. Always the Day waits, as crisis follows crisis, yet each of the prophets contributes some fragmentary elements to the pattern of the hope. Central in their message was the holding together of judgment and mercy, wrath and grace. The covenant God is a God of steadfast love, and so, beyond the final judgment, grace must still triumph.

The thought of the remnant which survives the purging fires of judgment holds the tension of wrath and grace. The early nature of Hebrew eschatology is demonstrated by its primary em-

---

[33] Vriezen, *op. cit.*, p. 360. Vriezen's whole discussion in this section is a welcome answer to the extreme position of Mowinckel.

[34] Johannes Hempel, essay on "The Contents of the Literature" in *Record and Revelation*, ed. by H. W. Robinson (Oxford: The Clarendon Press, 1938), p. 67.

phasis on the national group, on the people of God. The idea of individual and personal eschatology is a later arrival on the scene, and when it does emerge it is still bound up with the collective. Early Hebrew psychology emphasized the group above and beyond the individual, and had a sense of corporate solidarity which explains many of the phenomena of Israel's history.[35] Yet differentiation of the good and the evil at the individual level was also early, and hence the thought of a final purging of the nation and the emergence of a righteous remnant at the end-time soon found a place. This remnant hope signified both darkness and light. It spelled out judgment and emphasized responsibility as well as privilege—only those who were faithful to the covenant would survive. It held out hope and mercy—God would redeem his faithful ones. Yet the element of judgment is central.

Amos sees a purging so radical that it is as if only two bones and a piece of ear shall be saved from the lion's mouth (Amos 3:12; 5:3). With Isaiah, the remnant doctrine takes a clearer definition. The prophet is instructed to give his son the symbolic name "Shear-jashub" as a promise from God that a remnant of the nation shall turn to be saved. The apostasy of the people means that the nation as a whole cannot be the instrument of the divine purpose. Jehovah has brought up and nourished his children, but they have rebelled against him, showing a willful ignorance of which even the domestic animals are not guilty (Isa. 1:2-3). The judgment will descend, but the dross will be purged away, and the faithful remnant of the nation will be restored to Jehovah's purpose, so that Zion shall yet be called the "city of righteousness" (Isa. 1:25 ff.). Already we see the appearance of the personal aspect of the covenant relationship and the recognition that it involves an inward attitude. The continuity of this eschatological element with history is seen in Isaiah's own act, when he began to consolidate a remnant proleptically in the midst of a faithless

---

[35] For a discussion of this, cf. E. C. Rust, *Nature and Man in Biblical Thought* (London: Lutterworth Press, 1953), pp. 115 ff.; also any of the good theologies of the Old Testament cited in the footnotes of this chapter—Köhler, Jacob, Vriezen.

people by binding up the roll of his oracles and committing it to
a little band of disciples (8:16 ff.).

This same continuity with history is manifested by the centrality of Zion in Israel's hope. The restoration will take place on
the historical plane. Zion is here world-wide in its influence, but
such prophecy is not necessarily postexilic. Isaiah was steadied by
his faith in the inviolability of Zion. His prophecy aroused a
materialistic trust and false confidence with which Jeremiah had
to deal later in his famous Temple sermon (Jer. 7, 26). Isaiah's
logic is clear. Jehovah dwelt in his Temple in Zion, and therefore
his Temple must be inviolate. He had founded Zion and set a
cornerstone so that Zion should not be moved (Isa. 14:32; 28:16).
Thus historical confidence pointed forward to eschatological fulfillment. Assyria could not prevail against Zion, and Zion would
be central in the coming Kingdom. Yet Micah could still prophesy
that Zion would become as a plowed field (3:12), and Jeremiah
could remember this as, a century later, he prophesied the doom
of the Holy City (chs. 7, 26).

But the hope persisted. We have the prophecy of the mountain of Jehovah's house to which the nations shall flow and which
shall be exalted above the hills, where Jehovah will teach the nations his ways.[36] Ezekiel sees Zion as the center of a restored nation and pictures a healing stream which flows from the new
Temple and brings life to the nation and the land, including the
Dead Sea, which shall be cleansed of its salt that fish may live
again in its waters (47:1-12). God's glory will return to dwell in
the Temple on the same side from which it departed, from the
way of the East (Ezek. 43:2; cf. 11:23), and the name of the city
in that day shall be "The LORD is there" (48:35; cf. 37:27).

The more characteristic postexilic note appears in Deutero-
Zechariah, as the prophet sees the contours of the land being
altered by direct divine intervention and Zion's hill being elevated
in solitary splendor (Zech. 14:8-9). But Zion remains the center
of the glorious restored Kingdom. Here, however, as also in the
detached oracle of Isaiah 2:2-4, the world-wide emphasis appears

---

[36] Isaiah 2:2-4; cf. Micah 4:1-3.

more fully. All nations will center their life in the city and its Temple (Zech. 14:16-17). Already in Proto-Zechariah this note is appearing (8:21), however, and we cannot differentiate post-exilic eschatology so much on this basis as on the note of cata-strophic intervention and re-creation which seems to divorce the End more radically from the normal processes of history.

How is the creation of the remnant to become possible in the end-time? Here Jeremiah contributes to the fragmentary pattern. At first he seems to have seen the remnant in those who gathered around Gedaliah (Jer. 42:10-22), but soon he transfers his hopes to the exiles—it is in the "basket of figs" that the future rests (Jer. 24:4 ff.). Once more we see a measure of continuity, yet it is God's act that will make a remnant possible out of the darkness of the Exile. The prophet's own bitter experience drove him back upon the divine fellowship and brought a revelation in which he saw that the only hope lay in a transformed covenant relationship. In this "new covenant," the externals would be eliminated, and every true Israelite would share in the prophet's own personal fellow-ship with Jehovah (Jer. 31:31-34). God's law would be written on their inward parts, and they would know him individually and personally as forgiven men.

To match this comes Ezekiel's vision of an Israel re-created individually from within so that the individual Jew will be given a new heart and a right spirit (Ezek. 11:19; 36:27). With Joel the postexilic eschatology begins to emerge, but he continues the pre-exilic strain as he sees the remnant sharing individually in the Spirit which has normally been granted to the prophets (Joel 2:28 ff.). There will be a democratization of the prophetic con-sciousness with the concomitant divine fellowship. This will be God's re-creating act, for he will pour out his Spirit on all flesh.

Within this hope there is woven the messianic strand. As a technical term, the word "messiah" does not occur in the Old Testament record. It connotes generally "one who is anointed," and used in this sense could apply to kings, priests, prophets, patriarchs, and even Cyrus, the Persian conqueror. Undoubtedly the thought of an everlasting covenant with the royal house of David (2 Sam. 7:12) provides one root of the imagery now under

review. Another may well be the kingship ideology associated
with the enthronement ceremony. There is little doubt that the
king was regarded as the representative of the people before God,
and that his righteousness before God conditioned God's relation
to the nation as a whole. The current ideas of a corporate solidarity would lead us to expect this. The renewal of the king's life
before God in the ritual combat of the New Year's festival could
thus symbolize the renewal of the nation,[37] for under Jehovah
he would then secure justice in the heart. As the Davidic monarchy failed, hope would take the place of actuality. We cannot
accept Mowinckel's thesis[38] that this waited on the Exile, but
we can agree with him that the mythology of the New Year's
festival and, in particular, its emphasis on the place of the king
helped in the formation of the messianic hope.[39] It is wrong to regard it as the sole or even dominant source, but that it was under
the divine revelation seems highly probable.

It may well have helped in the formulation of the messianic
figure in the Isaianic oracles, especially if that prophet's call was
bound up with the New Year's festival.[40] The picture presented is
of a scion of the house of David who shall rule over the restored
remnant and upon whom the Spirit of Jehovah shall rest; he will
be a charismatic person, although the understanding of spiritual
gifts has been lifted to a high level. An idealized picture of the
Davidic monarchy as exercising justice and establishing righteousness, the source of peace and the center of concord, is thus put in
the center of the prophetic hope. The coming king will be unique
in his possession of superhuman powers, in his judicial decisions,
and in the unbroken peace of his reign—of his government there

---

[37] *Vide* Johnson, *op. cit.*, pp. 1 ff. and *passim*.

[38] *Vide* Mowinckel, *He That Cometh*.

[39] Cf. G. E. Wright, *The Old Testament Against Its Environment* (London: SCM Press, 1950), p. 64. "A theology of kingship evidently arose in
the court circles of Jerusalem, out of which the conception of the future
Messiah naturally grew. When the current kings betrayed their trust, God,
it was believed, would raise up an Anointed One who would fulfil the theological conditions on which the monarchy rested."

[40] Isaiah 6; *vide* Ivan Engnell, *The Call of Isaiah* (Uppsala: Lunde-
quistska Bokhandeln, 1949), *passim*.

shall be no end (Isa. 9:6, 7; 11:1 ff.). ". . . the royal rule shall be inflexibly just, because divinely inspired, and the spirit of concord shall not alone possess the hearts of men, but even extend to wild beasts, whose nature shall be radically transformed . . ." [41]

Jeremiah offers a similar picture, which emphasizes the justice of the Messiah's rule. Indeed, so much does the future ruler express the will of God that he can be called "The LORD is our righteousness," an illustration of the way in which the righteousness of the nation is bound up with that of its ruler (Jer. 23:5-6). So historical is the representation that some dispute an eschatological reference here and contend that it refers only to a future good king. G. E. Wright has pointed out that "the dividing line between the historical and the eschatological conceptions of kingship is . . . very difficult, if not impossible, to draw; the second was simply the extension of the first to the age of God's fulfilment of his covenanted promises." [42] Actually, however, the figure is so idealized that it must be linked up with the eschatological hope. Micah offers a late addition linking up the Messiah with the ancestral home of David, Bethlehem;[43] Zechariah and Haggai show how small a line divides eschatology from history in the prophetic hope, for each in his distinctive way binds up the messianic hope with the historical figure of Zerubbabel, who is designated the "signet ring" by Haggai (2:23) and "the Branch" by Zechariah (3:8; 6:12). We see here how easily an actual historical hope could move into an eschatological one and *vice versa*.

Deutero-Zechariah completes the pattern of the Messiah (Zech. 9:9-10). We see him entering Jerusalem, riding on an ass. It is Jehovah who establishes him on his throne. He is not riding a war horse to victory, for the victory is God's and he does not bring it. He is the passive recipient of it, and through it his dominion is world-wide. The emphasis falls on the lowliness which characterized our Lord himself.

We have not yet looked at the picture of the setting and life

---

[41] H. H. Rowley, *The Rediscovery of the Old Testament* (Philadelphia: The Westminster Press, 1946), p. 272.

[42] Wright, *op. cit.*, pp. 64 f.

[43] Micah 5:2-4; cf. the late Amos oracle 9:11.

of the restored remnant. Here we find again the sense of historical continuity, and also a picture of the return to paradise. It is quite clear that the picture of an initial "golden age" was present early in Hebrew thought. The Garden story occurs in J, our earliest source. This is of course paralleled by similar imagery among the oracles of other peoples. The theme of a return of the golden age had a cyclic and naturalistic connotation elsewhere, but the cyclic and naturalistic motif is replaced in Hebrew thought by its distinctive linear eschatological hope. The thought of the return of the initial state is thus lifted up and baptized into the Hebrew revelation. There can be little doubt that it played its part in the prophetic hope. Men will live long, and premature death will be barred.[44] Zechariah regards even one hundred years as young. Ezekiel sees a return of the primeval innocence and perfection, and uses this theme in his condemnation of Tyre and Egypt (Ezek. 28:13; 31:3). The stream of healing water that flowed in paradise will flow again in the redeemed community,[45] and on its banks will grow the tree whose fruit shall provide food and its leaf healing. The cosmic element appears in Isaiah's picture of the participation of the animals and the whole natural order in the messianic Kingdom.[46] The soil will recover its full fertility, and all shall share in its fruits. The heavenly bodies will become super-brilliant in their radiation.

It has been pointed out that not only the primordial story of the Garden but also the Exodus experience contributed at this point.[47] Hosea sees Jehovah calling Israel back into the wilderness and wooing her again as at the first (ch. 2). With Deutero-Isaiah, just because of the Exile, the Exodus theme becomes central. The returning exiles will cross the desert in triumphant procession, the wilderness itself being transfigured.[48] The water from the flinty rock is resurrected in the picture of the springs that

[44] Isaiah 65:20; Zechariah 8:4.
[45] Ezekiel 47:1-12; cf. Genesis 2.
[46] Isaiah 11:6-9; 30:19-26; 32:15.
[47] Cf. Edmond Jacob, *Theology of the Old Testament* (New York: Harper & Brothers, 1958), p. 326.
[48] Isaiah 41:18-20; 51:11. Cf. the detached exilic oracle in Isaiah 35.

gush forth. The leadership of Jehovah, symbolized in the pillars of cloud and fire in the first Exodus, is pictured again in the figure of God as the Shepherd going before his people.[49] Elsewhere in Isaiah the same imagery arises (4:5). The imagery of the initial creative triumph over the chaos monster, repeated in the triumph over Egypt in the Exodus, becomes basic in the assurance that Jehovah will deliver the exiles (Isa. 51:9-10).

Not only will the land and the people be restored, but also world-wide salvation is promised in some of the prophetic utterances. If Amos calls all nations to the bar of judgment and sees naught but condemnation (chs. 1 and 2), others offer hope for the nations as well as for Israel. Isaiah's promise that in the messianic age the knowledge of Jehovah will cover the earth (Isa. 11:9), the oracle that tells of all nations flowing to the mountain of Jehovah's house,[50] the hope of Zephaniah that there shall be a common pure language in which all peoples shall address Jehovah (Zeph. 3:9)—all these find their consummation in the missionary spirit of Deutero-Isaiah and his image of the "Suffering Servant."

Deutero-Isaiah's portrayal of the Servant draws together the loose threads of the redemptive aspect of Israel's hope. At the same time, it fills out the promise to Abraham that through his seed all nations should evoke blessing. In the midst of Deutero-Isaiah are the four Servant Songs in which are set forth the implications of his other oracles.[51] He paints a picture of a mysterious being, the Servant of Jehovah, through whose undeserved suffering others shall be redeemed. Various attempts have been made to identify the Servant.[52] He has been associated historically with a prophet like Jeremiah or Deutero-Isaiah himself or Moses. It is possible that the last-named figure played a part in the prophetic imagination since the prophet of the Exile uses the imagery of the

---

[49] Isaiah 40:11; 52:12; cf. Exodus 15:13.
[50] Isaiah 2:2-4; cf. Micah 4:1-3.
[51] Isaiah 42:1-4; 49:1-6; 50:4-9; 52:13—53:12.
[52] *Vide* Rowley, *The Servant of the Lord,* pp. 1-128; C. R. North, *The Suffering Servant in Deutero-Isaiah* (Oxford: University Press, 1948), *passim.*

first Exodus to describe in anticipation the return from Babylon to Palestine. Moses is himself styled the Servant of Jehovah,[53] and himself carries many of the distinguishing marks of the Servant— he is prophet (Exod. 6:6), intercessor (Exod. 32:11; Deut. 9:18-20), teacher (Deut. 4:10; 7:12), and covenant giver (Exod. 24:8). Yet this is undoubtedly only one strand, coming from the initial revelatory crisis of Israel's faith.

Other scholars take a corporate view of the Servant and regard him as a collective figure, representing either Israel as a whole or the righteous remnant. Yet others regard the figure as individual and messianic. The solution would seem to lie along the lines which take note of the peculiar Hebrew psychology. The Hebrew could move from the individual to the group, of which he was a constituent part and a representative figure, without change of tempo, ascribing to one the qualities and responsibilities and failings of the other. This sense of corporate solidarity and of extension of personality over a whole group has already been called to our attention and was a natural way of thinking in Israel. In the body of the prophecy, the Servant is identified with Israel. In the Songs, he seems at times to be the nation, at other times to be distinguished from it, perhaps as the remnant, and finally in Isaiah 53 to be a highly individualized figure. The Servant is a messianic figure who represents the nation and in whom the remnant is gathered up.

The picture of redemption through messianic suffering here begins to emerge. It is the Messiah who will effect the redemption on which Israel waits. The Servant will gather up the suffering of Israel in himself, identify himself with its judgment, and offer the overplus of suffering, which even Israel does not deserve, as a guilt offering on behalf of the nations of men. The universalistic note appears in its fullness. Through Jehovah's Servant, Israel will be a light to the Gentiles and the proclaimer of Jehovah's salvation to the ends of the earth (Isa. 49:6). The isles will wait on the Servant for instruction, and here the Servant may

---

[53] Exodus 4:10; 14:31; Numbers 11:11; 12:7; Deuteronomy 3:24; 34:5.

be the larger messianic figure embracing the remnant (Isa. 49:1 ff.).

The Servant fulfills a threefold role, bearing striking resemblances to the Mosaic pattern. He is king and leader. Both the beginning and the end of the fourth Song (52:13 and 53:12) emphasize his kingly nature. He is represented as an invincible ruler. Here the New Year's festival may make some contribution to the imagery. It is hypothetically believed to have had a ritual humiliation, death, and resurrection of the ruling king.[54] He is prophet, offering instruction and interceding for men (Isa. 49:6; 53:12). Was he *Moses redivivus?* The Servant is also priest and guilt-offering through whom the forgiveness of sins becomes a reality. Thus ideas of the cultus are gathered up with inspired insight in the figure of the Servant. As Jacob puts it: "All that myth and history taught about salvation he (Deutero-Isaiah) sees prophetically realized by a man who, because he is a living synthesis and a concentration of the elected people, will give back to the latter its sense of mission, for in the prophet's thought Israel never ceases to be the servant."[55]

The prophet manifestly sees the Servant extended into the faithful remnant, so that the totality of the redeemed with the redeemer are to minister to the isles and to be a light to lighten the Gentiles. Here we have a real missionary task portrayed. The true meaning of the promise to Abraham is made explicit. In the centuries that followed, however, Jewish life was to be dominated by increasing nationalism and preoccupation with their own future as the elect people. Jonah and Ruth stand out as two sublime examples of the true prophetic vision in the postexilic period. Generally we may say that the prophetic stream, which achieved final expression in Deutero-Isaiah, wedded universalism with particularism, for though all nations were to share in the glory, Zion

---

[54] Israel's ritual pattern is largely hypothetical, although Psalm 89:39 may hint at it; *vide* Johnson, *op. cit., passim.* The Babylonian ritual clearly allowed for the king's bearing the sins of the people in the ritual. Because of the Exile this may have been a contributing factor in Deutero-Isaiah's imagery.

[55] Jacob, *op. cit.,* pp. 340 f. I am indebted much to Jacob here.

was to remain the center. It was left for Ezekiel and the narrower viewpoint that sprang from his writings to major on the particularism. From Ezekiel's restored community all nations were to be excluded. The policies of the Nehemiah-Ezra period follow naturally. The most extreme expression of this viewpoint was the book of Esther.

This pre-exilic eschatology thus clearly regarded the final salvation as in some sense continuous with the historical experience of Israel. It did not radically divorce the "last things" from preceding history, and it regarded the Day of Jehovah as imminent, sometimes identifying the contemporary situation as its advance guard. Yet it did embrace a transcendent dimension in its portrayal of the End as a divine act, and fittingly clothed the act in imagery to signify its nature as divine inbreak. Further, it had elements of cosmic renewal alongside its hope of national restoration. With the Exile the transcendent and cosmic dimensions became mere event. The ultimate salvation became a transcendent act of God, and cosmic convulsions were to be succeeded by cosmic re-creation.

The period after the Exile saw the mood of depression settle upon the Jewish people. The near expectation of the Day, the failure of the historical fixation of the messianic hope on Zerubbabel, and the absence of great prophetic voices engendered a mood in which man doubted that God loved his people and that he had called them.[56] Men began to fix their eyes on a salvation beyond the plane of history. As Vriezen puts it: ". . . they first expected the destruction of this world and did not think salvation could be realized in this world unless it descended to earth from heaven; thus the time of salvation was moved to a new world, to the *'olam habba*."[57] We can trace this movement in the biblical testimony from Ezekiel through Joel, Isaiah 24-27, and Deutero-Zechariah (9:14), to the book of Daniel.

---

[56] This mood is combatted in Malachi 1:2. This prophet reasserts the eschatological note.

[57] Vriezen, *op. cit.*, p. 366.

4. Postexilic Eschatology—The Son of Man and the Age-to-Come

The postexilic prophets made the End thoroughly eschatological. Its inbreak was painted in purely supernatural and transcendent terms. It was to be a catastrophic cosmic upheaval. God would intervene directly rather than through historical intermediaries. This appears in Joel (ch. 3) and in Deutero-Zechariah (especially ch. 14). There began to emerge new insights which, unfortunately, in the intertestamental period developed into a deterministic and legalistic apocalypticism. Biblical apocalyptic, however, must not be confused with the latter as it is found in the Pseudepigrapha. Hence, we shall see that postexilic eschatology embraces elements which later developed into the fanciful symbolism and weird programs of the esoteric apocalyptic circles.

In this developed eschatology, the angelic element begins to function, while Satan and his demons find a place. Iranian influences here combined with earlier Semitic demonology. The phrase "the Kingdom of God" had hitherto signified God's kingship or kingly rule. This was a divine attribute with an eschatological significance, since it would be fully actualized in the messianic age. Now, however, it came to mean an eternal order in the heavens where God ruled from his throne over the hosts of angels who perfectly obeyed his will. For the pre-exilic prophet, the real eternal existent had been fundamentally the person of God, but the postexilic eschatology pictures an eternal and otherworldly order, which may be visited in visions, and which stands over against this world, where Satan and his demons are permitted to exercise authority.[58] History becomes one vast battlefield, stretching up into heaven, in which the Kingdom of God wars with the Kingdom of Evil. The fortunes of Israel and the destinies of the nations are bound up with the issue of this conflict, for they are respectively the representatives on earth of the two kingdoms. God is, however, in control. When his time

---

[58] Cf. Rudolf Otto, *The Kingdom of God and the Son of Man* (London: Lutterworth Press, 1943), pp. 36 f.

comes, his eternal order will invade this earthly scene, and, in a vast cosmic upheaval, defeat the powers of evil and dissolve the world in fiery judgment.

This raises several issues. The first is that history still centers in Israel as God's chosen people, but that the other nations come more into the picture than in earlier prophetic eschatology. They are no longer of significance merely as periodic executants of the divine judgment upon Israel or agents of its salvation. Their destiny, too, is bound up with the age-long conflict, in which Israel's destiny is being decided. Hence the final judgment is world-wide with the result that the new order may be universal in scope. It is pictured increasingly in the image of a great assize.

The second issue raised is a changed emphasis from the prophetic call to repentance—because the judgment is about to descend—to a comforting message of patience under trial and tribulation. The outcome of the conflict is sure and the faithful will be delivered by God and vindicated before all nations.

The third issue is that of individual survival. With the growing individualism of Jewish thought from the Exile on, and with the deferment of the hope, individual immortality became a problem. The pre-exilic prophets looked for a Day of Jehovah which would usher in God's Kingdom, and on which God would both judge and vindicate his people before all nations. So long as the idea of corporate personality held sway, the generations of the dead could participate in this consummation through their descendants. Hence, there was no incongruity in the thought of the Age-to-Come being staged on this earth.

With the increasing concern with the individual apart from his group, the problem became acute. How could the dead share in the glory-to-come? If God was dealing with each of them personally, then all should share in his promises. Why should frustration be the lot of the many, and the glory of the coming Age be the portion of the fortunate few? The Maccabean crisis precipitated the issue for the seer of Daniel. To him and the subsequent extracanonical apocalypticists was revealed, in and through the crises of history, the deeper truth that the covenant relationship extended beyond this earthly order. There must be a resurrection at the Day of Judgment, in order that the righteous of all ages might share in the glory of the Age-to-Come. The author of Daniel limited this participation to the righteous of his own day who were specially raised from the dead to share in its glory. Thereby the final judgment came to include the dead.

Parallel with this we find the increasing transcendentalizing and spiritualizing of the Age-to-Come itself. For Daniel its scene is still on this earth, although the other Old Testament apocalypses show belief in a cosmic convulsion and transformation ere it happens, and Trito-Isaiah speaks of a new heaven and a new earth (Isa. 65:17; 66:22). Slowly the framework of the Age-to-Come was being more fully set in a newly created and eternal order, and the idea of an eternal messianic kingdom on this earth was receding.

This period brought into the open an inner dialectic of history—the tension between the individual and the group. Just as the consciousness of corporate personality had taught Israel to look for a national restoration, so the developing sense of individuality brought the necessity for a personal eschatology. Was history to have as its meaning the redemption of the individual or the redemption of the nation? The solution lay in the remnant image. Israel maintained the tension in a hope that was both personal and corporate, individual and social. The Age-to-Come would mean the vindication of God's purpose for Israel because it was with the nation that he had made his covenant. But the consummation would be suprahistorical and supratemporal, so that the individuals constituting the restored nation would be those of all generations for whom the covenant relationship with God had been expressed in righteousness of life and loyalty to God's will.

With the vision of the Age-to-Come as the descent of an eternal order, the Kingdom of God with power, there came a transcendentalizing of the messianic concept. In the book of Daniel we meet with the enigmatic figure of one like unto a Son of Man who comes on the clouds of heaven. This figure is set in opposition to the four beasts who represent the successive world empires, and might, on that basis, be given a corporate signifi-

cance as representing the Kingdom of the saints of the Most
High. Many scholars have supported this viewpoint.[59] Others,
like H. H. Rowley,[60] argue that, although the figure is basically a
societary one, the seer must have envisaged a leader as he did for
the other kingdoms, and thus the title at the same time might
have been more narrowly messianic. Since the early king did
gather up the whole nation in himself and represent it, this would
raise no difficulty, especially because such representative ideas
persisted into the New Testament. Opinion now has room for an
even more narrowly messianic interpretation of the "Son of Man"
than this.[61]

Clearly the Son of Man is a transcendent celestial being who
comes before God and is sent from the heavenly order. This militates against total identification with the saints of the Most High,
who specifically are portrayed as being given the Kingdom of
God (Dan. 7:21, 27). The oscillation here between the corporate
group and the individual figure of the Son of Man would seem to
support the idea that he is a pre-existent figure who manifests
himself in human form, sent by God to give the saints the Kingdom.[62] Here we have no passive Messiah whom God sets on the

---

[59] *Vide* T. W. Manson, *The Teaching of Jesus* (Cambridge: University
Press, 1935), pp. 227 ff.

[60] H. H. Rowley, *The Relevance of Apocalyptic* (London: Lutterworth
Press, 1944), pp. 28 ff.

[61] E.g., W. F. Albright, *From the Stone Age to Christianity* (Baltimore:
The Johns Hopkins Press, 1957), pp. 378-380, contends that the Son of Man
is a transcendent messianic figure, a pre-existent heavenly being into whom
the Jewish messianic figure has been reshaped in the light of Mesopotamian
mythology. He regards it as ". . . very probable that Atrakhasis, the recurrent Mesopotamian savior of mankind from catastrophe, son of the god
Ea, yet explicitly called 'man,' was actually fused in Jewish-Aramaic tradition with the figure of the Messiah, as reconstructed from messianic prophesies in the Old Testament" (p. 380).

[62] In the Similitudes of Enoch (1 Enoch 37-70), the vision of Daniel
has been sharpened and the figure of the Son of Man made evidently
messianic in the narrower sense. The seer of Enoch also uses the titles "the
Righteous One," "the Elect One," and "the Anointed One." T. W. Manson
still thinks that the terms are collective (*op. cit.*, pp. 228 f.), and Messel
does likewise with those terms which he accepts as original (*Der Menschen-
sohn in den Bilderreden des Henoch.* Giessen: A. Töpelmann, 1922, pp.
3 ff.). The general consensus is, however, that they are messianic and that
all must be treated as original and not later interpolations. The Son of Man

throne, but a supernatural being who appears on the clouds of heaven and establishes the Kingdom, a transcendent figure who is also deliverer. Thus the Son of Man contrasts with the Davidic Messiah, and we have a completely new understanding of the messianic figure.

Bentzen has sought to provide an inner linkage between the Davidic Messiah and the Son of Man image by contending that both are related to an early myth of Adam as *Urmensch* and *Urkönig*. The prophetic emphasis on historical reality led to the eclipse of this idea of a primordial heavenly man in favor of a Davidic Messiah. Postexilic eschatology, however, struck once more the note of transcendence and turned back to the primordial image of the *Urmensch*. Bentzen contends that *ben 'adam* was originally a messianic title.[63] Jacob takes the same position. The Son of Man in Daniel is a real King, serving the same function as the Messiah, but his title carries a universalistic rather than a nationalistic flavor. As Adam is the prototype for all men, so the Son of Man will be the Messiah for all men.

Once more we find a partial insight being woven into the pattern of the promise. It may have been contributed partly by the dramatic imagery of Israel, and the idea of a first or heavenly man current in the atmosphere of the ancient world may also have influenced the figure. Yet what is significant is that, like so much else, it was lifted up into the central revelation and made significant for the understanding of the fullness of time. We agree with Jacob that this figure of the Son of Man "allowed Judaism to safeguard certain specifically religious and transcendent values."[64]

---

is pictured as a pre-existent being, sharing the throne of glory. He is thus a supramundane person, who is destined to be the savior of the righteous from their enemies (1 Enoch 62:13-14), and the one appointed to judge the world (1 Enoch 49:4; 62:2 ff.; 63:1-4, 11; 61:8 [angels]). One section of the Ezra apocalypse has a similar image (2 Esdras 13).

[63] Even Mowinckel, who interprets Son of Man corporately and denies that the title is narrowly messianic, believes that in Daniel's vision traditional material is being used (*He That Cometh*, p. 35). The seer was familiar with the image of a "heavenly man."

[64] *Ibid.*, p. 343.

5. The Emergence of Legalism

Many of the apocalyptists sprang from the Pharisees who had originated in the *Hasidim* of the Maccabean revolt, the pious who refused to fight on the Sabbath. So there grew up a group in Judaism zealous for the defense of the Law of Moses. They believed that, in the moral and ceremonial stipulations of the Torah, God had supplied all that the nation needed for the guidance of its life and the fulfillment of his will. Hence they sought to build up an earthly manifestation of the divine Kingdom, through obedience to the divinely given Law. Where the Law was too general or obscure, they compiled a system of interpretation which applied the stipulations to the changing conditions of life. This body of unwritten law or tradition consisted of the rulings of the great rabbis and slowly became more authoritative than the Law itself. So the Pharisees made "a fence for the Law." They surrounded it by cautionary rules which served the purpose of danger signals, warning a man when he got within distance of disobeying a divine statute. Further, as Moore reminds us: "When the exigencies of the time seemed to them to demand it, the rabbis in council or individually did not hesitate to suspend or set aside laws in the Pentateuch on their own authority, without exegetical subterfuges or pretense of Mosaic tradition." [65]

Here we have an attempt to re-create the remnant in a new form as the community of those who ordered their lives by the Law of God and meditated upon it day and night. Thereby they sought to establish themselves as a holy and separated people. In so doing they became so tied up in the jots and tittles of the Law that they lost the spirit which had moved them in their early days. In the political sphere they counseled patience and resignation. They concentrated upon a rigid observance of the Torah, written and oral, that they might be ready for the Day of the Lord and enter into the glory and inheritance of the Age-to-Come. In that Day, God would justify those who by the full per-

---

[65] George Foot Moore, *Judaism,* Vol. I (Cambridge: Harvard University Press, 1927), p. 259.

formance of the Law had a claim upon him, declaring them righteous before all nations and vindicating their righteousness, even though the events of this time seemed to deny such vindication.

Yet the Pharisees came to believe that they could save themselves by their own efforts, put themselves right with God by their own striving, share in the coming Age by virtue of their own righteousness. As the spirit departed, the Pharisees of Jesus' day became tied up with the letter, displaying their own bankruptcy. Once more the truth of man's sinful bondage was coming home to God's people and through them to the world. The eschatological vision of the prophets must be set over against the failure of the Law and the bankruptcy of the Pharisees.

So the faithful souls of Jewry looked and hoped. The remnant of which the prophets spoke had to some degree been actualized in the pious and poor of the Psalms (e.g., Pss. 11, 22, 42, 43) who cried up to heaven in their distress. Isaiah's disciples (Isa. 8:12-16) find their heirs among those to whom Malachi refers, the faithful ones whose names are written before God and on whom the sun of righteousness will rise with healing in its wings (Mal. 3:16; 4:1-3). Along with them we can think of the pious group of the Psalter, the *Hasidim* of the time of Daniel, and groups such as the discoveries at Qumran have disclosed to us. Often the remnant of one generation lost its identity and became ossified in the next, giving place to another who treasured in humility the hope and the promise. This happened to the Pharisees. But always the hope remained and the promise was borne in men's hearts until, in the fullness of time, the Day of the Lord dawned, and, with power and great glory, God acted to deliver men. At this inbreak of divine grace we must look in the next chapter. Let us not forget, however, that grace was already operative in the lives of the faithful remnant who treasured the promise in their hearts.

Before we leave the movement of revelation in the old covenant, let us remind ourselves how all turns upon the divine initiative. This was no instance of a waiting upon the development of the human race toward a more mature human response. The full-

ness of time dawned as God brought his people to the nadir of
moral and spiritual bankruptcy, to the realization of their utter
inability to save themselves apart from his gracious intervention.
The fullness of time is not the end-point of man's evolutionary
development at the religious level, but the final disclosure of
man's bondage and of God's grace. Here human moral impotence
and frustration, at the individual and the social levels, reached a
point at which the final divine disclosure as saving grace could
make its impact on the human soul, and the promise be fulfilled.

There is, however, an element of truth in the developmental
viewpoint. The period of the old covenant did have an educative
and preparatory significance in God's purpose. The story of Israel
is the story of God's preparing a people, educating them from
the primitive stage of belief and worship to higher stages, emanci-
pating them from lower understandings of himself, transforming
them from a loose confederation of wandering Bedouins into a
people for his own possession, making them aware of the pattern
of ideas within which the Christ could be understood, pointing
beyond man's sinful natural religious consciousness to the truth
that it had grasped in a broken and distorted form. Thus "salvation" gains a deeper understanding as God brings home to men
their true need.

In the early days "salvation" and its cognate words described
deliverance from earthly foes and national oppressors. As the significance of Israel's covenant relationship with Jehovah and its
implications were more truly grasped, it was seen that the main
issue was deliverance not from worldly enemies but from sin and
spiritual evil. The God who had been a "man-of-war" fighting
Israel's holy wars was also the God who dealt with the sin and
evil in men's hearts. Again and again in Israel's history, God
taught men through the natural order to move to the spiritual
and to grasp the deeper meaning of the images that are being
formed in their consciousness. The same could be said of the
whole sacrificial system which was bringing home to men the
truths of obedience and penitence for themselves and of sacrifice
as the medium of forgiveness. Even Israel's cultus was pointing
men to Christ, both in its insufficiency and in its basic pattern.

There is a divine economy in the movement in which the old covenant prepares the way for the new. We have studied it in the formulation of a pattern of the promise as the pre-exilic and postexilic prophetic eschatologies made their contribution under divine inspiration. We forfeit the historical nature of God's revelation when we sever the figure of Christ from the history of Israel. It is the totality of the old and the new covenants, brought to a focus in Jesus of Nazareth, which constitutes salvation history. The crises and accompanying spiritual insights of Israel's historical life were a preparatory revelation, necessary for the understanding of our Lord's work. It is true that God need not have thus prepared the way, but we are bound up with what he did. He bound himself to the particularity of history, and chose within the particularity of the historical existence of Israel to manifest his saving grace and to disclose man's historical destiny.

CHAPTER IV

SALVATION HISTORY—THE FULLNESS OF TIME AND THE KINGDOM OF GOD

The New Testament is dominated by the conviction that what Israel hoped and longed for has been fulfilled in Jesus of Nazareth. We have seen how the divine process in Israel's history was a sifting one, in which a remnant of pious and faithful souls kept alive the covenant faith and cherished the promise in their hearts.

The finest and noblest spirits in Israel became aware of its exceeding sinfulness before God. As Israel struggled to keep its heritage pure, it fell into narrow and nationalistic exclusiveness, into pride in its own achievements, and into the belief that in the last day it could lay a claim on God and be justified by obedience to the Torah. In the midst of the increasing bankruptcy, as crisis followed crisis, prophets lifted up their eyes and beheld the final crisis. Their interpretation of past history and of contemporary events waited for its vindication upon the mightiest of all God's mighty acts, a day like that day when first he had intervened to bring them up out of Egypt. Then judgment would be consummated, the promise fulfilled, and the glory of the Age-to-Come unveiled.

As the Day tarried, despair and secularism began to take hold. It was in such a time that postcanonical apocalyptists emphasized the glory of the Age-to-Come, and nourished a messianic hope in many forms. Ecclesiastes provides us with a clear example of the temper of those who had lost the prophetic hope and had come under the influence of Greek pessimism about history and the temporal order. Over against this pattern of hope and despair, of promise and bankruptcy, the New Testament church affirmed in its *kerygma* that in Jesus Christ the hopes and promises had been realized, the Age-to-Come had entered history, and the time had been filled.

In the Letter to the Galatians, Paul declares that "... when the time had fully come, God sent forth his Son ..." (Gal. 4:4). For the Old Testament witnesses, history was moving toward a goal when its time would be filled full. Since all times were in God's hands, he would so order the temporal succession of history that, at his appropriate moment, the old age would end and the new Age be ushered in. That appropriate moment would be the fullness of time. Our Lord himself describes his mission in such terms, according to the Synoptic traditions, and the burden of his message in the early days of his ministry was that "the time is fulfilled and the Kingdom of God is at hand." The old age had grown old, and its time was now filled full. Paul makes the same affirmation. In the inscrutable wisdom of God, the new Age was supervening upon it. It will be our task now to examine the New Testament testimony about the fullness of time.

1. *The Graeco-Roman World and the Fullness of Time*

In the biblical view, the time process must be measured in terms of the mighty acts of God and not of the evolutionary development of man. The *praeparatio evangelica* has often been associated with developmental ideas. It has been held that the progress of the human race had reached such a level that Christ was its natural climax. We must, at once, confirm our conviction that God is the Lord of history, controlling its events and movements in the interests of his purpose. Hence what he did with the Assyrians and the Persians in Old Testament times he could also do with the movements of the Graeco-Roman world. We cannot and dare not deny an overruling of what we have called secular history, and therefore of human sinfulness, in such a way that the situation was made ready for the final act of salvation. God so ordered world history that his final act of redemption could be actualized.

Hellenistic culture had become the basis of a world civilization, providing a common language, *Koine*, as a medium of communication, and a common atmosphere of thought in which ideas
could be promulgated. The Roman Empire had established by
military might a unified world, in which the Roman law provided
a common justice, in which Roman arms kept the peace and
broke down the barriers between national and racial groups, and
in which Roman engineers built their roads and established the
best means of communication that the world had known. The
way was set for the spread of a world-faith and the mission of
God's elect people. Yet all this was only one aspect of the
total situation, and much more fundamental was the moral and
spiritual state of humanity.

It is much more difficult to apply developmental categories to
the philosophical and religious atmosphere of the time. It is not
true to the facts to see a process of education by which men were
being led up to the level of the gospel. It was certainly not true
of the Jewish people, and still less does it hold of the Gentile
world. When Paul declared that the Law was a *paidagogos* to
bring men to Christ, he did not mean that the Law educated men
in preparation for the gospel. In any case, the *paidagogos* was a
slave attendant who conducted the boy to a suitable teacher, as
the Oxyrhynchus Papyri show. He was not a "schoolmaster." The
emphasis of Paul falls on the repressive measures and discipline
of the Law, its stern obligations. Thereby men were taught the
power of sin and their own moral impotence. For the Jews, the
Law brought men to Christ by demonstrating their bankruptcy
apart from him. In the same way, Greek philosophy was a *paidagogos*, because it demonstrated the bankruptcy of man's proud
reliance on his own reason. In the sphere of the intellect as much
as in that of morals, man had to learn that he can be justified only
by faith.

For Plato, the conversion of man must be intellectual, a turning about of the power of inner vision, so that man might be enabled to contemplate the eternal ideas and, above all, the Form
of the Good.[1] Sin and ignorance were almost equated, and salva-

---

[1] Cf. *The Republic*, VIII, 518.

tion was for the rational elite. Stoicism, founding its moral system on a rational basis, was fundamentally pessimistic about the mass of mankind. It saw no hope of moral progress in history, but took refuge in endless cycles of repetition in which there was nothing new under the sun.[2] This pride in human reason left the Greeks with a plurality of speculative systems. Blinded by their own diverse presuppositions, they had to learn that the only true presupposition with which philosophical thought may begin is a humble commitment to the living Lord, in whose service the rational powers may find their proper place. As it progressed, the Hellenistic culture showed the hopelessness of man's search for reality by his own rational powers. It is significant that, as nemesis settled upon the Graeco-Roman world, it should turn from the discursive intellect to the mystery religions with their offer of supernatural revelation.

At the political level, there were all the possibilities of a unified world without the dynamic of a common universal faith. The Romans could provide the law and order, the Greeks the language and cultural forms, and the Jews the world-faith which could bind them all together in one family around the throne of the living God. But the Jews were unable to emancipate themselves from exclusive nationalism, and the Gentiles, groping for the light, were in a bondage from which they could find no deliverance. With all its rich potentialities—political genius, universal culture, and world-faith—the ancient world lacked the power to weld them together.

Rome disregarded the Jews entirely and built upon the heritage of Greece. In its cultural and religious life, it drew its waters from the springs of Hellas. The gods of ancient Rome were identified with the Greek pantheon, and Greek mythology found its place in Roman life. The intelligentsia clothed their thought in Greek garb. But Rome had a genius for politics and government, and its law and discipline found no integrating faith in Greece.

Hellenism was essentially individualistic. Its best motive for goodness was, only too often, enlightened self-interest. In the days of the Greek city-state, this found political expression. It

---

[2] Cf. Marcus Aurelius, *Meditations*, XI, 1.

paid the individual citizen to be patriotic, for thereby the state would prosper and he would benefit. As the system of city-states broke up and showed its inner weakness, political concern began to decay, and such loyalty was transferred to all humanity. Plato's search for the righteous city in theory and in practice and Aristotle's emphasis on the duty of practical "politic" found little echo in the general philosophic atmosphere. Philosophy generally concentrated on goals less tarnished than those of earthly patriotisms. Hellenism contained the seeds of political indifference.

Most schools of Greek philosophy made little appeal to the Roman mind. Stoicism did, however—built as it was on the twin pillars of conscience and duty. Its broad, though self-centered, humanism taught a true brotherhood, a social responsibility, and an international spirit, which found echoes in the Roman spirit. Zeno, the Greek Stoic, had dreamed of a great and universal city bound together by the willing consent of its citizens under one divine law.[3] Marcus Aurelius proved a worthy successor, seeing the universe as the "dear city of God."[4] But Stoicism did not provide a faith strong enough to inspire political responsibility. Beneath its social idealism, the Greek idea of enlightened self-interest still persisted. Seneca held that living for others was the best way of living for oneself. Further, the pantheism prevalent in Stoicism made it pessimistic and fatalistic. The human reason participated in the all-pervading reason of the cosmos, and this immanent reason was the ground of the *lex naturae* manifested in the human conscience. The whole course of events was therefore predetermined, including affairs of state, and men had to subject themselves to the Roman law because it was a worthy copy of the divine pattern immanent in the whole.

In consequence, Rome sought elsewhere for a unifying faith. Attempts to resuscitate the ancient Roman religion in Greek dress having failed, its rulers turned to the Imperial Cult, deifying Rome and Caesar. The Hellenistic world had already practiced this under the successors of Alexander, and in the eastern

---

[3] Cf. W. W. Tarn, *Hellenistic Civilization* (London: Edward Arnold and Company, 1930), p. 73.

[4] Aurelius, *op. cit.*, IV, 23.

part of the empire it had some success. Yet ultimately it was little more than a political expediency. It became an instrument of totalitarian despotism, a useful means of binding together the diverse races and national groups of the empire. Thereby the bureaucracy at Rome retained its power, and any Stoic vision of universal brotherhood was replaced by an authoritarian rule in which Graeco-Roman culture found little expression.

In the midst of this situation, men turned in every direction for hope of salvation. There was an intense hunger abroad. With an air of toleration men were prepared to try every new faith and every new philosophy. This attitude went so far that they were embracing more faiths than one, recognizing one common deity in the varied forms of the different religions and speculating on the possibility of a common faith. Boundless vitality was matched by a universal craving for deliverance and a hunger for salvation. The Greek pride in the self-sufficiency of reason was undermined. The blind goddess Chance held many in her grip. Pliny[5] paints a picture of his contemporary world in which everything, adversity and prosperity alike, is ascribed to Chance, so that all is subject to her and she is the deity controlling life. The more philosophical preferred to speak in terms of Fate, feeling themselves bound to the wheel of cosmic necessity, controlled by stormy influences, and subject to the demonic world rulers of this darkness.

All longed for a savior who would deliver the soul, the divine spark within, from its prison house, the body, by which the spiritual forces of darkness in high places held it in thrall. They craved for some divine redeemer who would defeat or outwit the hostile powers and reunite them with the source of life, conferring upon them the gift of immortality. Mystery religions and systems of gnosis or esoteric knowledge abounded. The older Greek Eleusinian and Orphic mysteries were supplemented by newer imports from the Orient—the Phrygian Great Mother Cult, the Egyptian mystery of Isis and Seraphis, the Syrian Baal Cult, and later, Persian Mithraism. Emotionalism and superstition replaced the pride in the intellect. Astrologies and gnosticisms proliferated.

---

[5] Pliny the Elder, *Natural History,* II, 22.

Men went from one cult to another, passing through the initiatory rites, and hoping that by some means they might find in one of them the satisfaction they craved.[6] The very pursuit was a sign of man's awareness of a bondage from which he was powerless to escape without supernatural aid.

At the commencement of the Augustan period, Virgil[7] prophesied the advent of a divine child who would act as savior, ushering in the golden age. Some saw the dream fulfilled in Augustus himself. Others looked to the new mysticisms springing up on every hand. Gilbert Murray spoke of the Graeco-Roman world as suffering from a certain failure of nerve: "It is hard to describe. It is a rise of asceticism, of mysticism, in a sense, of pessimism; a loss of self-confidence, of hope in this life and of faith in normal human effort; a despair of patient inquiry, a cry for infallible revelation; an indifference to the welfare of the state, a conversion of the soul to God. It is an atmosphere in which the aim of every good man is not so much to live justly, to help the society to which he belongs and to enjoy the esteem of his fellow creatures; but rather, by means of a burning faith, by contempt for the world and its standards, by ecstasy, by suffering, and martyrdom, to be granted pardon for his unspeakable unworthiness, his immeasurable sins."[8]

Parallel to this we see the desperate moral situation. Paul's description of the moral chaos and anarchy of the pagan world in Romans 1:21 ff. can be matched from contemporary records. Moral hopelessness was very evident. The degrading effect of a slave population, the passing of the old religious sanctions, the absence of a unifying faith, the uncertainty of life—all contributed. The great cities, like Corinth and Ephesus, became sinks of iniquity. Some, believing the body to be evil, took refuge in libertinism instead of asceticism. Stoicism with its stern emphasis on duty was powerless to stem the flood. Lietzmann has described the situation thus: "Enjoy the good things of this world as long as

---

[6] Cf. the picture of an initiation into the Isis cult in Apuleius, *Metamorphoses*, XI.

[7] Virgil, *Eclogues*, 4; *Aeneid*, 6, 791 ff.

[8] Gilbert Murray, *Five Stages of Greek Religion* (Oxford: The Clarendon Press, 1925), p. 155.

you may, for afterwards you will collapse into dust and ashes. That was the answer given by many of the children of this world, and it re-echoes to us from many gravestones."[9] Hellenism begot egotism, and egotism began to assume its vilest forms.

· In such a world the people of God was called to fulfill its destiny. But the Jewish people were so bent upon a narrow nationalism and their own ultimate glory that they showed a mingled scorn and hatred to their Gentile neighbors, even while they availed themselves of the new commercial opportunities opened up by the Pax Romana. They could even draw into their own circles of thought ideas from the pagan philosophies, as the Alexandrian school of Jewish thinkers shows. The Diaspora, the growing edge of Judaism, required, however, that a man forsake his own people and become a Jew in order to share in the blessings of the Jewish faith and hope. Bankruptcy beset Jew and Gentile, Roman and Greek. The Jews looked for a Messiah, be he transcendent or Davidic, and hoped for a glorious coming Age. The Gentiles looked for a savior, who could assure immortality and escape from this present evil aeon. God brought all men to the point where the climacteric event of Jesus of Nazareth could burst upon a bankrupt world.

When the fullness of time came, however, it came in disguise, like a thief in the night. It was a hidden revelation. It seems highly probable that, in the early part of his ministry, many Jews did wonder if Jesus were the Messiah. The question of John the Baptist may well voice popular feeling. But the Jews still remained in political bondage to Rome, and Jesus died on the cross refusing to use violence or political measures to establish his Kingdom. Yet out of his death and resurrection there sprang a faith which affirmed that, beyond a shadow of doubt, he was the Messiah of God, and that he would come again on the clouds of heaven to judge the earth. In both cruder and more refined forms this faith dominates the New Testament writings. If the Greeks looked for a savior and the Jews looked for the divine Kingdom and the messianic deliverer, the hopes of both alike and of the

---

[9] Hans Lietzmann, *The Beginnings of the Christian Church* (New York: Charles Scribner's Sons, 1937), p. 226.

whole world were met in Jesus of Nazareth. In him Israel's true
destiny was fulfilled, and the people of God was reconstituted on
the basis of a new covenant that it might include those of all
nations and actualize God's purpose in the world of men.

2. The Apostolic Kerygma and the Fullness
of Time

We must now look at the message of the early Christian
church and see how their preaching presented Jesus of Nazareth
to the contemporary world.[10] To find this we must investigate
the early preaching in the Acts of the Apostles and fragments of
early creedal statements. A positive contribution of form criticism
has been its emphasis on the importance of preaching in the conservation of tradition. It is highly probable that the elements in
the life and teaching of our Lord contained in the Gospels owe
their form and their conservation to the preaching and teaching
activity of the early church.

Long before the Gospels were written, the early Christians
were proclaiming the *kerygma*. Indeed, the Gospels themselves
are really expanded forms of the *kerygma*. They are not biogra-
phies. They omit details about the personal appearance and characteristics of Jesus. They are not psychological studies of his motives, nor do they attempt to trace the developing consciousness
of his life's work. They are more *Geschichte* than *Historie*, more
concerned with the significant inner and eternal meaning of Jesus
than with the chronicle of his early life. Of course, this is the concern of the *kerygma*. The earliest material available for the study
of the *kerygma* is contained in pre-Pauline creedal and confes-
sional fragments,[11] embodied in Paul's letters, and in the Petrine

---

[10] *Vide* especially C. H. Dodd, *The Apostolic Preaching and Its Developments* (New York: Harper & Brothers, 1936), *passim*. This book is germi-
nal for all subsequent work and we have leaned on it.

[11] Romans 1:2-5; Galatians 1:3-4; 1 Thessalonians 1:9-10; 1 Corinthians
15:3 ff.; Romans 10:8-9; Romans 4:24-25. Possibly a creedal statement lies
behind Romans 8:31-34—as Dodd points out, a creedal statement emerges
—Christ Jesus, who died, and more, was raised, who is at the right hand of
God, who also intercedes for us.

sermons in Acts,[12] of which the most significant—Acts 10:34-43—is quite evidently based on an Aramaic source. A careful investigation of these various sources shows a common pattern in the *kerygma:*

(1) The declaration that the prophetic hopes have been actualized in history. The sermons in Acts cite specific passages. The basic element here is the declaration that the Age-to-Come has already dawned upon men, so that the things which God promised through his prophets have been fulfilled.

(2) The statement that this historical actualization has taken place in the life, death, resurrection, and exaltation of Jesus of Nazareth. Jesus is the promised Messiah, the Deliverer whom God has sent, whom he raised from the dead, and who is now exalted to be a Prince and a Saviour.

(3) The call for repentance and the reception of the salvation which Christ has brought.

By including Pauline material with the Petrine sermons in this analysis, we have shown that fundamentally Paul and Peter had the same basic *kerygma.* If it be pointed out that we have chosen pre-Pauline fragments at this point, let us remember that Paul had woven them into his own letters, indicating that he accepted them. In one instance he states this specifically; at the close of the statement of the received tradition he declares that this is the content of his preaching as much as of that of the other apostles—so *we* preach (1 Cor. 15:12). Furthermore, he defines his fundamental *kerygma* as ". . . Christ and him crucified" (1 Cor. 1:23; 2:2-6). This is the foundation that he laid, and here he is one with the other witnesses. The differentiation comes in the superstructures that he and others have erected on this foundation, the higher wisdom which can only be imparted when the fundamental gospel is firmly grasped (1 Cor. 3:10).

Let us look at the image of Jesus which the *kerygma* presents to us. He is the promised Messiah of the house of David, whom God has appointed.[13] He is described as God's Servant,[14] with

---

[12] Acts 2:14-36; 3:12-26; 4:8-12; 10:34-43; cf. Paul's sermon at Antioch of Pisidia, Acts 13:16-41.

[13] Acts 2:36; 3:20; 4:26; Romans 1:3.

[14] Acts 3:13, 26; 4:27, 30; cf. 13:47.

obvious reference to the prophecy of Deutero-Isaiah (Isa. 53), and his mission is described in terms reminiscent of the Servant—he is represented as concerned with the remission of sins in Acts 2:38; 3:19; God has raised him up as Servant to turn men from their iniquities—Acts 3:26; he died for our sins—1 Corinthians 15:3; he was put to death for our trespasses—Romans 4:25. Positively, the salvation he describes is associated with the promise by God of the pouring out of the Spirit (Acts 2:16-21, 33, 38) and with the sharing in the divine promises (Acts 3:24-25). Indeed, in Jesus the covenant made with Abraham is fulfilled, and the promise that all the families of the earth shall be blessed through the patriarch's seed is actualized. The image of the remnant reappears in the picture of the church as the New Israel, the community of those who are heirs of the prophets and of the covenant with Abraham. Along with the present realization we also find still a futuristic element. Jesus is the One whom God has ordained to judge the quick and the dead,[15] and the Christ is to come again that the new Age may be fully consummated and all things restored (Acts 3:21).

This pattern recurs throughout the rest of the New Testament. The Synoptic Gospels are expanded *kerygma,* making much of the passion tradition and thus showing how much of the early preaching was concerned with "Christ and him crucified." In Matthew we have a special concern with the Old Testament promises, and there are many quotations from the Hebrew text prefaced by the words "in order that that which was spoken by the prophets might be fulfilled." In Paul's letters, 1 Peter, the Johannine writings, and the Letter to the Hebrews, we find the same themes expressed in varying ways. In all of them Jesus is the Messiah in whom the promises have been fulfilled.[16] His death as an atoning and vicarious sacrifice echoes the theme of the Suffering Servant, although figures from the sacrificial system of Israel are also drawn upon.

Peter can identify our Lord with the Servant using almost the wording of Deutero-Isaiah (1 Peter 2:21-24), and can also de-

---

[15] Acts 10:42; 1 Thessalonians 1:10.
[16] This will be discussed in detail later.

scribe him as the precious cornerstone promised by Isaiah (1 Peter 2:6-7). He also uses the Old Testament messianic image of Shepherd to describe him (1 Peter 2:25). Paul can liken the deliverance at the cross and the empty tomb to that of Israel at the Exodus, using the Red Sea crossing as a type for baptism (1 Cor. 10:1-5). Matthew evidently makes the coming of Jesus the new Exodus—the foundation theme of his Gospel. Paul can write that Christ does away with the veil that hinders the true understanding of the old covenant (2 Cor. 3:13-16). The Letter to the Hebrews can describe Jesus as the Mediator of a new and better covenant (Heb. 9:15; 12:24).

The wisdom speculations of the Old Testament are used to fill out the understanding of the transcendence and otherworldly aspect of the Messiah, already implicit in the development of the Son of Man concept. There is indeed an increasing emphasis on the exaltation of Christ and on his transcendent person. A Christology is developed which emphasizes his pre-existence as Son and Word, and his final exaltation at the right hand of glory.[17] Yet the imagery comes from the old covenant revelation.

The church is identified with the people of God, with the remnant, and thus with the ongoing of the Old Israel. Peter even applies the description of the Old Israel to the New Israel, the church.[18] The image of Israel as God's son and the marriage image of Jehovah and Israel are filled with new meaning in the understanding of the Christian experience as sonship and adoption and in the picture of the church as the bride of Christ.[19] The author of Hebrews specifically identifies the church with the remnant of the old covenant, actualized in Isaiah's disciples (Heb. 2:13). The Holy Spirit is understood in terms of the eschatological promise of the old covenant.

It is true that this concern with the usage of Old Testament categories and images should not blind us to the insights which

---

[17] 1 John 1:1 ff.; Colossians 1:15-20; Philippians 2:5-11; 1 Peter 3:22; Hebrews 1:2 ff.

[18] 1 Peter 2:9-10; cf. Galatians 6:16; Philippians 3:3.

[19] Galatians 4:5; Romans 8:14; Hebrews 2:10; 2 Corinthians 11:2; Ephesians 5:22-33; John 3:29; Revelation 21:2, 9; 22:17.

are peculiar to the consummation. The images were often transformed and filled with the new content. But throughout the New Testament there is the conviction of fulfillment. The coming Age has dawned and the promises have been fulfilled.

This analysis will serve to crystallize the element of contrast between Jewish expectation and Christian fulfillment. First, although the Age-to-Come has dawned, history still goes on. The biblical witnesses had looked for a glorious fulfillment following a divine intervention in judgment and in mercy. Further, increasingly the sphere of fulfillment was regarded as an otherworldly order. The Christian church declared that the Age-to-Come had already supervened upon history. The prophetic promises referring to the messianic age were now being fulfilled. That age is actualized, the Messiah has come, and the gift of the Spirit is the sign that it is a present reality. Yet this present evil age with its sin and frustration still goes on. The human experience of the fulfillment is confined within the framework of this age. In some mysterious way the Age-to-Come and this present aeon were overlapping. The end of history, the *eschaton,* had paradoxically broken into history, but the historical experience of man was not thereby brought to an end. The redemption had become a reality, but sin and evil still continued their sway in the lives of men and society. Paul points to this fact when he argues that the historical experience of Israel paralleled that of the church ". . . upon whom the end of the ages has come" (1 Cor. 10:11).

Secondly, this does not mean that the overlapping will continue indefinitely and that there will be no final consummation. Throughout the New Testament there is an eschatological tension. The book has both a present and a future look. Jesus has inaugurated the Age-to-Come and he will come again to consummate it. The process of redemption inaugurated in the incarnation will reach its consummation in the *parousia,* of the imminence of which there is at first a *lively* expectation. This means that the messianic age is divided into two parts. One is that which supervenes upon and overlaps the process of history, and is ushered in by the life, death, and resurrection of Jesus. The other is the perfect and eternal consummation of that which has already begun, and will be ushered in by the *parousia* of the exalted Messiah who has been appointed by God to judge the quick and the dead. As the New Testament period proceeded and the *parousia* was delayed, we find an increasing tendency to emphasize the presence of the End in the first coming of Jesus and in his church and to show less concern with the hope of a final consummation. This change is especially evident in the later letters of Paul, in the Letter to the Hebrews, and in the Fourth Gospel.

Yet even here the same structure still remains. The belief in a final consummation, involving judgment and resurrection, persists (John 5:28-29; 12:48). As Hoskyns puts it: "He [the Fourth Evangelist] argues rather that those who know that there will be a day of resurrection unto life and unto judgment, and that there will be a final separation of those who have done good from those who have done evil, ought not to wonder and be surprised that the voice of the Son of God even now separates good from evil, exercises judgment and gives life."[20] The book of Revelation shows that late in the New Testament period the future expectation still played an important role, even in Johannine circles.

The third element peculiar to the Christian conception of the "fullness of time" is the centrality of the Messiah and the new interpretation of his mission. He is no longer incidental to the divine intervention, but the very center of it. The kingly act of God brings him with it and is embodied in him. He is the divine intervention in his own person. In his life, death, and resurrection the final act of God has come upon history. God's redemptive act centers in the Son. Thus although the humanity and the Davidic descent of Jesus are recognized as important, other threads in the eschatological pattern of the old covenant are also firmly grasped. The Messiah's task is interpreted in terms of suffering, death, and resurrection rather than in terms of what the world regarded as kingly glory. The image of the Suffering Servant becomes central in the interpretation of the messianic mission. If the Age-to-Come is to be one in which men are given a new spirit and their sin is

---

[20] Edwyn Hoskyns, *The Fourth Gospel*, Revised Edition, Francis Noel Davey, ed. (London: Faber and Faber Limited, 1947), p. 271.

remembered no more, God makes this possible through the sacrifice of Jesus. Even the sacrificial system of Israel is consummated in the messianic act.

In Jesus a new and spiritual remnant was created by a new covenant that was wrought out in his life, death, and resurrection. This emphasis on the Messiah as himself the center and agent of the divine intervention led to an increasing concern with his transcendence. The strands in later biblical eschatology that had given the Messiah a supramundane status were thus fulfilled in the New Testament image of the eternal and pre-existent Son of God. Into this image also was woven the Old Testament understanding of the Word and Wisdom of God as it developed in postexilic thought. Jesus was understood as God and was given the title "the Lord," hitherto reserved in synagogue practice for God alone and as a synonym for the sacred tetragrammaton, the unpronounced name of God.

Finally, the Christian church was seen to be the New Israel, the heir to the promises, and the remnant through which the divine act of redemption in Jesus would be made effective in all nations. It was not only Israel that was to be redeemed in the sufferings of the Messiah. Like the Servant, he was set to be a light to the Gentiles and for the salvation of the ends of the earth. Jew and Greek could find their hopes fulfilled and their needs met in the Anointed One of Israel. Clearly, through Jesus the remnant of the Old Israel is linked with the Christian church in one continuous stream. What began at the Exodus is consummated in the cross and the empty tomb. The promise to Abraham is fulfilled when in Christ there is neither Jew nor Greek, barbarian nor Scythian, bond nor free, but all are one in him. The destiny of Israel is accomplished in the new fellowship of the Holy Spirit. A New Israel is built not on racial blood but on the outpoured blood of the Redeemer, whose deliverance is effective for all men.

So the meaning of history enters the course of history and becomes effective redemptively within it. Christ is the midpoint and the goal of our human story. He is the *eschaton*, summing up its meaning in himself. He stands at its midpoint, his life,

death, and resurrection re-creating it from within and determining its course. He stands at its chronological end, as its *eschaton,* gathering up all things in himself. This is the New Testament
faith.

3. The Nature of Fulfillment

We have yet to consider the nature of fulfillment that we have
been discussing. Obviously we should not be satisfied with the
suggestion that the fulfillment is simply a useful hermeneutical
principle, whereby the old covenant supplies certain useful
analogies for our understanding of Jesus of Nazareth. The old
covenant promises were *promises,* and in some sense the history
of the old covenant is integral to the life, death, and resurrection
of Christ. The fact that our Lord incorporated the pattern of the
old covenant promise into his own person and teaching is an indication that we are dealing here with some form of historical continuity and not with mere hermeneutics.

Our view of prophecy would lead us to reject any suggestion
of accurate prediction or prediction in detail. The prophets did
not foretell the actual event that was to come. But they did share
enough in the pathos and counsel of the divine mind to have
some insight into the divine plan and declare some elements in
the ultimate pattern.

This view means that we must reject the old view, which
would treat the Old Testament as a book of prophecy and regard
all its utterances as prophecies.[21] For one thing, "prophecy" here
means the forecasting of a future event, and the fulfillment is the
occurrence of what has been forecast. This method led historically to a very arbitrary method of selecting passages that appeared to bear on the claims of Jesus Christ. Artificial interpretation and allegorizing, after the style of Philo and in the Hellenistic
tradition, meant that passages were often made to bear a forced
meaning, never in the mind of the original writer.

There is another way of regarding fulfillment. It is the Jewish

---

[21] For this and subsequent paragraphs, cf. also Rudolf Bultmann, *Essays*
(New York: Harper & Brothers, 1955), pp. 182 ff.

method of isolating the prophetic utterances about the messianic
age and associating these with Jesus. Insofar as prophetic means
accurate forecasting, we must discard this, too. The prophet was
not thinking in his messianic utterances of the actual event in
which we find their fulfillment.[22] Indeed, what matters is that we
grasp the meaning and significance of the event itself. It no
longer gains extra authority for us because it was "predestined
and prophesied."[23] The truth in this view is that, by divinely
given insight, the prophet did grasp something of the pattern of
what was to come. No one prophet grasped the whole pattern or
foresaw the actual event. It is doubtful that Deutero-Isaiah saw
how his image of the Suffering Servant could be woven into the
messianic expectation. Further, when the Christ comes to us in
existential encounter, he does so through the testimony and
kerygma of the early church and thus is clothed in the God-given
pattern of images that was framed in the prophetic consciousness
of the Old Israel. Finally, we are not speaking of some hermeneutical principle here, for we believe that the images were integral
to the person and mission of our Lord himself.[24]

In giving himself and disclosing his purpose, God gives the
images and forms in which he is to be apprehended. The fact
that these images recur throughout the biblical testimony is an
indication that there is an organic relationship between the history of the old covenant and the history of the new. This is no
accident. The events of the new covenant need the promises of
the old covenant if they are to be truly understood. Without the
promises through the prophets, it is difficult to understand our
Lord's person and mission. There had to be a *praeparatio evangelica*. The Christ-event is incomprehensible apart from the
covenant with and the promises to the Old Israel. Nor is this to
be understood merely at the hermeneutical level, as if it were
just an interesting array of resemblances between the life of Jesus

---

[22] Cf. *ibid.*, p. 185.

[23] Cf. *ibid.*, p. 187. We would not, like Bultmann, however, totally dismiss the viewpoint.

[24] Bultmann's concern with demythologizing leads to a failure to appre-
ciate this.

and the Old Testament promises. There is a theological continuity here, as if the whole were within the purpose and activity of God.

Hoskyns points out that "there is no event or utterance recorded of Him (Christ) which does not wholly proceed from a conception of the Messiahship smelted and sublimed from the ore of the Old Testament Scriptures; and that this complete Christological control is not imposed awkwardly upon the material, but underlies and penetrates every fragment of it."[25] The images are not chosen haphazardly. The elements in the prophetic promise are gathered up into a meaningful pattern in the person of our Lord because there is a principle of theological continuity in them. Indeed, there would seem to be a line of theological development in the history itself which is such that the Christ-event requires the previous movements, with their prophetic promises and their attendant images, for its true understanding.

In further development of this organic unity between the new and the old covenants as fulfillment and promise, we need to remember the significance of the prophetic word in biblical thought. The Word of Jehovah through the prophet, as it impinged upon the historical situation, had an objective concreteness such that it set in motion the forces which would bring about its accomplishment. Thus, as the prophet saw it, the promises and eschatological hopes which he uttered were, by their very utterance, ingredient elements in the history of Israel. In their utterance God's purpose began to move toward its actualization in history. In this sense, Jesus is the actualization of God's purpose, declared beforehand through his prophets and moving toward its full accomplishment in him as, through their personalities, it became integral to the life of the people. Here the emphasis must fall upon the divine activity whereby the organic unity of old and new covenant is continued.[26]

---

[25] Essay in G. K. A. Bell and Adolf Deissmann, eds., *Mysterium Christi* (New York: Longmans Green, 1930), pp. 70-71.

[26] As John Marsh has put it: "When the true prophet of Yahweh truly spoke the Word of the Lord, then a certain factor of dynamic power had been cast upon the stream of history. If it were a true prophecy, its passage

We are, of course, dealing with more than accomplishment of purpose. When we speak of Jesus in terms of fulfillment, we mean that he is the *perfect* accomplishment of the *divine* purpose in history. He is the *final* unveiling of the meaning of history and the destiny of man and the One through whom that meaning becomes actuality.

We have yet to emphasize the fact that the fulfillment in Christ not only fills in the pattern of the promise with historical actuality but, in some sense, transfigures and breaks it. There is in the pattern an element of polarity bound up with the images of the Suffering Servant and the transcendent Son of Man. In consequence the Messiah is no longer the passive recipient of the Kingdom, set on his throne by God, but the active agent whereby God's kingly rule breaks redemptively into history. Furthermore, the Age-to-Come breaks in upon this present age and the latter still continues, so the messianic age is divided into two parts.

Rather than regarding this polarity as a tension which arises out of the meeting of God and man in the incarnation, Bultmann carries it back to the prophets themselves and interprets it as a basic inner contradiction which pervades their hope.[27] He argues that the prophets brought the divine activity into line with the empirical history of the people rather than interpreting it in a transcendent and eschatological sense.[28] Prophecy always relates its promise to an empirical historical situation, yet implicit in such a promise is a contradiction, because the promise contains an eschatological idea which is unrealizable in history. We would take issue with this position at several points, even though it does contain a measure of truth.

For one thing, the prophetic hope did carry transcendent and cosmological elements signifying that the objective was the final realization of God's purpose by God himself. If "eschatological" describes this transcendent reference, it is clear that the prophet

---

into historical event was inevitable, and when that passage occurred, fulfilment took place"—*The Fulness of Time* (New York: Harper & Brothers, 1952), p. 81.

[27] Bultmann, *op. cit.*, p. 205.

[28] *Ibid.*, p. 206.

did not eliminate the eschatological from his thought. In pre-exilic eschatology there was more measure of continuity between the historical and the Day of the Lord, but there was also a tension. The Day had a transcendent reference. It would be the realization of God's purpose by God himself, even if he used historical agents. In postexilic eschatology the tension between the historical present and the eschatological event is more evident. But it is not contradiction.

In the second place, Bultmann speaks of contradiction rather than tension or polarity, because he tacitly assumes that the historical and the eschatological must ultimately be divorced. Bultmann rejects a true significance in secular history. Christ as the *eschaton* is apparently detached from this. The advent of the eschatological in Christ lifts men out of the world situation to a higher and transcendent level, radically transforming them and thereby making it possible for them to live triumphantly in the lower level of world history. The *eschaton* does not inaugurate a new historical development.[29] Eschatological existence in the world involves a withdrawing from the world.[30] This agnosticism to world history is in strange contrast to the biblical realism. How can eschatology sum up the meaning of history if it is withdrawal from history? Jesus Christ came to redeem and to affirm history. This absence of a cosmological sweep and historical realism from Bultmann's thought is the accompaniment of his process of demythologization. He understands the Christ-event and its accompanying myths as anthropological and not cosmological.

By mistakenly restricting the prophetic promise to the historical order, Bultmann can hold that there is a miscarriage and can speak of a contradiction in the promise because it cannot be historically fulfilled. We would hold that the tension was already present in the prophetic consciousness and thus no contradiction is involved. The really new element in Jesus was not just the eschatological inbreak, but the fact that this inbreak allowed the sin and the deviations of history to continue. This was the new revelatory content which poured into the mold of the Old Testa-

[29] *Ibid.*, p. 206.
[30] *Ibid.*, p. 207.

ment hope, breaking and transforming the very pattern itself. The Christ-event is fulfillment because the polarity in the promise is retained and given true meaning.

Bultmann does talk about fulfillment, and here he makes a contribution. He holds that the general miscarriage of Israel's history, its failure to achieve justification by works, carried a promise and constituted the basis for a fulfillment in justification by faith.[31] There is no doubt about the movement of the Old Testament age to bankruptcy, but it was this movement which provided the life situation within which the prophetic promises arose. Already the Old Testament seers saw from afar a redemptive inbreak of God. Jesus does fulfill the history of Israel by *negation* in Bultmann's sense, but he does not just negate it and all history. He positively brings that history to its fulfillment. He fulfills the tension between the historical and the eschatological in the prophetic promise by manifesting the eschatological redemptively within the historical and thereby claiming history, not destroying it.

Apart from the prophetic promises, can we find any *positive* organic continuity between the old covenant and the new? Does Jesus fulfill the history of salvation in the old covenant in any positive sense apart from the prophetic promises? What about the crisis events in the life of Israel? Certain characteristic patterns of events can be discerned. This thought is at work in the Old Testament itself, when the prophets bind together the primordial act of creation and the historical act of the Exodus in the same pattern of imagery—likening the creation of the nation and the triumph over Egypt to the shaping of the cosmos and the triumph over the chaos. Isaiah 51:9-11 goes further and sees a repetition of the same pattern in the return of the exiles from Babylon.

We see it in the New Testament where one theme in the Gospel of Matthew is clearly that, in the life, death, and resurrection of Jesus, a new Exodus has happened, a new people has been created, a new covenant has been cut, and a new law has been

---

[31] *Ibid.*, p. 208. *Vide,* for a developed critique, John McIntyre, *The Christian Doctrine of History* (Grand Rapids: Wm. B. Eerdmans Publishing Co., 1957), pp. 69 f.

given on the Mount. We see it in Paul's passage in 1 Corinthians 10:1-13 where he likens the historical pattern of the old covenant to that of the new, although he becomes allegorical in his identification of the rock with Christ (vs. 4). Our earlier discussion[32] would indicate that these patterns of events and the images bound up with them are not arbitrary and contingent, but grounded in the divine revelation and activity. In our time there has come a new appraisal of the essential truth in the typological method of exegesis. It is true that, in the hands of exponents like A. M. Farrer,[33] L. S. Thornton,[34] and Wilhelm Vischer,[35] this method sometimes goes too far, becomes fanciful interpretation, and ventures on the allegorical. Yet, in the hands of sober theologians, it is recognized as possessing true insight into the revelatory events and is not treated as a fanciful hermeneutic principle. Typology, unlike allegory, emphasizes the historical nature of the events of the history of the old covenant, but argues that these are so providentially ordered that they foreshadow the New Testament fulfillment.

It has well been argued that such a view, if not pushed too far, is rationally acceptable to the modern Christian of the post-critical age. God is the living God who makes all things new, absolutely free in his creation of and control over nature and men. But we may expect that he will, in his activity, disclose sometimes a repetitive pattern through which the new breaks. Since the old and the new covenants are alike under the aegis of God's revelatory activity, distinct and yet unified in their testimony to him as gracious Redeemer, we may expect, as H. H. Rowley suggests, ". . . the same pattern of revelation . . ." Rowley continues: "If both were revelations of the same God, as they claimed to be, then in the common pattern of the revelation . . .

---

[32] Chapter II.

[33] A. M. Farrer, *A Rebirth of Images* (London: Dacre Press, 1949).

[34] L. S. Thornton, *Revelation and the Modern World* (London: Dacre Press, 1950); *The Dominion of Christ* (London: Dacre Press, 1952).

[35] Wilhelm Vischer, *The Witness of the Old Testament to Christ*, Vol. I (London: Lutterworth Press, 1949); *L'ancien Testament Témoin du Christ*, Vol. II, *Les Premiers Prophètes* (Neuchâtel: Delachaux et Niestlé, 1951).

where neither could explain or control the other, we have the signature of God."[36]

We need to remind ourselves that a high Christology demands that the Word who became incarnate for us men and for our salvation was the agent of creation and of the revelation in the old covenant. It was he who spoke through the prophets and who guided Israel's history, so that the latter is permeated with the presence of the preincarnate Christ.[37] This applies not only to the prophetic promises, which took their shaping from the events of Israel's history. It applies also to the crisis events in Israel's history, especially the Exodus and the Exile, and also to God's dealings with persons like Abraham and Aaron. Since it is the living God, the same yesterday, today, and forever, who operates, we may expect that his work will manifest a recurrent pattern. His dealings with persons separated in time may yet show the same characteristics. To quote Reid: "As Aaron is by Moses anointed to a priesthood in the chosen people, and Christ at Jordan to a priesthood for all the world, so Christians at baptism are anointed into membership of the Church and a priesthood of all believers. There is a right kind of typology which is not mere fantasy, just as there is a real kind of prophecy which is not merely 'inspired guesswork'; and both rest securely upon the reiterated pattern of God's saving work."[38] It is because the living God is present as his Word in the history of the old covenant that salvation was a reality for the Old Testament saints. Because of the presence of the preincarnate Christ in Israel's history, we may expect that the ultimate pattern of salvation in the *eschaton* may be present proleptically for the people of the promise. Yet it still remains

---

[36] H. H. Rowley, *The Unity of the Bible* (London: The Carey Kingsgate Press Limited, 1953), p. 98.

[37] Cf. J. K. S. Reid, *The Authority of Scripture* (New York: Harper & Brothers, n.d.), p. 251. "If God saves in the time of the Old Testament, Jesus Christ is there, by whom he saves. It is indeed a Jesus Christ not yet incarnate, but the person in whom this pattern receives its final exemplification has not yet appeared."

[38] *Ibid.*, p. 252. The subsequent pages of this work develop the theme in an able way. Those desiring to pursue the matter further should consult this book. It is sober in judgment.

true, as the author of the Letter to the Hebrews saw, that they without us are not made perfect.

4. Jesus and the Kingdom of God

The pattern of the promise is actualized in the person and teaching of our Lord, which we have shown to be substantially presented in the Gospel traditions. We have supported the view that the Marcan framework must not be radically discredited and thus that the Gospels present us with some measure of *Historie* as well as with *Geschichte*. We shall now proceed to show how these aspects of the teaching of our Lord are borne out in the *kerygma* and testimony of the New Testament as a whole.

Jesus clearly made the image of the Kingdom of God central in his teaching. K. L. Schmidt[39] and T. W. Manson[40] have shown conclusively that the fundamental meaning of this phrase is not realm but rule or sway. The Kingdom of God is God's sovereign rule or power. It is thus a dynamic concept, associated with his intervention in his world, his acts. When the prophets associated the Age-to-Come with the Kingdom of God, they meant that in that age God's kingly rule would be fully exercised over all the beings whom he had created, and that the divine sovereignty over history and human life would be completely unveiled and consummated. There cannot be a king without subjects, and so in a secondary sense the Kingdom of God became associated with the hope of a remnant, already partially realized by the faithful in history, and with the glorious future realm in which the whole cosmos would manifest God's glory.

In our Lord's teaching, we face the tension between the presence of the Kingdom and its future coming. We have already criticized the "consistent eschatology" of Albert Schweitzer, who makes Jesus a thoroughgoing apocalyptist and puts the Kingdom in the future. Equally, however, we must criticize C. H. Dodd,[41]

---

[39] K. L. Schmidt, H. Kleinknecht, K. G. Kuhn, and G. von Rad, "Basileia," in Kittel's *Bible Key Words* (London: A & C Black, 1957).

[40] T. W. Manson, *The Teaching of Jesus*, pp. 116-141.

[41] C. H. Dodd, *The Parables of the Kingdom* (New York: Charles Scrib-

whose "realized eschatology" has become so fashionable. He contends that "the *eschaton* has moved from the future to the present, from the sphere of expectation into that of realized experience."[42] Hence he would dismiss the futurist apocalyptic images in our Lord's teaching as either the product of the early *kerygma* or an accommodation to the contemporary Jewish thought-world. W. G. Kümmel,[43] in a penetrating analysis, shows that neither aspect can be dismissed. In the thought of Jesus the Kingdom is both present and future.

The future aspect appears in sayings like that with which he began his ministry: "The time is fulfilled, and the kingdom of God is at hand. . ."[44] The word translated "at hand" here generally describes proximity in time, and might be rendered "coming near."[45] W. G. Kümmel holds that, in this and some scattered Q sayings, there can be no doubt that "Jesus proclaimed that the Kingdom of God had come near."[46] Other sayings reiterate this viewpoint. For example, Mark 9:1 records the saying: ". . . there are some standing here who will not taste death before they see the kingdom of God come with power." The prediction here is too evident for us to evade it.[47] Jesus is here assuring some of

ner's Sons, 1936); *History and the Gospel* (New York: Charles Scribner's Sons, 1938).

[42] Dodd, *The Parables of the Kingdom*, p. 50.

[43] W. G. Kümmel, *Promise and Fulfilment* (Naperville: Alec R. Allenson, Inc., 1957), *passim*.

[44] Mark 1:15. In the mission charge to the disciples we have a similar saying—Matthew 10:7-11; Luke 10:9.

[45] *Vide* J. Y. Campbell, *Expository Times*, 48, 1936-37, pp. 9 f. C. H. Dodd has argued that the passage should be rendered "the Kingdom of God has come." His position has found little support from philological study and Septuagint usage; cf. Kümmel, *op. cit.*, pp. 23 f., and R. H. Fuller, *The Mission and Achievement of Jesus* (Naperville: Alec R. Allenson, Inc., 1954), pp. 20 ff.

[46] Kümmel, *op. cit.*, p. 25.

[47] Dodd, *The Parables of the Kingdom*, p. 42 and pp. 53 f., endeavors to render the passage "until they have seen that the Kingdom of God *has come* with power," implying that the verb rendered "to see" must be interpreted as intellectual seeing, but the usage cannot be paralleled. Bultmann and Bornkamm would explain it as the creation of the early church as a word of comfort because the *parousia* had been delayed (*vide* Kümmel, *op. cit.*, p. 27).

his followers that they will escape the martyrdom which was predicted for others. There can be little doubt that it does suggest that the coming of the Kingdom is in the future, and that this is to be the final coming, for the phrase "with power" indicates this. Yet there is some suggestion that even though this final coming has been delayed far beyond the imminence implied in the saying, it may have been fulfilled partially at the exaltation of our Lord. Paul states that the Christ was ". . . designated Son of God in power . . ." after the resurrection (Rom. 1:4). Sayings like these must be set side by side with those which point to a final consummation and to the Day of the Son of Man.

There are other sayings of our Lord which evidently regard the Kingdom as a present reality. Thus Jesus declares: ". . . if it is by the finger of God that I cast out demons, then the kingdom of God has come upon you" (Luke 11:20), in reply to those who accused him of casting out devils in the name of Beelzebub. The Kingdom of God is evidently at work in him, and the powers of the Age-to-Come have been released in his ministry so that demonic forces are vanquished. Rudolf Otto sees in his person and work the advent and arrival of the Kingdom of God as a comprehensive redemptive event. This does not imply the "realized eschatology" of Dodd. Otto can describe the Kingdom as ". . . ready to break in with mysterious dynamis. From its futurity it already extends its operation into the present."[48] Thus he still retains a strong understanding of the futuristic aspect of the Kingdom.

In other instances Jesus says: "Blessed are the eyes which see what you see! For I tell you that many prophets and kings desired to see what you see, and did not see it, and to hear what you hear, and did not hear it."[49] That which the prophets and kings had longed to see was the glory of the Age-to-Come, the manifestation of the Kingdom, and this was now present in Jesus. We note the emphasis on hearing, which, as Kümmel notes,[50]

---

[48] Otto, *The Kingdom of God and the Son of Man*, p. 59.
[49] Luke 10:23-24; Matthew 13:16-17 (Q).
[50] Kümmel, *op. cit.*, p. 112.

implies that these words are not some eschatological promise that
has been taken over, but refer to a definite experience. The eschatological fulfillment is taking place in the present. Although it is
not explicitly stated, it is quite clear that the person and works of
Jesus are central here. In some sense the future Kingdom of
promise has become present in him.

When John the Baptist sent his disciples to Jesus with the
query: "Are you he who is to come, or shall we look for another?",[51] our Lord quoted the words of the prophets which refer
to the "good time coming" and applied them to the results of his
own ministry, thereby implying that the time of fulfillment had
come in him. Once more the good news of the coming Kingdom
is tied up with Jesus' own ministry. His acts and message demonstrate that the Kingdom is beginning in the present. The One
who will bring salvation in the last days is already present, and
now that which is expected of the eschatological future is taking
place.[52]

One other saying needs to be noted, the enigmatic utterance
which may be so variously interpreted—"The kingdom of God is
not coming with signs to be observed; nor will they say, 'Lo, here
it is!' or 'There!' for behold, the kingdom of God is ἐντὸς ὑμῶν"
(Luke 17:21 [L]). Jesus evidently intends to make it clear that
the Kingdom's coming is not heralded by observable cosmic signs,
as in the current expectation. He dismisses speculation as to time
and place for the future coming. Now ἐντὸς ὑμῶν may mean
either "inside you" or "among you." In the total context, the latter
meaning would seem to apply.[53] Then the significance of the saying is that the future Kingdom has dawned and is already in
their midst in the person and activity of Jesus. He is the sign, in

---

[51] Luke 7:18-20; Matthew 11:2-3 (Q).

[52] Cf. Kümmel, op. cit., p. 111. R. H. Fuller puts it this way: ". . . the verb
εὐαγγελίζονται in the answer to John must not be evacuated of its future reference. The proclamation of Jesus is part of the initial stages of the End,
but the End itself has not yet occurred. . . . With the healings and the
proclamation of Jesus the new age is dawning, but it has not yet arrived.
The decisive event still lies in the future" (op. cit., p. 37).

[53] So Kümmel, op. cit., pp. 33 f.

his humility, that the Kingdom is present. It has become effective proleptically in him.[54]

It is evident that the presence of the Kingdom is bound up with the person of our Lord and with his activity and words. It is significant that a comparison of the conditions of the entrance into the Kingdom with the conditions of discipleship shows that these are identical;[55] thus entrance into the Kingdom meant a loyalty to Christ as Messiah and obedience to his will. The disciples could already participate in the benefits of the Kingdom. It is noteworthy, too, that some scholars have come to the conclusion that the nonkerygmatic elements in the teaching of Jesus disclose a transcendent self identical with the person to whom the early *kerygma* bears testimony. Continually in the Gospel traditions we are being "turned away from the How and When of God's eschatological coming to the present messenger of this eschatological consummation."[56]

What did Jesus say about himself, and how did the early *kerygma* express the same truth? Let us at once note that our Lord came to fulfill a task and that we should not expect him to offer direct teaching about his own person. We do, however, find indirect references and certain characteristic phrases which throw light on his own position in the Kingdom. Our Lord identified himself with the expected Messiah and so transformed the messianic hope that he filled it with a new content, breaking the old pattern in filling it with its true meaning. He was not, like the Davidic Messiah of the prophetic hope, incidental to the Kingdom. He was the focal point of its operation, the agent of the inbreak of the Kingdom. Furthermore, his mission was to be fulfilled not in kingly power and glory but in suffering and death. Hence he refused to identify himself with a political movement. When they came by force to make him king, he evaded them and escaped to commune with his Father.[57]

---

[54] Kümmel writes: "the Kingdom of God has already become effective in advance in Jesus and in the present events appearing in connection with his person" (*op. cit.,* p. 35).

[55] T. W. Manson has studied this in detail, *op. cit.,* pp. 205 f.

[56] Kümmel, *op. cit.,* p. 111.

[57] John 6:15. This would appear to be an authentic tradition.

The story of the temptation may well mark the supreme struggle in his soul between the commonly accepted idea of messianic
kingship and his own conviction about his messianic destiny. If
we accept some degree of *Historie* in the Marcan framework and
the baptismal narrative be taken as authentic,[58] we may see here
some dawning conviction of his messianic task and its nature.
The voice which echoes in his consciousness combines a phrase
from a messianic Psalm with the ordination charge to the Suffering Servant.[59] Already in the time of Jesus, the titles "Son" and
"Son of God" had become messianic (cf. 2 Esdras). Is it fanciful
to see here the dawning of a messianic consciousness which saw
the future task in terms of the Servant image? Our Lord's identification of himself with men in the act of baptism is an indication
that already he saw his path as one of sacrificial service for the
many. His was a suffering messiahship as the Servant of the Lord.

As his ministry progressed and the power of sin and evil became increasingly apparent, the shadow of the cross fell more and
more across his path. He recognized that his messiahship could
not be consummated by preaching and healing, but by his dying
and rising on the third day (Mark 8:31; 9:31; 10:34). In Gethsemane we have the last dread agony, when Jesus faced the
Father's will for him and made himself obedient unto death. He
voluntarily accepted the cross and went forth to meet the powers
of sin and darkness which were gathered against him. It was a

---

[58] I am not very happy that some form-critical scholars dismiss the
Marcan outline in general and dismiss as legends the baptism and temptation stories in particular. Acts 10:38 shows that the baptism of our Lord
was an accepted part of the *kerygma* of the early church and that thus the
anointing by the Spirit was early associated with this experience of Jesus.
Bultmann adopts the historicity of the baptism by John, but rejects as
legendary accretion, due to Hellenistic influence, the reference to the descent
of the Spirit—*Theology of the New Testament,* Vol. 2 (New York: Charles
Scribner's Sons, 1951), p. 26. He has to face, however, the fact that this
element was very early a part of the church's *kerygma.* If the Gospels are
enlarged *kerygma,* then Mark's account of the baptism may go back to the
historical actuality. In any case, the suggestion of Hellenistic influences can
be countered by the obvious references to anointing by the Spirit in Isaiah
42:1 (cf. Isaiah 61:1), a Servant passage echoed in the mind of our Lord
at the ceremony.

[59] Mark 1:10-11. Cf. Psalm 2:7; Isaiah 42:1.

suffering Messiah whom he presented to the Jewish people, to them a stumbling block, but in very truth the power of God.

The peculiar nature of our Lord's mission is borne out in his use of the title "Son of Man." The phrase stands philologically for a literal translation into the Greek of the Aramaic for "man," and thus it could mean simply the first person singular, "I." In some of the sayings of Jesus it clearly has this meaning, but in most it carries deeper implications. In the book of Daniel this messianic image has a remnant reference, whereas in the Similitudes of Enoch it is solely and explicitly messianic. Some scholars[60] would derive our Lord's use of the title from these Similitudes,[61] but there is no evidence that our Lord had any knowledge of the elaborate and esoteric apocalypticism of 1 Enoch. Indeed, his deep grounding in Old Testament prophecy would militate against any interest in it or in the circle of persons in which it arose. Such sayings of Jesus as might be ascribed to the Similitudes can with equal plausibility be traced to the book of Daniel, and when Jesus quotes, it is from the latter that the quotations are derived. Other scholars[62] would find the source of our Lord's usage of the title in Ezekiel, where the prophet is himself described in these terms. Now it is true that the prophetic visions of Israel being resurrected in the valley of dry bones and of the restored community centering in the Temple and its healing stream are given to the prophet as Son of Man. Thus Ezekiel's visions of a restored and purified remnant may have influenced Jesus. It is difficult to see how the sayings about the death and the *parousia* of the Son of Man can find any ground in this source, however. Furthermore, we have to take note of the fact that our

---

[60] *Vide* especially Otto, *op. cit.*, where this thesis is elaborately developed.

[61] The authority of these chapters of 1 Enoch is doubted, however, because they have not appeared yet in any Greek ms. of the book. Many scholars hold that these sections are later Christian interpolations.

[62] *Vide* J. Y. Campbell, article on "Son of Man" in *A Theological Word Book of the Bible,* ed. by Alan Richardson (New York: The Macmillan Company, 1950), pp. 230 ff.; G. S. Duncan, *Jesus, Son of Man* (New York: The Macmillan Company, 1949). W. A. Curtis also supports the influence of Ezekiel—*Jesus Christ the Teacher* (London: Oxford University Press, 1944), pp. 137 ff.

Lord's actual quotations are from Daniel.[63] We are left, then, with the latter book as the source for the title. We have noted that, understanding it as messianic, its use in Daniel points to a transcendent heavenly being who comes from God to deliver and have dominion over the remnant, the saints of the Most High.

In the Gospel traditions, the "Son of Man" occurs in three different groups of sayings. The first is a general group[64] in which the phrase might be used just as a synonym for "I" or "man." The second group of sayings associates the phrase with the passion,[65] and the third group with the *parousia*.[66]

Of these latter two groups we may note that the references to death and suffering belong almost exclusively to the Marcan tradition, being found in the passion narrative or occurring as predictions of the passion. Further, the *parousia* utterances occur in both Mark and Q. Finally, the two groups never overlap, the passion utterances being completely detached from the *parousia* utterances. This has led Bultmann[67] to suggest that only the *parousia* sayings are authentic and that the passion utterances were the inventions of Mark. He then goes on to suggest that the *parousia* utterances are messianic, but that Jesus is not to be identified with the Son of Man. Jesus merely announces the coming of a glorious messianic figure. Apart from such extreme criticism, it is now the scholarly consensus that Jesus used the title of himself,[68] and few would follow Bultmann.

Eduard Schweizer[69] declares "that Jesus called himself the Son of Man remains extremely probable," on the ground that the use of the term is confined in the New Testament almost entirely to sayings of our Lord himself. Acts 7:56 indicates that the

---

[63] Cf. Fuller, *op. cit.*, p. 101.

[64] Mark 2:10; 2:28; Luke 7:34; 9:58; 12:10 (all Q); Matthew 13:37; Luke 19:10.

[65] Mark 8:31; 9:31; 10:33; 10:45; 14:21; 14:41.

[66] Mark 8:38; 9:9; 13:26; 14:62; Luke 11:30; 12:40; 17:24; 17:26 (all Q); Matthew 10:23; 13:41; 19:28; 24:39; 25:31; Luke 17:22; 17:30; 18:8.

[67] Bultmann, *Theology of the New Testament,* Vol. 2, pp. 30 ff.

[68] Cf. Mowinckel, *He That Cometh,* p. 445.

[69] Schweizer, *Lordship and Discipleship,* p. 40. Schweizer refutes the position of Bultmann in an excellent footnote.

earliest community thought of Jesus as the exalted Son of Man. Other scholars[70] would interpret Son of Man in the collective sense in Daniel and apply this collective sense to Jesus' use of the title. According to them the Son of Man represents Jesus and his disciples in both groups of sayings, and is a remnant concept. As W. G. Kümmel[71] notes, this interpretation "suffers shipwreck just on the eschatological pronouncements such as Mark 8:38, Luke 17:24 and most particularly on the texts . . . Matthew 10:23, 24:44, 25:31." He adds: ". . . that Jesus applied this veiled ascription of sovereignty to himself is shown indubitably by Mark 2:10, 28 and Matthew 8:20, 11:19; and the objections raised against these texts will not hold water." We too may conclude that "Son of Man" was used by Jesus to describe himself and his ministry.

The problem still remains of the contrast between the sayings about the passion and those about the *parousia*. If Daniel be the source of the title, the Danielic figure comes in glory. But in the teaching of Jesus, the Son of Man is presented as coming in glory and also as humiliated, rejected, crucified, yet rising on the third day. This, however, is no reason to deny the authenticity of the sayings. Because Jesus took the image from the book of Daniel, this does not mean that he would not fill it with new content while retaining its transcendent messianic reference. This is what fulfillment implies. There is a change of emphasis, a strange mingling of kingly glory and the humility of the Servant. As the prophetic messiahship is transfigured by the content of the Suffering Servant image, so also is the figure of the Son of Man. As Mowinckel puts it: "How Jesus reached this understanding of himself is his own personal secret, which cannot be penetrated by any attempt at psychological explanation. Jesus understood and fulfilled the thought of the unknown Messiah on earth in a manner entirely different from its presentation in the Jewish legend."[72]

---

[70] *Vide* Manson, *op. cit.*, pp. 227 ff.; "The Son of Man in Daniel, Enoch, and the Gospels," *Bulletin of the John Rylands Library*, 32, 1949-50, pp. 171 ff.; Vincent Taylor, "The Son of Man Sayings Relating to the Parousia," *The Expository Times*, 58, 1946-47, pp. 12 ff. This was my own position earlier—*The Christian Understanding of History*, pp. 146 ff.

[71] Kümmel, *op. cit.*, p. 46.

[72] Mowinckel, *op. cit.*, p. 447.

The title evidently has a double reference—his earthly passion and his future exaltation. The original insight is definitely the idea that the Son of Man will be rejected and suffer before his glorious exaltation and his coming on the clouds of heaven. To this we must add the element of fulfillment of the promise that through his suffering as Servant "the many" will be saved. As Stauffer puts it: "Jesus claims for himself all the heavenly majesty of the Son of Man. Yet this celestial glory belongs to a man who, as the height of improbability, treads the way of suffering. . . . The heavenly man in the form of a servant—that of the Son of Man of whom Jesus speaks."[73]

Again, Cullmann holds that Jesus' combination of the "Suffering Servant" with the "Son of Man" was "something completely new."[74] He continues: " 'Son of Man' represents the highest conceivable declaration of exaltation in Judaism; *ebed Yahweh* is the expression of the deepest humiliation. Even if there really was a concept of a suffering Messiah in Judaism, it cannot be proved that the suffering was combined precisely with the idea of the Son of Man coming on the clouds of heaven. This is the unheard-of new act of Jesus, that he united these two apparently contradictory tasks in his self-consciousness, and that he expressed that union in his life and teaching." We note that just as the Servant of the Lord represents the redeemed remnant, so the Son of Man represents redeemed humanity, so that the whole meaning of salvation history is gathered up in our Lord's unique combination of these two titles.

We might, at first sight, suggest that here we have a picture of an earthly sufferer who is later exalted and made the messianic Son of Man who shall return in glory on the clouds of heaven.[75]

---

[73] Stauffer, *New Testament Theology,* p. 109.

[74] Oscar Cullmann, *The Christology of the New Testament* (Philadelphia: The Westminster Press, 1959), p. 161.

[75] Mowinckel points out that the deeper insight of pre-existence is not present in the Synoptic traditions. At this stage the title refers solely to Jesus' earthly humiliation and eschatological exaltation. He believes this to be part of the enigmatic use of the title (*op. cit.,* p. 447). Eduard Schweizer evades the problem by regarding the *parousia* sayings as nonauthentic (*op. cit.,* p. 39).

R. H. Fuller[76] believes that Jesus' indirect use of the title for himself (e.g., Mark 8:38) arises from the proleptic element in his consciousness. He is not yet the glorified Son of Man. Between his humiliated and his glorified states there stands the event by which the Kingdom comes with power—the cross. Hence Fuller suggests that our Lord took the image of the Servant as fundamental for his earthly ministry and that of the Danielic Son of Man for his future glory. The Son of Man is therefore used proleptically when applied to his earthly ministry and his passion. We have yet to discuss the final significance of the cross, but this view commends itself as far as it goes. It still leaves us with the issue of transcendence implicit in the Danielic image.

What are we to say about the earthly and humiliated Jesus? That John later describes Jesus as Son of Man and makes it a favorite title is significant, especially because in the Fourth Gospel it implies pre-existence and transcendence. It is the insight of the postresurrection experience which came to John. This is true. But this does not make it less authentic, and we have no right to eliminate it from the consciousness of our Lord in the light of other descriptions of himself. There are tension and paradox here, but, as we have already noted, fulfillment involves these. The Son of Man who is a figure of kingly glory can yet be applied as a title by Jesus to his own lowly ministry with the humiliation of the cross. Paul shows that this can be understood only if the postresurrection exaltation and the future glorious coming are linked up with a heavenly pre-existence (Phil. 2:5-11). Then the humiliation does not lie only in the rejection of the cross and the lowly life of the present teacher. It lies in the divine glory itself, as God in his Son empties himself and takes the form of a servant. Mowinckel is right when he suggests that the tension in Paul's thought here goes back to the self-consciousness of Jesus "which finds expression in the daring way in which he transforms and uses the concept of the Son of Man."[77]

One more title used by our Lord requires investigation—the

---

[76] Fuller, *op. cit.*, pp. 103 ff.
[77] Mowinckel, *op. cit.*, p. 450.

"Son" and the "Son of God." In the Old Testament the phrase has a messianic significance, as Psalm 2:7 indicates, but it could also be applied to Israel.[78] The title is used in connection with both the baptism and the temptation. It certainly attests here to a messianic consciousness in our Lord, but does it attest to more? Here we need to remember our Lord's later mode of addressing God as *Abba*. Now the Aramaic reserves this style of address for the earthly progenitor, but expresses the proper address to God in the form "my father." There is a degree of familiarity here which suggests that Jesus was conscious of a peculiar and unique closeness to God. The familiar appellation had special significance for him and defined his own unique relationship.

In the parable of the Wicked Husbandman (Mark 12:1-9), Jesus is not a servant like the other prophets who are sent. He is the one beloved Son, the heir. This parable sums up the Old Testament history and centers it by implication in our Lord himself. It suggests once more the uniqueness of his relation to God. In Mark 13:32, the authenticity of which is often called into question, the Son occupies a place of lofty splendor above men and angels, subordinate only to God himself.

We are left with the notorious Q tradition, which seems like a "Synoptic bolt from the Johannine blue."[79] This is often rejected, yet we see no reason to doubt its genuine nature. It is as well supported as any logion from the documentary side. Further, are we to dismiss all the Johannine references to the Son as having no basis in the teaching of the historical Jesus? We find it very difficult to accept this radical suggestion. According to the logion under consideration, Jesus is not just the medium of the divine self-revelation. His sonship is unshared. He alone has true knowledge of the Father. Others can know the Father through him only. There is implied a uniqueness and an unparalleled nature about the filial consciousness of Jesus. His sonship is unique and marks him off from all others.

----

[78] Hosea 11:1; Exodus 4:22-23.
[79] Luke 10:22 ff.; Matthew 11:27.

William Manson[80] follows Harnack[81] in holding that Jesus' consciousness of sonship is primary to his messianic consciousness. He holds that "the Messiahship of Jesus comes as the final seal or imprint on the sense of revealing the Father which carried him into all his work for men."[82] Thus the drive in his messianic consciousness was the responsibility awakened in the deeper and more primary filial consciousness. The sense of his special relationship with the Father may well have been early, if the Temple tradition of his boyhood be authentic. In this there was a deep sense of responsibility which flowered into the characteristic form of the messianic consciousness of baptism.

Bultmann radically asserts that both the messianic and the sonship images were postresurrection products of *Gemeindetheologie,* and that the messiahship idea was prior to that of sonship. The evidence, as we have seen, is against his radical attack on the authenticity of the sayings. But equally it would reverse the order of the appearance of the two images. The messianic consciousness is set in the larger context of the filial. Such a view fits in better with the prophetic experience. Sonship was native to Jesus' consciousness, and because of it he saw his messianic task. His deep inner relation with God gave him the vision of his task.[83]

We thus see a Christology inherent in the very message of Jesus himself. It provided the roots from which the early church developed its thought on the incarnation. The presence of the Kingdom of God in the life, activity, death, and resurrection of Jesus had to be expressed in a form which preserved both our Lord's transcendent selfhood and his utter humanity. In him history had been consummated, the divine meaning of history was being actualized, the promises had been fulfilled. This Christocentric understanding of history found its expression in the vari-

---

[80] William Manson, *Jesus the Messiah* (Philadelphia: The Westminster Press, 1946), pp. 153-154.

[81] Adolf von Harnack, *The Sayings of Jesus* (London: Williams and Norgate, 1908), p. 245.

[82] William Manson, *op. cit.,* p. 109.

[83] Cf. Fuller, *op. cit.,* p. 85: "The Sonhood is the basis of his Messiahship, not the Messiahship of his Sonhood."

ous attempts to bring together the suprahistorical and the historical dimensions of the person and life of Jesus in the witness to the incarnation. The transcendent or suprahistorical dimension, already implicit in both Jesus' use of the title "Son of Man" and his unique filial consciousness, was now expressed in the image of the pre-existent Son of God and in the description of the risen Christ as "Lord."

CHAPTER V

SALVATION HISTORY—INCARNATION AND REDEMPTION

We must now examine the New Testament witnesses' understanding of the advent of the Kingdom of God in Christ and its significance. The all-embracing Christ-event contained the constituent elements of the life, death, resurrection, and ascension of the Lord. The whole is set against the backdrop of human sin and bankruptcy, of demonic bondage and divine judgment. When the first witnesses sought to express the personal and eschatological presence of the Kingdom of Jesus Christ, they did so in terms of incarnation. Thereby they were enabled to emphasize both the divine and the human elements in the Christ-event —its eternal dimension and its historical actuality. To this incarnational teaching we shall first turn our attention. We shall then consider the setting of the incarnation in the history of sinful and rebellious man. Finally, we shall consider the culmination of the divine act of redemption in the death and resurrection of our Lord.

1. The Kingdom and the Incarnation

Believing that the Kingdom had been actualized in the human life of Jesus, the New Testament witnesses sought to express this eternal dimension behind his humanity. This actualization was not only effected in him, but it had become potentially effective in all men. In the humanity of Jesus, God had lifted history, with all its sin, up into his redemptive purpose. He had joined issue with man's sin and demonic bondage in history itself through the medium of a historical life. The consequences of this act had been effective in the lives of the witnesses. Testifying from a postresurrection standpoint, they moved in faith from Calvary and the resurrection, the climax of God's redemptive act, to an understanding of the person of the Mediator. Like doubting Thomas, when the light from the risen Lord struck home to their souls, they cried: "My Lord and my God." They sought to express the truth that God was personally and uniquely present in the person of Jesus.

The primitive church early used the title "Lord" to describe Jesus.[1] This very word was used in the Greek Septuagint to translate the Hebrew name *Adonai*, which was regularly used in the place of the sacred tetragrammaton (YHWH) when the Scriptures were read aloud. For Paul, facing the Gentile world, the word was also used in Hellenism to describe the divine hero of a mystery cult. Hence, a word which undoubtedly had its origin in Jewish usage and clearly identifies Jesus with God could also provide a point of contact for declaring his deity to the pagan world. Paul used the title frequently,[2] and he implied by it the full deity of the Messiah. There is no adoptionism in his thought. In Romans 1:4 he declares that, at his exaltation, the Christ received the status that really belonged to him as Son of God. But the preceding verse indicates, by its use of "Son," that Christ is Son of God even before his birth of the seed of David. The conception involves more than did the official messianic name "Son." Paul and the other New Testament writers understand "Son" as an ontological title for Jesus and with the connotation of pre-existence. The title is not just bound up with a historical existence, and this passage cannot be used to support adoptionist ideas.

The Kingdom of God is present in Jesus in the sense that God himself is present personally and in his fullness. The fullness of the Godhead dwells in Jesus (Col. 2:9). One stream of thought which emphasizes this is evidently derived from the Wisdom speculation of Jewish thought. There is undoubtedly a prophetic

---

[1] E.g., Acts 2:36; 10:36. The usage is very frequent. Cf. Vincent Taylor, *The Names of Jesus* (New York: St Martin's Press, Inc., 1953), pp. 43 ff.

[2] Romans 10:12; 2 Corinthians 4:5.

note in the developing idea of the wisdom of God as first a personified attribute of God in Proverbs 8 and Ecclesiasticus 24, and
then a hypostatic being in God in the Alexandrian Judaism of the
Wisdom of Solomon (7:22-30; 9:9 ff.). Paul clearly has this
atmosphere of thought in mind when he describes Christ as
". . . the power of God and the wisdom of God" (1 Cor. 1:24).
The cosmic association of the idea is reflected in those passages
where Christ is described as a cosmic principle. Through him all
things were created and in him all things form a meaningful and
coherent whole (Col. 1:15-20). He is the unifying principle of
the universe, and it is the will of the Father that in him all
things shall be "summed up" (Eph. 1:10). As such, he is the pre-
existent Son who is before all things (Col. 1:1-17). The earthly
history of God's people is under his control. He is identified with
the Rock that followed Israel through the wilderness (1 Cor.
10:4). Thus, the Christ is one with God from all eternity. He can
be described as the Son of God's love, as God's own Son. Indeed,
he is the "image" of the invisible God, so that in him men know
the God who is invisible.[3] The resurrection reveals his divine
character, and because of this, every tongue confesses him "Lord"
to the glory of God the Father (Phil. 2:9-11).

The Fourth Gospel makes explicit what is implicit in the
Synoptic Gospels. It declares, like Paul, that the Father loves the
Son and sent him into the world. It goes beyond its Synoptic
parallels in affirming the uniqueness of the Son (John 1:14, 18;
3:16, 18). There is such a perfect identity between the Father
and the Son that, at the historical level, he who has seen the Son
has seen the Father also.[4] The Son thinks the Father's thoughts
and does the Father's will. This is more than moral identity. The
Son, like the Father, has life in himself (John 5:26). He is self-
existent and self-sufficient. There is an inner unity of love between Father and Son which is grounded in a community of
nature. Both are God, and both are love. As such, Jesus is the
pre-existent, transcendent Son in the flesh, and can say: ". . . be-

---

[3] Colossians 1:15; 2 Corinthians 4:4.
[4] John 5:19-23; 10:30; 12:44-45; 14:9 ff.

fore Abraham was, I am" (John 8:58). Here we have an ontological basis. A merely moral bond between Father and Son does not suffice. John puts in religious language what Nicaea expressed in metaphysical abstraction. He does, however, preserve the moral aspect of relationship. The Father loves the Son and the Son is obedient to the Father (John 5:19 ff.). As the Father works continually, so does the Son. Yet their identity is not just that of mutual moral commitment. It is an identity of essence. The Kingdom of God is personally present in Christ. There is an inner dimension of eternity in Jesus of Nazareth which unites him with God.

In the Prologue to the Fourth Gospel, this theme receives a rich expression. Here the characteristic description of the pre-existent Son is the "Word." Wisdom speculation may be influential.[5] But we cannot evade the influence of the Hebrew understanding of God's Word, in its creative and prophetic significance. The concrete realism with which the Hebrew envisaged a "word" meant that it was an extension of the personality of its utterer, carrying in it the latter's power and intention. Most of all was this true of the Word of God. The prophetic word carried the divine activity into a situation. This would seem to lie in the background of John's thought, for his emphasis is on revelation and the giving of light in Jesus. Christ's words are life and truth. But they are so because he is, in his person, God's Word.[6] In him the Word of God has completely clothed itself in human flesh. God has extended his personal being into his world and become personally active in a human life. Hence, the title becomes appropriate to describe the pre-existent Son. It is still more appropriate when we look at Genesis 1 and see the strong parallel between the Word of God at creation and the Johannine Word who is the agent of creation. So the Wisdom and the Word images of the old covenant find fulfillment and true content in Jesus of

---

[5] J. Rendel Harris suggests that we may have here a pre-Christian Jewish hymn to Wisdom which has been taken over by the Christian church— *The Origin of the Prologue to St. John's Gospel* (Cambridge: The University Press, 1917).

[6] John 17:17; cf. 14:6; 8:45, 47; 3:34; 15:24; Hebrews 1:1.

Nazareth, and provide a basis for the understanding of his pre-existence.

The influence of Philo on the Fourth Gospel is a debatable issue.[7] His Logos doctrine certainly merged the Hellenistic speculation of Platonists and Stoics with Jewish thought. It blended the Greek Logos concept with the Jewish image of Wisdom. Yet, as far as the Fourth Gospel is concerned, Philo should be regarded as a parallel indication that the Greek and Jewish worlds had a common point of contact in the idea of the Logos. Although for Christians the Logos had a peculiar and distinctive significance, the very use of the term made communication possible. For John, however, the Logos was no abstract rational principle, as with the Greeks, nor a personified and hypostatized divine attribute, as in Jewish Wisdom speculation. He was known in and through the person and life of Jesus Christ and was grounded in historical reality. God's Word had manifested his sovereignty over history in the old covenant, and now that Word had become flesh and the Kingdom was personally present.

The Word is described as "with God." As Cullmann reminds us, this means that he was not to be separated from God himself.[8] Further, he is not a second God, for he is *theos*, God. Hoskyns points out that this anarthrous predicate cannot be rendered adequately into English. "The Word of God is no neuter thing, no mere power: He acts with personal consciousness and will."[9] Thus he shares in the divine essence and yet is not merged in God. This is the highest Christology in the New Testament. The differentiation in God is one of function. The Word is God in his function as revelation. "The Logos is the self-revealing, self-giving God—God in action."[10] He is the sovereign will of God dynamically active in history and finally personally incarnated in Jesus.

The Prologue sets world history and salvation history in this

---

[7] *Vide* C. H. Dodd, *The Interpretation of the Fourth Gospel* (Cambridge: The University Press, 1953), pp. 54 ff.

[8] Cullmann, *Christology of the New Testament,* p. 265.

[9] Hoskyns, *The Fourth Gospel,* p. 141.

[10] Cullmann, *op. cit.,* p. 266.

framework of the revealing Word. We have a threefold movement of the Word into human history as Mediator of the divine
truth. He enters into the world which he created and whose life
he sustains. But he is light as well as life, and John uses this
image, hallowed by much usage, for the divine truth. This image
is dynamic. It implies that the higher reality is shining into this
world. The Word is God in action, seeking to disclose himself. If
the phrase ". . . coming into the world" in 1:9 is connected with
"the true light" and not with "every man," John would seem to
suggest that the truth has come into the world. It is immanent
within it, as the light which illumines the human conscience and
the reason, giving men some knowledge of the moral good. The
Word shines in the darkness and is not mastered by it (John 1:9-
10). But the world does not know him for what he is. It is not
able to grasp the truth by reason and conscience alone—a parallel
to Paul's declaration that men, able to know God, glorified him
not as God but, with a reprobate reason, made gods of their own
(Rom. 1:18 ff.).

Then the light came to his own (John 1:11-13), the Jewish
people, who are Jehovah's peculiar treasure.[11] Through the Old
Testament revelation and the prophets in particular, the living
light drew near to Israel, but "his own" received him not. So the
living Word which comes to all men in general revelation over-
rules also salvation history as promise. Here John sees a sifting
process, for some did receive the Word, and to them he gave
the title to become the children of God. Thus, proleptically the
remnant came into being. Yet even John the Baptist was not the
light. He and his predecessors only pointed to the light. At
long last the light entered history, personally (John 1:14). The
Word became flesh and tabernacled among us that we might behold his glory, full of grace and truth, and that seeing him we
might know God (John 1:18). So behind all history, creatively
and redemptively, is the Word in whom God is disclosing himself
redemptively, in whom he displays his sovereign grace.

---

[11] Cf. "Five possessions did the Holy One, blessed is He, take to Himself in the world; and these are they: the Law is one possession, and the
heaven and the earth are one possession, Abraham is one possession, Israel is
one possession, and the Temple is one possession"—*Pirke Aboth*, 6:10.

This emphasis on the eternal dimension in Christ is combined with an emphasis on his humanity, his historical actuality. The Kingdom of God has become flesh. God's personal presence and kingly power have been brought to a focus in a human life. Jesus was born of a woman and born under the Law (Gal. 4:4). Thereby he became a member of the human race in general and of the Jewish race in particular. He was made in the likeness of men and took the form of a servant (Phil. 2:7-8), so that he submitted to the servitude of sin even though he knew no sin. Hence, he can be described as made of sinful flesh (Rom. 8:3), that is to say, of creatureliness subjected to sin. He was as open to attack by the powers of evil and sin as were his brethren.

John was careful to preserve the humanity of our Lord, but he regarded it as a universal humanity, employing the title "Son of Man," so much used by our Lord himself. His Gospel was an attempt to safeguard the historical actuality and humanity of Jesus, while allowing the inner dimension of eternity to become evident within the historical life. Everywhere in the Gospel of John we meet the tension between the historical and the suprahistorical. John seeks to link together the traditions about the historical Jesus and to disclose the deeper rhythm and meaning behind the events in his life. He saw that *"Flesh, history, aye, the flesh and blood of Jesus, profiteth nothing,* if it be mere observable history, if it be that which was seen by the Pharisees, who also were eyewitnesses, if it be that which was seen by Pilate and by those others who neither believed nor knew." [12]

John is recording incidents in a serious historical sense and so attempting to supplement the other Gospels. But he is also seeking to unveil the inner meaning of the historical life. Hence the details are heightened and allegorizing tendencies are often introduced. As we have to employ distortion in order to present a three-dimensional scene on a two-dimensional canvas, so John heightens and distorts the *Historie* that the hidden meaning, the *Geschichte,* may be unveiled. He makes evident the manner in which the Kingdom is personally present and operative in the historical life of the Son of Man. The challenge to do this un-

---

[12] Hoskyns, *op cit.,* pp. 83-84.

doubtedly lies in the upsurge of Gnostic speculation in the church, of which recent discoveries in Egypt have made us very aware.[13] The temptation was to forsake the historical for super-history, the flesh for the Spirit, and to indulge in esoteric specula-tion. John rejected all such mystic flights from the historical. The only way into communion with the living Truth, with God, was by that faith which sees the glory of God in the historical life of Jesus of Nazareth, as disclosed by the Spirit. God's person and sovereign claims are known only through the Word made flesh, and the reality there disclosed is love—redemptive love (John 14:9; 3:16).

Hence Jesus is man, and as Son of Man he is representative man. Here we meet the true significance of the earthly life. John preserves the Synoptic emphasis in the title, namely, its associa-tion with eschatology and with soteriology. As Son of Man, Jesus will judge men in his Day (John 5:21-29; cf. 12:47). There is a heightened sense of the Kingdom as a present reality, but the future reference is still present. The attitude to the Son of Man in the present determines a man's final judgment.[14] The final eschatological decision is made proleptically in the flesh and blood of the Son of Man, his historical existence and mission. Here and now he comes to give his life for the many, and yet John sees the cross as the road to glorification, the path to the throne. The emphasis falls on the exaltation of the Son of Man. The glory of God is disclosed through the sacrifice and sufferings of Jesus (John 8:28), and the "lifting up" of the Son of Man upon the cross becomes the "lifting up" into glory (John 12:28 ff.). In the triumphant sacrifice and exaltation of the Son of Man, all men may share. Through his historical death and lifting up, eternal life—the life of the future age—is communicated to men (John 3:13-15). They enter the Kingdom. As Son of Man, Jesus makes possible a new humanity which is incorporated in him

---

[13] *Vide* Jean Doresse, *The Secret Books of the Egyptian Gnostics* (New York: The Viking Press, Inc., 1960); W. C. van Unnik, *Newly Discovered Gnostic Writings* (Naperville: Alec R. Allenson, Inc., 1960); R. M. Grant, *The Secret Sayings of Jesus* (Garden City: Doubleday & Company, Inc., 1960).

[14] John 5:24; cf. Matthew 25, also John 3:18.

(John 6:27; cf. 15:1-9). The title conveys the full divine glory of the Messiah, but it also discloses his full humanity. There is the suggestion that he is a pre-existent being who descended from heaven (John 3:13), and that in his exaltation he ascends to where he was before (John 6:62). Yet as archetypal man, all men may have life in him. He is true man, for they have life in themselves only as they eat the flesh and drink the blood of the Son of Man. They must abide in him as the branches in the vine. As Barrett points out: "The Son of Man in John is thus not only a mediator in that he is the redeemer of men, but is also a mediator in an ontological sense, since he is related both to God and to men."[15]

Paul discloses the same ideas without using the title. Jesus is "the Man." It is possible, as Cullmann suggests, that John was nearer to the Synoptic tradition than Paul and stands in the line of the Jewish Hellenistic group associated with Stephen, which seems to have preserved the original teaching of our Lord.[16] If this be the case, a Son of Man Christology might have been especially significant for John. We have already demonstrated the presence of a Logos Christology in both John and Paul. It would seem that there was a Son of Man Christology also woven into the early traditions. Its use is evident in Paul as well as John, even though Paul does not use the title. Attempts to trace the influence of Philo on Paul's thought are not too successful.[17] The New Test-

---

[15] C. K. Barrett, *The Gospel According to St. John* (London: S.P.C.K., 1955), p. 61. Barrett also notes that John has slightly transmuted the meaning of the terms "Son of God" and "Son of Man" (in the Synoptic tradition). He writes: "Superficially it might seem that the two are almost reversed in meaning, for while in the synoptic gospels 'Son of God' draws attention to Christ's obedience to God and 'Son of man' means a heavenly being, in John 'Son of God' means at times one who shares the nature of God, 'Son of man' one who shares the nature of man. To draw the contrast so sharply would however be misleading"—*ibid.*, p. 60.

[16] Stephen is certainly the only one in Acts who speaks of the exalted Jesus as Son of Man; cf. Cullmann, *op. cit.*, pp. 183 f.

[17] The Hellenistic myth of the "heavenly man"—*vide* R. Reitzenstein, *Die Hellenistischen Mysterienreligionen* (Leipzig: B. G. Teubner, 1927), and W. Bousset, *Kyrios Christos* (Göttingen: Vandenhoeck & Ruprecht, 1913)—undoubtedly influenced Philo. He set the ideal man of Genesis 1:27 over against the second, historical Adam of Genesis 2:7. The first is the cosmological blueprint by which the second is modeled from the earth.

ament interest was soteriological, not metaphysical. In Philo's thought, the heavenly man comes first and the interest is cosmological. In Paul's thought, the heavenly man comes second and the interest is eschatological. The Danielic image of the Son of Man[18] was probably much more influential with Paul. Indeed, it would seem that Paul's teaching has been shaped by Jesus' own use of the title "Son of Man" with its implicit transcendence and heavenly glory and with its representative aspect. Christ will come again on the clouds of heaven (1 Thess. 4:17). He is the new man, the life-giving Spirit, through whom a new humanity comes into being (1 Cor. 15:45 ff.). He restores and completes man's destiny, representing in his own person a restored humanity. Just as Adam's task was to manifest the image of God, so Christ is the image of the invisible God, the true man.[19] He succeeds where Adam failed, and, in his representative humanity, a new humanity is created. In Jesus, true man in God's image becomes a historical actuality. The Kingdom of God is actualized in history in human life, and the meaning of history is both revealed and realized.

It is an open issue how far the heavenly man idea influenced Paul's interpretation of our Lord's pre-existence. Cullmann, influenced by Barth's unusual speculation about a pre-existent humanity of Christ in the heavenly order,[20] believes that it was influential. He believes that all humanity has lost the divine image except "the Heavenly Man, who already existed at the beginning, but not on earth; who came only much later (ἔπειτα) as an incarnate, earthly 'man.' "[21] The hymn of Philippians 2:5-11[22] might

---

[18] The background of this figure—the *Urmensch* myth—has been discussed earlier.

[19] Colossians 1:15; 2 Corinthians 4:4.

[20] Cf. Karl Barth, *Christ and Adam* (New York: Harper & Brothers, 1957), *passim*. *Vide* also his *Church Dogmatics*, II, 2, pp. 94 ff., and *The Humanity of God* (Richmond: John Knox Press, 1960).

[21] Cullmann, *op. cit.*, p. 170.

[22] Ernst Lohmeyer (*Kyrios Jesus, Eine Untersuchung zu Phil. 2:5-11*) believes it an ancient Christian Aramaic Psalm. J. Héring in *Le Royaume de Dieu et Sa Venue* (Neuchâtel: Delachaux & Niestlé, 1959), pp. 162 f., traces it to an original Jewish gnostic hymn concerned with the heavenly man and his descent to earth.

support Cullmann's thesis if it be regarded as written around the theme of the heavenly man. Whatever its origin, however, Paul has made it his own and colored it with his own distinctive thought. Cullmann, with Héring, would make the phrase "the form of God" synonymous with "the image of God" and thus a reference to Genesis 1:26. Then Christ's being in the form of God does not refer to his deity but to his representative humanity. Unlike Adam, he refused to grasp at equality with God but maintained his divine destiny to be in the image of God. In the place of Adam's arrogance, he followed the path of humiliation and took the form of a servant, accepting our bondage and becoming fashioned as a man.

Here the theme of the Suffering Servant, already bound up by our Lord with the image of the Son of Man, enters the Pauline picture. The true meaning of incarnation is thereby made plain. The obedience unto the death on the cross meant that Adam's disobedience was undone. The heavenly man accepted the ignominy and rejection of the worst death that may befall sinful man. As representative Suffering Servant he thus, by his obedience, corrected the disobedience of humanity. So our Lord's association of the Son of Man title with his own passion finds expression in Paul's thought. The humiliation, the emptying of the heavenly man, implies both that *the* man became *a* man, and that he assumed the role of the Servant of the Lord.[23] Here the important theme of *kenosis* enters theological thought. This is the cross before the historical cross, the process which begins in eternity and is brought to a climax in Calvary. He emptied himself.

The hymn finishes with the exaltation of the heavenly man and the humiliated Servant to full lordship over all. The cosmic *via dolorosa* leads to the place of divine honor. Jesus' obedience as Son of Man brings him to that equality with God at which he refused to grasp. God confers on him the title "Lord." He receives God's name, and thus returns to a higher glory than that of his pre-existent state. God "*more* than exalted" him. This does not mean adoptionism, for being in the form or image of

---

[23] Cf. Cullmann, *op. cit.*, p. 178.

God is tantamount to oneness of essence. What is added is not nature but function, "complete equality with God in the exercise of divine Sovereignty."[24]

So the redemptive meaning of the incarnation as the Kingdom manifested in a mighty act of salvation becomes plain. The two central witnesses here are Paul and John. For Paul, the emphasis falls on the self-emptying and humiliation of the Servant as representative man. For John it falls on the exalted Christ, reflected proleptically in his earthly life so that always, through the humanity, the deity is evident. Both are sure that the living God has tabernacled among men and so brought to a climax the long course of salvation history, disclosing the full meaning of the human story. Both emphasize the full humanity of Jesus. For both, Jesus is archetypal man, and for both he is earthly man—re-created. There is no Platonic idea of archetype and copy. There is real incarnation. As Barrett expresses it: "Being truly God and truly man, and being also the image of God and the archetype of humanity, he [Jesus] is an ontological mediator between God and man; he is no less a mediator of true knowledge, and of salvation."[25]

2. The Background of Secular History—Sin and the Flesh

The New Testament witnesses, like the Old Testament prophets, understood the redemptive act of God in relation to sin. Our Lord conceived the Kingdom as operating in himself against the forces of sin and evil. He understood his task in terms of the image of the Suffering Servant, whose human task was concerned with the sin of Israel and the nations. If sin produced the impotence and frustration of the chosen people, then with sin the Messiah must deal. Hence Jesus came not to call the righteous, but sinners,[26] and identified himself with publicans and sinners.[27]

---

[24] *Ibid.*, p. 181.

[25] Barrett, *op. cit.*, p. 62.

[26] Mark 2:17 and parallels. Luke adds the explanatory gloss "to repentance" (5:32).

[27] Luke 7:34 ff.; Matthew 11:19 (Q).

He saw that Israel had failed because its emphasis had been on outward behavior and not inward attitude. The old covenant had to be replaced by a new covenant, in which God's law would be written on men's inward parts. Indeed, our Lord allowed his disciples to neglect the ceremonial washings prescribed by the Mosaic law.[28] Sin was an inward thing, and the outward must be traced to its source in the human heart.[29] With this inner uncleanness man was powerless to deal. Men could not get into right relations with God nor were they fit to share in the Age-to-Come until their hearts were right. Love of God and neighbor had to become a natural attitude. Pride and selfishness had to be cast out.

Now for such a new inner state to become a reality, God must act. Men could not go to God as the righteous making a claim. They could not earn salvation by their own merits for it was solely the outcome of divine grace.[30] The Servant's task was to justify the many, and our Lord understood his mission as this gracious act, making intercession for the transgressors and bearing their iniquities (Isa. 53:11-12). If the Age-to-Come was to descend upon men, it had to bring to them divine forgiveness and restore them to that fellowship with God for which they were created. The Kingdom would be manifested in the changed attitude of men's hearts. During his ministry Jesus was effecting this in a few lives, but it was a proleptic act. If we ask when the Kingdom came with power, we have to point to the event of the cross and resurrection, in which man's redemption was finally effected. Over the earthly ministry of Christ this event cast its shadow. Those who would not see death before they saw the Kingdom of God come with power were not promised a vain thing.

The New Testament witnesses agree with unanimity that history is the sphere of universal sin. The Old Testament traditions set world history in such a framework with the story of the Gar-

---

[28] Luke 11:38 (L); Mark 7:2 ff.
[29] Mark 7:20-23; Matthew 7:17 ff.
[30] This is the theme of parables like the Prodigal Son (Luke 15:11-32), the Laborers in the Vineyard (Matthew 20:1-16), the Great Supper (Luke 14:16-24), the Pharisee and the Publican (Luke 18:9-14).

den. The world is not as God intended. Human history is under God's wrath and judgment. The New Testament, in varying ways, affirms the same viewpoint. All men have sinned and come short of the glory of God, and none is righteous (Rom. 3:23; 3:10). Every man deceives himself if he declares that he has not sinned (1 John 1:8, 10). Men exist in contradiction (Rom. 7:19). There is in them all a fixed attitude of character which only the grace of God can set free, a deliberate choice of a way of living out of harmony with the will of God.

Hence, the life of historical man is described as being in Adam. The hallmark of humanity and of secular history is a universal sinfulness which entered the race in Adam's sin. Paul teaches that through the sin of the first man there arises a corruption which extends throughout the race. Man thereby becomes involved in death. The Apostle does not suggest that the guilt of Adam's sin rests upon his descendants. Each man is responsible for his own sin.[31] Death (physical death) obtained a lodgment in the race through the sin of Adam, and has passed to all men *because* all men have sinned. The primordial sin produces a corruption which involves men in death (cf. 1 Cor. 15:21-22). Man's organic continuity with Adam makes this possible. More than death is indeed involved in this corruption. There is a mark left by Adam's disobedience which makes sinful rebellion universal. One man's disobedience made all the rest sinners (Rom. 5:19 ff.). Because of Adam, in some way, all men become sinners and therefore die. An inherent propensity toward sin becomes a part of man's nature. We need to remember the Hebrew background here, with its lively sense of corporate solidarity. In Paul's thought, Adam was the representative man, "the archetype of all humanity, what happens to him happens to all men."[32] If we overstress this solidarity, individual responsibility ceases to count. But Paul does not do this. In some way we have to allow for individual responsibility within a corporate solidarity of sinfulness. There is no idea of imputed guilt.

---

[31] This is the implication of Romans 5:12 on its best exegesis.

[32] Johannes Weiss, *The History of Primitive Christianity*, Vol. I (London: Macmillan and Co., Limited, 1937), p. 434.

There may be a clue in the complementary concept of the flesh. To be "in Adam" is to be "in the flesh." Flesh is more than physiological. It stands for the whole sphere of the creaturely and the outward. It is the visible, material aspect of man and also the whole earthly and visible realm in which he is involved. It describes the transient order of creation and is synonymous with the "world," the "cosmos," the ordered whole in which man's historical life is lived. If we live for this visible and outward order of things, we live "in the flesh." A man's nature is described by the sphere in which he moves, the horizon of what he does and experiences. Hence man may live in the flesh, but he may also live in the Spirit. He may fix his eyes on the outward, but he may, on the other hand, have his horizons and goals provided by his interior world, the inward dimension that belongs to Spirit.[33]

This does not mean that the flesh is inherently evil. It is a sign of man's creatureliness. It covers not only his own outward being, but also his historical environment. It can describe what we mean by the term "history." Secular history is the realm of the flesh. But flesh does take on psychical aspects which may impair the functioning of man's true personal being. It can be the seat of sin. The "mind that is set on the flesh" (Rom. 8:7) means that the mind, under the influence of the outward, may set itself against God. So the desires of the flesh can be described as evil,[34] and these include many that belong to the mental and spiritual realm as well as those that belong to the physical and sensual.

The inner man, the seat of his freedom and personal being, may become dominated by the outward. All men have to live in the flesh, to live the life of a creature. But when they walk "according to the flesh," they live as sinners.[35] The Christian has still to live in the flesh,[36] but he should not live according to the flesh.[37] Thus in secular history redeemed man is the center of a tension between the flesh and the spirit (Gal. 5:16-23). As Bult-

---

[33] Cf. Bultmann, *Theology of the New Testament,* Vol. I, p. 235.
[34] Rom. 13:4; Gal. 5:16, 19, 24.
[35] Bultmann makes this distinction usefully—*op. cit.,* pp. 235 ff.
[36] 2 Cor. 10:3; Phil. 1:22; Gal. 2:20.
[37] Gal. 4:23; 2 Cor. 1:17; 5:16; 10:2-3; Rom. 8:4.

mann puts it, flesh "... stamps an *existence or an attitude* not as natural-human, but *as sinful.*" [38] The flesh is not inherently evil, but it tempts to self-assertion and worldly values. Historical man becomes self-reliant, putting his trust in his own powers and in the outward things which he can control.[39] He boasts after the flesh, glories in worldly things, becomes wise in the worldly sense, and refuses to sacrifice his wisdom before God, letting it become foolishness. Thus to be "after the flesh" is to be subject to desire, to live for worldly ends. The Genesis story suggests the same thought. Man's control over the visible and his involvement in it tempt him to turn his back on God. In itself morally neutral, the flesh is yet the medium through which the human citadel may be attacked. To live in the flesh is, apart from the grace of God, to live according to the flesh. This is secular history.

There may be some indication of the connection between universal sinfulness and the primordial sin in the phrase the "mind that is set on the flesh." This might be better rendered the fleshly *yezer,* and should be understood in the light of developed rabbinical thought. The latter spoke of an evil *yezer* or imagination inherent in man. Paul speaks of a principle in man's members which rebels against the law of God (Rom. 7:21-23; 6:13-14). It is a sinful inclination, an openness to sin, and it has its seat in the flesh. Man's flesh is under pressure from a sinful principle. The non-Christian writer of 4 Ezra later connects the presence of this with Adam's disobedience. Paul does not do this, nor does he follow the rabbis and locate the principle in the heart. It is in the flesh. It is the mind that is set on the flesh, and yet this phrase may also imply that it brings the mind under the domination of the flesh.

3. The Kingdom in Secular History— Judgment and the Christ

New Testament thought binds up such an understanding of sin with judgment. The Kingdom of God, the sovereignty of God,

---

[38] Bultmann, *op. cit.,* p. 237.
[39] Cf. *ibid.,* p. 240.

is manifested as judgment in secular history. Man the sinner stands under the wrath of God. We have seen how, in the Old Testament, the idea of divine judgment is brought to a focus in the eschatological hope of Israel, increasingly so in postexilic eschatology. The judgment of God in history would be consummated in the final act of judgment, which would at the same time be a purging and re-creation of Israel. As the emphasis on the individual emerged within the concern for the resurrection of the nation, we find the idea of an individualized judgment in the last time which is yet also concerned with mankind as a whole. In the New Testament this remains, but it is filled with new understanding. The eschatological judgment remains at the core of the witness. But the Messiah has come, so this judgment is already being realized in his person. The last judgment is already coming proleptically upon men.

Jesus himself manifests this dual aspect of judgment and sustains the tension which it involves. On the one hand, he speaks of judgment as the final reality, as one aspect of the descent of the *eschaton.* In this sense it is future, and so we have those pictures of the final consummation in which men will be ultimately judged by the relation they bear to Jesus, the Messiah, in the present.[40] In a well-known passage, it is declared that every generation will be judged by its attitude to the particular manifestation of the Kingdom in its own time. The divine endowment of Solomon's wisdom, the preaching of Jonah, and the advent of the Kingdom in Jesus are the determining factors in the judgment on the men of these different generations (Luke 11:31 ff. [Q]). Since Jesus has come, the relation to him must be the criterion upon which the final judgment turns. No racial privilege, no membership in the chosen people, will avail. The awesome reality of the last judgment is, indeed, in the center of our Lord's teaching.[41]

On the other hand, the eschatological judgment has drawn near with the advent of the Kingdom in the Messiah. Judgment is a present reality. History is a realm of judgment, and the di-

---

[40] Mark 8:38; cf. Luke 12:8 (Q); Luke 17:23-30 (Q); the parable of the Sheep and the Goats, Matthew 25:31-46 (M).

[41] Mark 9:43-48; Matthew 5:21 ff.

vine wrath is operative in history. On the eve of the crucifixion, the judgment will descend in the form of a scattering of the disciples because they have been offended in him (Matt. 25:31 ff.). Our Lord appears to have uttered predictions about the inevitable outcome of the situation in which his own ministry was exercised. In his trial he was accused of stating that he would destroy the Temple (Mark 14:57-58), and Mark 13:2 makes it clear that he did make some prediction about it.[42]

A careful analysis of the catena of sayings in Mark 13 shows that some of the sayings appear to apply to contemporary or immediate future history, rather than to the ultimate eschatological judgment. Men are enjoined to flee to the mountains,[43] and it is indicated that the disaster befalling them will be so sudden that they will have no time to take apparel for their flight. The straits in which the pregnant and the nursing mothers will find themselves suggest a state of war (Mark 13:17-18).

It is significant that the Lucan parallel specifically associates the saying with Jerusalem's being encircled by camps[44]—although probably unauthentic, this at least indicates that Luke made a specific reference to a judgment in history, possibly Rome's siege of Jerusalem. There is the reference to the one being taken and the other left.[45] This may, of course, indicate the selective judgment of the last Day, so that the *parousia* steals upon the private lives of people and cuts across all human relations in its discriminating determination of human destiny. Its setting could certainly make it mean this, but C. J. Cadoux's comment is relevant: the sayings " . . . look like more warnings about the arbitrary and uncertain horrors wrought by an invading soldiery . . ."[46] It would

---

[42] For a full discussion of the nature of Mark 13 see *infra.*, pp. 280 ff.

[43] Mark 13:14; cf. Luke 17:31-32.

[44] Luke 21:20 ff. T. W. Manson believes this form is more authentic and original than the Marcan form—*The Mission and Message of Jesus* (London: Ivor Nicholson and Watson Limited, 1937), pp. 621 f. The Q passage of Luke 17:22-37 also contains passages better understood as references to judgment in history than as references to the *parousia.*

[45] Matthew 25:40 ff.; Luke 17:34 ff.

[46] C. J. Cadoux, *The Historic Mission of Jesus* (London: Lutterworth Press, 1941), p. 274. Generally dated and outmoded, this book often has useful insight.

appear that Jesus saw the doom of the Temple and the destruction of Jerusalem as events within history in which the inevitable judgment of God would be evident. For him, as for the prophets before him, the eschatological judgment could cast its shadow before, and powers like Rome could be the unwitting instruments of the divine wrath. So he apostrophizes Jerusalem in moving words, which finish with the declaration: "Behold, your house is forsaken" (Luke 13:34-35), an evident reference to that Temple which should have been a house of prayer for all nations but which had become a den of thieves.

In the thought of the New Testament witnesses, the same dual reference is evident. For Paul the wrath of God is an eschatological concept which is also regarded as proleptically active in the present. For him the final judgment as a future event is certain. God will judge the world (Rom. 2:5, 16; 3:6, 19), and by "world" Paul means both angels and men (1 Cor. 4:9). The judgment of God will extend to the angelic powers, including the demons. Sometimes it is Christ who will judge and at other times, God. We must all appear before the judgment seat of Christ (2 Cor. 5:10) or of God (Rom. 14:10). This is in keeping with the sayings of the Gospel traditions. The Messiah is indistinguishable from God in the operation of the divine wrath, and men will be judged on the "Day of Wrath" in the light of their relation to Christ. The judgment will be a day of unveiling. When the Lord comes he "... will bring to light the things now hidden in darkness and will disclose the purposes of the heart" (1 Cor. 4:5). Paul's gospel includes the element of judgment in the Day when God shall judge the secrets of men (Rom. 2:16). Paul speaks about the judgment as according to works,[47] yet this is not a denial of "justification by faith." The salvation of a Christian is assured, though his works be burned as by fire (1 Cor. 3:15; 5:5). Thus there is a final judgment for Christians on the basis of works.[48] Faith in Christ is demonstrated to be a reality by a man's works, as James saw (James 2:14-26), and a man's salvation will be manifested by his life according to the Spirit.

---

[47] Romans 2:6; 2 Corinthians 5:10.
[48] Colossians 3:25; 1 Corinthians 9:27.

John often is accused of overemphasis on the present reality of the Kingdom as judgment, but he also emphasizes its final consummation (John 5:28-29).

Because the final judgment is bound up with faith in Christ, and because in him the Kingdom has already drawn near, the wrath of God is already operative in present history. God's wrath has been manifested against the ungodliness and unrighteousness of man (Rom. 1:18). This is Paul's justification for the gospel in the Letter to the Romans, and later in the same chapter he defines the wrath of God as God's giving men over to the sin of their hearts (Rom. 1:24, 26). One difficulty arises at this point, because Paul uses "the wrath" absolutely, although "of God" is implied. C. H. Dodd[49] argues that therefore Paul does not think of wrath as the personal reaction of God to sin, but rather that the wrath represents an impersonal law of cause and effect. In a moral universe, sin works or produces its own consequences. The universe is so created that God has set limits to man's sinful rebellion. Let a man or a society overstep these bounds and those forces will be set in motion by which the judgment inevitably descends.

But we may not so interpret the wrath of God without doing violence to the personal relationship between God and his creatures. Even the righteous anger or moral indignation of good men and women may be a pointer to a deeper quality in God himself, and we may not easily reject the idea of personal divine wrath as anthropopathic. Did not our Lord, the perfect man, manifest this very reaction to those who offended the little ones (Mark 9:42), to the money changers of the Temple,[50] and to the hypocrites among the Pharisees?[51] That there is a process of judgment in the universe is true, but we have no more right to explain this in impersonal terms than we have the regularities of nature.

Nature, throughout the biblical testimony, manifests the personal presence of the Creator God, and its regularities are the ex-

---

[49] C. H. Dodd, *The Epistle of Paul to the Romans*, Moffatt Commentary (New York: Harper & Brothers, n.d.), pp. 20 ff. A. T. Hanson takes a similar view in *The Wrath of the Lamb* (New York: Harper & Brothers, 1957), *passim*.

[50] Mark 11:15 ff.; cf. John 2:14-16.

[51] Luke 11:42 ff.; cf. Matthew 6:2 ff.

pressions of the habitual operation of his personal sustaining will. In the same way, the process of judgment in history is the normal expression of God's personal attitude and response to the sin of man. The fact that sin and suffering are bound together, that evildoing reaps its consequences, is no expression of an impersonal law. Looking at it horizontally, we may interpret it in terms of cause and effect. But, at every point of the process, there is an invisible vertical dimension. It leans back on the will of God, who sustains it. Secondary causes operate under the direction of the first cause. The biblical men were very aware of this. There could be no process if God did not set it going and sustain its operation. Behind judgment is his personal reaction to sin. Paul was too much of a Hebrew to forget this, whereas Dodd and others are in danger of replacing the Hebrew by the Greek Platonic way of thinking. Paul saw a personal God giving men over to the sins of their hearts and thereby hiding his face from sinful man.

For Paul, Jew and Gentile are alike without excuse (Rom. 1:18-32; 2:8-9). The living God approaches all as absolute demand, all have rejected him, and all are subject to his wrath (Rom. 3:9-18). All have sinned and all are children of wrath (Eph. 2:3). The present operation of wrath is elaborated in Paul's thought at both the personal and the social levels. Man's whole existence is subject to judgment. His heart is darkened (Rom. 1:21-22). His body is prone to sickness and to death.[52] Even his world is under judgment and subjected to corruption and frustration.[53] The wrath of God is also operative in and under the power of the state, so that Rome can become the agent of the divine judgment (Rom. 13:4-5).

This present judgment is operative in relation to Christ.[54] Here the other New Testament writings make the same point. John especially emphasizes the present reality of such judgment (John 3:18-19; 9:39; 12:31). To reject Christ's preaching and to hate the light mean that the wrath of God becomes operative here and now (John 3:36; 3:18-20). Even in the celebration of

---

[52] 1 Corinthians 11:30; Romans 6:23.

[53] Romans 8:19-23 (interpreting "creation" here as the realm of nature).

[54] Romans 2:6; 2 Corinthians 5:10.

his Supper, Christ's judgment can be operative (1 Cor. 11:29).
The cross of Jesus is indeed the great divide of judgment. In this
crucial act, judgment has entered the world.[55] To accept Christ
now precludes the verdict of the last Day (John 12:48). Paul can
declare that our attitude to Christ now is the assurance of future
deliverance in the end-time (1 Thess. 1:10). Therefore, we can
be confident in Christ that God has not appointed us to final condemnation.[56]

The book of Revelation contains a rather unique picture of
the judgment. Here the Christ is pictured as judge. How exclusively the seer's picture is concerned with the future is a matter
of debate among scholars. Our own view is that he regards the
end-time as beginning with the death and resurrection of our
Lord. In that case, the vivid images of the messianic woes, the
pictures of the judgments that are to descend as signs of the
pending final judgment, are John's attempt to picture in symbolic
form the judgments in the contemporary scene. They include
famine, war, pestilence, and death, as the four horsemen show,
and they might be a sad comment upon the realm of secular history. Here is a representation of the demonic which is at the same
time the agent of the divine wrath. The prophetic vision of judgment taking place within history and at the hands of historical
occurrence finds expression once more. Yet it is the personal action of God as well as a process in history.

E. F. Scott tries to interpret the wrath in Revelation along the
same lines as the view of C. H. Dodd already criticized. He argues that, although the judgment in history is the work of angels
who break the seals of the book of destiny, yet behind the imagery
"we can discern the thought that evil judges itself, containing in
it the germ of those events by which it will be processed."[57] Thus
Rome is to fall finally by the return of one of its emperors as antichrist and with his overthrow by the kings whom he has used to
work his will. He exalted himself above his station and placed

---

[55] 2 Corinthians 5:21; Romans 1:18.
[56] 1 Thessalonians 5:9; Romans 8:1; cf. 1 John 4:17.
[57] E. F. Scott, *The Book of Revelation* (London: SCM Press, 1939),
p. 164.

himself in the seat of his Creator, and that act of sinful arrogance spelled his doom. "The righteousness of God," writes Scott, "consists in His thus ordaining that good and evil should produce their fitting results." Once more we would not deny the horizontal dimension of process but would affirm the vertical dimension of personal, divine reaction to sin.[58]

As we have seen, judgment is related to Christ throughout the New Testament, but only in Revelation do we find the phrase "the wrath of the Lamb" (6:16). In the Apocalypse little remains of the humanity and gracious approach of the historical Jesus, even though the seer is careful to emphasize his historicity and his human life. The emphasis falls upon his transcendence and the awfulness of his dimension of eternity. Even his humanity has been transcendentalized. His face shines like the noonday sun, his eyes flash like flames of fire, his hair is white as snow, his feet glow like metal red-hot from the furnace, his voice is like the sound of the waterfall. His radiance is overwhelming. The God shines through the man. He is the wrathful one who, in crowned splendor, sits on a cloud and wields the sickle of judgment (Rev. 14:14 ff.). He comes on the clouds of heaven, a warrior king, to do battle for the saints (Rev. 19:11 ff.), and out of his mouth comes a sharp sword. He will shepherd all the nations with an iron rod (Rev. 12:5). He is the exalted judge who holds in his hands the scroll of destiny and unlocks the secrets of human history (Rev. 5).

Yet in all this and running through the Apocalypse like the undertones of a tremendous symphony, the Christ is pictured as the Lamb that was slain. If Christ comes as the Son of Man with his sickle, he is also pictured as one who comes with his garments dipped in redeeming blood (Rev. 19:13). The wrath of God operative in history can be pictured as an angel treading out the wine press until the blood of sinful men flows like water (Rev. 14:19-20). But the Christ who comes in triumph, arrayed in bloody garments, is the one who treads the wine press of the fierceness of the wrath of God (Rev. 19:15). This picture is an

---

[58] This whole theme is discussed later in more detail, pp. 303 ff.

obvious borrowing of the imagery of Isaiah 63:3, where God
comes as victor trampling over the blood of the conquered. Is this
a picture of Christ himself entering under the wrath and expiatory mission? Alan Richardson suggests that the meaning of this
passage is that "Christ has conquered through his own blood and
the last reference in the New Testament to the divine ὀργή shows
us the Christian picture of God as himself providing the means
of the propitiation of his wrath."[59]

The final judgment is depicted in the Apocalypse in vivid
images, but the significance of the book lies in more than this. It
lies in the deep insight into the reality of the wrath of God, its
operations in the present historical context, and its close connection with the Lamb that was slain. The victorious Christ delivers
men from judgment.

4. The Demonic Bondage of Historical Man

Closely bound up with the themes of sin and the judgment is
the understanding of the demonic. The New Testament witnesses,
like our Lord himself, have a lively sense of the cosmic background of evil. Jesus knew that his struggle was with Satan and
the powers of darkness. His healing miracles are clearly bound
up with both the sin of the individual and the domination of the
demonic. He believed that his mission was concerned as much
with the latter as with the former. Sin, suffering, disease, and
death were signs that men were living in an evil age in which the
demonic exercised its sway. If the prophetic promise of the Age-
to-Come involved the end of suffering, disease, evil, and (sometimes) death, then the proof that this Age had dawned must be
seen in their defeat.[60] When our Lord casts out demons this is a
sign that the Kingdom has drawn near. Paul's thought is particularly concerned with this dimension of cosmic evil. Many New
Testament scholars have demonstrated that for him sin (in the
singular) is a demonic power rather than a human act, an evil

---

[59] Richardson, *An Introduction to the Theology of the New Testament*,
p. 78.

[60] Hence Jesus' answer to John's question, Luke 7:20-22 (Q).

force that takes possession of the individual.[61] Man is thus more than a creature who sins, for his sinful decision has sold him under sin like a bondman (Rom. 7:14). He has become its thrall.[62] Sin's point of entry is man's flesh, his creaturely nature. Moreover, sin is not the only demonic power that takes up its residence through the flesh. Because sin has entered, death and corruption enter. Adam's sin, the primordial and original sin, has made possible man's domination by death and a whole host of demonic forces.[63] These are variously labeled the elements of this world, principalities, the princes of this world, spiritual rulers of darkness in high places, powers of the height and depth. Paul seems to have thought of a world of angels, in rebellion against God and holding men in bondage. There are possible relations in his thought to the Hellenistic belief that the stars were personal powers in the heavens which controlled the destiny of man, and to later Judaistic teaching about the angels who were the guardians of the nations.[64] Possibly the latter circle of ideas was the more influential, for in it the angels were regarded as the authority behind the earthly rulers.[65] Thus the power of the state and of various aspects of the social life become demonic to the degree that they manifest the authority of angels in rebellion against God.

History becomes for Paul a scene of bondage, in which individual man and society alike are under the "princes of this world," the "world rulers." Cullmann believes that the New Testament understanding of the state is grounded in this late Jewish view that each people has its angel.[66] Such demonic powers hold sway over all history and use human beings as their instruments. Along-

---

[61] His vocabulary is distinctive here. Sin as a demonic power is *hamartia*. Sin as a human act is *adikia*. The former word rarely occurs in the plural.

[62] Romans 6:20; Galatians 3:22; cf. John 8:34.

[63] Romans 5:12; 1 Corinthians 15:56; Romans 5:21.

[64] Daniel, Ecclesiasticus, 1 Enoch.

[65] Cf. Oscar Cullmann, *Christ and Time* (Philadelphia: The Westminster Press, 1950), pp. 192 ff.

[66] *Ibid.*, p. 193. This is the meaning of 1 Corinthians 2:8. The verse does not refer to earthly rulers but to the rebellious spiritual powers behind them.

side sin we must see the angelic powers. Thereby individual man and corporate humanity, at the social and political levels, become subject to the demonic.

Yet such demonic power is also bound up with the divine judgment. The wrath of God shuts men up in their sin and gives them over to this demonic bondage. Thereby the demonic becomes the executant of the divine justice, and rebellion in its cosmic aspect is made to serve the purpose of God. To describe man's individual and corporate subjection to the demonic is also to describe his judgment. He is not big enough to figure out his rebellion alone. It is suggested to him from a rebellion of a greater order, yet even the latter is still within God's control and can serve his purpose for humanity.

We see this in the New Testament understanding of the Law and of death. Let us look at the Law first. Even the Law has become demonic for Paul. Once more his insights have tremendous significance for the understanding of history. The Law is good. It expresses God's claim on men, and so it is holy (Rom. 7:12), yet it is a yoke of bondage. Our study of the Old Testament reveals that the claim of God should lead to life, but in its legal form it serves but to show the bankruptcy of the human heart. For Paul, it fails on two scores. On the one hand, its very injunctions increase coveting (Rom. 7:5-9). It serves to awaken desire. On the other hand, it increases pride, for it makes a man believe that by obeying it he has a claim on God (Rom. 3:20). This is a very profound analysis of the function of the moral law in human life. The Law brings to light the fact that sin is in possession and itself becomes demonic, because man sets the Law in the place of a God of grace and interprets God as a taskmaster. Sin is demonic in the way it makes use of God's Law for its own advancement (Rom. 7:13). The Law serves its true end when it shows up the demonic nature of sin as absolute hostility to God. But then the Law itself becomes demonic, because it tempts man to believe that he can have a claim on God. So man enters under bondage to it, and the Law, detached from God, holds sway in its own right. The Law, too, becomes a tyrant, from which man needs to be delivered. Is not human history just this story of man's seeking to establish a claim, to lift himself to heaven by his own bootstraps? But this demonic bondage is also his judgment.

Further, we have the reality of death as a demonic power. Like sin, death is an invasive force which holds man in thrall. When sin entered humanity through Adam, it made an entrance for death, and, because all men sinned, universal corruption became their lot.[67] In the biblical testimony as a whole, sin and death are closely bound together. All corruption and decay are regarded as in opposition to God. Death is not regarded as a natural thing, a liberation from prison, as with the Greeks. It is unnatural and contrary to the divine intention. It represents a process set up in creation because of sin. In the Garden story, man can continually renew his life at the tree of life, but sin bars him from the Garden, deprives him of contact with the divinely given source of renewal, and makes him subject to death. This explains the fear of death that pervades the period of the old covenant. Men lived under the shadow of death, and death meant separation from God, as the Psalms make abundantly clear. Only as sin is dealt with, however, can death be vanquished. As Cullmann puts it: "In this Biblical view, death and continued life after death do not constitute a continuous organic natural process; rather, mighty powers stand in conflict. When in the Bible life comes out of death, a miracle is necessary."[68]

From the biblical point of view, death has no place only when man is truly related to God. It is natural and inevitable for man as we know him, man the sinner. If Christ is man as man ought to be and if his resurrection body is indicative of man's existence as God intended it, then death was *not* natural to him. He tasted death *for us.* The transfiguration scene is in its right historical context[69] prior to the crucifixion, for it indicates that death, by rights, had no hold over Jesus. His body was a perfect instrument where ours is crippled by sin and subjected to death. The sug-

---

[67] Romans 5:12 ff.; 1 Corinthians 15:21-22.
[68] Cullmann, *Christ and Time*, p. 234.
[69] Cf. Rudolf Bultmann, who would dismiss the historical authenticity of the transfiguration and describe it as a postresurrection event.

gestion would seem to be that because of sin the abrupt separation and judgment of death has taken the place of the process of transfiguration of the physical elements. Everywhere sin and death are concomitants in our world, and because death has come, disease, corruption, and decay have beset our humanity. Our Lord's healing miracles are reminders that for him the triumph over disease and death, the staying, if only temporarily, of the process of corruption and decay, was bound up with the forgiveness and removal of sin. Healing was in some sense a partial resurrection.

It is in the light of this that we must understand the New Testament view of death. Paul can tell us that the universality of sin means the universality of death (Rom. 5:12). Death is indeed the "wages of sin" (Rom. 6:23). When the demonic power of sin has men in its thrall, it rewards its slaves with the wages of death. *Death is indeed sinful man's judgment.* Sinners deserve death (Rom. 1:32). Paul works out the mechanics of this judgment in keeping with his view of judgment as a process which works itself out in men's lives when God gives them over to the sin of their hearts. The process is set going by the personal reaction of the divine wrath.[70] Sin entering into the flesh produces death as its inevitable concomitant. The Law is given for life, but it arouses desire in man, increases sin, and leads to death.[71] Because sin dwells in it, man's body of flesh becomes also a "body of death" (Rom. 7:24). As Bultmann has said, "Sin's 'deceit' (Rom. 7:11) consists in deluding man to think that if he follows his 'desire' he will gain life, whereas he only acquires 'death.'"[72] For Paul, therefore, death is man's last enemy. In some sense, it is the executant of the divine wrath, but its power has to be broken. Hence, it awaits its final destruction (1 Cor. 15:26). In the Apocalypse, death is the rider on the pale horse who victoriously gathers his prey until the world becomes a scene of death and destruc-

---

[70] Romans 1:24. I cannot agree with Bultmann (*op. cit.*, pp. 246 ff.) that this view of death as the organic concomitant of the presence of sin is incompatible with Paul's other view of death as a punishment for sin.

[71] Romans 7:5, 9-11; cf. 6:21.

[72] Bultmann, *op. cit.*, p. 248.

tion, a vast mortuary (Rev. 6:8). But finally death, too, must be vanquished and cast into the lake of fire (Rev. 20:14).

One last element in the New Testament thought on evil is that evil is brought to a focus in the devil, or Satan.[73] In him the powers of darkness are organized. This principle of evil is variously described. For Paul he is the "god of this world" (2 Cor. 4:4). For John he is the "ruler of this world" (John 12:31; 14:30; 16:11). Paul can also describe him as the "prince of the power of the air" (Eph. 2:2) and as the "evil one."[74] His power is limited to this present evil age, but of this he is the center, so that John can write: " . . . we are of God, and the whole world is in the power of the evil one" (1 John 5:19). The cosmos, in the sense of humanity, is under him (John 12:31), and it is he who is responsible for the death of Jesus.[75] Our Lord prays that his own shall be protected from the evil one (John 17:15), whom John regards as the primary source and originator of sin.[76] The devil is a murderer from the beginning, for his tempting of men brought death, a parallel to the ideas just developed above. Yet even the devil is God's instrument. His bondage is also judgment. The lifting of the divine judgment becomes also the breaking of the bondage.

5. *The Cross and the Kingdom*

It was against this backdrop of sin and demonic bondage that the early church set the work of our Lord. He himself regarded the cross as the climax of the mighty act in which the Kingdom broke into history in his person. Each in his own individual way, the New Testament witnesses make a like affirmation and endeavor to interpret the central act of Calvary. Let us look, first of all, at the association of the cross with the advent of the Kingdom in the thought of Jesus and in the testimony of the church.

---

[73] 1 John 3:8; Romans 16:20.

[74] 2 Thessalonians 3:3; cf. 1 John 2:13; John 17:15.

[75] John 14:30; cf. 1 Corinthians 2:8, where Paul uses the plural "rulers," as discussed earlier.

[76] 1 John 3:8. The phrase "from the beginning" refers probably to Genesis 3 and thus provides a parallel to Paul's reference to the beguiling of Eve by the serpent—2 Corinthians 11:3.

The teaching of our Lord makes it evident that the cross was
no mere afterthought, due to the development of hostility and a
realistic recognition of the facts. The tendency to overemphasize
the humanity of Jesus has caused a misinterpretation of his
death.[77] We need to remember that his human life is like ours and
yet utterly different in its devotion to God's purpose. The baptism
tradition suggests that from the beginning Jesus understood his
messiahship in terms of the Suffering Servant. Our Lord seems
always to have seen his suffering and death as the climax of the
drawing near of the Kingdom in his own person. As R. H. Fuller
has expressed it: "This mystery [the mystery of his impending
death] is that Jesus has been sent not only to announce the coming of the Reign of God, but to perform the decisive event
through which God will inaugurate that Reign."[78]

We have already argued that the chronological framework of
Mark in its broad outlines should be regarded as authentic.[79]
Peter's confession provides an enlightening turning point in our
Lord's ministry. Up to that time he had proclaimed the advent
of the Kingdom and shown it to be proleptically present in his
own healing ministry. The nearness of the event is indicated by
his prophecy that some of his hearers would not taste death until
they had seen the Kingdom come with power (Mark 9:1). After
Caesarea Philippi, he talked openly about his death. Peter's recognition of his messiahship made it necessary for our Lord to show
the nature of his death—the representative Son of Man is also
the Suffering Servant. Is it that his death and resurrection are to
mark the advent of the Kingdom with power?

It has been shown by many scholars that the phrases in the
passion sayings—"set at nought," "be rejected"—are strikingly

---

[77] Cf., Cadoux, *op. cit.*, pp. 260 f.

[78] Fuller, *The Mission and Achievement of Jesus*, p. 77.

[79] Cf. Bultmann, *op. cit.*, pp. 29 ff. Bultmann dismisses it as unauthentic,
and leaves us with a string of *pericopae* and detached units of teaching,
fitted into an artificial framework for kerygmatic purposes. The confession of
Peter at Caesarea Philippi and the transfiguration become misplaced resurrection appearances, while the baptism and the temptation are regarded as
legends.

parallel to Isaiah 53:3.[80] Further, the notable utterance "to give his life as a ransom for many" is strangely reminiscent of the declaration that the soul of the Servant shall be made an offering for sin (Isaiah 53:10) and of the references to "the many" at the end of the final Servant Song (Isaiah 53:11).[81] Our Lord implies a voluntary and vicarious giving of his life to release the many from the doom which overhangs them. He clearly thought of his death as some kind of sacrifice in which the suffering of the innocent avails for the guilty. We note that the phrase "for many" has in the Greek a substitutionary flavor and is better rendered "in the stead of many." Thus, Jesus held that he was the ransom in the place of the many. Combined with this is the idea of representation already noted in the Servant and Son of Man traditions. What our Lord did was a substitutionary act but it was also representative; it could not be effective in a man's life until it was appropriated. In dying he not only did something for the many that they could not do but also represented them. He did it "in their name" as well as "in their stead."

---

[80] *Vide* especially Vincent Taylor, *Jesus and His Sacrifice* (London: Macmillan and Co., Limited, 1937), pp. 85 ff.; Fuller, *op. cit.*, pp. 56 ff.

[81] The word translated "ransom," *lutron*, is a good Greek equivalent to the Hebrew word for "offering," *asham*, in Isaiah 53:10. It is true that the idea of "service" is connected with our Lord in a Q passage, Luke 22:24 ff. Rashdall and others would regard this as the more original and contend that the Marcan saying under discussion is the result of later theological interpretation—cf. Hastings Rashdall, *The Idea of Atonement in Christian Theology* (London: Macmillan and Co., Limited, 1919), pp. 49 ff. R. H. Fuller holds, on the contrary, that the Q passage is the later and secondary, reflecting "the concern of Hellenistic churches with the differentiation of the members in the local congregation" (*op. cit.*, p. 57), and employing words used in this latter connection in Hebrews, 1 Timothy, and 1 Peter. It is argued by some that "ransom" is a Pauline idea. But Paul does not use this word. He uses "redemption," *apolutrosis*. The connection of "ransom" with "offering" noted above suggests a direct relation to the Servant passages. Now our Lord evidently leaned on this tradition. We have seen that Paul is naturally influenced by it, but it is noteworthy that he does not use its vocabulary except in quoting primitive Christian traditions received by him. On the balance Mark 10:45 would seem to be the more original and authentic. Vincent Taylor holds that "it is better to conclude that Jesus has furnished a theme for later Pauline developments rather than that Mark has introduced a Pauline sentiment into the words of Jesus" (*op. cit.*, p. 105), and quotes Lagrange in support.

Luke provides us with a significant saying from his private tradition. It is our Lord's answer to Herod: "Go and say to that fox, Behold, I cast out demons and perform cures to-day and to-morrow, and the third day I am perfected. Nevertheless I must go on my way to-day and to-morrow and the day following: for it cannot be that a prophet perish out of Jerusalem."[82] The phrase "I am perfected" suggests more than the chronological end of a ministry. It seems to indicate the culmination of our Lord's mission, its completion in the deeper sense of end. Clearly our Lord intends it to be understood that his exorcisms and healings are only signs of what has yet to be accomplished. The "must" in the next sentence indicates an inner compulsion which moves Jesus toward the culmination of his ministry, his approaching death at Jerusalem. Here, as Fuller points out, is a saying free of *Gemeindetheologie* and yet indicating a basic connection between our Lord's ministry and his dying. "By stating that it is as a 'prophet' that he is to perish at Jerusalem, Jesus brings his death into organic relation with his prophetic proclamation, 'the Reign of God has drawn nigh.' "[83] This Lucan saying is of similar import to the Marcan saying: " . . . the Son of Man *must* suffer many things . . . " (Mark 8:31). There is the same sense of inner compulsion, of divine necessity. "Must" (*dei*) signifies here the inner constraint of our Lord's messianic vocation.

One more saying should be noted among the many that can be cited—the utterance at the Last Supper. Here we have two versions—the Marcan and the Pauline.[84] The Marcan seems the

---

[82] Luke 13:32-33, American Standard Version. Wellhausen, supported by R. H. Fuller (*op. cit.*, p. 62), suggests that the phrases "on the third day I am perfected" and "today and tomorrow" should be eliminated from vs. 32 and vs. 33 respectively, on the ground that their omission produces a smoother text. The idiom is familiar in Hebrew thought, however, as indicating a short but divinely ordained span of time, as in Hosea 6:2, and we see no heavy reason for rejecting it; cf. Vincent Taylor, *op. cit.*, pp. 168-171. T. W. Manson likewise finds the original form of the saying internally coherent and writes: "There is . . . no fundamental inconsistency in saying 'I shall continue my work in Galilee for some time yet' and 'In the next few days (or weeks) I shall be moving out of Galilee' " (*op. cit.*, p. 569).

[83] Fuller, *op. cit.*, p. 63.

[84] Mark 14:24; 1 Corinthians 11:23-25.

original form,[85] but both versions speak of a covenant which will be established by the "blood" of Jesus, and both declare that the cup is the symbol of this covenant. The covenant with Israel was a gracious relationship initiated by God and constituting Israel a nation. Yet Jeremiah saw that this relationship had been broken by Israel's sin, and promised a new covenant in which the relationship would be restored (Jer. 31:31-34). As before, God would initiate this covenant and, in so doing, would reconstitute his people by an inner and individual re-creation of man. Paul brings out the Jeremianic reference by inserting the word "new." This new covenant would involve a forgiveness of iniquity and an erasing of the memory of sin. The reference to the "blood" probably points back to the sacrificial covenant rite on Sinai, which sealed the covenant of God with Israel.[86] In any case, the word connotes sacrifice. Further, we cannot separate the saying from the Servant tradition, for in one of the Songs the Servant is described as having been given for "a covenant to the people" (Isa. 42:6).

Once more we find ourselves in the realm of sacrificial categories. Our Lord seems to be binding in the Jeremianic promise of a new covenant with his messianic mission as the Servant, and implying that his sacrificial death will make this new covenant

---

[85] Jeremias believes the Pauline to be the later of the two. He points to the Hellenistic tendency and the removal of Semitism. He also believes it to be a revision of the longer Lucan form which he regards as original. *Vide* Joachim Jeremias, *The Eucharistic Words of Jesus* (New York: The Macmillan Company, 1955), pp. 87 ff. Jeremias regards the Marcan text as the authentic original but believes Luke 22:15-18 to be an original duplication. R. H. Fuller thinks that Paul was here revising the original saying himself (*op. cit.*, pp. 65 f.). He here follows A. J. B. Higgins, *The Lord's Supper in the New Testament* (London: SCM Press, 1952), p. 34. All three scholars are agreed that the Marcan version is the earlier and more authentic. Vincent Taylor provides a valuable discussion of the same issues —*op. cit.*, pp. 114 ff.

[86] Exodus 24:8. Jeremias would find a closer reference here to the paschal lamb—*op. cit.*, pp. 136 ff. The Passover is indeed central for this scholar's understanding, but his attempt to demonstrate that the Last Supper was the Passover meal is not satisfying—*vide* Vincent Taylor, *The Gospel According to St. Mark* (London: Macmillan & Co., Ltd., 1952), pp. 644 ff. Vincent Taylor believes this explanation of Jeremias the less probable inference—*Jesus and His Sacrifice*, p. 139.

possible. God's people will become an actuality through his dying. Again, the death is linked with the advent of the Kingdom in power or fulfillment. Jesus as Servant will mediate a new covenant through his sacrificial death and he will do this for the many. Although we have not accepted Jeremias' identification of Jesus' understanding of his sacrifice as that of the Passover Lamb, we can agree with the burden of his comment: "Jesus ... describes his death as this eschatological Passover sacrifice: His vicarious (περί) death brings the final deliverance into operation." [87] Again he writes: " ... His death is the vicarious death of the Servant, which atones for the sins of the πολλοί, the whole world, and ushers in the beginnings of final salvation." [88]

The Marcan tradition of the Last Supper also preserves the vow of Jesus that he will not drink of the fruit of the vine until he drinks it anew in the Kingdom of God. [89] Jeremias interprets this as an oath of renunciation, made to reinforce our Lord's prayer that the Kingdom should come. [90] Fuller[91] holds it to be a solemn resolve *either* to consecrate himself totally to the Father's will and accomplish his messianic task *or* to drink the cup of suffering to its dregs (Mark 14:36). Jeremias' suggestion that the abstention is to force God's hand does not meet the case. We agree with Fuller that it is an act of consecration which envisages his sacrificial death. Fuller holds that "this saying is an additional proof that Jesus regards his death as the decisive event in and through which God will inaugurate the End."

The cross is the climacteric event that ushers in the end-time. Already proleptically present in our Lord's person, his words, and his deeds, the Kingdom comes redemptively in the cross and the empty tomb. In his death Jesus establishes a new covenant, re-creates the people of God, and brings the dawn of the Age-to-Come. In his own words, the death is inseparable at this point from the resurrection. The two together constitute the mighty act of God, the dawn of the end-time.

---

[87] Jeremias, *op. cit.*, p. 148.
[88] *Ibid.*, p. 152.
[89] Mark 14:25; cf. Luke 22:18 (L).
[90] Jeremias, *op. cit.*, pp. 168-172.
[91] Fuller, *op. cit.*, pp. 76 f.

The New Testament witnesses also make an affirmation that the cross is the climax of the incarnation. For Paul, God's sovereignty is described as God's righteousness, and this righteousness is, as with the Old Testament men, a saving righteousness.[92] The Jew had hoped that by fulfilling the Law in every jot and tittle he would be justified, declared righteous by God. The term "justification" is a forensic term, borrowed from the law courts. It means to be declared righteous, to be acquitted. Hence the Jew believed that he could earn his status of righteousness. His salvation lay in justification on the basis of his works, the conferring of a merited status of righteousness upon him by God, the righteous judge. Such justification was eschatological. It waited upon the ultimate manifestation of God's sovereignty. Paul declares that such justification has become a reality, but that it is entirely different from the Jewish hope. All are sinners, even the strict Jew, but all have been declared righteous in the sacrifice of Jesus Christ, irrespective of merit on their part, provided they have faith. No man can establish a claim on God, but God has shown his righteousness, his kingly power, by graciously justifying sinners in the self-giving of his Son. This is the gospel, in which the righteousness of God is revealed (Rom. 1:16 ff.). God's Kingdom is a saving Kingdom centering in the cross.

Paul also uses the figure of reconciliation to associate the cross with the advent of the Kingdom. God's Kingdom may be manifested as wrath, but it is finally manifested as grace. Man is alienated from God. The negative removal of condemnation, which justification implies, is in this figure transformed into a positive relationship to God. Paul speaks even of justification in positive terms. It brings peace with God (Rom. 5:1), and this is synonymous with reconciliation. The latter image, however, draws out the emphasis on personal relationship. The Kingdom of God, his saving righteousness, comes into action as reconciliation. God was in Christ reconciling men to himself (2 Cor. 5:18). Here his grace breaks through his wrath, and the present reconciliation saves men from the wrath to come. The eschatological

---

[92] Isaiah 56:1; Psalm 98:2.

event is again proleptically realized in and through the death and resurrection of Jesus. The Kingdom has drawn near, the wrath has been overpassed, and the mercy of God has been manifested. We are reconciled through the death of his Son (Rom. 5: 10-11).

The *auctor ad Hebraeos* paints a picture of *Heilsgeschichte* which is dominated by the theme of sacrifice. The Levitical system with its atonement for sin provides the background, and the theme is ritual and ceremonial rather than prophetic. The emphasis falls on the priestly, even though the letter commences with the affirmation that in former times God spoke through the prophets in diverse portions and manners (Heb. 1:1). The eternal world is imaged as God's eternal temple (Heb. 8:2), of which the realm of the historical is a promise and a foreshadowing. But the author has a real sense of the historical, and does not take refuge in Platonism, despite the Alexandrian influences that play on his thought. The common pattern of New Testament eschatology is present. The dawn of the Age-to-Come in history is a significant part of his thought. As C. K. Barrett puts it: "God has begun to fulfill his ancient promises; the dawn of the new age has broken, though the final day has not yet come. The Church lives in the last day but before the last days."[93]

The priesthood and sacrifices of the old covenant were copies of the heavenly original, and the tabernacle in the wilderness was on the pattern of the heavenly temple shown Moses on the Mount (Heb. 8:5). But none was effective in cleansing men from sin and bringing them near to God. The priesthood could provide no permanent mediation between God and man (Heb. 7:23; 9:6-8). But now the perfect high priest had been manifested, and the perfect sacrifice had been made in history (Heb. 9:11-12). The eternal order had entered the temporal, and men could share in the Sabbath rest of God (Heb. 3:14-15). The sovereignty of God is expressed in priestly imagery, but the point is clear. His King-

---

[93] C. K. Barrett, "The Eschatology of the Epistle to the Hebrews," *The Background of the New Testament and Its Eschatology*, ed. by W. D. Davies and D. Daube (Cambridge: The University Press, 1956), p. 391.

dom is now manifested in history, establishing a new covenant. Men may strive to enter into their rest.

The central point is the sacrifice of Christ. The Kingdom is brought to its climacteric revelatory and redemptive activity in the cross. By Christ's sacrifice, men may taste of the powers of the Age-to-Come (Heb. 3:1; 6:4-5), and draw near with boldness to the throne of grace (Heb. 4:16). He has opened up a living way to the divine presence (Heb. 10:20). Yet he is still the forerunner (Heb. 6:20). He is now seated at the right hand of God (Heb. 8:1) and is high priest forever (Heb. 7:24-28), ministering in the eternal sanctuary (Heb. 8:2 ff.; 9:11, 24). Thither by faith we may *finally* follow him into the unhindered communion with himself that God has promised. So we lay hold of a hope set before us. The author is still living in an atmosphere impregnated with the eschatology of the primitive church. The Age-to-Come has dawned in the sacrifice of Jesus, but its fullness is yet before us. It has, however, dawned with power, and the promise is in part realized, as it was not for the heroes of faith in the Old Testament. In the eleventh chapter, the long history of faith in the old covenant is consummated in the Christian church, and the center is Jesus, who endured the cross to take us with him into the presence of God.

The author of the Johannine corpus likewise emphasizes the centrality of the cross in the inbreak of the Kingdom. For John, history is salvation. It is the removal of death, darkness, and hatred, and thus the advent of the Kingdom in Jesus can be pictured as the entrance of life, light, and love. In Christ, eternal life breaks in, and the characteristic emphasis of John is that such life is released through a life laid down. The life of the Age-to-Come is released through death. The cross is Christ's path to glory, and it brings the dawning of the Age-to-Come among men. His death was inevitable, if his mission was to be completed. So Caiaphas can declare that it is expedient that one man should die on behalf of the people (John 11:50). When men lifted up the Son of Man on the cross, it became a revelation of the Kingdom (John 8:28; 12:32, 34.)

6. The Sacrifice of the Son of Man

In its understanding of the person of the Lord, the early
church had emphasized both his humanity and his deity, drawing
on the imagery of both the heavenly Son of Man and the pre-
existent Son of God. In like mannner, when it sought to interpret
the climacteric event of his death, it saw him as both representative sacrifice for sinful humanity and divine victor over man's
demonic bondage. Had not Jesus bound up the Servant theme
with his messianic consciousness as heavenly Son of Man? Had
he not further declared that the Son of Man came to give his life
a ransom for the many? The sacrificial theme, focalized especially
in the image of the Suffering Servant, became central as the New
Testament witnesses expressed their inspired insight into the
relation of the cross to human sin. Later we shall see that from
this sacrificial center they moved out to the victory of the cross
over the power of evil which held men in thrall. Christ was both
victim and victor. Here we shall concern ourselves with the sacrificial theme. Yet in this theme the representative humanity is
matched by the personal presence and activity of God in his Son.

The emphasis in the sacrificial imagery of the New Testament
falls upon the divine initiative. This is no appeasing of an angry
God, for the Father delivered up the Son for us (Rom. 8:32), and
he sent his own Son as an offering for sin.[94] The Lord Jesus gave
himself up for our sins according to the will of our God and
Father (Gal. 1:4). God sent his Son to be an expiation for our
sins (1 John 4: 10; cf. 4:14). God loved us and initiated the sacrifice of his Son.

At this point, we need to look at the word so often rendered
"propitiation." God's grace has already triumphed over his wrath;
he has appeased himself in sending his Son. The Greek word
hilaskesthai and its parallel forms cannot be made to mean that
God was propitiated by the sacrifice of Jesus. Septuagint usage
helps us here. In pagan Greek usage the word could be translated

---

[94] Romans 8:3. Septuagint usage indicates that the phrase *peri hamartias*
here refers to the sin offering; *vide* William Sanday and Arthur C. Headlam, *The Epistle to the Romans*, I.C.C. (Edinburgh: T. & T. Clark, 1895).

as "propitiation," but in the Judeo-Christian tradition it is God who provides the sacrifice. This is true also of the Levitical sacrifices of the Old Testament, where the Hebrew word *kipper*, "to atone," is rendered in the Septuagint by the Greek verb *hilaskesthai*. Scholars are agreed that Hebrew and Septuagint usage carry the note of expiation.[95] The sacrifice is made not to propitiate an angry God but to expiate, to wipe out or cover up sin. In Romans 3:21-26, Paul uses the word *hilasterion*, an adjective derived from the noun *hilasmos*, and this would appear to mean "pertaining to expiation" or "expiatory." The *auctor ad Hebraeos* uses the same word in Hebrews 9:5 to describe the mercy seat, the cover of the ark in the holy of holies,[96] which was sprinkled with the blood of the sacrifice on the Day of Atonement. The same thought of covering sin is implied, and the sprinkling of the blood on the mercy seat may well be in Paul's mind, too, since he accompanies the word with the phrase "by his blood." Christ's sacrifice is a means of expiation, and the "mercy seat" of the old covenant was, in this sense, a promise of what was to come. When we remember that the blood in Hebrew thought represented the life-principle, we may say that our sin is covered by a sacrifice in which Christ poured out his life unto death. His sacrifice was "a life sacrificially released by death." John uses a word in the same Greek family when he declares that the death of the cross is an *hilasmos*, expiation for our sins (1 John 4:10). God loved us and initiated this expiatory act, a clear indication that the word must not be rendered "propitiation." God provides the means of covering sin whereby his forgiveness can operate. So the blood of Jesus Christ, his life poured out to death, cleanses us from all sin (1 John 1:7).

This must not be interpreted as a minimizing of the divine wrath. This remains a reality outside of Christ. The point is that God has determined to show himself as grace in the sacrifice of

---

[95] C. H. Dodd, *Journal of Theological Studies*, Vol. XXXII, 1931, pp. 352-360, has undertaken a detailed examination of this and shown that the verb means "to perform an act whereby guilt or defilement is removed." He supports the idea that it should best be rendered "to make expiation."

[96] Cf. Exodus 25:17; the Septuagint uses the same word—*hilasterion epithema*.

Christ. He has set forth the expiation. The coming of Christ means
that God has found a way whereby his holiness and righteousness
are not infringed upon, yet he may be gracious to sinners. The
wrath becomes here transfigured into grace, and in Jesus men
know that the face of wrath is truly a face of mercy. Only in this
sense may we speak of propitiation. God propitiates himself by
providing a means of expiation for sinful men. He is not appeased
like an angry man, and we must not, at this point, transfer to him
our human analogies.

Paul is clearly defending the divine righteousness (Rom. 3:
21-26). This might seem to be impugned by God's failure to punish the sins of past generations. But God's forbearance was in the
light of the sacrifice that was to come. In setting forth Christ, his
own Son, as a means of expiation, he showed that he took sin
seriously and yet could bring men within the sphere of his righteousness by a gracious acquittal or remission of sins. This does
not imply a change in the divine intention. The cross was in the
mind of God from the beginning, and God's action was determined by its pattern. In Calvary that pattern was actualized in
history.

What constituted the heart of the sacrifice? The emphasis
falls on the obedience of our Lord (2 Cor. 10:5). In the hymn on
the *kenosis* of the Servant Son, Paul emphasizes the obedience
unto the death of the cross as the significant element in the self-
giving (Phil. 2:8). Elsewhere, he stresses the obedience of Christ
which cancels the result of Adam's disobedience for all who have
faith in him (Rom. 5:13-19). The one act of righteousness by
which the many are justified was Christ's obedience, his sacrifice
on the cross in accord with the will of God.[97] Although stressing
the priestly aspect, the *auctor ad Hebraeos* unites the prophetic
with it in his portrayal of the sacrifice of Christ. It is the sacrifice
of perfect obedience which makes the cross effective (Heb. 10:
5-10). Thereby the new covenant is effected. Indeed, when he
stresses the "blood" (Heb. 9:13-14, 22), this is no more for him

---

[97] This is made clear by the parallelism of vss. 18 and 19. The "one act
of transgression" and the "one act of righteousness" in vs. 18 correspond
respectively to the "disobedience" and the "obedience" in vs. 19.

than for Paul a synonym for a "bloody death." The context shows that the main emphasis is on a " ... life freely surrendered, applied, and dedicated to the recovery of men."[98] The offering of Christ is the offering of himself for men in complete obedience to the Father's will. It is not, however, just the obedience that expiates, but the obedience that issues in sacrifice.

The obedience of Christ is the perfect fulfillment of God's redemptive will for men, and by that will " ... we have been sanctified through the offering of the body of Jesus Christ once for all" (Heb. 10:10). Sacrifice is the divinely appointed way of dealing with sin, and in obedience to the divine will Christ goes this way. The emphasis on the sinlessness of Christ and on the sacrifice being made " ... through the eternal Spirit ... " (Heb. 9: 14) may help to penetrate more deeply here. Denney suggests that the sacrifice of Christ without spot had an absolute or ideal character, and that the phrase last quoted means that "it was something beyond which nothing could be, or could be conceived to be, as a response, a spiritual response, to the divine necessities of the situation."[99] Once for all, in history, love triumphed over evil with an absoluteness and a qualitative perfection which give God the right to forgive sins.[100]

The sacrificial imagery is not confined to the Servant concept. We have a clear reference to the Passover sacrifice. Paul declares that Christ, our Passover, has been sacrificed (1 Cor. 5:7). In the Johannine corpus it is not clear whether our Lord's description of himself as the Lamb of God (John 1:29, 36) is to be understood in relation to the Passover lamb or to the Servant who is led as a lamb to the slaughter (Isa. 53:7, 10).[101] It seems fairly certain,

---

[98] Vincent Taylor, *The Atonement in New Testament Teaching* (London: The Epworth Press, 1945), p. 123.

[99] James Denney, *The Death of Christ,* reissued in abridged form, ed. by R. V. G. Tasker (London: The Tyndale Press, 1951), p. 150.

[100] Cf. Leonard Hodgson, *The Doctrine of the Atonement* (New York: Charles Scribner's Sons, 1951), p. 83.

[101] Scholars point out that the Aramaic for "lamb" could also mean "servant." *Vide* Walther Zimmerli and Joachim Jeremias, *The Servant of God* (Naperville: Alec R. Allenson, Inc., 1957), p. 82. C. H. Dodd holds that the "Lamb of God" is a messianic title equivalent to the "king of Israel," and radically denies any connection with the Passover imagery. He

however, that the Passover theme did not influence the Johannine dating of the crucifixion on the Passover night.[102] The Lamb who was slain provides the abiding theme of the Apocalypse. One emphasis may be moral-martyrological here, but there is deeper metaphysical redemptive concern.[103] The death of Christ encouraged the Christian martyrs, but those martyrs were also purchased with his blood (Rev. 5:9). And "blood" here seems to have the connotation of the blood of the sacrificial lamb. We are loosed from our sins by his own blood (Rev. 1:5). The themes of the Passover lamb and the covenant sacrifice are echoed respectively in the Petrine references to our redemption by the precious blood of Christ as of a lamb without blemish and without spot,[104] and to the sprinkling with the blood of Jesus Christ.[105] The *auctor ad Hebraeos* turns almost entirely from the Servant theme to that of the Levitical sacrifices, and Paul at times reflects this same kind of imagery. Thus, he speaks of Christ as having given himself up for us as a sacrifice to God "for an odor of a sweet smell."[106] On the whole, however, the Servant theme is central, as with our Lord himself, and the other imagery serves to enrich it.

Clearly the death of our Lord is a vicarious sacrifice,[107] but it is also envisaged in representational terms. Paul's thought of Christ as the second Adam means that Christ acted as the inclusive representative of the new humanity. He summed up in him-

---

thinks that, as in Revelation, the phrase is borrowed from the apocalyptic imagery of the ram as military leader—*The Interpretation of the Fourth Gospel*, pp. 230 ff. Dodd does, however, think it possible that the Servant theme may have influenced John's thought (*ibid.*, p. 238). He adds that any Servant concept is retained in a very sublimated sense, and seems to deny that our Lord's death has an expiatory significance in the Fourth Gospel.

[102] Cf. Dodd, *op. cit.*, p. 234.

[103] Cf. Ragnar Leivestad, *Christ the Conqueror* (New York: The Macmillan Company, 1954), pp. 22 ff.

[104] 1 Peter 1:18-19; cf. Exodus 12.

[105] 1 Peter 1:2; cf. Exodus 24:1-8.

[106] Ephesians 5:2; cf. Exodus 29:18, 25; Leviticus 1:9, 13. Peter seems to imply the same idea in declaring that Christ himself bore our sins in his own body on the tree, probably contrasting Christ with the high priest who laid the sins of the people upon the scapegoat in the Levitical ritual and with the whole practice of that ritual—1 Peter 2:21-24; cf. Leviticus 15:20 ff.

[107] Cf. 1 John 4:10; 3:16.

self those who by faith in him should enter into filial relation with God. His achievement was theirs and his obedience was theirs. He died for all, and all died in his representative death (2 Cor. 5:14). The representative nature of our Lord's act is stressed in the high priestly prayer of John 17 (especially vss. 17-19). Jesus sets himself apart for the service of God and thus for the act of obedience which leads to his death on the cross. Yet he does so for "the others." The object of his own utter self-dedication is that "they" may also be consecrated. His act of obedience becomes an "earnest" of theirs, and he is the first link in the chain of dedicated lives consecrated to and by God. Through his representative sacrifice, those who abide in him may go out in dedicated service to the world. So in the Apocalypse the saints in the time of tribulation may already share in benefits established by the Lamb who was slain and may be partakers of his Kingdom.

7. The Triumph of the Son of God

Christ is sacrificial victim but he is also victor. The representative heavenly man is also the Son of God who has triumphed over every demonic power that holds men in thrall. His sacrificial act both covers sin and sets men free. The major view of the New Testament would seem to be that God must deal with individual sin and cosmic evil in a way befitting God. He who created and sustains by his Word can also withhold his creative Word. Then the universe would be ended. But this would belie God's nature as love. Again, he who is omnipotent could compel subservience, but this would belie both his nature as love and the freedom which he has freely given to his creatures. Hence, he must deal with sinful men and a rebellious universe in a way that respects such freedom and is consonant with his own righteousness. In some sense, in dealing with individual sin he breaks the power of cosmic evil. The two aspects of the cross are one act. God becomes man and meets sin and evil where they can meet him, as it were, on equal terms. Man has been defeated as man. So God empties himself and meets evil as man, in the likeness of sinful flesh.

This is Paul's theme, and it is taken up by Irenaeus.[108] Christ's victory is the natural consequence of the incarnation. As Wingren puts it, commenting on Irenaeus: "God's victory over Satan is realized in the humanity of Jesus, and therefore in the Crucifixion. Only by entering into Adam's condition could Christ achieve his purpose, and in so doing he has defeated death by his resurrection, which is the end of all Creation, and the means of fulfilling this end for all Creation."[109] But Irenaeus learned this from the New Testament. In covering sin, our Lord also broke men's demonic bondage. As victim, he is also victor.[110]

Paul's favorite word for describing this aspect of the cross is "redemption," *apolutrosis*, an image borrowed from the slave market. Yet no more than in its Old Testament antecedents is there much thought of a price or ransom being paid.[111] The emphasis is more on men being set free, on "deliverance." Man is delivered by Christ from the powers of darkness. The theme is the same for Paul whether he is dealing with sin, death, the demons, or the tyranny of the Law. He probably provides the fullest understanding of this triumph in the New Testament. Yet the theme occurs throughout the New Testament.

There is a once-for-allness about the triumph of the cross which secures the redemption of men. A new situation has been created objectively in history, independent of individual men.[112] The decisive battle has been fought and the ultimate outcome is sure. Paul can tell us that the rulers of this world are destroyed (1 Cor. 2:6), because Christ has dealt the decisive blow (Col. 2:15). John makes much of the triumph of Jesus over the Evil

---

[108] Irenaeus, *Adversus Haereses*, V, 21, 1: "as our species went down to death through a vanquished man, so we may ascend to life through a victorious one."

[109] Gustaf Wingren, *Man and the Incarnation* (Philadelphia: Muhlenberg Press, 1959), p. 122.

[110] The New Testament material on this theme is dealt with in Leivestad, *op. cit.* This book has as its background the seed book in historical study, Gustav Aulén, *Christus Victor* (New York: The Macmillan Company, 1931).

[111] The idea lingers only in the use of the phrase "bought with a price" —1 Corinthians 6:20; 7:23; and possibly Galatians 3:13.

[112] Cf. C. A. A. Scott, *Christianity According to St. Paul* (Cambridge: The University Press, 1927), p. 53.

One. He is so sure that the Age-to-Come has dawned with the death of Jesus that he sees the final overthrow of the devil and the judgment of men as present realities (John 12:31). When our Lord faces death, he declares that the prince of this world is coming but has no power over him (John 14:30). Indeed, the Paraclete can come because the prince of this world has been judged.[113] This theme of the triumphant Christ finds its quintessent expression in the Apocalypse, which is dominated by the vision of Jesus as the victorious Messiah. He is no longer the suffering Jesus but the heavenly Lord. The humanity of Jesus is clothed in awesome majesty and the lowly Son of Man is the heavenly victor coming on the clouds of heaven.

We note certain important elements in the New Testament understanding of the triumph of the cross. First of all, there is the emphasis on the reality of the incarnation. The incarnation provided the vantage ground in which the issue could be joined. Redemption was possible because the Son of God chose to encounter the demons in the territory where they could attack him as they attacked all men. The demonic powers gain entrance to man through his flesh, his creaturely stuff. Christ took upon himself this constitution. He took the likeness of sinful flesh (Rom. 8:3). Being thus made of a woman, he came into hostile relation with the demonic powers (Gal. 4:4). He was without sin, but he did experience all their power and artifice (Heb. 4:15). Thus, sin was a reality to him.[114] Although he knew no sin, he was "made sin." As C. A. A. Scott puts it: " . . . in all else that belongs to man's relation to sin except consent to it, Christ was partaker through his Incarnation."[115]

Even the Law is demonic, for it has imposed a curse on

---

[113] John 16:11. Such ideas must not be taken in support of realized eschatology. For John, the ultimate consummation is still in the future. The point is that ultimate outcome is proleptically present in the triumph of Jesus. The hour is coming and *now is*, when the dead shall hear the voice of the Son of God and shall live—John 12:31. But the *now* is *pari passu* the future. The resurrection unto life and the judgment are still to come— John 5:28-29.

[114] We are using "sin" here in Paul's sense of an invasive demonic power, not a human act.

[115] C. A. A. Scott, *op. cit.*, p. 52.

man.[116] But Christ has dealt with man's subjection to the Law
(Gal. 4:4-5). He has redeemed men from the curse by becoming
a curse for them (Gal. 3:13). Again, this was possible only because of the incarnation. Christ became a Jew. He was made under the Law, for in identifying himself by birth with the Jewish
race, he accepted their form of bondage. Thereby he was able to
redeem those under the Law (Gal. 4:5). Even the Apocalypse,
which transcendentalizes the figure of the Messiah, retains the
reality of the incarnation. Without this the Lamb could not be
victorious. He is the Lion of the tribe of Judah, the root and off-
spring of David (Rev. 5:5; 22:16).

In the second place, the death on the cross becomes crucial.
In dying, our Lord stripped off the flesh in which the incarnation
had involved him (Col. 2:15) and through which the powers of
darkness could join issue with him. When they crucified the Lord
of glory, they overreached themselves (1 Cor. 2:6-7). He escaped
from their dominion. When Paul speaks of our Lord's taking the
form of a Servant (Phil. 2:7), this may well refer not only to the
Servant theme but also to his placing himself in the position of a
thrall (howbeit unconsenting!) to the forces enslaving men.
Hence he died to sin (Rom. 6:10), in the sense that he died from
under its demonic power, thereby condemning sin in the flesh. He
died from under the servitude in which the incarnation had involved him. This point of view is particularly evident in Paul's
thought.

In the third place, the triumph of the cross is bound up with
the resurrection. In this aspect of Calvary, the cross and the resurrection constitute a single event. Without the latter, the former
would be defeat. The resurrection of Jesus sealed the doom of the
powers of evil. He escaped their dominion in death and rose from
the dead to declare his triumph. By his resurrection he conquered
sin, living unto God. He also conquered death. Sin brought the
demonic power of death in its train, as its wages. In dying Christ
defeated death, for death was robbed of its prey in the resurrection. The demonic tyranny of the Law, too, was broken. Christ

---

[116] Galatians 3:10; cf. Deuteronomy 27:26.

"broke the power of the Law as a yoke of bondage by first realizing in His own Person the utmost extremity of its authority, and then by breaking forth from its domination in the newness of the resurrection life."[117]

In the Fourth Gospel the cross becomes the path to glory, the way to the throne, because John sees it from a postresurrection perspective. The Fourth Evangelist even gives a secondary place to Paul's emphasis on the cross as humiliation and obedience unto death. He sees the cross as intimately bound up with the resurrection and the ascension. All three constitute different facets of the one act of glorifying the Son. In three passages the lifting upon the cross is associated with the lifting up to heaven.[118] Leivestad suggests that the Fourth Gospel covers by a single term, "to lift up," what the Synoptic tradition expresses in the two antithetical phrases "suffer" and "enter into his glory" (Luke 24:26). He comments: "The Son of Man must die. But this lifting up symbolizes his exaltation from earth to heaven, his glorification."[119] The connection of the cross with the resurrection and the ascension turns it into a present power and guarantees the continued activity of the Redeemer's work. Seen in the light of the resurrection, the cross is not a limitation but an exaltation. It meant the release of pent-up activities, and the procession to Calvary becomes a triumphal procession. This triumph spells the overthrow of the Evil One.

When the hour of Christ's death was come, the devil put it into the heart of Judas to betray him (John 13:2). But, at that moment, our Lord remembers that he comes from God and re-

---

[117] C. A. A. Scott, *op. cit.,* p. 40.

[118] John 3:14; 8:28; 12:32-33. There has been considerable debate about the significance of the phrase "to lift up" in these passages. Burney and Abbott, on the basis of the Aramaic, hold it to mean exaltation (*Journal of Theological Studies,* July 1919, p. 337). J. H. Bernard disputes their findings—*Gospel According to St. John,* Vol. I, I.C.C. (Edinburgh: T. & T. Clark, 1928), pp. 113 ff. Vincent Taylor points out that much of this debate loses its point when it is recognized that the cross is the exaltation. "The death *is* the exaltation, the liberation of the Son from the self-imposed conditions of mortality into the freedom of the Spirit"—*The Atonement in New Testament Teaching,* p. 147.

[119] Leivestad, *op. cit.,* p. 199.

turns to God, that his death is the return to heaven of the divine emissary. The devil was occasioning not the defeat but the glorifying of the Son of Man, the fulfillment of his mission. Our Lord can declare that the prince of this world is now cast out and immediately speak of his being "lifted up" from the earth (John 12:31-32). The Son of God was manifested to destroy the works of the devil, and the cross marked the termination of this process (1 John 3:8). It became the throne. John reads the resurrection back into the cross. Paul makes the former the sign of triumph and the cross the place of humiliation. John sees the cross itself as an unveiling.[120]

The Christ of the Apocalypse is the triumphant risen Lord, and yet, as such, he is still the Christ of Calvary, the Lamb that was slain. For the seer of Revelation, the cross and the resurrection are intimately bound together in the triumph over cosmic evil. Christ was dead and he is alive forevermore. He has conquered death. He is the first-born from the dead (Rev. 1:5), bearing the keys of Hades and exercising lordship over the realm of death (Rev. 1:18). In the Apocalypse death and Hades serve a double role. They are both executants of the divine judgment (Rev. 6:8) and evil powers that must finally be thrown with the devil into the lake of fire (Rev. 20:14). The resurrection secures for Christ the keys of Hades and opens the gates of death for those who believe.

Chapter 12 is enigmatic. The child mysteriously born in the wilderness is evidently Christ, and the woman would appear to be the remnant of the old covenant. The cross, resurrection, and ascension are reflected in the child's being caught up to the throne. In consequence, Satan is defeated and thrown down to earth. The devil is now left on the earth to persecute the saints, but they triumph in the triumph of Christ. The decisive blow to the powers of darkness has been dealt, and the Lamb becomes the military leader. His triumph on the cross and in the resurrection gives him the right to be the warrior who descends to avenge his martyrs.

---

[120] Cf. *ibid.*, p. 200.

Here we come to the fourth element in the victor-theme—its close association with the victim-theme. The two cannot finally be separated. This is evident in Paul's thought, but it is also evidenced by the sacrificial language filling the book of Revelation. The victor-theme is dramatic and pictorial, but its rationale lies in the sacrifice. Atonement means fundamentally the reconciliation of men to God. The inner core of the triumph over demonic evil in the cross and resurrection was the atoning sacrifice in which God reconciled men to himself. The reconciliation set men free from their evil bondage and defeated the powers of darkness. Hence the Apocalypse makes Christ share the throne of God as the victorious Lamb (Rev. 5:5 ff.). He alone is worthy to unlock the secrets of history because he has redeemed men by his blood (Rev. 5:9 ff.). The forgiveness of sins means the breaking of the powers of evil. God deals with them justly. He uses the demonic to execute his judgment. He allows it to operate on him through the incarnation, and by the sacrifice of the Son makes forgiveness possible within the realm where sin reigns as king.

The core of atonement is thus forgiveness, but the cross and the empty tomb have a wider and more cosmological background, which the dramatic picture of conflict preserves. More was involved than just the reconciliation of man. The cross was cosmic in its sweep.

8. The Resurrection and Exaltation of the Crucified Lord

Earlier we have defended the historicity of the empty tomb and the objective nature of our Lord's resurrection body. Here we face mystery, and so the early church regarded it. The resurrection was a miraculous inbreak from beyond in which the normal procedure of nature was contravened. Of Christ's bodily appearance, Alan Richardson remarks: "No attempt is made by the New Testament writers to explain these things. If they could be explained by us, the mystery and miracle of the resurrection would be quite other than it is, and the Christian faith would be a different thing from what it has been throughout its history.

Christianity is a religion of miracle, and the miracle of Christ's
resurrection is the living center and object of the Christian
faith."[121] Hence the earliest apostolic preaching can declare that
God raised up Jesus (Acts 2:24, 32). Paul reiterates the same
faith again and again.[122] Peter can speak about having confidence
in the God who raised Jesus from the dead (1 Peter 1:21), and
the *auctor ad Hebraeos* can invoke the God of peace who brought
again from the dead our Lord Jesus Christ (Heb. 13:20). The
resurrection is God's act and is an integral part of the incarnation
as the inbreak of God's saving power.

The New Testament regards the resurrection as a new and
utterly unique act, breaking the habitual patterns of God's providential activity. In so doing, it dismisses both metaphysical speculation about the natural immortality of the soul, of which Christ
then becomes a supreme manifestation, and occult ideas which in
every age are produced by psychic enthusiasts. This act of God
was the inbreak of the *eschaton*, the unveiling and the dawn of
the actualization of the final meaning of history. It was the event
which transformed the seeming defeat and humiliation of the
cross into triumph and exaltation. It was the sign of the divine
victory over sin, death, and every demonic power, the sign that
ultimately all things would be put in subjection under God (1
Cor. 15:26), the sign that death had already lost its dominion
(Rom. 6:9), the sign that Christ's atoning death had brought forgiveness to men.[123]

In the cross and the resurrection we have the mighty act of
God which crowns and fulfills all his acts, marking the dawn of
the Age-to-Come. Hence, it is pictured in terms of two preceding
mighty acts. It can be likened to a new creation (1 Peter 1:3), so
that Christ is the second Adam, the originator of a new humanity
through the resurrection.[124] It can also be described as the new
Exodus, and is so regarded in the First Letter of Peter (1:18-21;
2:9). All the powers of God, already released in the initial act of

---

[121] Richardson, *op. cit.*, p. 197.
[122] Cf. Romans 6:4; 1 Corinthians 15:15.
[123] Romans 4:25; Philippians 3:9-11.
[124] 1 Corinthians 15:45; cf. 2 Corinthians 5:17; 4:5-6.

creation and redemptively present creating a people in the Exodus from Egypt, have now been released in their fullness in the empty tomb. The Kingdom has come with power. The divine intention behind creation and the calling of Israel are actualized in and through Jesus' death and resurrection. The dawn of the Age-to-Come has broken. Hence, Christ is declared to be Son of God with power by the resurrection from the dead (Rom. 1:4).

The unity of the cross and the resurrection is essential to the *kerygma* of the New Testament. This is explicitly present throughout the New Testament testimony. The gospel is a resurrection gospel. This, incidentally, is why both events have to be, in some sense, historical, even though the resurrection appearances were private and to the disciples only. Easter sets the seal on the atonement and transforms black Friday into Good Friday.

So for Paul the doctrine of redemption is incomplete without the resurrection, for "the work of Christ is not finished and salvation history does not reach its goal,"[125] until God raises Christ from the dead.[126] Death, too, is triumphant until the resurrection. If Christ is not raised, then we are of all men the most miserable, and death is still victor. Our hope is vain. Paul's logic is clear (1 Cor. 15:12-19). Death is not natural to man. It is the result of sin. Thus Christ, the true and sinless man, tasted death for us, that he might deliver us from death. In the resurrection he broke its power. The descent and humiliation of the Servant-Son reached its lowest point on Calvary. The resurrection confirmed the Servant as Saviour, and his foes were scattered (Acts 2:24). He was crucified in weakness, but raised by the power of God (2 Cor. 13:4).

The resurrection signified for the New Testament witnesses the dawn of the new Age. It was an act of God which began a new creation. The resurrection body of the Lord was the sign of a resurrected universe. Not only would the believer be resurrected in a body of glory (1 Cor. 15:42 ff.), but the whole creation was groaning and travailing, waiting for this final unveiling of the

---

[125] Stauffer, *New Testament Theology,* p. 137.
[126] Romans 4:22-25; 1 Corinthians 15:17.

sons of God (Rom. 8:17-23). Then it, too, would be resurrected, and a new heaven and new earth would appear (Rev. 21:1). Thus, the resurrection was the sign of a cosmic triumph, the assurance that the Age-to-Come had already broken in. The uniqueness of the resurrection lies in the affirmation that it is the key to all history. It is the divine redemptive act whereby sin and death are defeated. It is the eschatological event in history in which the meaning of all history is made plain, and in which the distortions and perversions of the whole created order and of man's creaturely existence are decisively dealt with. Heim can write of the resurrection appearances that the disciples "knew that in a small space for a little while they had been granted a view into the Reality which contained the destiny of the whole world to come, the future of nature and the world of men."[127]

The resurrection is not separated in the early preaching from the ascension and exaltation of the Lord. We need to note at once that the ascension, in a major part of the New Testament tradition, is not treated as an event detached from the resurrection but is intimately bound up with it. It represents the complementary aspect of that all-embracing Easter event which centers in the resurrection. That event is both triumph over death and the declaration that Christ has become the Son of God with power by being raised from the dead.

Luke separates the ascension from the resurrection by forty days of resurrection appearances.[128] He separates it also from the subsequent descent of the Spirit, which took place seven weeks after the resurrection of Christ (Acts 2:1-3). At the ascension, the disciples are told to await the gift of the Spirit. The longer ending of Mark (Mark 16:9-20), generally held to be late and to reflect Luke 24:13-52, records the same tradition and makes the ascension a detached event.[129]

Conzelmann, in a stimulating discussion of Luke's theology, has clearly shown what many other scholars hold, that Luke's

---

127 Heim, *Jesus the World's Perfecter*, p. 171.
128 Luke 24:50-51; Acts 1:9-11.
129 Mark 16:19; cf. Luke 24:51.

Gospel is basically a theological writing.[130] Luke regards the forty days of resurrection appearances as "a sacred period between the times," in which the appearances "do not take place from heaven." The later appearances, for example at Damascus, presupposed the ascension and "are of a different kind, for they establish no relationship with the Lord in the special sense that the Resurrection appearances do."[131] Conzelmann thus sees a theological motif in the Lucan tradition. The ascension marks the end of the story of the risen Lord on earth and the beginning of his heavenly reign. Henceforth the Spirit becomes the substitute for his real presence, and the waiting for the Spirit introduces yet another chronological duration into Luke's version of *Heilsgeschichte*.

As Alan Richardson has pointed out, Luke is using the historical "to convey the truth of history by means of an imaginative reconstruction of historical happenings."[132] Actually the Fourth Gospel follows the same method. It, too, is concerned to make the inner and spiritual significance of the historical revelation plain by presenting the history in a form that brings out that inner meaning.

Luke's theology conditions his presentation of the events. Actually the events, apart from the empty tomb, are inner and private events. They belong to the inner side of history, to its invisible side which is grounded in the acts and intention of God. They are testified to by the experience of the witnesses; but always we find in history the effects of the events and not the events themselves. Luke puts them into chronological history to express

---

[130] Hans Conzelmann, *The Theology of St. Luke* (London: Faber & Faber, 1960), *passim*.

[131] *Ibid.*, pp. 203 ff.

[132] Richardson, *op. cit.*, p. 117. He also writes: " . . . Luke-Acts would seem to present the truth of the Gospel by means of a brilliantly stylized presentation of history which brings out profound theological truth in story form." J. G. Davies in an excellent treatment of the doctrine of the ascension suggests that Luke derived his idea of a bodily assumption after forty days from the significance of such a period in sacred history and from the Elijah saga. ". . . in Acts he [Luke] would appear to be using the Elijah saga and he points the connection by referring to a forty day period"—*He Ascended into Heaven* (London: Lutterworth Press, 1958), pp. 52 ff. Cf. A. M. Ramsey, "Ascension," *A Theological Word Book of the Bible*.

a theological meaning, to express their meaning as he sees it. He
clearly sees that the resurrection does not mean that Christ now
shares the divine throne, but only that Christ has conquered
death. Hence he separates the resurrection and the ascension to
draw out the difference of theological meaning.

Involved in Luke's thought also is the three-tier universe of
contemporary cosmology. Jesus is taken up into heaven; he parts
from the disciples. Although we must dismiss this three-tier structure as outmoded and prescientific cosmology, the truth remains.
Even the Hebrew did not localize God, though he did house him
above the heavens, for the highest heaven could not contain him
(1 Kings 8:27). The Hebrew cosmology was not scientific, concerned with observable phenomena, like that of the Greeks. It
was through and through theological, and it presented in pictorial
form the theological understanding of God and of God's relation
to man. It is true that Luke himself was not a Jew, but the same
motif underlies his thought. How literal he meant the picture to
be is, of course, an open issue, but, as J. G. Davies says, "When
St. Luke came to describe the Ascension, which to him . . . was
the occasion of Christ's entrance into the divine presence, he did
so pictorially—Christ was taken up."[133] He points out that fact
and interpretation are so closely welded as to be inseparable and
that the translation of the Hebraic imagery into abstract terms
does not *ipso facto* make the result any more accurate.

The ascension does not spiritually and theologically mean
a translation in space. It means a change in the mode of existence.
This is symbolized in the cloud which receives Christ out of the
sight of the disciples, for the cloud in biblical thought veils the
presence of God's glory. The Lord has moved from the state of
humiliated and crucified Servant-Son to that of victorious Lord,
to share in the power and glory of God (cf. Phil. 2:9 ff.). As
Ch. Biber has written: "The 'ascension' expresses a real assumption of power, not a miraculous journey . . . the words 'He ascended into heaven' express a political rather than a meteorologi-
cal ascent (W. Vischer), for heaven is the place where God

---

[133] Davies, *op. cit.*, pp. 57 f.

reigns and which will always be higher than any human authority." [134]

Luke is thus neither naive nor untheological, but is seeking in a pictorial way to present a theological truth which is the final meaning of the resurrection appearances, the presence of the Holy Spirit, and the manifest lordship of the historical Jesus.

Now the Johannine tradition makes the ascension-exaltation theme an integral part of the resurrection itself. The ascension is not a detached event, as it is in Luke's theology, separated in time. Luke, for the sake of theological interpretation, has broken up the primitive tradition, which John retains. Paul, Peter, and the primitive preaching bind the resurrection and the ascension-exaltation together, while carefully differentiating between their theological meaning.[135] The victory over death in the resurrection and the kingly session at the right hand of power signified by the ascension are two constituent elements of the one Easter event. The resurrection and ascension-exaltation constitute together the divine vindication of the sacrifice on Calvary.[136] John holds closely together the lifting up on the cross and the exaltation, the lifting up into glory.[137] He preserves a tradition which declares that the risen Lord appeared to Mary Magdalene, forbidding her to touch him and enjoining her to tell the disciples that he was ascending to the Father (John 20:17). According to earlier teaching in the Gospel, the Holy Spirit, the other Paraclete, could not come until Jesus ascended (John 7:39). But when Jesus appears to the disciples after the Mary Magdalene incident, he imparts the Holy Spirit to them (John 20:19 ff.). Further, he tells Philip that he may touch him. The implication is that, between the morning encounter with Mary and the evening visit to the disciples, he has ascended. Thus for John the resurrection, the ascension, and the gift of the Spirit belong together and happen in the all-embracing event of the first Easter Day. Paul seems to take a

---

[134] Ch. Biber, "Right Hand," *A Companion to the Bible*, ed. by J.-J. Von Allmen (New York: Oxford University Press, 1958), p. 372.

[135] Ephesians 1:20; 4:9-10; 1 Timothy 3:16; 1 Peter 3:21-22; Acts 2: 32-33.

[136] Romans 8:34; Philippians 2:9.

[137] Cf. *supra*, p. 210.

similar view. This would explain why he does not differentiate
between the resurrection appearances of the Lord to the disciples
and the appearance to himself on the Damascus Road in 1 Corinthians 15. They are all postascension appearances. It would also
fit in with John's own theological view of the cross. The lifting
upon the cross is the beginning of the ascent to the Father (John
16:28).

What is the significance of the exaltation for a theology of
history? It is, first of all, the assumption of power. The Christ now
shares the divine throne, and to him all power is given. Through
his death, resurrection, and ascension, he has been installed as
king by God. The background of this would seem to be the enthronement ritual of Old Israel, of which Psalm 110 formed a
part.[138] The real day of enthronement of God's Messiah had now
come. Israel's annual enthronement ceremony had hailed Yahweh
as king, but the earthly king and the chosen people had alike
failed him. Now the true Messiah had made possible in history a
true people of God. The day of enthronement had become an
actuality, and God had established his Messiah on his throne.

The theme of Psalm 110 is used again and again in the New
Testament. In the Psalm, the anointed king has vanquished his
foes and has been installed as king over God's people, acting also
as high priest (Ps. 110:1-2, 4). In Acts 2:34 and the Letter to the
Hebrews the Psalm is explicitly quoted, but the frequent use of
the phrase "at the right hand of power" indicates how implicitly
present is its theme.[139] God had shared his authority with the
ascended Son and given him a name above every name (Phil.
2:9). Christ now rules as the Lamb in the midst of the throne
(Rev. 5:6). So triumphant is he that the New Testament witnesses see him as the one through whom God created, through
whom he sustains and judges, and in whom he will consummate

---

[138] There is a useful summary of this and its relevance to the ascension
thought of the New Testament in Davies, *op. cit.*, pp. 19 ff. For detailed
references see our own discussion earlier.

[139] Romans 8:34; 1 Corinthians 15:25; Colossians 3:1; Ephesians 1:20;
Hebrews 1:3; 8:1; 10:12; 1 Peter 3:22; Acts 2:34; 5:31; 7:55; Revelation
3:21.

human history.[140] It is as this sublime Mediator of creation and redemption that the Christ now sits at the right hand of power and shares the divine authority.[141] He is Lord of history, and ultimately all his enemies will be put under his feet (1 Cor. 15:24 ff.). The final subjection will only take place at the end of the days, but the beginning has already been made.[142] Indeed, it has already taken place in the death, resurrection, and exaltation of the Lord, for the ultimate outcome is therein assured (Eph. 1:20 ff.). Cullmann comments that "this subjection at the moment is rather merely a 'binding' for they must once again be defeated at the end."[143] He continues: "Here again the tension which is so important for characterizing the present redemptive period emerges into view." Christ has all authority now in heaven and on earth, and he is with his church even to the end of the age (Matt. 28:18 ff.).

Because he is King, his own may now share with him in his glory. They, too, may sit in heavenly places with Christ Jesus.[144] They have become a Kingdom.[145] For he is the second Adam, in whom all the new humanity is gathered up. He is the forerunner who has gone before into heaven (Heb. 6:20). In him our lost humanity has attained its goal. He has taken to heavenly places a victorious humanity which he actualized in history and which is increasingly being actualized in those who are incorporated in him. Thus his lordship in history is expressed specifically in and through his church, for his saints reign with him. This present period of history is the reign or Kingdom of Christ. There is already in history the eschatological realization of the kingship of Christ in the church. He rules it from heaven, sends it his Spirit, and allows it to share his throne. It is with him and in the world, in the Spirit and in the flesh, raised with him where he sits above and yet sharing the lot of sinful man below.

[140] John 1:1-14; Colossians 1:16-20; Hebrews 1:2-3.
[141] Romans 8:34; Hebrews 1:3; 1 Peter 3:22; Revelation 3:21; Colossians 3:1.
[142] Mark 14:62; Revelation 3:21; 14:14; Hebrews 2:8-9; 10:12-13.
[143] Cullmann, *Christ and Time*, p. 153.
[144] Ephesians 2:6; cf. Colossians 3:1; 1 Corinthians 4:8.
[145] 1 Peter 2:9; Revelation 1:6; 5:10.

The other theme of the exaltation is the intercessory high priesthood of the exalted Jesus. He has ascended as priest, taking with him his sacrifice on Calvary. This is the theme of the Letter to the Hebrews.[146] This does not mean a continual re-enactment of the sacrifice on an eternal altar. The sacrifice has been made once-for-all, an event in eternity as well as in time. Christ sits now as the triumphant Lamb at the right hand of God. But he has the right to intercede for us and to be our high priest, because he won this right in the sacrifice on the cross. As A. M. Ramsey has finely expressed it: ". . . his sacrifice, which was once-for-all wrought in history upon the Cross, remains forever in virtue of his presence with the Father."[147] The exaltation of Christ means that the expiatory sacrifice in human history becomes an event in eternity; man's sin is covered. The Christ ever lives to make intercession for us, and in him the church, though sinful, may live in the presence of God, offer its worship, and do the Father's will. Christ is our advocate at the right hand of God. Stauffer paints a fanciful picture of Satan standing on the left of God's throne as our accuser and adversary, and seems to find this meaning in Romans 8:33-34. His final comment is, however, significant: "Christ and Satan—these two engage each other before God's throne for the future of the Church. But Christ has the last word —that much is certain to the whole NT (cf. John 12.31 f.)."[148]

---

[146] Hebrews 4:14-16; 7:25-26; cf. Romans 8:34.
[147] Ramsey, *op. cit.*, p. 28.
[148] Stauffer, *op. cit.*, p. 139.

CHAPTER VI

SALVATION HISTORY—THE CHURCH AND ITS ESCHATOLOGICAL FRAMEWORK

We have emphasized the life, death, resurrection, and exaltation of Jesus Christ as the turning point of human history and have found that in this all-inclusive event the *eschaton,* the end, has entered history. For the Hebrew prophets, the *eschaton* lay at the chronological end of history and would usher in a golden age. Likewise, in postexilic eschatology with its transcendentalizing tendencies the *eschaton* lay at the chronological end and was to be ushered in with a transformation and glorification of the whole created order.

The two must not be differentiated too much, since the pre-exilic prophets manifest unmistakable evidence of a transcendent and cosmological reference in their understanding of the end. Hence, the description "eschatological" must not be confined to the postexilic witnesses but must also describe the prophetic hope. Both pre-exilic eschatology and that of the postexilic period are unanimous in believing that the inbreak of the *eschaton* would mean a judgment and purging of history, a removal of sin and the destruction of evil, the renovation or re-creation of nature, and the emergence of God's people as the perfect community.

The Age-to-Come would mean the cessation of this present age, and the Kingdom of God would take the place of the kingdoms of this world. Now the New Testament testimony seems quite clear that the Age-to-Come has dawned and the Kingdom of God has come with power. But here is the paradox. Sinful history still goes on, this present age still continues, and the kingdoms of this world still exercise their power. Here was the issue which was faced by the first Christian witnesses. They still anticipated a final consummation in which the process of sinful history would be wound up chronologically. They were equally sure that the Age-to-Come had dawned and that the powers of that age were already at work in their lives. The death, resurrection, and ascension of the Lord had released those powers, and the Spirit of the Lord was operating in the Christian fellowship as an earnest of their future inheritance. Thus the Kingdom of God was both present and future.

We turn now to the issues raised by this eschatological framework and the nature of the Christian life in the Body of Christ, his church.

1. The Christian Eschatological Framework

The New Testament is grounded essentially in the Old Testament, no less in its view of time than in other aspects of its thought. Time is basically viewed from the point of view of content, as in Hebrew thinking. The Hebrew was a realist. He took history seriously, and his view of time was realistic and existential. Time had to be reckoned with, and there was no escape from its inexorable procession. Man lived in a world where the experience of time was meaningful. Time was bound up with his decisions and was given to him that he might decide his destiny.

There is no Greek flight from the realm of becoming to the world of timeless being, of eternal ideas. The world was not merely a moving image of a timeless eternity and thus of no ultimate significance. The Greek might adopt this position, but the Hebrew believed that this world is a realm into which the eternal order breaks and discloses itself. It is not a mere changing order, striving to be a copy of an eternal and unmoving original. It is a sphere of activity in which the eternal order is dynamically at work and in which man may encounter the living God. God, for the Greek, sat above the flux of time and change. By rational dialectical and mystical insight he might be known; and for this insight man must rise above the temporal order of becoming. History was cyclic, a series of repetitions, achieving nothing. For the

Hebrew, God is the living God who lifts the temporal order into his purpose and actualizes his will within it. History is linear, even though cyclic elements are involved in it, such as the return to the golden age. It has a goal and is dynamically directed.

This understanding has its repercussions on the Hebrew words for time and eternity. Time as a chronological abstraction was not of interest to the people of the Old Testament. The characteristic word for time, 'eth, denotes filled time, time that is known and remembered by what happens in it. Time is what meets one in life, the eventful moment in which often a decision has to be made.[1] Thus it may be filled with happenings of the natural order or of the physiological functionings of the human organism. Again, it may have as its content the decisions which arise out of human relationships. Most of all, it matters when its content is fraught with divine-human encounter, at the individual or corporate level. Man's times which are most significant are those fraught with a decision which affects his relation to God and God's purpose. Indeed, all man's times of crisis and decision are related to God and so also are those of nations and social groups. God confronts men in times of decision.

For the Hebrew, two times were especially significant—the time of the Exodus when Israel's election was sealed, and the time of the ultimate consummation when God's sovereignty would be unveiled. The day of deliverance in the past was matched by a like day in the future, the Day of Jehovah. The prophets speak of the supreme "time" behind them, in which God had shown his saving power and in which the actualization of his purpose began. They speak of the "other" time, still for them in the future, in which God would surely consummate the purpose behind his election of and covenant with Israel, purging and remaking the nations. The imagery of the end-time reflects that of the first time. So all history is ordered by God's sovereign will.

---

[1] Cf. H. W. Robinson, *Inspiration and Revelation in the Old Testament*, p. 112. Dr. Robinson's whole treatment of time and eternity in Hebrew thought should be consulted. Also *vide* the author's article "Time and Eternity in Biblical Thought," *Theology Today*, Vol. X, October 1953, pp. 354 ff.; John Marsh, *The Fulness of Time, passim;* and Cullmann, *Christ and Time, passim.*

Israel's history begins in a time that is filled with his activity. It will be consummated in a time again filled with his activity. In between, every filled time becomes pregnant with decision and alive with God's presence in judgment and in mercy. It is within this framework of election and eschatology, of times filled with the sovereign and redemptive activity of God, that the Hebrew time-consciousness must be understood.

What of the order that shall supervene upon human history in the Day of Jehovah? In the pre-exilic prophetic hope, its scene is this earth and there is no indication that time will cease. It will mark the end of the present historical order, but temporal language is used to describe it. It is enough, for the purpose of differentiation, to think of the coming Age as marked by a quality of permanence which the present order lacks. Judah shall abide forever and Jerusalem from generation to generation (Joel 3:20). The child shall die a hundred years old (Isa. 65:20). Even at evening time there shall be light, for there shall be no sunset (Zech. 14:7).

With the postexilic eschatology the belief in individual resurrection appeared, and the new order was increasingly transcendentalized. The scene of the consummation was shifted, in the developed apocalyptic of the post-Old Testament period, to a totally new world order. "Age-to-Come" became the characteristic phrase by which to describe this new order. It was the realm of resurrection, and its setting could be described as a new heaven and a new earth. Yet often the latter could be pictured as a glorification or re-creation of that which had preceded it, and there was some sense of continuity involved. In the radical apocalypticism of the intertestamental period, views fluctuate, but some solid core of truth remains, derived from postexilic biblical eschatology. It would appear that the Age-to-Come is to be for the resurrected faithful, to possess in a glorified form some measure of continuity with that which has preceded it, and not to be a negation of time—whatever more may be involved. Insofar as the coming era will reflect the life of God whose will it fulfills, there may be some indication of its temporal nature from the meaning of "eternity" in Hebrew thought.

The characteristic Hebrew word for "eternity" *('olam)* does not imply the negation of time. In the common expressions "for ever" or "from everlasting," eternity implies both remoteness and the absence of any borders to the duration.[2] It can thus cover the whole span of the time of creation, the period of nature and history. History is made up of "generations," but all the successive generations arise out of the primeval time, *'olam*. Eternity is the whole that embraces all times, the permanent background through all the changing times, the depth immanent in every time. Pedersen writes that "eternity [*'olam*] is not the sum of all the individual periods [of history], nor even this sum with something added to it; it is 'time' without subdivision, that which lies behind it, and which displays itself through all times."[3] Eternity is the whole, present behind every time, and may be especially concentrated in any one time. As Pedersen suggests, the declaration that the throne of David is established forever means that it will pervade the successive generations because it is grounded in primeval time.

To understand God's time or eternity, we must grasp the significance of this secular usage of *'olam*. God's eternity is the whole that embraces all other wholes, such as the primeval life of the fathers and all individual times. It is certainly not timeless being as in Plato's thought, and God is no unmoved mover as with Aristotle. If God is the living God, it is understandable that the Hebrew connected him with time. Eternity has a temporal quality, and thus can be rendered everlastingness. So, too, God's life has a temporal quality. History has meaning for God, and the temporal is an aspect of the divine experience. With the thought of everlastingness is implied the idea of permanence. God's ways are as of old (Hab. 3:6). He is the ancient God, the "ancient of days,"[4] and he is also the high and lofty One who sits enthroned forever (Isa. 57:15). His eternal being is described in terms of pre-existence (Ps. 90:2) and postexistence (Ps. 102:26 ff.). His

---

[2] For a discussion of this, consult Robinson, *op. cit.*, p. 113.

[3] Johannes Pedersen, *Israel*, I-II (London: Oxford University Press, 1926), p. 491.

[4] Genesis 21:33; Daniel 7:9, 13, 22.

unending being stands over against the time of the world, limited
as it is by creation and the Day of Jehovah.

So far, God's eternity might be described as time without
limits. Yet it is not subject to the ambiguities, transitoriness, and
frustrations of creaturely time. God's glory does not fade (Ps.
104:3), and his covenant love is unchanging (Ps. 103:17). His
word is unchanged forever, so that the will it expresses is contrasted with the transitoriness of nature (Isa. 40:8). God's life is
thus more than succession. There is an enduring unity which
binds succession in a whole. Eternity involves time and yet transcends it. God's Kingdom is the kingdom of *'olamim,* of indefinite
and unlimited periods of time (Ps. 145:13). The latter phrase is
an intensifying plural of majesty. God's eternity is not like the
'olam that may be predicated of earthly things. God's creative and
all-embracing permanence is the ground for all creaturely time.
He is the rock of *'olamim* (Isa. 26:4). His mode of being is far
different from our creatureliness, but our times are real to him.
He transcends them in his inner being, but their succession has
significance for the fulfillment of his purpose. He has life in himself. His eternity, his time, is his self-determined life, completely
unconditioned, the expression of his sovereign will in action. But
it is dynamic, not static, for he is the living God. Succession becomes meaningful to him.

Our times have meaning insofar as they are grounded in God's
eternity, just as our life is derived from him. So all our times of
opportunity and decision are significant because he gives them to
us. Hence the Hebrew piled up the plural *'olamim* in describing
God. Such a literary form of expression means little if taken
literally, but, taken poetically, it conveys the sense that time is,
in some way, an indication of the nature of God's life as dynamic
will and purpose, and yet that his life transcends our transience
and the ambiguities of our existence. By poetic insight we may
move beyond the temporal language and grasp something of that
whole which is the life of God, a whole which embraces our
created times and yet rises above their succession.

If the Age-to-Come has a life akin to that of God, then it will
not be a timeless existence. Equally it will not be filled with the

ambiguities and transitoriness that characterize our historical time in this order. This is exactly the kind of picture which the prophets endeavor to convey in their oracles. At the end of history stands a "time" that will be filled with God's presence, his kingly power in judgment and in mercy. The Day of Jehovah will usher in and mark the dawning of the new Age. Whether that be on this earth or a totally new order, it is no timeless realm such as mystics delight in, but a realm of bliss in which life, action, and time still have their place.

In the New Testament, too, time is considered from the point of view of content. The characteristic word for this is *kairos*. It stands for filled time, the time of decision with its opportunity for action. In its secular usage, it means a time especially propitious for some particular activity. It may be anticipated long before, even though its date is not fixed. Hence Cullmann[5] suggests that, in modern jargon, it is describable as D-day.[6] The general emphasis in the New Testament is theological, and the idea of the human determination of time fades into the background. God fixes the times and through them challenges men to a decision concerned with their salvation. Just as Old Testament history is gathered around special "times" of divine activity in judgment and in mercy, so the New Testament continues this thought in the doctrine that God's plan requires special *kairoi*. He determines these, and in them the meaning of history is actualized. It should be noted that the New Testament Greek has a word for abstract clock time, *chronos*. Thus both *Historie* and *Geschichte* have a place in its vocabulary.

The *kairos* of all *kairoi* is the time of Jesus. His is filled time in a unique sense. Jesus regarded it as filled full with God's sovereign presence, the messianic time fixed in the hope of the Old Testament saints, the time of the re-creation of Israel. In Jesus and his time, God's sovereign power is uniquely and savingly manifested. Peter can describe the prophets as searching what *kairos* or what manner of *kairos* the Spirit of Christ which was in them did point

---

[5] Cullmann, *Christ and Time*, p. 84.
[6] Such secular usage also occurs in Paul's interviews with Felix (Acts 24:25).

to, when it testified beforehand the sufferings of Christ, and the glories that should follow them (cf. 1 Peter 1:11). The New Testament, then, with unanimity regards the life of our Lord together with his death and resurrection as the supreme *kairos*.

Within this totality of duration, our Lord himself differentiated certain times as significant *kairoi*. He clearly regarded his passion as the culminating *kairos* of his earthly mission, and evidently believed that here his conflict with sin, evil, and death was brought to a decisive issue. The demons whom he cast out before this final triumph can ask: "Have you come here to torment us before the *kairos?*" (Matt. 8:29.) In preparation for the Last Supper, he declares that his *kairos* is now at hand (Matt. 26:18). In the agonizing of Gethsemane, he tells the sleep-filled disciples that his hour is at hand (Matt. 26:45). The Fourth Gospel is filled with like reference. The Evangelist reminds his readers that no man laid hands on Jesus because his hour was not yet come (John 7:6, 8). Later, we are told that Jesus acted as he did because his hour was come (John 13:1; 12:23; 17:1). The New Testament witness emphasizes the cross and resurrection as the advent of the Kingdom with power, the dawning of the Age-to-Come. The future age for which the prophets hoped had become a present reality in history.

But there is a radical transformation of thought here. In prophetic and postexilic eschatology, the Day of the Lord marked the end of history. The Christians believed that the Day was upon them, that the Age-to-Come had dawned, yet history went on. Into the midst of history the end had broken. Historical time with its decisions and opportunities still went on, and yet its true meaning had burst into it. The time was already fulfilled, and the inner and eternal significance of history was disclosed in historical garb. No longer had men to wait on the end, for the end, the *eschaton*, was actualized in the life, death, and resurrection of Jesus. Henceforth every succeeding "time" could be loaded with this fulfillment, with judgment and salvation, with the call to decision. The supreme *kairos* in Jesus Christ cast its shadow over, and became decisive in, all present *kairoi*.

Christians were able to discern the times aright, since they had recognized the supreme *kairos* in which their redemption was wrought. A Christian must indeed redeem the *kairos*,[7] that is to say, he must interpret every present *kairos* in terms of that supreme *kairos* which is the death and resurrection of the Lord. So he must find a place in the divine scheme of salvation for himself and his fellows. The supreme *kairos* is thus renewed in every Christian existence, and historical man is called upon to recognize and respond to its claims (Rom. 13:8-11). Because of what was done in Christ, the present era of history is potent with destiny.

Hence we have the emphasis on the "now." Paul can write: ". . . *now* is the acceptable *kairos* . . . *now* is the day of salvation" (2 Cor. 6:2). The "now" of the New Testament is filled time, while the "now" of the Old Testament is not. Every individual who comes to recognize this thereby passes decisively into God's "now," the present period of temporal existence in which men may taste the powers of the Age-to-Come. We are living in God's "today" in which the *kairos* of Jesus Christ is effective unto salvation. We dare not harden our hearts as Israel did in the wilderness, for we must hearken unto the voice of God (Heb. 3:7 ff.). "Now" is the period of the divine redemption. Actually the judgment of the last Day is on men now, its purging and sifting is at work, the salvation of the remnant is proceeding. The cross and resurrection mark the dawn of the coming Age, and the present period of history is in it.

The Day of the Lord is already casting its shadow upon the historical scene, and God is now making up the roll of his elect through the redemption wrought on Calvary and in the empty tomb. The New Testament clearly uses the phrase "last days" to refer to this period (Acts 2:17). Indeed, there seems a variety of usage at this point,[8] for the last time, the time of the end, began with the death and resurrection of Jesus Christ, and it will end in a series of last times (2 Tim. 3:1) that will usher in the last Day, the Day of the Son of Man, the *parousia*.

---

[7] Ephesians 5:6; Colossians 4:5.

[8] Cf. John Marsh, "Time," *A Theological Word Book of the Bible*, p. 265a.

All present *kairoi* are within this last time, God's "now." They
are constituted by the *kerygma*. In this the supreme *kairos* of the
death and resurrection becomes contemporaneous, and men are
either redeemed or judged by their response. God constitutes the
present as a *kairos* in which the unbeliever is confronted with the
gospel of salvation. Peter can remind his readers: "For the *kairos*
has come for judgment to begin with the household of God; and
if it begins with us, what will be the end of those who do not
obey the gospel of God?" (1 Peter 4:17.)

The Day is upon us, and the Age-to-Come has dawned. Here
we come to the use of the Greek word *aeon*, which is largely
synonymous with the Hebrew word *'olam*. Its major use in the
New Testament has a temporal reference. Like *'olam* it may describe both a limited and an unlimited period of time. In its
former use, our present historical era may be described as this
present evil *aeon*.[9] As such it stands in contrast to the coming
aeon, the Age-to-Come. The latter is a period which, if temporal,
is at least fixed at one end, namely where it conjoins this present
evil *aeon*, but it extends forward indefinitely into the future. The
two ages meet in the Day of the Lord, which marks the transition
from one to the other.

In the Jewish Apocalyptic of the first century A.D., for example
2 Esdras and Slavonic Enoch, we find this thought expressed in
parallel terminology. According to such apocalyptic thought, the
new *aeon* was to begin with the resurrection of the dead. The
Christian church declared that, with the resurrection of Jesus
Christ, this *aeon* had already begun. The resurrection of Christ
marks the beginning of the general resurrection. He is the first-
fruits from the dead (1 Cor. 15:20, 23). The descent of the Holy
Spirit was a sign that the last days were upon man (Acts 2:16-
17). Christians who were still living in this present evil *aeon*
were yet saved from it and had tasted the powers of the coming
aeon.[10] The "now" is the period when the ends of the *aeons* have
come together, that is to say, the *aeons* have overlapped. Man

[9] Ephesians 1:21; 2:2; Matthew 12:32.
[10] Galatians 1:4; Hebrews 6:5.

lives in the old *aeon*, but he may also, by faith, share in the life of the new.

For the later Jewish apocalyptists, the coming Age had been almost the negation as well as the end of history. The emphasis had often been so heightened that there had arisen a certain pessimism about history itself. The Age-to-Come was transcendent, eternal, supernatural. In the New Testament, it is the prophetic emphasis that shines uppermost. There is a radical transformation of both prophetic and postexilic eschatology, but the emphasis is on the value of the historical.

In declaring that the coming *aeon* had already begun in Christ while history still went on, the Christians became true heirs of the prophetic consciousness. History was not negated but fulfilled, and the movements of history found a new meaning and significance in the supervention of the Age-to-Come. The *end* of history, the meaning of all history, was "now" being actualized. The glorious consummation had supervened upon this present evil age, and so a new kind of historical tension had been created.

Christians live in the flesh still, but not after the flesh. They are in the world, but not of the world. They are in this present age, but they are also in heavenly places with Christ Jesus (Eph. 2:6). They must live soberly and godly in this present age because their devotion is to the other age (Titus 2:12). As Trocmé has finely put it: "Their life is thus a perpetual tension between a present which is potentially closed and a future which is already present."[11]

Although it has supervened on this present evil *aeon*, the coming *aeon* remains hidden, and its presence is known only to faith. To every man there comes a *kairos* of faith, a time of decision, when he may choose to live in the coming *aeon*, even while still living in this present evil *aeon*. In so doing a man differentiates between his present and his past. "At that time" becomes the mark of life in this present evil age prior to the *kairos* of faith. "Now" marks the life which, though still in this present evil age,

---

[11] E. Trocmé, "Time," *A Companion to the Bible,* p. 426.

is not of it, but belongs to the Age-to-Come. *At that time* we did the things of which we are *now* ashamed (Rom. 6:21). *Now* God has graciously made open to us the mystery which was hidden from the generations before the supreme *kairos*. Now we may experience "Christ in [us], the hope of glory" (Col. 1:27). Hence, we are living in God's "today" in which the *kairos* of Jesus Christ is effective unto salvation and in which we may by faith share in the life of the Age-to-Come. *Aeon* and its adjective *aeonios* can be used also to describe, like *'olam,* the eternity of the living God and of our Lord as the pre-existent and glorified Son. Hence the life of the Age-to-Come is, as in the late Jewish thought, akin to the life of God himself. Although history goes on, men may share in the life and powers of God's eternity. So for the Fourth Evangelist, eternal life, the life of the *aeons,* becomes a present possession by faith in Christ.

Because this experience is a hidden one, open only to faith, the New Testament has a futuristic emphasis in its eschatology. The *eschaton,* the end of history, has already come in Jesus Christ, and time has already been filled with eternity, yet the very hiddenness of the *eschaton* implies that this period of hiddenness must end in a final consummation when the full glory shall shine forth. *Then,* what is happening in the present period of history, when the *aeons* overlap and the powers of the coming *aeon* are at work in historical time, will be summed up and made plain. *Then,* the judgment that is already supervening upon men and the salvation that is already effective in their lives will be gathered up into a fully consummated eternal order, and history will be no more, for its purpose will have been accomplished. *Then,* the Christ, whose glory is known only to faith, will shine forth in his supernatural splendor, and the mists of history will be taken up into the clear atmosphere of the eternity of God.

In the Synoptic tradition, the Kingdom of God is a present reality in the person and works of our Lord, coming to a focus in his death and resurrection. It also has a future reference as the unclouded and unambiguous manifestation of the sovereignty of God. It is, in this sense, synonymous with the Age-to-Come. Outside the Synoptic tradition, this future significance is usually attached to the phrase.[12] Yet it is also a present reality for the New Testament witnesses, even though hidden. Some scholars differentiate its present reality by employing the phrase "Kingdom of Christ,"[13] but Cullmann acknowledges that such differentiation is not absolute.[14] Paul certainly refers to the present period as the Kingdom of the Son,[15] but he also speaks of the "Kingdom of Christ and God."[16] The Kingdom of Christ is simply the Kingdom of God expressed in the form of this world in which the two *aeons* overlap.[17] It emphasizes Christ because the divine sovereignty is now manifested in his redemptive activity through his Spirit. The Kingdom is both present and future, and already the end-time has begun, the Kingdom has supervened upon us, moving on its triumphant way to the full realization which is its unveiling in the *parousia*.[18]

So the New Testament writers look for a second advent, a *parousia*, the appearance of Christ in his glory, no longer hidden by the humility of the flesh and the ambiguities of our temporal experience. This final *kairos*, like the supreme and central *kairos* of Jesus Christ and all the *kairoi* of salvation history, is utterly under the control of God. Such *kairoi* are his own, and he alone knows and determines the day and the hour. Meantime, whether the *parousia* be remote or imminent, we are those who live by faith and in hope, waiting for that day when faith shall become sight, and when we shall enter into full possession of that inheritance of which already we have an earnest in the gift of the Holy

---

[12] Galatians 5:21; Ephesians 1:5; 1 Corinthians 6:9-10; 2 Thessalonians 1:5.

[13] E.g., Oscar Cullmann, "The Kingship of Christ and the Church in the New Testament," *The Early Church* (Philadelphia: The Westminster Press, 1956), pp. 105-140.

[14] *Ibid.*, pp. 115 f.

[15] Colossians 1:13; cf. 1 Corinthians 15:23-24.

[16] Ephesians 5:5; cf. Revelation 11:15.

[17] Cf. Schmidt *et al.*, "Basileia," Kittel's *Bible Key Words*, p. 37: ". . . there can be no question of the *basileia* of Christ being mentioned apart from God."

[18] Cf. Joachim Jeremias, *Jesus' Promise to the Nations* (Naperville: Alec R. Allenson, Inc., 1958), p. 75. He speaks of "an eschatology in process of realization."

Spirit. Even the Christ knows not this "time."[19] The Father has it in his own authority and fixes it according to the necessities of his saving purpose (Acts 1:7).

In our present experience of time we are painfully aware of the same tension as were the biblical writers. Our time is filled with transience, with pain, anxiety, and death. It is broken and separated time, in which the transient present alone has reality, separating on its razor edge the past from the future. The future is continually committing suicide upon that razor edge and tumbling into the realm of the "already become" with its irrevocability. Only in the present—the "now" of this flux of becoming—is decision possible, yet its pattern is the pattern of death. In some measure we are able to rise above this transience, to hold the past by memory and to anticipate the future in imagination, yet true and full integration eludes the natural man. He is the slave of *chronos*, of the deadly succession of the "nows," in which his hopes are frustrated and his pasts seem irrecoverable.

Yet his "now" and its decisions do open the way to true integration. It is here that his creatureliness is yet manifested as grounded in God's eternity. The decision of faith and the experience of being "in Christ" imply a process toward an integrated personality. Salvation means this. This integration involves our experience of time. In Christ the past is no longer irretrievably lost and inexorably gone. He gives the guilty conscience peace and transforms the past, turning the scars of sin into signs of grace. As A. A. Bowman has written concerning repentance: "We are . . . forced to the conclusion that something from the present spreads back over the past, transforming the latter with new and dynamically active meaning. . . . The call to repentance is an injunction to accept responsibility for our own past . . . and there is profound insight in the characteristically Christian notion that when we repent our past misdeeds, so far as *we* are concerned they are wiped away and undone. In other words, they are *transformed* as elements in the continuum of an experience which in-

---

[19] Mark 13:33; 1 Thessalonians 5:2.

cludes them along with the act of repentance."[20] Equally in Christ the future becomes knit with the present and is seen in the will of God. Anxiety is transformed into an unashamed hope because we already have the guarantee of our future inheritance. This inheritance does not reveal what we shall be, but we know that when Christ is made manifest, we shall be like him. Already we have Christ in us, the hope of glory.

If this is, in a pale and broken way, a reflection of life in the heavenly order, in the Age-to-Come, then the latter and God's eternity, too, are qualitatively different.[21] They have none of the quality of the broken and separated temporality which marks our sinful humanity. Our time, with its pattern of death, of before and after, with the fleeting transience of the present, is a pale indication of God's eternity. In its present manifestation the coming Age has to conform to this time form, yet already Christian experience shows how in Christ the ambiguities of this form are in part resolved and its borders broken down. In Christ we are delivered from death. We remain in this time form, but we have been delivered from *bondage* to it. A new experience of time has become ours, an experience that belongs to the Age-to-Come.

God's eternity involves both wholeness and succession. It is not the negation of time, and the succession of historical *kairoi* is significant for him. They relate our time to his time. The events in our time in which his purpose is actualized are also events in his eternity, his life. Their succession is meaningful to him as the completion of purpose. There is a temporal element in the references to God's intentions before the foundation of the

---

[20] A. A. Bowman, *A Sacramental Universe* (Princeton: Princeton University Press, 1939), p. 356.

[21] Cullmann (*Christ and Time, passim*) envisages the Age-to-Come in purely temporal terms and identifies eternity exclusively with unending time. In consequence eternity has no qualitative otherness and the Age-to-Come has not presently supervened in this present order but still lies in the future, being realized only proleptically. This attributes too naive a view to thinkers like Paul. Even apocalyptic speculation recognized a qualitative otherness in eternity (e.g., Slavonic Enoch). To understand the temporal images employed poetically rather than literally does not make the Age-to-Come and eternity timeless or deny the significance of time for eternity. More mature biblical thought should be understood at this level.

world.[22] We are concerned here not with a timeless eternity, but with an eternity not wholly other than our temporal experience. The ambiguous and disintegrated nature of the latter, its death-pattern, cannot belong to God's essential being. The succession of the *kairoi* and their unity in the fulfillment of purpose have their place in God's eternity. Their division—their separation into past, present, and future—cannot. In some way, God's eternity transcends succession, and does not negate it. It must involve a form of simultaneity that finds place for succession. The ambiguities of our succession are replaced by an interpenetration of past, present, and future. There is no past of God which does not possess his present and future, no present in which his past and future are not present. He is love, dynamic and moving, living from himself, ordering his own time or eternity. No static simultaneity suffices, and yet simultaneity is involved in the movement. It is life of this quality in which we come to share through Christ. Then, hidden in our broken time-form, we have the life of the Age-to-Come.

2. The Gift of the Spirit and the New Humanity

In the "now" God's purpose is being actualized in history. The turning point is the resurrection of Christ. Christ was raised for our sakes (Rom. 4:25). His resurrection affects us individually as radically as it affected his own corporeal earthly existence. In it the will of God is expressed redemptively for his creation. The resurrection spells the end of our sinful humanity and miraculously ushers men into a new and risen way of life.

In our world, death has been defeated decisively in Christ. Christ has triumphed over sin, but sin still appears to hold the world in thrall, and, because sin has a hold over us, so has death. The created order is a realm under the shadow of death, which casts its dark and seemingly triumphant form over the universe.

The Second Law of Thermodynamics is generally acknowledged by all scientists to be the regnant description of the ulti-

---

[22] *Ibid.*, pp. 70 ff. *Vide* especially 1 Peter 1:14-15; Revelation 18:8; Ephesians 3:4; 1:4-5.

mate outcome of that cosmos which science studies so diligently and which manifests such brilliant rational structure. Disorder and chaos will ultimately return to a universe which is called out of them by the divine fiat. Even our own sun is growing old and is in the initial stages of decay. Dissolution lies before us, a deep abyss in which all things will be swallowed up, and along with all things all our human history and achievements. As Karl Heim puts it, the universe is trembling before an "avalanche of death."[23] Individually we men too must perish and our works mold in the dust of the ages. What then has Christ done? If he has defeated death, where are the signs of his triumph? Inexorably mortality and corruption move on their seemingly victorious path.

The New Testament witness affirms that to stay this triumphant progress one man stepped forth in the power of God. Death failed to hold him in its thrall, and his resurrection deprived sin and mortality of their triumph. The tide was stemmed, and life moved forward to its ultimate victory.

The Christ could do this because he was man in a unique and all-embracing sense. He was representative man, so that his victory over sin and death was in principle the victory of all men. If, in the old humanity, death is regnant, in his new humanity all men are made alive (1 Cor. 15:21). Christ is a life-giving Spirit, for in him death has lost its sting. All who are descended from Adam are one with him by common descent. He is the first man and he is also every man, for he lives on in those who stem from him.

In Hebrew thought, the primeval time of the patriarchs was a whole that embraced all times. The most ancient past was also present, and events of the past were still effective in the living present. So all men, the many, were embodied in one man, Adam. They shared in the sin and death that entered the race in him.[24] Now a new man had come. In the resurrection a process of re-creation moved to completion. A change took place in human history, for the risen and victorious humanity was an incorporating humanity, a life-giving Spirit (1 Cor. 15:45). Christ embraces in

---

[23] Heim, *Jesus the World's Perfecter*, p. 175.
[24] Romans 5:12-21; cf. *supra*, p. 184.

himself all who by faith are united with him. They are now "in Christ," buried with him into his death and raised with him to newness of life (Rom. 6). They have put away the old man with its growing corruption and put on the new man created in righteousness (Eph. 4:22-24).

The Fourth Evangelist expresses the same thought in different imagery. His emphasis falls here more on the incarnation than on the resurrection.[25] Those who abide in Christ find that he and the Father abide in them, and this mutual indwelling means that they are perfected into one (John 14:23; 15:1-10; 17:23-24). A new humanity which is a unity of love appears among men.

This new humanity is the creation of the Spirit of Christ and is indwelt by his Spirit. In the New Testament the continuing work of the risen and exalted Lord is described as the activity of the Holy Spirit. He is at work in quickening power against the "avalanche of death" and the demonries of sin. The foretaste of our ultimate resurrection is the earnest (*arrabon*) of the Spirit (Rom. 8:23). It was through the Spirit that God effected the resurrection of Christ,[26] and he is now operative in the inner life of the believer (Eph. 3:16). Through the Spirit men may abide in Christ and Christ in them (John 14:20). He safeguards their orthodoxy (1 John 5:7) and guides them into the truth about Christ (John 14:26; 15:26; 16:13). Because of the presence of the Spirit, the inward man is being daily renewed against that avalanche of death in which the outward man is perishing (Rom. 7:14, 25).

Men are transformed by the Spirit into the image of the Lord, the new man, from glory to glory, so that the glory of the original creation is restored (2 Cor. 3:18). The Spirit is the Spirit of glory, and, as Christians participate in him, they share in the reproaches of Christ and are blessed indeed (1 Peter 4:14). In the Spirit, the end is already partially realized. Men have still to die, and the body is still subject to corruption, but already the risen life of Christ is at work in his Spirit. They have the gift of eternal life,

---

[25] Richardson, *An Introduction to the Theology of the New Testament*, p. 244.

[26] Romans 1:4; 1 Peter 3:18.

the life of the Age-to-Come, even though they still wait for the end, the raising of the body (John 6:39-40, 44, 54).

We need to remember that life is an eschatological concept in biblical thought. Like the glory of God, it belongs to the *eschaton*.[27] For John, the Spirit is the life-giver. The Christian has been reborn through the Spirit (John 3:5-8). This rebirth is something man cannot perform or even induce. The words of the Son effect the re-creation of life by the operation of the Spirit (John 6:63). The Spirit also imparts knowledge (John 14:26; 15:26; 16:13), but in imparting knowledge he imparts life (John 6:47). For knowledge means, as throughout the Bible, existential knowledge that arises in personal commitment. To know God in Jesus Christ is to be reconciled. It is to have the life of the coming Age. So the Spirit of truth is the Spirit of life. His function is revelatory, but, in being so, he is also redemptive and creative. He is indeed an eschatological reality. God's promise saw the advent of the Spirit as the sign that the last days had come upon men. Peter's sermon declares that the promise has been fulfilled (Acts 2). Man may now share in the life of the *eschaton*. So the resurrection and the operation of the risen Lord through his Spirit imply a new creation, effective in history.[28]

The resurrection and the gift of the Spirit created a fellowship of new men. The old creation had broken apart. Babel had been a sign and symbol of a broken humanity. Now a new humanity has been created in which the old divisions are no more. In this new creation there is neither circumcision nor uncircumcision (Gal. 6:15). Christ has made peace, uniting the divided humanity and creating in himself, of Jew and Greek, one new man (Eph. 2:11-16). All become one man in Christ Jesus, even male and female (Gal. 3:28). So the social and racial barriers are overridden by God's new creative act. By faith in Christ, men put on a new humanity in which Christ is all in all (Col. 3:10-11). As man and woman were created to be in the image of God and the image is a societary one, so the new man is a societary image of

---

[27] Cf. the intertestamental apocalypses for the same view in Jewish thought.

[28] 2 Corinthians 5:17; John 3:5-8.

God, a new whole in Christ. The Spirit of Christ is, indeed, a unifying presence. He creates fellowship, building men together and enabling them to transcend the separation caused by sin.

This separation is made more realistic by the body of flesh. But, in the end, the Spirit will so pervade all created things that fleshly matter will be replaced by glorified substance, akin to Christ's glorified body. Then full fellowship will be possible. Our bodily forms will not separate and hinder fellowship, but they will embody us in Christ, who will be all in all. In the meantime, the Spirit is creating such fellowship, though we are still in this present evil *aeon* and have fleshly bodies. The world remains divided. It cannot receive the Spirit, but within believers he is the *alter ego* of Jesus, continuing the presence of the historical Jesus with his disciples (John 14:14, 16-17). Through the Spirit, men are being made one in Christ, a fellowship (Phil. 2:1). As the church, they constitute a temple built together by God to be inhabited by his Spirit.[29] Just as the presence of the Spirit in the primitive church meant that the early Christians had all things in common (Acts 2:44-47), so there is still one body of believers because there is one Spirit (Eph. 4:3-4). Thus, in Christ a true sonship has become possible. We are adopted as sons into God's family. God places men in a relation to him in which they no longer need be afraid (Rom. 8:15). They are restored to the position occupied by Adam. God has sent forth his Spirit into their hearts, so that they are no longer slaves of the demonic powers, but sons.[30] The new humanity means that we have been adopted into the divine household as joint heirs with Christ (Rom. 8:12-17).

This present period of history forbids all mystic flight into the invisible order. The meaning of history is being actualized here and now. This is the significance of the resurrection. Just as the appearance of the risen Lord was only to believers, so the en-

---

[29] 1 Corinthians 3:16-17; Ephesians 2:22.

[30] Galatians 4:6-7. The true meaning is not that they are first sons and then receive the Spirit, but that they are sons because God sends his re-creating Spirit into their hearts. Verse 7 shows this. Verse 6 should read "that ye are sons (manifests that) God has sent the Spirit of his Son into your hearts."

counter with the risen Lord is hidden and mediated, and only to those with eyes to see is the truth made manifest. At the moment of his resurrection, had there been a public manifestation of the glorified Lord, there would have been enforced acknowledgment. The divine purpose of love in creating men with freedom to respond would have been defeated. The strategy of grace would have been replaced by one of overwhelming power. The resurrection and exaltation of Christ had to take place so that "his incognito before the world is not broken."[31] It is in this world that our destiny has to be worked out. Even though our order seems doomed to dissolution, it has been redeemed in Christ. Under its surface he is creating his new humanity. That, too, lives incognito. It is in the world and imprisoned in flesh. But it is not of the world and does not live "according to the flesh." Here we find our salvation, and wait still for our final redemption into the fullness of God's new order. But meantime, in history, God's new humanity, his fellowship of love, is being created.

3. The Church and the Reign of Christ

This brings us to a discussion of the new humanity as the "people of God," the church, and of its function in the world. The Greek word *ecclesia*, translated "church," must be understood in terms of its Septuagint usage. In ordinary Greek it is best rendered "gathering" or "assembly," meaning a popular assembly. But in Septuagint usage it was equivalent to the Hebrew word *qahal* which described Israel as the gathered people of God (e.g., Deut. 9:10). Thus, the Christian use of this concept conveys the idea that the new humanity in Christ claimed to be the true people of God, the heirs of Old Israel, the fulfillment of the promises, and the people of the new covenant.

Jesus, according to the Synoptic traditions, intended the church, although the word is used rarely. He chose twelve disciples as a sign that he intended to rebuild the twelve tribes of Israel. He may consciously have followed Isaiah's action in form-

---

[31] Heim, *op. cit.*, p. 161.

ing an inner group of disciples which should actualize the hope
of the righteous remnant of Israel. Our Lord's messianic consciousness would certainly imply a people over whom he should
rule. There can be no messianic shepherd without the sheep, and
it is significant that the disciples were addressed as "little flock"
and sent forth as "sheep."[32] Just prior to the crucifixion, our Lord
quotes the passage from Zechariah: "I will strike the shepherd,
and the sheep will be scattered." He continues by promising that,
after his resurrection, he will go before them, like a shepherd (so
the verb means), to Galilee.[33] The group thus formed proleptically would be reconstituted after his resurrection.

The theme of the New Israel of God is found throughout the
New Testament. It is used by Paul in developing his interpretation of history.[34] He offers a picture of the church as the true
Israel which includes both Jew and Gentile. The church can be
described as the sons of God—another Old Testament description
of Israel[35]—who have been released from bondage and can pray
"Father" (Gal. 4:6). From the beginning, faith in God has been
the determining factor, and now, by faith in Christ, Jews and
Gentiles alike may become the "children of Abraham," the sons
of God by adoption, members of the true Israel. They are blessed
with faithful Abraham (Gal. 3:9). In Old Israel a process of se-
lection was at work, for the visible Israel was not necessarily the
true Israel, the chosen of God. Thus, of Abraham's seed, Isaac but
not Ishmael, Jacob but not Esau, were chosen.

The old covenant presents a history of rejection because of
pride and disobedience. This continued until the Christ came,
and Paul employs rabbinical casuistry to argue that Christ is the
seed of the original promise. In him the rejection reaches its consummation. In his cross Israel stands rejected and yet marvelously
re-created by God's grace. The Christians have taken the place of
Old Israel. Elsewhere Paul can describe them as the circumcision
(Phil. 3:3). The physical practice which characterized the Jewish

---

[32] Luke 12:32; Matthew 10:16.
[33] Mark 14:27-28; cf. Zechariah 13:7.
[34] Galatians 3:7-16; Romans 9-11.
[35] Hosea 1:10; Deuteronomy 14:1.

people has been lifted to a spiritual level in the church. The Christians have been spiritually circumcised. They have put off the old man.

Images and expressions used to describe Israel in the old covenant can now be applied to the church in the new covenant. If Israel was God's vineyard,[36] or God's vine,[37] Christ can be described as the true vine and his disciples as the branches (John 15:1-5). He is clearly thought of as the Messiah, and the disciples are the people of God. Ezekiel pictures the end-time as one in which the Shepherd will gather his flock,[38] and the Fourth Gospel speaks of Christ as the Shepherd and his followers as the sheep (John 10:11 ff.). This image once more emphasizes the inclusiveness of the new people of God, for all, Jews and Gentiles, will be gathered in the one fold (John 10:16). Peter sees the church as the fulfillment of Hosea's hope; it is God's people.[39] He can describe the church as a people for God's own possession, a true Kingdom of priests[40]—expressions used of Israel also (Exod. 19: 4-6 [LXX]). The seer of Revelation echoes the picture when he portrays the church as a nation of priests consecrated to mediate between God and the world (Rev. 1:6; 5:10; 20:6).

The author of Hebrews transfers to the church the Old Testament images of "Mount Zion," the "heavenly Jerusalem," and the "city of the living God" (Heb. 12:22). All through his epistle there is the image of the church as the inheritor of the promises (Heb. 11). It is gathered around the perfect high priest and the perfect sacrifice, Jesus, in whom the sacrificial system of Old Israel is both abrogated and fulfilled. The church is the New Israel. Hence we can understand why the theme of a new Exodus dominates the Gospel of St. Matthew, with its new covenant and its new Law on the Mount. Paul, too, presents us with this picture of a new Exodus in which God has delivered and created a new

---

[36] Isaiah 3:14; 5:1-7; Jeremiah 12:10.

[37] Jeremiah 2:21; Ezekiel 15:1-6; 19:10-14.

[38] Ezekiel 34:1-19. The Shepherd, at first, appears as God himself; later he is identified with the messianic prince—34:23. Cf. Micah 5:4; Isaiah 40:4.

[39] 1 Peter 2:10; cf. Hosea 2:23.

[40] 1 Peter 2:9 ff.; cf. Titus 2:14.

people, who drink of the living water from Christ himself (1 Cor. 10:1-4).

In Paul's letters we find the word "church" in both the singular and the plural. This might invalidate our identification of the church with the unity of the New Israel. Careful consideration shows that in the singular the word refers to the whole body of Christians, whereas the plural refers to the local Christian community, sometimes just a home church. The idea of an inclusive people of God runs throughout the Apostle's usage. Moreover, the church is not just a summation of all the local communities. An organic picture is involved. The church is a whole which embraces all its local manifestations but is more than they.

The Hebrew organic view persists in the New Testament, and modern biology reinforces our understanding. Just as the principle of wholeness in a biological organism pervades and is regnant in every part, so the church in its wholeness is present in every local community of believers.[41] What can be said of the whole can be said of the parts embraced in the whole. Paul emphasizes this corporate unity of the local communities in phrases like "the whole church,"[42] "all the churches."[43] Even the local community bears the marks and characteristics of the people of God. The phrase "the church of God which is at Corinth"[44] is best rendered not "the Corinthian church" but "the church of God as present in Corinth." As A. G. Hebert has written: "The mystery which is 'Israel' is present in Corinth, having its local embodiment in the Christian community there, as it similarly has in other places where there are those who call on His name."[45]

Paul requires his readers to "give no offense to Jews or to Greeks or to the church of God" (1 Cor. 10:32), clearly regarding the church as a third race alongside the other two. Paul can also describe the church collectively as the "saints" (Col. 1:2, 26). As the church they are localized at Philippi, Colossae, Rome, and

---

[41] K. L. Schmidt, "The Church," *Bible Key Words,* p. 10.

[42] Romans 16:23; 1 Corinthians 14:23.

[43] Romans 16:4; 1 Corinthians 7:17; 14:33; 2 Corinthians 8:18; 11:28.

[44] 1 Corinthians 1:2; 2 Corinthians 1:1.

[45] A. G. Hebert, *The Throne of David* (London: Faber and Faber Limited, 1941), p. 230.

Jerusalem.[46] They are those to whom has been manifested the mystery of ". . . Christ in you, the hope of glory," so that they are those who partake of the inheritance of the saints who dwell in light (Col. 1:26-27). The phrase is clearly synonymous with "sons of God" and "Israel of God."

Paul is especially concerned with this mystical unity of the church. In Ephesians this one divinely created reality occupies the center of his thought, and here especially is the church described as the "body of Christ." The image is first used in Romans (12) and 1 Corinthians (12:4-11), and here it would seem to be applied to the local Christian community. The church is many and the church is one. Like the members of the human body, it has a diversity of gifts, yet it is one in Christ. Just as the organs of the human body constitute a co-ordinated whole, so the members of the church are mutually interrelated in Christ (Rom. 12:5).

In Colossians and Ephesians, the image is applied to the whole church. The risen and exalted Lord effects a new unity in a separated and disintegrating world. No matter what their race or tongue, their social status or political standing, their spiritual gifts and talents, Christians are built together in Christ into a co-ordinated whole. They are built into his body, where they are members one of another. To be in Christ is to be in his body, the church. To be united by faith to him is to be bound into the unity of his body and the fellowship of his society. The Christological and ecclesiological aspects of Christian thinking are bound together in this image. We are told that as the church is the body, so Christ is the head. Christ is the center of coherence of the universal church. He guarantees its oneness, for he is Lord over all distinctions of race, sex, learning, or social status.

Hebrew psychology helps us to understand Paul's use of the image. In Hebrew thought the body stands for the whole man and represents him.[47] In English idiom, the same thought is con-

---

[46] Philippians 1:1; Colossians 1:2; Romans 1:7; 1 Corinthians 16:1; cf. also 2 Corinthians 9:1, 12.

[47] Cf. L. S. Thornton, *The Common Life in the Body of Christ* (London: Dacre Press, 1950), p. 254.

veyed by the words "somebody" and "everybody." Hence Paul
is suggesting that Christ *is* the church. He is the head of the
church and he is the whole body, including in himself those members which constitute the parts of the body other than the head.
The body is one and so is Christ. He is both the One and the
many. He died in his body of flesh, and he was raised in a glorious spiritual body, a perfect humanity which he took to the
heavenly session. But Paul suggests that by his resurrection he
also gained a new body in the Spirit and in history, a body into
which he is incorporating those who have been raised with him.
L. S. Thornton would differentiate at this point between the glorious risen body of the Lord and the mystical body which is the
church. The redeemed order derives its meaning from the risen,
glorified Lord, and in history he is able "to impart the substance
of his risen life to us now in our present condition."[48] Hence Paul
speaks of the church as growing up in all things into the head,
from which, on the other hand, all growth proceeds (Eph. 4:15-
16).

In Hebrew idiom, "head" like "body" could represent the
whole personality. It dominated the body as a center of life, and
the separate organs of the body, in subordination to the head,
contributed to the whole personality. So Christ is the Saviour of
the body (Eph. 5:23), preserving it from harm, saving it from
the disintegration which sin would cause were it not for his grace.
As head he is the source of bodily growth, and Christians must
hold fast to the head.[49]

We can, using this figure, describe the church as the continuation of the incarnation. Yet we must remember that we are dealing with an image and must not give it ontological status. The
organic analogy can be pressed too far. J. A. T. Robinson[50] would
identify the church with the resurrection body of the Lord and
argue that the resurrection bodies of believers must be understood not individually but as inclusion in this resurrection body.
He does attempt in this way to safeguard the social and inclusive

---

[48] *Ibid.*, p. 302.
[49] Colossians 2:19. Cf. the Johannine figure of the vine and the branches.
[50] J. A. T. Robinson, *The Body* (London: SCM Press, 1952), pp. 81 ff.

aspect of redemption, but he majors too much on consistency in Paul's thought. The latter's Hebrew background would surely lead him to believe that the resurrection body was, in some sense, just as the physical body, a differentiating and individualizing medium by which communication and fellowship are possible. Our Lord's resurrection body showed such aspects in their perfection. Through the risen body of glory, the believer retains his individuality and yet can enter into full and perfect communion with his Lord and his fellows. The identification of the mystical body, the church, with the glorious resurrection body of Christ may lead to real theological difficulties.

It is noteworthy that, in Ephesians, the image of the bride is set alongside that of the body as a description of the church. We have Christ including the church as his body but the church also standing apart from him as his bride. As one with Christ the church is complete, yet apart from him it is in a process of growth and has a duty of obedience. If we absolutize the figure of the body at this point, we stress only one side of this paradoxical relation of Christ to his church. To speak of the church as the extension of the incarnation is a useful analogy, but it must not be made an ontological statement. The sinless nature of the incarnate Christ finds no replica in the checkered history of the church, and we have to ask whether the sufferings of the church can atone for the sins of men. To speak of the church ontologically as the continuation of the incarnation may endanger the historical once-for-allness of the work of the incarnate Lord.[51] This is the danger in forms of Roman Catholicism and is seen both in their understanding of the church as the body and in their interpretation of the Mass. The church is the fullness of Christ only eschatologically. The actual church is not Christ's perfected humanity, but it will become the perfect manhood of Christ eschatologically.[52] The "body" is a useful figure, but it is only one among many, and we absolutize it only by doing violence to the exegesis.

Over this body, the church, Christ reigns as head. If we ask

---

[51] Cf. E. H. Best, *One Body in Christ* (London: S.P.C.K., 1955), p. 197.
[52] Cf. Richardson, *op. cit.*, p. 256.

how Christ effects his reign in his church, the New Testament
employs the figures of the Word and the Spirit. The Holy Spirit
is the continuing presence of Jesus Christ in the midst of his
church. He is the subjective aspect of the reign of Christ, the fulfillment of the promise: "... lo, I am with you always, to the
close of the age" (Matt. 28:20). He is the presence of Christ in
the life of the fellowship, his immanence in the lives of his people.
He guides them without overriding their personality (Rom. 8:
14). He empowers them so that they can attempt tasks beyond
their natural powers.[53] He enlightens them so that they are led
into the truth.[54] It is his testimony within that assures them of
their membership in God's people (Rom. 8:16). He removes the
veil that covers men's hearts, interpreting the testimony of Scripture (2 Cor. 3:14-18).

Without such inner testimony, the preaching of the church
is vain. The Spirit always testifies not of himself but of Christ,
and makes the living Lord manifest under the written or spoken
words of the church's witness. Indeed the letter of the written
Scriptures is dead; it is the Spirit who makes alive (2 Cor. 3:6).
He produces in their lives his fruit in the supernatural virtues of
love, joy, peace, long-suffering, tenderness, goodness, meekness,
and self-control (Gal. 5:22). It is his presence in their hearts, his
travailing with them within, that makes true prayer possible
(Rom. 8:26-27). He prays with them and intercedes for them. So
the Christian shows that he is under the lordship of Christ by
walking in the Spirit (Gal. 5:26; cf. 5:18). It is the leading of the
indwelling Spirit that makes him manifestly a son of God (Rom.
8:9, 14).

It is this supernatural presence that creates men into a fellowship of love.[55] So Christ reigns over his church in love, binding
believers together by the bonds of love in his Spirit. There is a
communion in which reigns "... the unity of the Spirit in the
bond of peace" (Eph. 4:3). Christ, as the bond of peace (cf.

---

[53] 2 Timothy 1:7; 1 Corinthians 2:4.
[54] John 14:26; 16:13; Revelation 1:19.
[55] 2 Corinthians 13:14; Philippians 2:1-2.

Eph. 2:14), binds his members together in mutual concern and responsible love, nourishing his body through his Spirit.

Objectively Christ confronts his people in the Word. In the New Testament the Word stands for the preaching, the gospel or the *kerygma,* as well as describing the pre-existent Christ himself.[56] He who was before all things and the principle of their creation, who became flesh and pitched his tent among men, is identified with the message of the church. The preaching is in some sense the extension of the exalted Risen Lord into the midst of his people, and thus is akin to the Word of God through the prophets in the old covenant. In Hebrew thought, the Word was an event, and so in the New Testament, the preached Word is an event, an act of Christ, in and through which men confront the living and exalted Lord. When the Word is preached, a new situation is created for the hearers. Yet there has to be the subjective aspect, the moving of the Spirit in their hearts to convict and convince men of the truth which the proclamation offers (1 Cor. 2:4). "The preaching of the Church consists not so much in recalling and declaring the words of Jesus as in proclaiming Jesus himself. To preach the Word is to preach Jesus Christ."[57] As he is present as Lord in the preached Word, so he is present in the sacraments. In the Lord's Supper, in acted Word of broken bread and outpoured wine, men confront the Lord himself. The prophetic symbolism of the old covenant gives a key to this proclaiming of the Lord's death until he comes. In the Word and the sacraments the Christ reigns in his church.

There is a further aspect of the reign of Christ in his church. His saints reign with him. They are a Kingdom of priests (1 Peter 2:9-10), the fulfillment of the promise made at Sinai. They are sealed together with Christ at the right hand of God (Col. 3:1). This is an eschatological concept, and as always in the New Testament, it has both a future and a present aspect. The saints shall judge the world and judge the angels (1 Cor. 6:2-3), fulfilling the Danielic promise about the saints of the Most High.

---

[56] 1 Corinthians 1:18; 1 Peter 2:8; 2 Timothy 2:9; Revelation 1:9.
[57] J.-Ph. Ramseyer, "Word," *A Companion to the Bible,* p. 462.

If they suffer with Christ, they shall also reign with him (2 Tim. 2:11-12).

But this future hope is also a present reality. Already, all things belong to the saints, since they are Christ's and Christ is God's (1 Cor. 3:21). To the first man, Adam, was given the reign over the world as God's vicegerent. Now in the second man, Christ, men succeed where hitherto they had failed. They are free under God, free to rule the world and to judge the world. The Kingdom is theirs now and it is manifest in the quality of life which they possess. They will receive the crown of life (Rev. 2:10), but already they possess eternal life. They will reign in the life of the Age-to-Come with Christ, but already that quality of life is theirs (Rom. 5:17).

In Revelation the tension is held, despite the futurist emphasis. The saints *are* a Kingdom and they *shall* reign on this earth—the millennial idea (Rev. 5:10; 1:6). The future will, however, see the unveiling of their glory. He who overcomes shall share the throne with the victorious Lamb (Rev. 3:21). The image of the millennium is an attempt to preserve this truth as a goal of history.

Since the reign of the Christ is the reign of the Servant-Messiah, the kingship of his saints will be characterized by their capacity for service. They will be called on to make up what is lacking in the sufferings of Christ.

4. The Church in the World—The Mission to the Nations

The last thought brings us to the relation of salvation history to secular history in this present time. The true life of the church as the Kingdom of the saints, the people of God, and the rule of Christ in it are hidden and not openly manifest. How does the Kingdom operate in this present age? Cullmann[58] rightly sees that Christ's kingship—the divine sovereignty—is exercised both in the church and in the world, in two realms. We are concerned now with the divine lordship over secular history.

---

[58] Cullmann, *Christ and Time*, p. 188.

This is exercised first of all through the proclamation and testimony of the church. When our Lord sent forth the Twelve (Mark 6:7-13), he prefigured the task of the church. The Greek word for "sent forth" (*apostellein*) is the Septuagint rendering of the Hebrew *shaliach*. This verb in the Old Testament usage places its emphasis on the sender rather than on the person sent. The latter is the representative of the sender, an extension of the sender's person for the time being.[59] His presence is equivalent to that of the one whom he represents.[60] Actually the term *shaliach* is one of functon rather than status. Further, the *shaliach*, insofar as his function was religious, was confined in range to Jewry. He could not exercise missionary activity. In the same way, an apostle (Mark 6:30) is sent and commissioned by Christ for a special task, to proclaim the gospel. The Twelve share in their Lord's powers, even that of exorcism, and their mission is confined to the bounds of Israel.[61] They are to proclaim the advent of the Kingdom (Luke 10:9), and he who receives them receives Jesus.[62]

Let us look at Jesus' own mission as testified to in the Synoptic tradition.[63] He seems to have condemned Jewish proselytizing activity in a solitary utterance, condemning the Pharisees for compassing sea and land to make one proselyte.[64] Our Lord even suggests that such proselytizing corrupts Gentile converts and makes them more evil than in their pagan days. This is of one piece with Jesus' own instruction to his disciples. They, too, during his lifetime, were not to preach to non-Jews.

There are references to the preaching of the gospel to all nations (Mark 13:10; 14:9), but these seem to be eschatological and

---

[59] Cf. A. R. Johnson, *The One and the Many in the Israelite Conception of God* (Cardiff: University of Wales Press, 1942), p. 10.

[60] Cf. *The Mishnah*, Berakoth, V, 5—"He who is sent by a man is as he who sent him."

[61] Matthew 10:5-6. Jeremias notes that the saying occurs only in Matthew, is based on Aramaic tradition, and is definitely Palestinian—*op. cit.*, p. 20.

[62] Matthew 10:40 ff.; Luke 10:16. The Lucan sending of the Seventy is obviously a doublet of the sending of the Twelve in Luke 9:1 ff.

[63] We shall use here the arguments of Jeremias, *op. cit., passim.*

[64] Matthew 23:15. Jeremias regards this logion as Aramaic and authentic—*ibid.*, pp. 17 f.

future. Even Jesus himself seems to have limited his ministry to
Israel. Jeremias would dismiss any idea that rejection by the Jews
led our Lord to change his mind in the latter part of his ministry
and to go to the Gentiles.[65] The keynote for Jesus' whole ministry
was set by the early Aramaic logion: "I was sent only to the lost
sheep of the house of Israel."[66] The story of the Syrophoenician
woman (Mark 7:24 ff.) might contradict this, yet she is harshly
dealt with, and her request is granted only when she acknowledges the ordained division between God's people and the Gentiles. The incident of the centurion's servant (Matt. 8:5-13) likewise portrays a brusque refusal by Jesus and a yielding only on
the basis of the supplicant's faith. Jesus' visit to the district of
Tyre (Mark 7:24, 31) was no turning to the Gentiles because of
rejection by his own people. He never went beyond the bound-
aries of a Jewish population even here.[67]

Within this narrow context Jeremias elaborates three positive
aspects.[68] (1) Jesus removed the idea of vengeance and narrow
nationalism from the eschatological expectation. The note of hate
never appears.[69] (2) He promises the Gentiles a share in salvation. The Ninevites, the Queen of Sheba, the inhabitants of Tyre
and Sidon, Sodom and Gomorrah, will have part in the resurrection.[70] All nations are to stand before the throne of the Son of
Man (Matt. 25:31 ff.), and the repentant and believing Gentiles
are included among those who shall inherit the Kingdom. (3)
The redemptive activity and lordship of Jesus includes the Gentiles. Here Jeremias especially emphasizes the title Son of Man

---

[65] *Ibid.*, pp. 26 ff.

[66] Matthew 15:24. Jeremias notes that this was preserved in the tradition of a church dedicated to the Gentile mission, an indication of its authenticity.

[67] So Jeremias, *op. cit.*, pp. 32 ff. Jeremias notes that topographical considerations support his thesis, quotes Albrecht Alt in support, and argues
that Matthew introduces Gentile elements to support his own theological
position.

[68] *Ibid.*, pp. 40-54.

[69] E.g., Luke 10:25-37; 9:55 (when he condemns hate against the in-
hospitable Samaritans); 13:1-5 (Jesus shows no trace of hate but makes
the falling of the tower a summons to Israel to repent).

[70] Luke 11:31-32; 10:14; 10:12; Matthew 10:15.

and the central theme of the Servant. All nations are to serve the Son of Man, according to Daniel 7:13, while the Servant is to be a light to the nations (Isaiah 42:6; 49:6) and to sprinkle many nations (Isaiah 52:15). Yet in the former case the role is reversed. Jesus who serves the nations as Son of Man is also the Servant of the Lord.

Jeremias[71] finds the solution to the issue of a mission to the nations in the eschatological setting of our Lord's ministry. A noncritical assessment of the Old Testament passages which deal with the eschatological hope—and the men of our Lord's time would read them without taking account of critical procedures—makes central a pilgrimage of the nations to Zion to share in the messianic banquet and to worship at the world sanctuary. Further it always directs this movement to Zion. The divine epiphany will take place at the holy mountain and the Gentiles are not to be converted where they are. Thus, the nations are to share eschatologically in the promises to Israel and to be incorporated in the redeemed community. In the Matthean tradition Jesus' saying envisages the Gentiles participating in the messianic banquet in the place of those Jews who have refused.[72] The saying is evidently based on two Isaianic oracles (Isa. 49:12; 26:6-7), and the picture shows the Gentiles joining the true remnant of Old Israel, the patriarchs and prophets, in the glory of the Age-to-Come. The parable of the Sheep and the Goats (Matt. 25:31-32) likewise sees all nations gathered before the throne of the Son of Man, while we have the image of the new Temple in which all nations may worship.[73]

If Jeremias be right, and his case is well supported, our Lord drew a line between his own mission to Israel and the proclamation of the gospel to the nations, because the Kingdom had not yet come with power. His death and resurrection were to usher in the new Age. The ingathering of the Gentiles belonged to the

---

[71] Jeremias, *op. cit.*, pp. 57 ff. Cf. W. J. T. P. Phythian-Adams, *The Fulness of Israel* (London: Oxford University Press, 1938), pp. 178 ff.

[72] Matthew 8:11-12; cf. Luke 13:28.

[73] Mark 14:58; 12:10. The story of the cleansing of the Temple in Mark 11:17 involves a direct reference to Isaiah 56:7.

dawning of the last time and thus it must follow the lifting up of
the Son of Man. Only when he was so lifted up would he draw
all men unto him, as the Johannine tradition makes clear. In two
passages[74] there is a reference to the gospel being preached to
all the world, and in a third it is declared that the gospel must
first be preached to all nations before the end, the *parousia,* comes
(Mark 13:10). Clearly our Lord anticipated that in the end-time,
when the Kingdom had been manifested with power, there must
be a proclamation of the good news to all peoples.

Jeremias holds that for Jesus the preaching to the nations
meant an angelic proclamation. He interprets the passive usage
"the Gospel shall be preached to the whole world" as a circum-
locution to avoid the divine name. The preaching is an eschatological act of power, "the great final manifestation of God's free
grace."[75] Jeremias thus makes the ingathering of the Gentiles to
the messianic banquet at Jerusalem a transcendent act through
angels. His justification of the latter medium is somewhat lacking.
He seems to take away from our Lord any unique and peculiar
contribution, and would appear to suggest that Jesus' thinking
was conditioned and even determined by the Old Testament pattern. Yet surely our Lord, with his unique vision of a reconstituted people of God, could envisage the very strategy which his
church was to undertake. Was he so bound to an Old Testament
pattern?

Jeremias' interpretation is further influenced by his close association of the resurrection and the *parousia* in the thought of
Jesus.[76] Either the resurrection and the coming are identified or

---

[74] Matthew 24:14; Mark 14:9.

[75] Jeremias, *op. cit.,* p. 70.

[76] Cf. the comment of W. G. Kümmel, *Promise and Fulfilment,* p. 67
and n. 155. Jeremias seems to imply that the separation of the resurrection
and the *parousia* arose out of the eschatological outlook of the early church,
not in the mind of Jesus. Cf. his discussion of the effect of the delayed
parousia upon the early church's treatment of Jesus' parables—*The Parables
of Jesus* (London: SCM Press, 1954), pp. 38 ff. Jeremias holds that "Jesus
lives in the expectation of the great catastrophe, the final πειρασμός (Mk.
xiv, 48), the last crisis of history which his death will introduce"—*ibid.,* pp.
32 f. Cf. p. 44, where Jeremias states that for Jesus the incidence of the
final *peirasmos* "would be ushered in by his passion."

there is no appreciable lapse of time between them. Hence the eschatological act of the last days must be a transcendent act through angelic proclamation and not human agency. However true this may be of the Old Testament pattern, our Lord broke that pattern. It is by no means clear that, in his thought, the exaltation and the *parousia* are to be either identified or separated by only a small interval of time. The imminence of the *parousia* in Jesus' thinking could still leave room for his intention with regard to his church. Jeremias seems overly concerned with the realized eschatology of C. H. Dodd at this point. Yet he is prepared to admit that the early church did separate the *parousia* from the resurrection, and hence that the practical outcome of the thought of Jesus was the proclamation by the church itself. Surely if the church recognized that its own task was the proclamation of the gospel, it did so because this was in the intention of our Lord himself. Then the passages in Matthew 24:14, Mark 14:9, and Mark 13:10 take on a new meaning, for they provide the church's task with an eschatological motif.

The church stands between the dawning of the Kingdom with power in the cross and resurrection and its full consummation in the *parousia*. Further, the church's preaching is not just a demonstration that the Kingdom has come with power as Jeremias holds.[77] It is a precondition for the final glorious unveiling of the Kingdom. The Gentiles must be gathered in before the Lord comes in glory. Until Christ rose from the dead, Jonah stayed in the belly of the great fish and Israel was prevented from its missionary task. Now the new Age has dawned, the end-time is upon us, the reign of Christ has begun, and the grace of God has become available to all nations. The vicarious death and triumphant resurrection of the Lord were an act of service to the Gentiles. But the church's proclamation does more than demonstrate that this has happened. The full consummation cannot be made manifest until all nations have heard the good news. Cullmann brings

---

[77] Cf. Jeremias, *Jesus' Promise to the Nations*, p. 75: *"The missionary task is a part of the divine fulfillment,* a divine factual demonstration of the exaltation of the Son of Man, *an eschatology in process of realization"* (cf. *The Parables of Jesus*, p. 159).

this out very forcibly. The end is already being realized in history, and we agree with Jeremias when he speaks of "eschatology in process of realization." Yet the full realization waits on the accomplishment of the world mission.

This is the theme of Paul in Romans 9-11, in many ways a commentary on Mark 13:10: "The gospel must first be preached to all nations." In Romans 10, Paul contends that God is following an exact plan. There must be offered to all an opportunity to hear the gospel (Rom. 10:14). The Jews have already heard it, but not all have received it. Therefore the call now goes to the Gentiles, before finally, at the end, the Jews do enter. For Paul, who is called especially to preach the gospel to the Gentiles before the present time ceases in the *parousia,* this is all in God's purpose. The full plan is surrounded with mystery, but within that mystery he clearly sees his own calling as apostle to the Gentiles (Rom. 11:13). Elsewhere he underlines the bond between his own apostolate and the mystery of the divine economy (Col. 1:22-29). He is an element in the working out of the mystery among the Gentiles and thus in the final consummation. So, also, Paul feels compelled to preach the gospel (1 Cor. 9:16) and declares that he is a prisoner of Christ for the Gentiles (Eph. 3:1). The time is short. The last time is upon us and the *parousia* is near. But Paul and his fellows are ambassadors for Christ, standing in his stead, and pleading with men that they be reconciled to God (2 Cor. 5:20). For the full number of the Gentiles must be made up (Rom. 11).

This understanding of Paul is supported by Johannes Munck in his study of the Apostle.[78] Munck contends that concern for the Gentiles dominated the early church. He finds two parties— a group gathered around the twelve apostles which stayed in

---

[78] Johannes Munck, *Paul and the Salvation of Mankind* (Richmond: John Knox Press, 1959), *passim.* Munck shows convincingly that the Hegelian influence of the Tübingen school underlies the customary view of the early church as developing two factions—a conservative party of Jewish Christians regarding the Law as obligatory; a liberal party of Hellenizing Jews, concerned with a Gentile mission and not holding the Law mandatory for Gentiles. Paul and a law-free gospel should not be set over against Peter and Jewish Christianity.

Jerusalem and a group gathered around Paul which was actively engaged in work among the Gentiles. He holds that these two parties are not to be differentiated by their view of the relation of the Law to non-Jews. Neither held the Mosaic commandments to be obligatory for Gentile converts and both held them binding on Jewish Christians. Their difference lay in the attitude to the mission task. The Jerusalem party held that the time was not yet ripe for the mission to the Gentiles. They were waiting for the acceptance of the gospel by Israel. The Pauline group went out on a Gentile mission because they hoped that, by so doing, Israel would be stirred to envy and would accept Christ. Munck holds that Paul believed that his mission to the Gentiles was a necessary stage in *the ushering in* of the Kingdom. This savors too much of futuristic eschatology. The last time *is* upon us, and the Kingdom has dawned, to be partially realized in the historical scene. Yet the *parousia* does lie ahead, and the duration of the end-time would seem to turn upon the kind of thesis that Munck has developed. Did Paul see what the others did not? The vacillation of Peter may indicate a growing conviction that Paul was right, and that only by taking the gospel to the Gentiles would all Israel be saved. There are many weaknesses in Munck's position,[79] but we do not have to accept it in its totality in order to adopt some of its insights. The Law may have played a larger part in the relationship of the groups, but the real issue between them may well have been not so much a matter of principle as a matter of timing.

Cullmann supports the idea that the *parousia* waited upon the preaching to the nations. "You shall be witnesses" is an imperative, not an indicative. God takes the initiative in the cross and the resurrection, and through his messengers he now offers his gospel to the world before the end. "In this work the apostles

---

[79] He does not always deal trenchantly with the framework of Acts as later did Conzelmann in *The Theology of St. Luke.* He dismisses it as secondary in authority compared with Paul's letters, and yet uses it at other times uncritically. He does violence to the material in seeking to uphold his view of the legalistic issue. It is not clear that this issue played no part in the relationship of Paul to the Jerusalem church. Munck believes that the Judaizers who attacked Paul in Galatia were Gentiles who wanted to make the Law and circumcision binding.

are only the executive instruments of the eschatological plan of salvation."[80] Cullmann offers the suggestion that the phrases "that which restrains" and "he who restrains" in 2 Thessalonians 2:6-7 should be understood in this connection.[81] "That which restrains" the final manifestation of lawlessness and the advent of the Day is the mission preaching of the end-time. "He who restrains" is Paul himself with his lofty consciousness of mission. We shall discuss this in detail later.

As the *parousia* was delayed, it would seem that the eschatological motif dropped into the background. Luke portrays the mission to the nations as a developing plan. It moves in concentric circles from Jerusalem. Conzelmann[82] makes much of the place of Jerusalem in Luke's thought. It was the city of revelation. Here the passion and resurrection had taken place. But the city lost its place in redemptive history by Jewish unbelief and the killing of Jesus. Its destruction by the Romans prior to Luke's writing his Gospel completed the picture. "As far as the Christian hope is concerned, the city has forfeited its function by its own conduct."[83] Jerusalem no longer had a redemptive function, and Luke regards the Jerusalem church as of little account. Now the Law and the Temple are left behind, and the thought of a mission to the Jews has disappeared. Munck suggests that this viewpoint characterized the subapostolic age. As he puts it, the later Gentile church "has no idea that the salvation of the Gentiles is connected with the salvation of Israel before Christ's coming in glory."[84] The movement is now from Jerusalem to Rome and so to the ends of the earth.

Even so the church's missionary task is part of the final fulfillment. Its preaching is God's act through the testimony of his people. The nations are now being invited to the eschatological feast by God's gracious activity in Christ and in the Spirit through the church. This "now," this "end-time," is the period of grace for

[80] Cullmann, *Christ and Time*, p. 162.

[81] *Ibid.*, pp. 164 ff.

[82] Conzelmann, *op. cit.*, pp. 132 ff.

[83] *Ibid.*, p. 134.

[84] Munck, *op. cit.*, p. 276. Munck's argument would be both strengthened and amended had Conzelmann's work been available.

the nations. The church by its preaching has the last word to the sons of frail humanity.[85] Men are judged or saved by their attitude to this proclamation. Their sins are remitted or retained according to their acceptance or spurning of the church's message.[86] "The Church is apostolic because she is called . . . to go and make disciples of the nations."[87]

5. The Church in the World—The State and the Cosmic Powers

But the church not only preaches to the nations. It is also called upon to make known the mystery of God to the cosmic powers (Eph. 3:10). It is indeed to judge the angels (1 Cor. 6:3). At once we come to the relation of the church and of the Kingdom of God as manifested in the Day of the Lord to the powers of the state and the structure of the common life.[88]

In the Septuagint version of the early song of Moses (Deut. 32:8 [LXX]), we read that when God divided up the nations and chose Israel, he fixed the number of the people on the basis of the "sons of God," the angelic hosts. Thus Jehovah himself accepted direct responsibility for Israel, but entrusted the others to angelic guardians. This meant that the fortunes of a nation were bound up with the angelic powers to whose mediating rule it was entrusted. This theme occurs also in the book of Daniel (Dan. 10: 13, 20-21; 12:1) and the book of Enoch (1 Enoch 89:59-60), both of which picture the angelic princes of the nations withstanding the living God. In Daniel, the archangel Michael stands forth as God's champion against the angels of the nations that oppose Israel.

---

[85] Cf. R. H. Strachan, *The Fourth Gospel* (London: SCM Press, 1941), p. 329.

[86] John 20:22-23. John gives no hint of Paul's hope but indulges in a polemic against the Jews.

[87] T. W. Manson, *The Church's Ministry* (London: Hodder & Stoughton Limited, 1948), p. 52.

[88] *Vide* especially Cullmann, "The Kingship of Christ and the Church," *The Early Church*, pp. 120 ff.; *Christ and Time*, pp. 190-210; *The Christology of the New Testament*, pp. 230 f.; *The State in the New Testament* (New York: Charles Scribner's Sons, 1956), pp. 50-114.

In Enoch there are, as per conventional usage, seventy angels of the nations. These are permitted within limits to exercise God's judgment on Israel, pictured as sheep. The apocalyptic setting is that of a nation in distress and under foreign domination. In looking to God for deliverance, it traces its undeserved persecution to the rebellious angels of the nations. Thus the conflict on earth becomes also a rebellion in heaven, a theme that openly recurs in the Apocalypse of John, but that is evident also in Paul's thought of principalities and powers and spiritual rulers of the darkness in high places.

We must link Paul's belief in the cross as a triumph over demonic powers with the current idea of the angels of the nations and their states. Our interpretation of 1 Corinthians 2:8 confirms that the rulers of this world who crucified the Lord of glory were the demons. We may interpret the rulers as both earthly rulers and cosmic demonic powers. The political powers of our Lord's day and the demons that guided and possessed them became involved in the attempt to defeat Christ and were themselves judged and defeated. As Cullmann has written: "By 'the rulers of this age' Paul manifestly means *both* the invisible 'princes of this world,' who are often mentioned as such, and their actual human instruments, Herod and Pilate."[89]

In another passage in 1 Corinthians, Paul discusses the issue of the Corinthian Christians settling their disputes in the law courts on the ground that the law courts are under control of the angels of the nations on whom one day the church itself will sit in judgment (1 Cor. 6:1 ff.). The emphasis, at first sight, appears to fall on the magistrates, but the additional statement about the judging of the angels indicates that the Apostle's attitude is de-

---

[89] Cullmann, *Christ and Time*, p. 190. In a definitive discussion of the whole position, Clinton D. Morrison, in *The Powers That Be* (Naperville: Alec R. Allenson, Inc., 1960), pp. 23 f., points out that Cullmann's position is also held by Günther Dehn in "Engel und Obrigkeit," *Theologische Aufsätze, Karl Barth zum 50. Geburtstag*, ed. by Ernst Wolf (München: Chr. Kaiser Verlag, 1936), p. 104. Dehn like Cullmann disagrees with the exegesis of Dibelius who interprets "the rulers of this world" purely as spiritual powers. He believes that there is in this passage a coincidence of heavenly and earthly activity—Pilate, the high priests, and the angelic powers were all involved.

termined by the relation of the state and its legal system to the angelic powers. Paul justifies his warning against the church members' taking court action by the fact that the church is sitting in heavenly places with Christ Jesus and will judge the world powers in the final consummation.

This passage leads immediately to a more controversial one in the Letter to the Romans—Romans 13:1 ff., in which Paul enjoins his readers not to resist the powers since they are ordained of God. There is considerable debate among scholars as to what interpretation should be given to the word "powers" in this context. The traditional interpretation identified it with the earthly authority of the state and its representative magistrate, and this has been supported by many modern scholars on diverse grounds.[90] Perhaps the most recent is Karl Barth who originally agreed with the identification of the "powers" in Romans 13:1 with the angelic and demonic rulers.[91] More recently[92] he would contend that there are three interdependent yet distinct usages of the word. First, and here he cites Romans 13:1 and Titus 3:1 as examples, the word refers to the power of the state itself as ordained by God and accepted by men. Second, and here he cites Colossians 1:16, 2:10, Ephesians 1:21, 3:10, and 1 Peter 3:22, it refers to the spiritual powers which provide the background for human powers, including the state. These powers are created and ordained by God, and are servants under his rule fulfilling his purpose in Jesus Christ. Third, as in Colossians 2:15 and Ephesians 6:12, it has reference to demonic powers which imitate and usurp the place of the spiritual powers and challenge their authority in the world. Now Paul is not a systematic thinker, but we need to remember the contemporary Jewish background of the Apostle's thought, which did accept the doctrine of the angels of the nations under whom earthly authority was administered. Perhaps more serious is Barth's preoccupation with his distinctive

---

[90] Morrison gives a careful and searching analysis of these points of view —*op. cit.*, pp. 40-54.

[91] Karl Barth, *Rechtfertigung und Recht* (Zollikon-Zurich: Evangelischer Buchhandlung, 1938).

[92] Karl Barth, *Die Kirchliche Dogmatik*, III, 3 (Zollikon-Zurich: Verlag der Evangelischen Buchhandlung, 1950).

and weird doctrine of the Nihil or the Nothing, which is the
ground for Satan and the demons. He does not believe that an
angelic being can fall, and so takes refuge in a speculative doctrine which involves him in far more eisegesis than exegesis.

In determining what Paul meant, we have to consider the
state of mind of his readers who were not Jewish. It is argued
that Roman readers who were Gentile in outlook would not understand Paul's use of the word in the sense of angelic powers.
But actually this background was common to Jew, pagan, and
Christian.[93] The Graeco-Roman concept of the state in the cosmos
also held to a divine ordering of the authority of the state. The
Graeco-Roman world did believe that the emperor was under the
guardianship of a *daimon*. There was indeed a popular *Weltan-
schauung* compounded of astrological teaching, a widespread, if
nebulous, monotheism, and this belief in guardian powers and
daimons. The last constituent was the most significant. *Daimons*
were thought to exercise guardianship over individuals and over
states and their rulers. Pagans like Porphyry and Christians like
Origen both held such a view.[94] Thus, there seems agreement between pagan and Christian as to the character of the world structure but not as to its theological content. As Morrison says: "Their
differences are almost exclusively theological; the Christian Gospel has never been based on a particular cosmology, but was proclaimed as intelligible to the accepted views of its own age."[95]

We shall not, therefore, assume that Paul used "powers" only
in a secular political sense in Romans 13:1 ff. His own Jewish and
Christian outlook has a counterpart in popular Hellenistic ideas.
His readers would understand that he meant more than emperor
and magistrates and that he was referring also to the spiritual
forces which operated behind them. Paul's references apply both
to the invisible powers and to the civil authorities, and we do not
understand the full implication of his utterances without this
double reference. What matters, moreover, is not Paul's back-

---

[93] *Vide* Morrison, *op. cit.*, pp. 63-101.
[94] Cf. *ibid.*, pp. 83-87. We have not space to examine the position or
authorities in detail, and refer the reader to this monograph.
[95] *Ibid.*, p. 87.

ground in Jewish and Hellenistic thought, but the use to which he puts it in drawing out the implications of his Christian faith.

On this basis, Cullmann and others contend for a Christological foundation for the state. Christ's rule over the state is determined, like that over the church, by his triumph on the cross. His lifting up on the cross, which initiated his lifting up onto the heavenly throne, gave him the victory over the cosmic powers and ensured that their rebellious activity must be subservient to his authority. If the cross was cosmic in its sweep and the state is regarded as possessing a background of cosmic powers, then Romans 13:1-7 must be interpreted in terms of Paul's understanding of the victory of Christ over the demons.

There is also another Christological facet to the understanding of the world powers. The New Testament understands the preincarnate Son, the pre-existent Word, as the agent of creation. Paul can therefore assure us that all things were created in him, including the things in the heavens, the things invisible, which the Apostle proceeds to define as the heavenly powers (Col. 1: 16). Clearly then (*vide* Barth's interpretation *supra*) the heavenly powers shared in the original goodness of God's creation and, like all creation, are dependent upon the Son for their authority. What he did on the cross was therefore to deal with his rebellious creation at the cosmic level and assert his control over "all things" created in him. Thereby he became the head of all principalities and powers (Col. 2:10), and thus invisibly of all earthly states. He is head of the state as he is head of the church, except that in one case his headship is hidden and unacknowledged, whereas in the other case it is manifest and acknowledged.

This does not involve a condemnation of civil power as such. The cosmic background of the state is also a divine creation, and the cosmic angels of the nations are servants of the divine will. This is evident in the Old Testament picture of God as surrounded by the heavenly council, the sons of God who are the angels or gods of the nations. That they should become demonic and rebel against God does not, for Paul, do away with the divine control. The state and the Law still serve God. The angelic powers serve God in being, along with their civil and earthly counterparts, the instruments of his redemptive plan. They play their part in the drama of redemption[96] and they also serve God's purpose in this period when the ages overlap. They serve the task of restraining evil, preserving order, and making the church's proclamation possible. The gospel can be preached and received because the powers that be serve God in maintaining peace and some measure of social justice.

God's control over the powers of the cosmos and their instrumental civil authorities was re-established through the cross. They acted there in ignorance, and brought about their own defeat. Because of Christ's triumph they now unwittingly serve God's plan. The idea of a Christian state is, indeed, a contradiction. In the consummated Kingdom of God such authority will be abolished and God will be all-in-all. In God's "now" the state unwittingly serves the gospel, even though it does not acknowledge the gospel. It does to some degree see its duty to act justly and to serve its place in God's plan. Yet it is still a manifestation of rebellious powers.

Despite this victory of Christ over the cosmic powers and their earthly instruments, the latter do not manifestly exhibit signs of his triumph. They remain rebellious, even though they maintain order. They serve God in spite of themselves. Indeed, the state and its guardian powers have pretensions to power and rebellious inclinations which may become demonic. They may become the "beast," envisioned by the seer of Revelation. They may persecute the church, even while they make its proclamation possible. An unleashing of the demonic power is still possible. We need to remember that Christ's triumph on the cross is a decisive triumph, a once-for-all victory, but that it does not immediately issue in the abolition of rebellion at the human or cosmic level. As John saw, the powers of this world are passing away, but they still are a power to reckon with. Something of this insight lingers in the Apocalypse, where the demonic powers are pictured as bound and yet released to exercise a catastrophic final bid for power ere the final consummation. This is thoroughly apocalyptic, but it preserves a real insight.

[96] Acts 4:25 ff.; cf. 1 Corinthians 2:8.

In the present period, the triumph of the cross marks the commencement of a movement toward the actualization of the divine meaning in history. This occurs in the life of the church and will be consummated in the *parousia*. The outcome is sure because the decisive battle has been fought on Calvary. This latter was a manifestation of the Kingdom with power and the dawn of the Age-to-Come, yet the present age remains so that the actualization of the meaning of all history may proceed in the life of the church. The present is a process of realization in which the triumph of the cross is actualized in the church as the people of God, the true Israel. Hence we have the unusual tension of this "now." The cosmic powers have been subjected;[97] they will be subjected[98]—just as the end has come and will come. Between the cross and the *parousia*, the cosmic powers serve their purpose and yet still exercise their rebellion.

Insofar as the cosmic powers and their earthly counterparts serve God's purpose and maintain law and order, the Christian must acknowledge their authority under God. To pay to the state its taxes and dues (Rom. 13:7), to honor its officers (Rom. 13:7; 1 Peter 2:17), to pray for its welfare (1 Tim. 2:1 ff.), are Christian responsibilities; the writer of 1 Timothy notes that such prayer is made that the state ensure a tranquil and quiet life. The state plays its part in God's plan of redemption, and must be honored as so doing.

When the state's demonic nature comes uppermost and it becomes beastlike the Christian must refuse acknowledgment, for he serves the Lord Christ. Yet normally he may serve Christ in acknowledging the authority of the state and its guardian powers, which also unwittingly serve God. As Cullmann puts it: "The Christian attitude is perfectly clear, the most loyal subjection to the State as such, granting it everything that is its due and which it needs for its existence and security, but relentless opposition once it deifies itself."[99] Thus, for the author of the Apocalypse, the state's claims for the imperial cult and the worship of Caesar,

---

[97] Colossians 1:16 ff.; 2:15; Philippians 2:10; 1 Peter 3:22.
[98] 1 Corinthians 15:24-25; Acts 10:13.
[99] Cullmann, *The Early Church*, p. 122.

its manifestation as the beast, call down the wrath of the Lamb. The saints resist and become martyrs. When the state leaves the area that is Caesar's and penetrates into the area of overlordship which belongs to Christ alone, the attitude of the Christian is unequivocally determined. Only Christ is Lord. The Christian must obey God rather than men and suffer in so doing (Acts 5:29).

The state cannot finally free itself from subjection to Christ, in whom its angelic guardian was created and through whom the rebellion of both has been dealt with. Indeed, the Christian is more sensitive to the injustice and demonic pretensions of the state than the non-Christian. For his conscience, educated in Christ, assures him when the state oversteps its limits and infringes on the prerogatives of its overlord, Christ himself. Because he knows that Christ is Lord even of the state, he has to rebel and oppose infringement on such lordship. Normally the state exists to enable the church, the area of Christ's visible rule, to lead a tranquil and peaceable life.

The triumph of Christ is thus brought to a focus in his church. The Christians, too, have conquered the cosmic powers. They sit with Christ in heavenly places far above principalities and powers.[100] They have come to fullness of life in him who is the head of such powers (Col. 2:10), and they have died with Christ to the demons (Col. 2:20). Hence they are more than conquerors (Rom. 8). The Christians stand in grace and freedom, their life hid with Christ in God. They serve the state as a service to God, acknowledge its restraining power, and pray for its welfare. But they do not fear it, for they rule it invisibly. Its power of death, its persecution, its demonic manifestation, can have no final influence in their life. Indeed, the church judges the cosmic powers and their earthly instruments, while acknowledging their earthly assistance to the progress of its mission. In persecuting the church instead of providing a framework of order, the state spells its own doom. The blood of the martyrs cries to heaven and the beast is headed for final destruction. This is the theme of the Apocalypse,

---

[100] Ephesians 2:5-6; Colossians 3:1-3.

which has the same picture of the cosmic guardians of the nations and of cosmic rebellion and conflict.[101]

The same idea underlies the apparently contradictory injunctions of Paul—Christians are to be loyal to the state (Rom. 13:1 ff.), but they are not to use its law courts to settle their own disputes (1 Cor. 6:1 ff.). In the church Christ is Lord, and here the power of the state reaches its limits. The Christian can settle his disputes in the fellowship of the church and under the procedures of ecclesiastical justice. Yet in so doing he does not weaken the state's influence, for the justice of Christ should be more fully manifested in the church. Further, it does not threaten the state's existence. As Cullmann points out, the Christian and the church cannot "take over the other affairs of the State."[102] The life and existence of the church as the manifest area of Christ's lordship sets limits to the powers of the state and the guardian powers of the nations over which his lordship is hidden. That the latter may still become demonic in no way denies the triumph of the cross. It belongs to the period in which God has granted a measure of freedom, even to the cosmic powers, so that his purpose in history may be actualized through the identification of his church with Christ's triumph.

Morrison makes the point[103] that the New Testament Christian submits to the governing powers of the state as a man of faith. He does it in Christ. Hence his relationship to the state and its obligations is at a deeper level than that of unredeemed man. He has been released from the demons, and hence his acknowledgment of the authorities must be that of one who is committed to the exalted Christ. He must not fall under the domination of the guardian powers and thus be subject to the rulers, as if Christ had not set him free.

If a man is in Christ, he is committed to the proclamation of the gospel to all peoples. But the whole cosmic order was created in Christ and subjected in him to the same end. Hence to believe in Christ means to support that world order which also supports

---

[101] Cf. Cullmann, *The State in the New Testament*, pp. 72 ff.
[102] *Ibid.*, p. 61.
[103] Morrison, *op. cit.*, p. 123.

the end for which the cosmos existed. Obedience to the guardian powers means co-operation with them in a common end which they serve in their own way. Such obedience is a matter of conscience and not a way of avoiding trouble.[104]

A man must examine his conscience in Christ to determine the point at which for him loyalty to the state conflicts with loyalty to the Lord. The Christian is more sensitive to injustice and tyranny than the non-Christian. His conscience is sensitized, by faith, to Christ's lordship over the state. Where the policies and demands of the state will no longer support the church's mission under Christ, the church rebels. Until then the two co-operate. Indeed they are mutually complementary. God's purpose is actualized in this end-time in the church, because the state provides a framework of order. To obey the state is indeed a real, even if lower, manifestation of that love which Christ came to actualize among men as the bond of the people of God. For obedience helps an order which makes for the welfare of all, independent of their deeper reconciliation to God.

---

[104] *Ibid.*, p. 125.

CHAPTER VII

SALVATION HISTORY—THE PAROUSIA AND THE CONSUMMATION

The biblical understanding of history ends as it begins in historical image, in symbolism and poetry, for this is the only way in which the impingement of the invisible upon the visible, in origin and in termination, can be pictured. The end means the taking up of our creaturely, historical time into God's time with its quality of eternity. We can express such an event only in symbolic form. Parabolic pictures, not abstract concepts, will best express it. This is the viewpoint of the New Testament, which already, in the Old Testament eschatology, had a wealth of imagery on which to draw. The fact that such imagery was historicized in our Lord himself, both in his own teaching and in the *kerygma* of the early church about him, made it natural that the imagery should be applied also to the final consummation.

1. Jesus and Apocalypticism

The sayings of Jesus about the *parousia* of the Son of Man, when examined by the form and source critical techniques, cannot be easily dismissed. As we have already argued, these may not be dismissed as unauthentic because they reflect the primitive *kerygma*. We must now examine them and seek some kind of pattern among them.

Let us commence with the so-called little apocalypse of Mark 13. This is a gathering of sayings with a seemingly apocalyptic framework. The issue is whether such a catena of sayings would have been preserved in the tradition from the time of our Lord's earthly ministry. Many doubt this, because the structure has strong relationships to the apocalyptic elements preserved in the Thessalonian correspondence and the book of Revelation. Scholarly treatment varies from extreme liberal criticism to conservative efforts to ascribe most of the material to Jesus.

We must examine how far an apocalyptic outlook can be ascribed to our Lord himself. He certainly showed familiarity with the book of Daniel, and seems to have derived from it the image of the Son of Man. Yet it is by no means evident that he was dominated by or employed the ideas of the apocalyptic literature current in his own time. General ideas like the transcendentalizing of the Age-to-Come were undoubtedly present in his thought and in that of the church.

Schweitzer's view that Jesus was a consistent apocalyptist has been discredited, but he still has a following.[1] Undoubtedly eschatology in its late Old Testament form made a contribution to the divine activity of revelation in history. Extrabiblical apocalyptic, however, manifested a pessimism about history which is not reflected in the general outlook of our Lord himself. The early church had the problem of reconciling a prophetic acceptance of history with elements ingressing from this apocalyptic pessimism about history. It was the prophetic understanding that predominated. The Kingdom of God was to be actualized in the "now" of history, the end-time which came with the cross and the empty tomb. The dawning of the Age-to-Come had taken place in history and not beyond it. No longer must men despair of history but find their redemption within it. This seems to be the view of Jesus himself.

We must not set the postexilic and pre-exilic forms of prophetic eschatology in total contrast. Many elements in the latter viewpoint were preserved in the former, but much more transcendentalized with apocalyptic strands that developed later into full apocalypticism. Both languages are present in the New Testament. The apocalypticism of the intertestamental period accepted, as its stock-in-trade, a deterministic plan of history and

---

[1] Schweitzer, *The Quest of the Historical Jesus*. Martin Werner still contends that Jesus was a thoroughgoing apocalyptist—*The Formation of Christian Dogma* (New York: Harper & Brothers, 1957).

an emphasis on vision. The latter was accompanied by characteristic symbols and images and a distinctive vocabulary. A common
pattern emerged in it—the woes of judgment preceded the advent of the Messiah and the glories of the coming Age. At places
in the New Testament, such elements do appear, but the eschatology is basically prophetic. We find a realistic view of history as
the scene of the actualization of God's purpose as contrasted with
the pessimism and determinism of apocalyptic, even though some
of the imagery is employed.

We believe that this is true of the church's witness because it
was true of the thought of our Lord himself. He, too, was essentially the prophet, and the seemingly apocalyptic strands that
did influence his thinking were from the Old Testament and were
baptized into his unique viewpoint. The attempt of Otto[2] to prove
that Jesus was influenced by the esoteric apocalypticism of the
book of Enoch has met with little acceptance. J. W. Bowman[3]
suggests that our Lord's worship in the synagogue would make
him familiar with both rabbinical teaching and the apocalyptic
terminology. The Pharisees were particularly interested in the
esoteric and speculative writings of the apocalypticists. If Jesus
was to make a point of contact with them, he must use a vocabulary they understood. Yet, as Bowman points out, apart from the
canonical apocalypses, especially Daniel, Jesus never refers to
any of the apocalyptic literature, nor does he ever appear to quote
it.[4] Bowman even suggests that, since the church was familiar
with and quoted extracanonical apocalyptic, the fact that extant
traditions of Jesus' teaching show no such familiarity or usage
demonstrates "the Church's faithfulness in transmitting his teachings in the form in which he gave them." [5] Our Lord's skill as a
teacher led him to baptize some of the central biblical apocalyptic terminology into his own distinctive gospel of the Kingdom.

---

[2] Otto, *The Kingdom of God and the Son of Man, passim.*

[3] J. W. Bowman, *The Religion of Maturity* (Nashville: Abingdon-Cokes-
bury Press, 1948), pp. 237 ff. The chapter on "Jesus and the Apocalypticists"
is a rebuttal of the thesis that Jesus was essentially apocalyptic in his outlook. The present writer does not agree always with the argument.

[4] *Ibid.,* p. 238.

[5] *Ibid.*

But we do not find the visionary element or the deterministic pattern of history. As Kümmel points out,[6] our Lord speaks of or assumes the general resurrection as a preliminary condition of the judgment, but he does not describe the process of resurrection, nor does he give more than hints about the postresurrection state. He rejects efforts to fix the time of the end.[7] He uses apocalyptic imagery, but he gives no detailed vision of the renewal of the world and of the new creation, while into the description of the world judgment he introduces distinctive elements of his own (Matt. 25:31 ff.). Bowman holds that in none of the eschatological passages "does our Lord claim to have seen a vision and so to have learned therein of coming events, particularly of those of the Messianic age."[8] Bornkamm holds that Jesus cannot be completely fitted into any category. He "differs from the customary ways of the prophet . . . and nowhere does he use the ancient prophetic formula. Even less do we find any trace of that self-justification typical of the apocalyptic visionaries of later Judaism, who claim the authority of ecstatic states of mind and visions, secret revelation of the next world, and miraculous insight into God's decrees."[9]

Only in the case of Mark 13 might real questioning arise. At first sight, this chapter shows some of the characteristics of thoroughgoing apocalypticism. Many scholars, including Albert Schweitzer,[10] have dismissed it as a creation of a Jewish-apocalyptic order and not the utterance of our Lord at all. More moderate critics have, in varying degrees, seen genuine sayings of Jesus within the catena of teaching, but have contended that an unauthentic apocalyptic framework has been imposed upon these. Thus T. W. Manson points out that the individual sayings, apart from the setting, can mostly be paralleled by other sayings in the Synoptic tradition, but holds that they have been arranged to give a wrong impression as to the eschatological teaching of Je-

---

[6] Kümmel, *Promise and Fulfilment*, pp. 89 f.

[7] Luke 17:20-21; Mark 13:32, 35; Matthew 24:43-44; 25:1-2.

[8] J. W. Bowman, *The Intention of Jesus* (Philadelphia: The Westminster Press, 1943), p. 53.

[9] Bornkamm, *Jesus of Nazareth*, p. 56.

[10] Schweitzer, *op. cit.*

sus.[11] Kümmel is more cautious in assigning sayings to Jesus, but holds that some may be authentic, although "no details can be established with certainty."[12] He dismisses other sayings much too cavalierly because he is concerned to eliminate all traces of apocalyptic from Jesus' teaching. He dismisses Mark 13:7, 8, 12, 14-20, 24-27, arguing that they show apocalyptic terminology not present in the rest of Jesus' teaching. They contain phrases like "for the elect's sake," "abomination of desolation," and so on. Nowhere else in our Lord's eschatological sayings do we find "the description of the catastrophe before and at the end of the world, as well as the exhortation to find safety before the final catastrophe, of the lamentation over those who, when the end comes, will be physically encumbered and of the thought of gathering the elect from the four ends of the earth."[13] Kümmel concludes that "these texts drop out of the otherwise reliable tradition."

A more conservative estimate of Mark 13 has been provided by G. R. Beasley-Murray,[14] who desires to retain something of the apocalyptic flavor for our Lord's own teaching and who is anxious to preserve the authenticity of all the sayings together with their framework. After a careful analysis of the sayings, he concludes that either (1) "the original discourse that followed Mark 13:3 has been expanded by sayings uttered on other occasions," or (2) "the discourse was spoken on one occasion, but it was reproduced in a fragmentary condition, either through its narration at various times by the apostles or because it was too long to be remembered in its entirety." His work must be taken into account, especially his valuable exegesis of individual sayings.

He acknowledges that the central section—Mark 13:14-20—constitutes predictions of historical judgments upon the Temple and Jerusalem. We have evidence elsewhere that our Lord prophetically declared the judgment of the holy city (Luke 13:1-5;

---

[11] T. W. Manson, *The Teaching of Jesus*, p. 262.

[12] Kümmel, *op. cit.*, pp. 98 ff.

[13] *Ibid.*, p. 103.

[14] G. R. Beasley-Murray, *Jesus and the Future* (New York: St Martin's Press, 1954) and *A Commentary on Mark Thirteen* (New York: The Macmillan Company, 1957).

19:41-44; 23:28 ff.), and the references in this section would well fit in with a coming historical conflict. Beasley-Murray even endeavors to identify the abomination of desolation[15] with the setting up of some idolatrous Roman insignia in the confines of the Temple. He draws instances of this already extant in Jesus' time, including the possible use of a standard in the garrison castle of Antonia within the Temple precincts, a usage which Pilate had to give up because of Jewish protest. With his prophetic insight, Jesus inevitably would see the ultimate outcome of disaster if such profanation recurred, as it was bound to do.

The other sayings of this section fit in with a historical situation like a siege of Jerusalem, and there is no reason to doubt their authenticity. We would accept this analysis. Beasley-Murray goes beyond this and identifies such historical judgments with the apocalyptic woes. He thus gives them eschatological significance as signs of the end and links them up with the preaching to the Gentiles (vs. 10) as another sign of the end. Now Paul does indicate that God's rejection of the Jews provided the setting for the mission to the nations (Rom. 11:15; cf. 11:25-26). Further, if Matthew 23:39 be an authentic utterance, and here we have no major skepticism,[16] our Lord believed that the destruction of Jerusalem and the desolation of the Temple might lead to the ultimate repentance of the Jews and their acceptance of the Messiah.[17]

It must be confessed that this interpretation is cogent. It preserves the apocalyptic flavor without indulging in thoroughgoing apocalypticism. Our Lord is offering encouragement to those for whom he foresees persecution and distress if they are to be his witnesses. We are not offered an apocalyptic program, and the

---

[15] Cf. Daniel 9:27 where it refers to the profanation of the Temple by Antiochus Epiphanes.

[16] Kümmel (op. cit., pp. 80 f.) regards it as an independent saying of Jesus in the oldest tradition. K. L. Schmidt, J. Schniewind, T. W. Manson, C. H. Dodd, and Joachim Jeremias do likewise.

[17] Kümmel would interpret the judgment in this verse as referring to the removal of the Messiah until he shall return in glory and be acknowledged with benediction (op. cit., p. 81). Beasley-Murray accepts the context of the verse and more reasonably associates it with the historical judgment on the holy city.

time sequence can be shown to be far less significant.[18] Our Lord, as a prophet, saw that both judgment for Jewry and distress for his witnesses must happen before the *parousia,* but he is careful to avoid more than such general statements. Apocalyptic details are avoided. Our Lord would not give the exact date of the *parousia.*

J. W. Bowman[19] endeavors likewise to preserve the coherence of Mark 13, but with an overconcern to eliminate all apocalyptic elements. The discourse was offered as an anti-apocalyptic to combat the contemporary apocalyptic pursuit of signs. Jesus prophesied the destruction of the Temple and the fall of Jerusalem, and he gave signs relative to such historical events, but he gave no sign regarding the end of the world. The main body of Mark 13 is concerned with historical events, and only verses 24-27 point to the end. The latter, Bowman contends, would come without sign or warning of any kind. Bowman rightly indicates that many phrases indicate that our Lord refused to give precise signs and that he warned against seeking for them.[20] But this does not mean that Jesus did not understand something of the general strategy. Must we reduce him just to a prophet and forget his divine sonship! He was no apocalyptic visionary. True! He did not pinpoint the *parousia* chronologically, nor is there in Mark 13 any deterministic view of history. But he did use some of the apocalyptic apparatus to portray his understanding of future events. He saw that the judgment of Jewry and the proclamation of the gospel were necessary precursors of the consummation of the *eschaton,* and he employed the common apocalyptic-woes pattern to express this insight. This does not make him an apocalyptist, but it does indicate that he gave some general direction about the movement of history and its consummation. This is what Bowman

---

[18] This may, indeed, be one point at which the *Gemeindetheologie* has been at work. Cf. Beasley-Murray, *Jesus and the Future,* pp. 214 f.

[19] Bowman, *The Intention of Jesus,* pp. 55 ff.; also *The Religion of Maturity,* pp. 245 f.

[20] Bowman cites expressions like "the end is not yet" (vs. 7), "they shall lead many astray" (vs. 6; cf. vs. 22), "believe it not" (vs. 21), and vss. 32-33 (*The Intention of Jesus,* p. 57).

would deny, and yet we find the apocalyptic elements too evident
to deny their presence. We cannot completely separate the historical judgments of Mark 13 from the references to the *parousia*.

2. Jesus and the Parousia

Our Synoptic traditions contain a series of *parousia* sayings—
Mark 8:38; 13:26; 14:62, and parallels. The setting of Mark 13:26
is contained in a section, Mark 13:24-27, which appears to refer
to the end. It cannot be denied that it has a real apocalyptic
flavor. It is true that cosmic convulsions are found in the pre-
exilic and postexilic eschatology of the Old Testament as well as
in later apocalypticism. But the reference to the gathering of the
elect from the four corners of the earth raises difficulties. It is
seemingly dependent on the Greek and not the Hebrew text of
Zechariah 2:6.[21] This suggests that *Gemeindetheologie* may have
colored the section and made it more apocalyptic.[22] Such a criticism, however, need not apply to Mark 13:26, for this must be
considered in relation to the other two passages cited.

All three would appear to have as their background Daniel
7:13, where the Son of Man comes with the clouds of heaven to
the Ancient of Days. Now this evidently refers to an ascension to
the heavenly throne rather than a descent to earth.[23] Hence,
some scholars[24] would interpret Mark 14:62 as an affirmation of
the exaltation and ascension, not the *parousia,* and would dismiss
any reference to the *parousia* in the other two sayings as the crea-

---

[21] The Greek reads "From the four winds of heaven will I gather you."
The Hebrew is "I spread you abroad as the four winds of heaven."

[22] Beasley-Murray (*A Commentary on Mark Thirteen,* pp. 87 f.) does
not agree, but his argument here does not bear much weight. It is true that
the gathering of the elect is part of the Old Testament hope—Deuteronomy
30:4; Isaiah 11:11; 27:12; Ezekiel 39:27; Psalm 106:47. But only special
pleading would seem to evade the LXX usage. Jeremias would seem to support the authenticity too—*Jesus' Promise to the Nations,* pp. 23 f. and 69.

[23] *Vide* T. W. Manson, "The Son of Man in Daniel, Enoch, and the
Gospels" in *Bulletin of the John Rylands Library,* XXXII, 1950, p. 174.

[24] J. A. T. Robinson, *Jesus and His Coming* (Nashville: Abingdon
Press, 1957), pp. 43 ff.; T. F. Glasson, *The Second Advent* (London: Epworth Press, 1945), pp. 63 ff.; Duncan, *Jesus, Son of Man,* p. 174.

tion of the apocalypticism of the early church. But we find it difficult to understand what our Lord meant by the high priest's *seeing* the Son of Man in his glorified state. The *parousia* seems implied even in this verse.[25] Actually our Lord places the description of his enthronement before his coming on the clouds of heaven and appears to differentiate between the two.[26]

When we turn to Mark 8:38, we find that Glasson[27] sets this saying parallel to Matthew 10:32-33, which makes no mention of the *parousia*, but suggests the same criterion of relationship to Jesus and clearly refers to the heavenly session. He would make the Marcan saying an apocalypticized expansion of the Matthean and thus unauthentic.

But need the two sayings be thus dependent? Our Lord may well have said things of a similar nature, and thus both these sayings may be authentic. Again, just because he used the imagery of Daniel, that does not mean that he was always bound to use it in the same way. If there was an element of uniqueness in his message, he might well use the imagery of the Old Testament and fill it with new content. He did this often—why not here? The danger in so much criticism is that we prejudge the issue by the presuppositions with which we begin. Jesus was not confined to the straitjacket of Old Testament imagery. In fulfilling it, he also broke it.

The same contention applies to Mark 13:27. It is obviously a *parousia* utterance, and it is not unauthentic either because it misuses Daniel or because it has an apocalyptic setting. The latter, as we have seen, may arise in part from *Gemeindetheologie*. The former points to our Lord's unique understanding of himself as Son of Man. After all, in the Old Testament imagery the clouds are God's chariot in which he exercises his judgment and his redemption (Ezek. 1). Our Lord was also heir to this and to the tradition in which the clouds disclose and hide God's glory.[28]

---

[25] Luke omits the description "see" (Luke 22:69), possibly because a delayed *parousia* led to concentration on the present enthronement.

[26] Cf. Oscar Cullmann, *Peter: Disciple, Apostle, and Martyr* (Philadelphia: The Westminster Press, 1953), p. 149.

[27] Glasson, *op. cit.*, pp. 74 f.

[28] Exodus 34:5; Psalm 18:11; Isaiah 19:1.

Let all this imagery be gathered around our Lord's unique mission and something distinctive may emerge. Not only would he go on the clouds to be enthroned, but he would come again to exercise his kingly role, riding as God's representative on the cloud chariot.[29] He comes on the clouds to consummate the divine work of judgment and redemption.

This suggests that the *parousia* sayings are authentic. Even Bornkamm believes that at least Mark 8:38 "can be traced back without a doubt to Jesus himself,"[30] and yet he does not believe that Jesus identified himself with this future Son of Man. We have already sought to show that the Son of Man tradition was an aspect of our Lord's own self-consciousness. Other indications support the contention that the *parousia* of our Lord as Son of Man belongs to the very teaching of Jesus himself.[31] The parable of the Robbed Householder and the saying which follows it stress the unexpectedness of an eschatological happening. The Son of Man will come like a thief breaking through the mud wall of a house, coming in judgment into the world upon a generation unprepared.

The *parousia* is described as an event which takes the world by surprise. It will be a revolutionary event—not the result of an evolutionary process. Men do not know the hour (Mark 13:33-37). Because of this, they must take heed to themselves. This is an existential issue, and no matter for idle questioning. Bornkamm reminds us that "in Jesus' preaching, speaking of the present means speaking of the future, and vice versa."[32] The coming of the *parousia* is likened to a thief in the night, to lightning out of heaven, to the catastrophic flood in the time of Noah, and to the judgment on Sodom in the days of Lot.[33]

---

[29] Cf. Paul Minear, *The Christian Hope and the Second Coming* (Philadelphia: The Westminster Press, 1954), p. 125.

[30] Bornkamm, *op. cit.*, p. 176.

[31] Matthew uses the word *parousia* in Matthew 24:3, 27, 37, 39, but the verses are Matthean insertions into Marcan material. It is doubtful whether Jesus himself used it.

[32] Bornkamm, *op. cit.*, p. 93.

[33] Luke 12:39 (Q); 17:23-30 (Q). The phrase "days of the Son of man" is peculiar. Its parallelism in vs. 26 with the "days of Noah" suggests

The *parousia* will also be judgment in which the issue will be decided by the relation of men to Jesus, their loyalty to the Messiah in the present.[34] The Matthean parable of the Sheep and the Goats makes this the final criterion.[35] In this parable there are distinctive features peculiar to the teaching of Jesus—the placing of the Son of Man on the judgment seat, the relating of the verdict of judgment to the treatment of "the least of these my brethren" and the association of the angels with the Son of Man.[36] The frame of the picture would seem to be conventional Jewish apocalyptic, but these features stamp authenticity upon its essential content.[37] The King and the Son of Man are not specifically identified, but, although Jesus does not elsewhere designate himself as King, the messianic consciousness of our Lord included awareness of his kingship.[38] Probably Jesus used the title "King" here because the parable had an eschatological setting.[39] At the *parousia* this title would succeed that of the Son of Man.

We note that in this parable Jesus' brethren would appear to be not the disciples but the needy.[40] Works of love and mercy

---

that it means the last days culminating in the Day of the Son of Man—so T. W. Manson, *The Mission and Message of Jesus*, pp. 434 ff.

[34] Mark 8:38; cf. Luke 12:8 (Q); 17:23-30 (Q).

[35] Matthew 25:40, 45 (M). The parable undoubtedly contains apocalyptic elements, but this is no ground for dismissing it.

[36] Kümmel, *op. cit.*, p. 92.

[37] Cf. T. W. Manson, *The Mission and Message of Jesus*, p. 541; Jeremias, *The Parables of Jesus*, pp. 143 f.; Kümmel, *op. cit.*, p. 95. T. F. Glasson would eliminate the eschatological reference and confine the parable to the process of judgment in history—*op. cit.*, pp. 130 ff.

[38] Cf. Jeremias, *The Parables of Jesus*, p. 143. T. W. Manson characteristically identifies the Son of Man with the corporate whole, Jesus and the group of brethren, and then regards Jesus as the King who incorporates and represents the brethren—*The Teaching of Jesus*, p. 270.

[39] Cf. Theo Preiss, *Life in Christ* (London: SCM Press, 1952), p. 47.

[40] Cf. Jeremias, *op. cit.*, p. 143. While "brethren" can describe the disciples and Jesus (Mark 3:33-34; Matthew 23:8), it can also be used figuratively of a man's neighbors (Matthew 5:22-23; 7:3 ff.; 18:35). Kümmel would identify the "brethren" with "the poor" of Matthew 5:3. He holds it unlikely that the judge is inquiring about the attitude of the heathen to Christians, who surely would be included in "all the nations" and "the righteous." He concludes that the reference is to those in need of help—*op. cit.*, p. 94; cf. Preiss, *op. cit.*, p. 52.

toward the afflicted will guarantee a share in the eschatological
Kingdom. In caring for the needy, even the heathen are obeying
the Messiah's law of love and serving him. Indeed the bearing of
this parable would seem to be the fate of the nations (Matt.
25:32). They are justified on the ground of love, since the ransom
has been paid for them also.[41] In another well-known passage,
Jesus makes the same point (Luke 11:31-32 [Q]). Every generation will be judged by its attitude to the particular manifestation
of the Kingdom in its own time, so that the divine endowment of
Solomon's wisdom, the preaching of Jonah, and the advent of the
Kingdom in Jesus are the decisive elements in the judgment of
the men of those different generations. Since Jesus has come, relation to him and his redemptive work must be the final criterion
upon which the judgment turns, and no racial privilege or membership of the chosen people can avail against it.

Clearly the judgment will be universal in scope. Judgments in
the course of history will be validated at the end. Indeed, it will
then be more tolerable for Sodom and Gomorrah, Tyre and Sidon,
than for the cities of Galilee which reject the messengers of the
Kingdom (Luke 10:12-15). Jew and Gentile will stand then on
the same basis, and things will even be turned upside down. The
sons of the Kingdom, the Jews, will find themselves outside in
darkness and despair, while the patriarchs, the prophets, and the
faithful Israelites of every generation will share the final bliss
with men from every corner of the world.[42] The last shall be first
and the first last. The same theme is reiterated in the parable of
the Great Feast (Luke 14:15-24 [Q]). Jesus is the "servant" who
comes to announce that the feast is ready. The guests, the Jews,
excuse themselves, and the mission goes to the outcast Israelites
and the Gentiles. The latter are constrained to come in by in-
sistent hospitality. There is no thought of divine compulsion
here.[43] It is the attitude to the Servant now which is determina-

---

[41] Cf. Jeremias, *op. cit.*, p. 145.
[42] Luke 13:28-29 (Q). The Matthean form is a conflation with a parable about a wedding guest and shows allegorizing tendencies—Jeremias,
op. cit., p. 53.
[43] So T. W. Manson, *The Mission and Message of Jesus*, p. 274.

tive, and the verdict at the end confirms the sifting process that goes on in God's "now."[44]

We note that the idea of conflict and ultimate triumph which characterizes the contemporary apocalyptic of Jesus' time is replaced in our Lord's thought by the moral triumph of the *parousia*. There is no picture of a tremendous conflict in which the world powers shall be overthrown. Rather the final consummation is portrayed as a great assize, in which the central figure is Jesus himself and in which his balances are weighted with mercy. There is no narrow exclusive nationalism here. This is the triumph of a Kingdom of grace over the powers of evil. The coming of Christ in glory is also judgment, the moral triumph of good over evil. In it this present evil age ends, and everything hostile to the Kingdom is eliminated.

One point of significance is the imminence of the *parousia* in the thought of Jesus. He refused to predict the time of his coming, but several sayings seem to indicate that it was thought by him to be imminent. Mark 9:1 speaks of some hearers not tasting death until they see the Kingdom of God come with power. The coming of the Kingdom with power may refer to the dawning of the new Age in the cross, resurrection, and exaltation of Jesus.[45] We must not, however, oversystematize, and other attempts to identify the coming with power with the transfiguration,[46] the descent of the Holy Spirit at Pentecost,[47] the creation of the church,[48] must not be dismissed.

Our ideological schemes can so often miss the truth here. For our Lord, the Kingdom was both present and future. His whole time was time filled with the Kingdom, but it moved in his own historical lifetime toward the supreme *kairos* of his death and

---

[44] Jeremias would eliminate the eschatological reference; he regards the missionary motif as *Gemeindetheologie*—*op. cit.*, p. 37.

[45] Jeremias links the *parousia* so closely with the cross and resurrection that he regards the third day of resurrection as also the Day of the Son of Man, when the Kingdom came with power.

[46] So Chrysostom.

[47] So H. B. Swete, *The Gospel According to St. Mark* (New York: The Macmillan Company, 1898).

[48] So Vincent Taylor, *The Gospel According to St. Mark*, p. 386a; cf. J. W. Bowman, *The Religion of Maturity*, pp. 254 f.

resurrection. Here the Kingdom became redemptively present in a climacteric sense. It could be said to be present with power but in a veiled form. But this would be true also of all subsequent *kairoi* from Pentecost onward. The powers released in the resurrection were active in them, still in veiled form. The power that was hidden would be unveiled at the *parousia,* and the secret meaning of history, now being actualized, would be made manifest. If our Lord intended such an interim period and intended his church, in some sense the saying was fulfilled from the cross and resurrection on through Pentecost and the church's life. Yet this does not completely satisfy. We are left with an enigmatic utterance, a prediction not outwardly fulfilled apparently. Schweitzer makes much of this. It would appear that the *parousia* is also involved and that Jesus did expect it to occur in the lifetime of at least *some* of his contemporaries—at most a period of some decades.[49]

The saying in Mark 13:30 is by no means clear. Cullmann insists that it does not deserve the importance attached to it.[50] Some would have it refer only to the historical events with which the center of the discourse is concerned—the destruction of Jerusalem and concomitant happenings.[51] Other scholars seek to evade the issue of the imminence of the *parousia* by interpreting differently the word customarily translated "generation." "Race"[52] and "kinds of men"[53] have been suggested as alternative renderings. But elsewhere in the Synoptic tradition, the word is best rendered by the customary translation. It would seem that we have to render the phrase as the generation contemporary with Jesus,[54] and then the issue of imminence at once is raised.

---

[49] Cf. Cullmann, "The Return of Christ," *The Early Church,* p. 152.

[50] Cullmann, *Christ and Time,* p. 88. He says the same of Mark 9:1 and Matthew 10:23.

[51] Cf. W. Michaelis, *Die Herr vorzieht nicht die Verheissung* (1942), pp. 30 ff.

[52] Cf. Julius Schniewind, *Das Evangelium nach Markus, Das Neue Testament Deutsch* (Göttingen: Vanderhoeck & Ruprecht, 1933), p. 167; Friedrich Busch, *Zum verständnis der Synoptischen Eschatologie,* 1938, pp. 133 f.

[53] Cf. Michaelis, *op. cit.,* pp. 30 ff.

[54] Cf. Beasley-Murray, *A Commentary on Mark Thirteen,* p. 100.

Schweitzer[55] interpreted Matthew 10:23 as indicating that our Lord did not anticipate the return of the disciples from their missionary journey prior to the dawn of the new Age. When they returned and the new Age had not come, Jesus decided to go to Jerusalem and compel the advent of the Kingdom by his own death. Kümmel[56] has demonstrated, however, that the second part of verse 23 is detachable from the first, which refers to the behavior of the disciples under persecution. The reference to the imminence of the end would thus appear to be a detachable logion. Actually Luke quotes it in quite a different connection (Luke 6:40), and the saying may well not be connected with its Matthean context. Then the logion would mean that the *parousia* will occur before the disciples shall have finished proclaiming the gospel to Israel. Once more, however, we cannot evade the matter of the imminence of the end in Jesus' consciousness. If we follow Kümmel, the reference of this saying is to the complete discharge of the disciples' missionary commission. This might be after Jesus' death, but in the lifetime of his hearers.

Mark 14:62, the saying before the high priest, seems quite explicitly to imply the imminence of the end. Yet it also allows for an interval between the resurrection and the *parousia*, for it separates the exaltation to the right hand of God from the return of the Son of Man.[57] The condition of the preaching of the gospel to all nations carries the same implication. Our Lord's creative imagination reaches its heights in the parable of the Vineyard,[58] and here again a lapse of time between the death of the son and the final consummation is indicated. When the son is killed, the vineyard will be given to others, presumably the Gentiles, until the end comes.

All the evidence thus goes to indicate that our Lord anticipated an imminent return of himself as Son of Man subsequent to his death and resurrection. It would happen in the life-span of

---

[55] Schweitzer, *op. cit.*, pp. 357 ff.

[56] Kümmel, *op. cit.*, pp. 61 f.

[57] Cf. Cullmann, "The Return of Christ," *The Early Church*, p. 152. Ct. the view of Jeremias criticized *supra*.

[58] Mark 12:1 ff. Vincent Taylor, Julius Schniewind, and C. H. Dodd accept its authenticity despite allegorical traits.

his contemporaries. In estimating the significance of our Lord's understanding at this point, certain points need to be borne in mind. First of all, we have to remember the peculiar nature of eschatological thinking. The Old Testament prophets indulged in a shortening of the historical perspective in their prediction of future events, because they were so sure of the ultimate divine outcome.[59] In the same way, the profound conviction of our Lord that God must be victorious and his certainty that there must be a final consummation lie behind and are symbolized in the sense of immediacy that characterizes his references to them. The ultimate consummation is so certain that the sense of temporal duration is lost in the conviction that eternity is so near. Looking at the event *sub specie aeternitatis*, religious genius would tend to regard it "as proximate and swift as lightning."[60]

In the second place, we have to remember our Lord's true humanity. His ignorance would be a sign of his full humanity, not a denial of his true divinity. He was a man of his time, accepting the contemporary viewpoint at the level of secular knowledge. Modern science, contemporary critical knowledge of the Bible, the methods of modern psychology, were hidden from him as man. He treated Jonah as literal history, accepted the Davidic authorship of the Psalms, and interpreted psychological symptoms in terms of demon possession. Only so could he be true man. Yet such limitations at superficial levels of knowledge did not hinder him from truly understanding the Old Testament revelation or going to the heart of man's trouble and effecting its cure.[61] His insight into the heart of the revelation of the old covenant was unique, even though he had no modern critical tools. As with past events, so too with future ones. The date and nature of the *parousia* are not to be confused. Our Lord could have shared with his contemporaries the expectation of an imminent Day of the Lord, and yet still have had a unique insight into its nature.

---

[59] Cf. Dodd, *The Parables of the Kingdom*, p. 71.

[60] Thus Friedrich von Hügel, *Selected Letters 1896-1924*, ed. by Bernard Holland (New York: E. P. Dutton & Co., Inc., 1927), p. 159.

[61] Cf. T. W. Manson, *The Teaching of Jesus*, p. 283.

Third, we have to remember our Lord's clear affirmation that all his utterances about time were under and subject to the Father's decision. This conditioning factor would apply to his sayings about the imminence of the end. God alone had the initiative and thus here could correct the statements of the Son.[62] The latter were provisional at this level.

But the reality of the second advent does not fall with the failure of the expectation of its imminence. The early church was quick to learn this. The Christian hope did not rest upon a future event, but upon something that had already happened. The guarantee for the hope of final victory lay in the completed act of Christ, crucified and risen. The delay of the *parousia* could not eliminate such a hope. Its ground was not in any future actualization. We anticipate the future both because of the past and because that past is effective in our present. The end has burst into historical time in Jesus. The future is a present reality for the man of faith, and its delay does not impair its certainty. There is truth in both realized and futurist eschatology. There is a "now" as well as a "then" about the Kingdom of God. The Kingdom was proleptically present before the death and resurrection of Jesus in his own person, words, and deeds; it dawned decisively and redemptively in the cross and the empty tomb; it was manifested in the crisis of Pentecost; it is present in the preaching and sacraments of the church; it discloses itself in the activity of the Holy Spirit in the fellowship; and it shall be fully manifested in the last Day. The end of history will contain nothing that was not present in the incarnate life and acts of the Lord and that is not present now to believers as they encounter the risen Lord through his Spirit.

3. The Parousia in the Apostolic Witness

Our Lord saw history moving toward a consummation, centering in his *parousia*. When we move from his teaching to the *kerygma* of the early church, we have to remember that we have

---

[62] Cf. Beasley-Murray, *Jesus and the Future,* p. 189.

entered the postresurrection era. Cullmann reminds us that the difference between the hope of Jesus and the hope of the New Testament church lay in the fact that the decisive event had taken place.[63]

It is to be noted that, in the writings of Paul and the Apocalypse, the chief sources for the eschatology of the *kerygma,* we find stronger apocalyptic influences than in the hope of our Lord. The early church at times employed the apocalyptic imagery of contemporary Judaism, but it transformed it because of the crisis-event, the filled time of Jesus. The imagery came to possess a new content, for the *eschaton* had already supervened upon history. The New Testament witnesses saw that there could be nothing in the temporal end of history which was not already disclosed in its teleological end, the redemptive act of God through his Son. Paul thus placed increasing stress upon the life of Age-to-Come enjoyed here and now. Yet he still spoke of being saved by hope and of the Spirit as the earnest of our future inheritance. The hope of the *parousia* was never absent from his thought. Those critics who label the Thessalonian Letters as naively apocalytic often take refuge in the later captivity Letters and are even glad to claim Ephesians as Pauline for the sake of what they regard as its more mature nature. Actually, it is by no means clear that Paul ever forsook his so-called "early apocalypticism," although he may have felt that the *parousia* would not occur in his own lifetime as the years came and went.

The early church and its contemporary Pharisaism lived in a common atmosphere of apocalypticism, stimulated by the Roman occupation of Palestine. Jewish apocalypticism influenced the thought of the Christian community, and we must not be surprised if occasionally elements that were more Jewish than Christian found their way into its eschatology. As we have seen, our Lord's apocalyptic images were taken from the late Old Testament eschatology. He made himself as Son of Man the center of the final consummation and pictured the Day of the Son of Man as an assize. But Jewish apocalyptic, influenced by the conflict

[63] Cullmann, "The Return of Christ," *The Early Church,* p. 154.

imagery of Ezekiel's vision of Gog from Magog and dominated by a narrow nationalism, spoke of a final dread conflict toward which it saw history moving along predetermined lines. We can see two factors present in the postresurrection *Gemeindetheologie.*

First of all, our Lord's judicious use of apocalyptic imagery was extended until a Christian apocalypticism was fully developed under the influence of contemporary apocalypticism. We find this in the Apocalypse, where the picture of a final dread conflict is developed and a complicated system of apocalyptic woes is offered on the Jewish model. Thus a retrograde movement in Christian thought back into Jewish apocalyptic was evidently present.[64]

In estimating the significance of such changes, we have to consider the second factor. The church viewed the last things from the postresurrection vantage point, and thus the triumphant faith in the risen and exalted Lord dominated its thought. We should expect, therefore, that its theological testimony would have a much more Christocentric emphasis than we find in the original sayings of our Lord, colored as they were by his natural reticence. Thus, we may find in Matthew 24 a tendency to heighten the Christocentric emphasis of Mark 13 as well as a tendency to cast it in a more apocalyptic framework.

Both these factors are at work in the case of the early Pauline eschatology as reflected in the Thessalonian correspondence. Let us, first of all, summarize its viewpoint. It is often said that the second Letter is but a pale ghost of the first, but this difficulty is removed if we reverse the order of their writing.[65] Then the eschatology becomes clearer. A young and enthusiastic community is living under the shadow of an imminent Day of the

---

[64] Cf. J. E. Fison, *The Christian Hope* (New York: Longmans Green & Co., 1954), p. 147. J. A. T. Robinson has shown such a process at work in Matthew 24, the Matthean version of Mark 13. He also points out that sayings are slightly altered so as to separate Jesus from the Father and to associate the angels and the final retribution more with our Lord—*op. cit.,* pp. 108 ff.

[65] This has been advocated by Johannes Weiss and T. W. Manson. This is not, of course, the general consensus.

Lord. Persecution raises questions about the delay of the *parousia*, and this delay threatens to undermine their faith. Paul writes 2 Thessalonians to meet this challenge. He warns them that evil must make one more convulsive effort before the end. The man of sin must come. The Thessalonians then become concerned about those who die before the delayed *parousia* occurs. To them (1 Thessalonians 4:1—5:11) Paul outlines his doctrine of the resurrection of the dead.

Both letters are dependent upon some source of Old Testament testimonies which was circulating in the early church.[66] The latter indeed drew much of its rich imagery from the testimony of the old covenant and its promises. This is to be expected, for our Lord was himself steeped in Holy Scripture, and used it to describe his own person and mission. The Thessalonian passages tend to employ the more apocalyptic elements in the Old Testament, but this does not discredit them. Our Lord also made use of such elements. The danger is that we should ascribe all such creative activity to the early church, and forget that the new images and the new content that fills the images is inexplicable without a creative personality like our Lord at the center.

A careful analysis shows that the Thessalonian passages are closer to Matthew 24 than to Mark 13.[67] J. A. T. Robinson argues against any direct dependence, holding that Matthew 24 marks the end of an apocalyptic development in the Synoptic tradition, and that the Pauline letters show that the same tendency was at work elsewhere. His position is vitiated by his dismissal of the authenticity of the general pattern of Mark 13 and by his contention that the *parousia* hope is a creation of *Gemeindetheologie*. Hence he argues that the eschatological content of the Thessalonian Letters gives us no contact with the original teaching of Jesus.[68] We do not dispute that secondary tendencies are at work, but we contend that the central core of the Thessalonian eschatology preserves the *parousia* hope of our Lord himself and fills it with postresurrection insight.

---

[66] *Vide* Glasson, *op. cit.*, pp. 172 ff.

[67] Cf. Robinson, *op. cit.*, pp. 106 ff.

[68] Cf. *ibid.*, p. 111.

It cannot be disputed that 2 Thessalonians 1:6—2:10 is colored with contemporary apocalypticism, but veiled in this imagery there may be truths that we must heed. Three odd phrases call for attention at this level. The first is the picture of a falling away, an apostasy, that must precede the *parousia* (2 Thess. 2:3). In apocalypticism this word acquired the meaning of a world-wide rebellion against God which was to be associated with the messianic woes. The same kind of association is evident in Thessalonians, although Paul seems to have held the same viewpoint apart from such apocalyptic associations (Acts 20:30). Actually, allowing for later apocalyptic coloring, Mark 13:22 would indicate that our Lord expected such a falling away in the interim before the *parousia*. A shrewd prophetic insight into the future, such as he possessed, would see such a possibility, if not a certainty. Thus the phrase may reflect our Lord's own mind, although it may have been set in a developed apocalyptic framework by the church.

The second phrase describes a "man of sin" who must be unveiled before the end comes. This figure is typical of Jewish apocalypticism. As archenemy of the Messiah, he is characterized by sin or lawlessness and is presented sometimes as the last great human ruler[69] and sometimes as a supernatural being (Belial or Satan).[70] Ezekiel's figure of Gog from Magog[71] and Daniel's image of the Fourth Beast (Dan. 7:21-27; cf. 11:36) undoubtedly provided grounds for the first presentation, and the second has its roots in the Zoroastrian Satan and his evil spirits, often called Belial in Jewish apocalyptic. Apocalyptic thought came to regard the human figure as the incarnation of the supernatural.[72]

In the second half of the first century of the Christian era, a third strand was woven in, derived from the Nero redivivus myth —the "man of sin" was identified with the return of Nero. Paul's thought follows the characteristic Jewish apocalyptic pattern. The

[69] Cf. Apocalypse of Baruch 39; 2 Esdras 5:6.
[70] Cf. Testament of Judah 25; Ascension of Isaiah 2.
[71] Ezekiel 38-39. A similar final assault on Jerusalem is portrayed in Zechariah 14:2 ff., without mention of a leader.
[72] Sibylline Oracle 3:63-74; Ascension of Isaiah 4:2-4.

man of sin shows the same blending of the human and the supernatural. He will proclaim himself to be God, will gain followers by
performing miracles, will have a gospel which is a lie, and will
bring widespread apostasy from the church. The mystery of lawlessness is presently at work, but it is being restrained. Once the
restraint has been removed, the power of darkness will be unveiled in the antichrist, who will usurp the place of God in the
Temple. He will be a counterfeit messiah claiming allegiance that
belongs rightly to Christ. Paul seems to be working with a currently accepted circle of apocalyptic ideas with which his readers
are familiar.[73]

Yet despite this apocalyptic dressing, with its abnormal imaginative pattern, revelatory insight may still be conveyed. John, in
his Letters, identifies antichrist with those who deny that Jesus is
Christ, or who deny the Father and the Son, or who do not confess that Jesus Christ came in the flesh (1 John 2:22; 4:2-3). He
uses the plural and declares that up to this time there have been
many antichrists. In other words, every day manifests its incarnation of evil, its embodiment of blasphemy. But such embodiments
are to be understood only in relation to the *parousia,* when Christ's
hidden reign will be made manifest and evil will be overthrown.

The third phrase appears in successive verses as "that which
restrains" and "he who restrains." There is some power which
restrains the outbreak of lawlessness in the advent of the man
of sin. This power can apparently be regarded as an impersonal
force or as a person. Here apocalyptic parallels are difficult to
find, while various interpretations have been offered. Some[74]
identify the restraining force with Rome, which had protected
the Apostle from Jews and pagan mobs. Dibelius[75] interprets "to
restrain" as "to hold in bonds," and suggests that antichrist or
Satan is bound by a friendly angel but will be released in due
time.

---

[73] Cf. Leivestad, *Christ the Conqueror,* p. 90. "His readers know the
clue. They know the *shibboleth* by which anti-Christ will be identified.
Those who are enlightened will recognize him."

[74] Cf. J. E. Frame, *The Epistles of St. Paul to the Thessalonians,* I.C.C.
(New York: Charles Scribner's Sons, 1912), pp. 259 ff., for various positions.

[75] Quoted in *ibid.,* p. 261.

Cullmann takes "to restrain" in the temporal sense of "to delay."[76] He argues that "that which restrains" is the mission preaching of the end-time. He gets over the difficulty of the masculine and neuter genders by suggesting that the former refers to a restraining person who is to be identified with the Apostle himself. We have already discussed the eschatological significance of the Gentile mission, and it is noteworthy that, in rabbinical thought, the delay of the Messiah was frequently laid at the door of "the still unfulfilled repentance of Israel."[77] Further, Cullmann's interpretation might be supported by Paul's own lofty sense of mission which is itself eschatological. Here the muddied waters of apocalypticism close over us, and a final verdict is difficult.

Paul left this apocalypticism behind, but to the end he retained his *parousia* hope. As the extreme apocalyptic coloring recedes from view so also does the emphasis on the imminence of the *parousia*. In the Corinthian correspondence there is still the note of urgency. The Apostle is still concerned with those surviving death when the Day dawns (1 Cor. 15:51-52), and his advice about marriage and domestic relationship is conditioned by the conviction that the time is short (1 Cor. 7:29). The sentence ". . . death is at work in us, but life in you" (2 Cor. 4:12) may mean that he will die but that some of his readers will survive until the end. Even in Romans he can declare that ". . . the night is far gone, the day is at hand" (Rom. 13:11-14), but the long and sustained argument of the Letter makes no appeal to an imminent *parousia*. The emphasis is on the life of the Age-to-Come as being proleptically realized here and now. The consummation can be awaited without urgency, for the substance of our hope is already a present possession (Rom. 8:18-39).

In the captivity Letters, Paul gives concrete ethical teaching. The *parousia* hope remains. Christ will be manifested, and we shall be manifested with him in glory (Col. 1:27; 3:4). Christians still await a Saviour from heaven (Phil. 3:20-21). The church is,

---

[76] Cullmann, *Christ and Time*, pp. 164 ff.

[77] Cf. *ibid.*, p. 165, quoting from *The Babylonian Talmud, Sanhedrin*, 97b. *Vide* also *ibid.*, p. 159.

however, a colony of heaven, and the heavenly life may be enjoyed here and now. We have now been quickened together with Christ, even though we await the final resurrection.[78] The tension remains and the hope is not relinquished, but the Apostle is concerned with the present life in Christ in all the complex of personal and social relationships (Col. 3:18—4:1).

In the hope of the *parousia,* the New Testament witnesses also emphasize its aspect of final judgment. Sometimes we find a note of harshness characteristic of Jewish apocalyptic. The *parousia* will be a rendering of vengeance to the disobedient and unbelieving, their eternal banishment from the face of the Lord. Yet this ultimate wrath is present in our Lord's own teaching! Our Lord is himself usually the center of the final judgment. We must all appear before the judgment seat of Christ (2 Cor. 5:10). In that day God will judge men's secrets by Jesus Christ (Rom. 2:16). Thus, the judgment will center in men's relation to Christ, as in our Lord's own sayings.

The final Day will confirm the present reality of justification that faith makes possible. Even Christians will then be purged from the stains which weakness and blindness can still leave on their lives. Faith secures the all-embracing verdict, yet the believer must still undergo judgment. He will be saved not by his achievements, of which he may be so proud, but in spite of them. Indeed, he may have a hairbreadth escape (1 Cor. 3:13-15). The judgment will be concerned with inward motives as well as outward action. It will make manifest the inmost secrets of our hearts (1 Cor. 4:5). The final judgment will mark the end of a process of judgment, in which God personally operates in history. Its outcome is either eternal life or death. In 2 Thessalonians (1:9), Paul speaks of eternal destruction from the face of the Lord and the glory of his might.

It might superficially be argued that both the Fourth Evangelist and the author of the Letter to the Hebrews have transferred all attention from the future to the present. But, as we discussed earlier, this is not true. The eschatological note remains, although

---

[78] Colossians 2:12-13; Ephesians 2:5.

very much subordinated to this present period of history. Any
elements of apocalypticism have disappeared. God's plan is being
actualized here and now, but the city of God is still ahead of
the faithful. Christ is the ". . . high priest of the good things that
have come . . ." (Heb. 9:11). There will be a final shaking, in
which God will *yet once more* shake the things that can be
shaken, that the things which cannot be shaken may remain
(Heb. 12:26 ff.). The *parousia* is still regarded as imminent (Heb.
10:25), but there is more concern with the tasting of the powers
of the Age-to-Come, here and now. There is here no static dual-
ism between the real and the phenomenal worlds, such as Plato
postulated. Even Hebrews suggests a dramatic movement of redemption to a final consummation. It is eschatological.[79]

In the Apocalypse, however, apocalypticism seems to take
over. In the rest of the New Testament, the prophetic and moral
aspect of eschatology is central, and apocalyptic elements are
subordinated to it. The idea of a final consummation centers in
the *parousia* and is pictured not as a terrible conflict striking
from heaven down to earth but as a great assize. The elements of
conflict present are spiritualized, centering in the moral triumph
of the cross over the spiritual powers of darkness and reaching a
culmination in the manifestation of the Lord upon the judgment
seat.

Paul, with his cosmic emphasis, never approaches the idea of
a gigantic flesh-and-blood conflict on earth.[80] John denies such a
possibility when he records the saying that Jesus' Kingdom is not
of this world, else would his servants fight for it (John 18:36).
But in the Apocalypse we see the unique eschatological outlook
of the Christian revelation battling with the eschatological outlook of Jewish apocalyptic. Gog, Magog, and Armageddon be-

---

[79] Cf. C. K. Barrett, "The Eschatology of the Epistle to the Hebrews,"
The Background of the New Testament and Its Eschatology, W. D. Davies
and D. Daube, eds., p. 389.

[80] Where our Lord takes issue with the demonic powers there is no comparison with the Jewish ideas of messianic conflict; e.g., 1 Corinthians 15:24
ff. The spiritualization of the imagery removes Paul's thought from the realm
of crudely realistic apocalyptic. Cf. Hans Windisch, *Der Messianische Krieg*
(Tübingen: J. C. B. Mohr, 1909).

come dominant motifs. The suffering Lamb of God, the Servant of the Lord, becomes the wrathful figure who reaps with a sickle, treading the winepress of wrath, and riding victoriously into the conflict, seated on a white horse, a sharp sword in his hand. The Christ won his triumph on the cross by moral and spiritual power. But here the Lamb who was slain becomes a terrible figure who rules the nations with a rod of iron, a despotic avenger.[81]

Thus, in the Apocalypse, we see the symbols and images of the new faith struggling with those arising in the nationalistic and apocalyptic stream of Judaism. Later Christian apocalyptic succumbed completely to the latter, throwing the hope of deliverance upon the final cataclysm and presenting a note of vengeance against the oppressive persecutors. Persecution and martyrdom created a situation increasingly receptive to the historical pessimism and narrow exclusiveness of Jewish apocalyptic. John the seer manifests these influences at work.

The Apocalypse is much more open to the dominant themes of apocalypticism—the messianic woes, the dread conflict that was to be fought on earth as well as in heaven, the ultimate millennial reign of the saints. The Christian eschatological outlook prevails a little more in the first two chapters—the letters to the seven churches. After this, Jewish apocalypticism becomes more evident.[82]

The seer pictures Christ as making war on the Gentiles and slaying the pagan and unbelieving enemies of the church in a real military campaign. A flesh-and-blood battle will be joined, and the slain will wallow in their gore on the battlefield. This is no spiritual conflict with the demonries, and no amount of casuistry can evade the fact that Satan, incarnated in the man of sin, leads a human army into actual conflict. Yet the balances are weighted, and the battle is not joined on equal terms. It is really execution. This is Jewish messianism in which "the Messiah is identified

---

[81] Leivestad, *op. cit.,* p. 247, suggests that we have here an unbearable contradiction that destroys the moral identity of the historical Jesus and the eschatological Christ.

[82] Cf. Fison, *op. cit.,* p. 147.

with the crucified Christ and Israel with the Church."[83] We have here a distorted picture of Christian eschatology, in which the symbolism of the battlefield replaces that of the great assize.[84] We have moved from the picture of Paul and John. This does not mean that there is no real insight in the Apocalypse.[85] The book is a drama of history and judgment amid the tangled skeins of which essential meaning is contained.

Various attempts have been made to solve the enigma of the book and its impression of chaos rather than orderliness.[86] The problem is especially acute with regard to the repetitive messianic woes, arranged in three successive sets of seven—the Seven Seals, the Seven Trumpets, the Seven Bowls, each complete in itself. Three times the judgment on the earth seems to reach its consummation of destruction. John repeatedly declares that the end has come, only to start a fresh development of woes (e.g., 8:1; 10:6-7; 11:15 ff.). This would suggest that we have here not progressive movement but repetition of events in new ways for the sake of emphasis.[87] The seer was a poet and a visionary with pastoral concern. He was anxious to impress upon his readers an expectation of persecution in increasing measure, for this would inevitably be their lot. But he was also concerned to give them a triumphant faith in God. Hence he multiplied the woes to bring out the severity and terror of the final judgment and to encourage the Christians to meet them undaunted because they were in the victorious movement of the divine purpose. The final judgment was certain.

---

[83] Leivestad, *op. cit.*, p. 246.

[84] Cf. Fison, *op. cit.*, p. 148.

[85] Austin Farrer, *A Rebirth of Images*, presents a fascinating survey on the basis of his peculiar theory of revealed images. He argues that the book is a great and vividly imagined poem which gives a key to the thought of the later New Testament age.

[86] Some attribute all the visions to the seer and attempt a rearrangement to the original order which has been disturbed, e.g., John Oman, *The Book of Revelation* (New York: Cambridge University Press, 1923). Others suggest that the seer culled his material from different apocalyptic sources and put it together, e.g., E. F. Scott, *The Book of Revelation*.

[87] Cf. Martin Kiddle, *The Revelation of St. John*, Moffatt Commentary (New York: Harper & Brothers, 1940).

As the seer portrays it, this ultimate world judgment is preceded by a process of historical judgments that lead up to the end.[88] He makes the latter center in Rome. The victorious path of this mighty empire was beset by the wars, famines, and pestilences which characterize some of the woes. Martyrdom and death for the church did attend its triumphant way. The seer sees these as preparing the way for yet more convulsive manifestations of evil in which the supernatural will be more evident—the cosmos will be convulsed and heaven rolled up like a scroll. We can learn from this that the judgments in history will be summed up in the judgment at the end of history, however much we have to re-express the imagery and however difficult we find it to describe the final assize in symbols that must not be taken literally. The process of judgment in history will lead inevitably to the fall of Rome. At this point Jewish apocalyptic takes over, and the final judgment supervenes.

The final assize is replaced by a field of battle which, in its gory detail, ill befits the redeeming love of Calvary, even though Christ is still the center of the finale. In Armageddon the evil forces of the pagans led by antichrist join issue with Christ and his angels. The moral and spiritual triumph of the cross is thereby climaxed in the horrors of physical conflict and in a bloody vindication of the martyr host at the expense of the world which Christ died to save (Rev. 19:13 ff.).

In this connection one phrase requires our attention—"the wrath of the Lamb." We have the grim picture of the mighty of the world hiding from "the wrath of the Lamb" (Rev. 6:15-17). This picture seems bound up with other imagery which associates the Lamb that was slain with the Lion of Judah (Rev. 5:5 ff.). The latter figure is represented in Hosea as one who shall tear and devour (Hos. 5:14). It would seem that the phrase portrays a divine wrath in which the Lamb has turned Lion. Hanson believes that the phrase is not purely eschatological but describes a

---

[88] A. T. Hanson (*The Wrath of the Lamb,* pp. 159 ff.) contends that the picture of judgment in the Apocalypse is the most profound in the New Testament. We have already criticized his view of the wrath as a process in which God is not personally involved.

process stretching from the cross to the *parousia* in which "the consequences of the rejection and the crucifixion of the Messiah" are worked out.[89] This attractive hypothesis is invalidated, however, by the image of the Warrior-Christ, with his garments dipped in blood.[90] A warrior messianism seems at times to replace the messianism of the Suffering Servant, and suffering and redemptive love appear to give place to tendencies of vindictiveness and exclusiveness.

Within the scheme of woes, Cullmann would find another insight besides the general emphasis on the reality of judgment. When the First Seal is broken the three horsemen representing war, famine, and death are accompanied by a fourth whose identity is not so clear (Rev. 6:1-11). He comes on a white horse, and his figure is not sinister like those of the other three. Rather he is luminous and crowned, suggesting a beneficent power—a heavenly attribute in the Apocalypse—and, since he comes forth conquering and to conquer, Cullmann suggests that he is representative of divine activity. Hence this scholar would identify the figure on the white horse with the preaching of the gospel to the world. This may be supported by the later vision of the angel who appears with the eternal gospel and issues a final call to repentance to the pagan nations (Rev. 14:6-7). Once more we are reminded that, apart from all apocalyptic schema and messianic woes, the preaching of the gospel, as well as the processes of historical judgment upon sin, is a necessary precondition of the end.

4. The General Resurrection and the Age-to-Come

In the New Testament hope the *parousia* is bound up not only with the final judgment but also with the general resurrection. Perhaps this is brought out most of all in the Pauline correspondence, but it is evident throughout the testimony of the church. In our Lord's thought, the consummated life of the Age-to-Come is realized at his *parousia*. He shows a general reticence about this

---

[89] *Ibid.*, p. 170.
[90] Revelation 19:13 ff.; cf. Isaiah 63:1.

life, but glimpses of light shine through his teaching. It will be like the life of the angels in heaven.[91]

Our Lord affirms that the dead are raised, quoting from the Torah but basing his affirmation finally on the nature of God. God is the God of the living and not of the dead (Mark 12:27). Those who live in fellowship with him have eternal life.[92] There is no suggestion of the resurrection of the flesh. It is life like that of the angels. The whole point is the survival of personality in its totality, and the resurrected share in the glorified garb that befits the sons of God.[93] The glorified body will express the perfect inward beauty of those who live with God.[94] They are "perfect images of the heavenly Father."[95]

Jesus paints a picture of the new order as a sphere of greater opportunities and enlarged responsibilities. Its life will bring abundant joy and satisfaction. Hence we have the pictures of the wedding feast and the great feast.[96] The disciples will sit at the table of the Son of Man (Luke 22:29-30 [L]), but they will also share the responsibility of the coming Kingdom, for they will sit on the twelve thrones and judge the world. The responsibility of the new life is indicated also in the parable of the Pounds (Matt. 8:11 [M]), where the good servant is given responsibility over ten cities. The Age-to-Come is a continuation of the historical order in a glorified form, freed from its evils, its rebellious sin, and its limitations.

When we turn to the postresurrection testimony of the church, we find a similar belief in personal resurrection, reinforced by the resurrection of the Lord. Paul will have nothing to do with the immortality of the soul. This Greek idea is repugnant. We must not be found naked (2 Cor. 5:1-4), but the personality must be

---

[91] Mark 12:25. Luke 20:34-36 may be from a separate tradition.

[92] Luke 20:36. Luke seems to imply in his version the resurrection of the righteous only; cf. Philippians 3:11. Was this a Pauline touch?

[93] In our Lord's time, contemporary apocalypticism shows a wide variety of speculation about the nature of the resurrection body. Undoubtedly he was familiar with it.

[94] Cf. Willibald Beyschlag, New Testament Theology, Vol. I (New York: Charles Scribner's Sons, 1895), p. 212.

[95] Ibid.

[96] Matthew 22:1-14; Luke 14:15-24.

clothed with a body of glory. This is thoroughly Jewish. For the Jew, the body was an essential constituent of human personality, its outward manifestation. Without a body, existence would be stunted, not exalted. In this world the personality inhabits a tent, and when we die we receive a heavenly tent or habitation. Paul changes the figure and speaks of the body as a kind of robe or wrapping. After death, we are clothed with a body suited to the spiritual order. Death, the last dread enemy, is able to inflict on us the state of being found naked. But the Apostle takes courage in the rememberance that he and his fellows have the earnest of the Spirit. They will be at home with the Lord. Thus, for the believer, the state of nakedness is equivalent to being asleep in Christ. Even before the *parousia* and the resurrection, therefore, Paul can desire to depart and be with Christ (Phil. 1:23).

The nature of the resurrection body is discussed most fully in 1 Corinthians 15. At the *parousia*, the dead will arise with a spiritual body (vs. 44) which bears the marks of the heavenly (vs. 49). Those still alive will have their bodies appropriately transformed (vss. 51-52). The body of flesh will not arise, for flesh and blood cannot inherit the Kingdom of heaven (vs. 50). The outward material substance with its psychical accompaniments is not fitted for the resurrection life. It will be replaced by a glorified substance. Paul does not seem to regard this as immaterial, but rather as stuff that provides a more adequate medium for expressing life in the new order. The adjective "spiritual" defines it as a body that answers to the vital functions of spirit and forms a complete embodiment for redeemed humanity. It does not imply a body composed of spirit, but it does imply something other than the crudely material and fleshly tent of this order.[97] It is a body of glory, fashioned like the resurrection body of the Lord (Phil. 3:21).

There is a continuity of personality. The change has an inner identity, as Paul's analogy of the seed demonstrates. The new body is God's gift, and Paul suggests that the Spirit prepares the inner man for this new dwelling (2 Cor. 4:16 ff.). Even affliction

---

[97] Cf. James Moffatt, *The First Epistle of Paul to the Corinthians* (New York: Harper & Brothers, n.d.), p. 260.

and trouble only serve to prepare the personality for a body heavy with splendor (2 Cor. 3:18). We have died already and been raised with Christ, and the presence of his Spirit is the guarantee of our full resurrection.[98]

But what of the interim period between the death of the individual and the *parousia*? Paul says that even to be unclothed, to be absent from the body, is to be present with the Lord (2 Cor. 5:8). In 1 Thessalonians 4:14 ff. Paul bedecks his view with the typical dressing of the apocalyptic—the trumpet, the shout, the voice of the archangel, the gathering of the elect. Actually this has Old Testament roots and strongly reflects the little apocalypse in Isaiah.[99] The same theme of the awakening trumpet recurs in 1 Corinthians 15:52. Since the resurrection accompanies the *parousia*, Paul and the other New Testament writers hold to an intermediate state in which the temporal tension between the present and the future is not yet resolved. The dead in Christ, those who fall asleep in Jesus, are not yet clothed with the resurrection body, but they *are* in Christ. The fellowship with him and the energizing presence of his Spirit are not impaired by death. The resurrection life of Christ is in them, guaranteeing that they shall rise when he comes. They are still in this interim period in which the ages overlap, enjoying the fruits of Christ's resurrection and awaiting his *parousia*.

As Cullmann puts it: "The connection with Christ, which is established through the Holy Spirit and is already effective even while we are still in our physical body, becomes—not yet complete, to be sure—but nevertheless more intimate as soon as we put off this physical body."[100] So the Father has his abiding places and the Lord is preparing a place for his own (John 14:1-3). The seer sees the martyred souls waiting under the altar, covered by the sacrifice of the Lord, but they are still subject to the tensions of the interim, and they too await the *parousia* (Rev. 6:9-11).

The New Testament hope attests the cosmic nature of this

---

[98] 2 Corinthians 5:5; cf. Romans 8:11.

[99] Isaiah 24-27. Cf. Glasson, *op. cit.*, p. 170.

[100] Cullmann, *Christ and Time*, p. 240.

final consummation. Paul sees nature corrupted, subject to frustration, groaning in pain together, and eagerly waiting for the final unveiling. In the final glory of the Age-to-Come, the created order will be redeemed, delivered from the bondage of corruption into the glorious liberty of the children of God (Rev. 19:1-8). John the seer contemplates a new heaven and a new earth watered by the stream that flows from the throne of God and the Lamb (Rev. 22). But this re-creation and restoration of harmony stretches up to heaven. The discord in heavenly places, which figures in Paul's picture of the demons and in the seer's portrayal of Satan and his hosts, will also be overcome. The universe is presently a scene of conflict and discord stretching from earth to heaven. Nature and man alike are in thrall to the demonic powers. There is confusion in the invisible as well as the visible order, and the original divinely created harmony is broken.[101] Already this rebellion has been dealt with on the cross, so that the rulers of this world are being deprived of their power and are coming to naught (1 Cor. 1:28; 2:6). But the ultimate consummation will see their final defeat. Christ is reigning now, visibly in his church, invisibly in the world. And he shall reign until all the powers are in subjection to him (1 Cor. 15:24-28).

Actually, the church is already disclosing to the angelic rulers and authorities the full sweep of the divine purpose. Through the existence and unifying work of the church, they are learning that their conspiracy to crucify Christ was their defeat and not their triumph (Eph. 3:10 ff.). Already, before the end, the divine redemption of the universe is in process. At the *parousia* the cosmos will once more find its center, and the preordained harmony will be restored once for all. The principalities and powers will be deprived of their authority, and all things will be subjected to God who shall be all in all (1 Cor. 15:28). It is not clear whether Paul envisages the demonic enemies as being destroyed or recon-

---

[101] Cf. E. F. Scott, *The Epistles of Paul to the Colossians, to Philemon and to the Ephesians*, Moffatt Commentary (New York: Harper & Brothers, n.d.), p. 147. Johannes Weiss suggests that behind Paul's thought there is a myth of cosmic apostasy and thus the need of cosmic redemption—*The History of Primitive Christianity*, p. 527.

ciled. In 1 Corinthians 15 he speaks as if they are to be abolished,
but in Colossians and Ephesians they are to be gathered up in
Christ. He declares that it is God's purpose so to order things that
in the fullness of the times he will sum up in Christ all things on
earth and in heaven (Eph. 1:9-10). His apologetic against early
Gnosticism, with its ranks of intermediate semidivine beings, is
to affirm that God willed to reconcile all things to himself in
Christ, including the things in the heavens (Col. 1:20). All these
powers of the air will be gathered up in Christ as the source and
center of all things, the one in whom all God's fullness dwells
(Col. 2:9).

Within this re-created and glorified universe with its restored
harmony, the saints will reign in glorified resurrection bodies.
Indeed, insofar as the Christ is taking visible form in his church
(Gal. 4:19), they already rule with him invisibly (1 Cor. 4:8),
and, at the *parousia,* they shall share in the judgment, judging the
world and the angels (1 Cor. 6:2-3). In the glorified community
the fruits of history will be gathered up. The "full number of the
Gentiles" will be gathered in, and "all Israel" will be saved. The
first phrase would seem to indicate "those who are elected," and
the "all" must be understood in a corporate rather than a numeri-
cal sense. This is in keeping with the rest of the New Testament,
and would seem to indicate that Paul was no universalist, although there remains the tantalizing statement of Romans 11:32
that God has shut up all in disobedience so that he may have
mercy on all.

In the New Testament, the Apocalypse alone borrows the
image of a millennium from contemporary apocalypticism. Some
would find the idea in 1 Corinthians 15, but such exegesis is
highly disputable.[102] However, its presence in the Apocalypse is
beyond dispute. The seer places a messianic Kingdom on earth
between the *parousia* and the end (Rev. 20:2 ff.). In it the elect
shall sit on thrones and share in the rule of Christ himself. Because the last judgment follows this millennial reign of Christ,
this does not mean participation in the final judgment, but only

---

[102] *Vide* Beyschlag, *New Testament Theology,* Vol. II, pp. 260 ff.

in the exercise of Christ's kingly power. For this period, only the faithful dead are raised, and the general resurrection will follow it.[103]

The resurrection of the faithful is, however, to immortal existence. Death persists for the inhabitants of the earth, but it has no power over them. Thus the millennial kingdom, even though it is taking place on this earth, has a supernatural quality about it. It is in history, it is pictured in historical imagery; yet it has a suprahistorical quality—it is life in the Age-to-Come. The Apocalypse echoes the Pauline theme of the destruction of the demonic powers at the end of the millennium. The final judgment supervenes, ushering the redeemed into the glorious life of the new Age in a re-created cosmos. This image of the millennium is an attempt to declare that, in some sense, the reign of Christ that began at the resurrection and exaltation will be consummated in history. When he appears, his reign will become fully manifest and be consummated. In one sense, the millennium is on us now. We have already been raised with Christ and can sit with him in heavenly places. But we cannot leave it there. In some sense, the consummation must keep the meaningfulness of history.

The *parousia*, whatever its poetic symbolism may mean, must imply a consummation that is both within and beyond history. There is no pessimism about history, no tendency to defeatism in the Christian hope. It is bound up with the final manifestation in history of the One who has become incarnated in history and redeemed it. We do not here abandon hope in this world by taking refuge in another.[104]

There must be a final consummation, otherwise the Kingdom of God becomes an empty dream. Cullmann has used the vivid picture of D-day and V-day. There has to be a V-day in which the consummation is accomplished, because there is D-day, a

---

[103] Revelation 20:6. Probably only the martyrs are meant here, as many commentators suggest.

[104] Cf. Fison, *op. cit.*, p. 148. He describes the millennium as "an attempt to safeguard the double element of both *telos* and *finis*, which is essential to any truly Christian eschatology" and as "a valuable corrective to merely individualistic and other worldly interpretations of the Christian hope."

decisive day, in which the final outcome of the conflict is assured. Jesus was very much of a realist, world-affirming and not world-denying. He did not advocate mystic flight from this visible order but rather wrought his redemption in it. His resurrection, and its precursory sign of the transfiguration, are indications that he was concerned with the redemption of this world. His healing miracles show that, for him, redemption was of the body as well as the spirit, the outer as well as the inner, of personality in its psychosomatic totality. The incarnation meant that God was actualizing his purpose in flesh and blood and lifting up history into his own life. Christ's redemption involves the cosmos and man's historical existence in its totality. History must be consummated in its totality. It is not just a case of pilgrim souls traversing its course to their home in the spiritual order. Nature and history in their totality have a part in God's purpose that centers in the incarnate and risen Lord. The redeemed community will be consummated in a redeemed universe.

This consummation is the *parousia,* the final encounter of history and its cosmic setting with the One who is the midpoint of history. Such an encounter is a purging and a judgment. But it is also resurrection and re-creation: resurrection and re-creation that is concerned not with individuals but with humanity as a corporate whole, with the gathering up of the fruits of historical and social life; resurrection and re-creation that is cosmic in its sweep; resurrection and re-creation that provides for a more perfect continuance of that fellowship and encounter of persons with one another and with God which shall consummate the purpose of history.

INDEX OF AUTHORS

Abbott, 217
Albright, W. F., 128
Allmen, J.-J. Von, 224, 225, 239, 257
Alt, A., 260
Althaus, P., 86, 87
Anderson, H., 72
Apuleius, 140
Aristotle, 138, 233
Aulén, G., 214
Aurelius, M., 137, 138

Barrett, C. K., 179, 182, 206, 301
Barth, K., 39, 82, 180, 269, 270, 271
Bartsch, H. W., 40, 71
Beasley-Murray, G. R., 281, 282, 283, 284, 290, 293
Bell, G. K. A., 151
Bentzen, A., 37, 129
Bernard, J. H., 217
Best, E. H., 255
Beyschlag, W., 306, 310
Biber, Ch., 224, 225
Bornkamm, G., 72, 73, 84, 158, 280, 286
Bousset, W., 179
Bowman, A. A., 242, 243
Bowman, J. W., 279, 280, 283, 289
Bright, J., 97, 98, 101, 109
Brunner, E., 80
Bultmann, R., 38, 39, 40, 41, 42, 45, 46, 54, 70, 71, 72, 76, 84, 87, 149, 150, 152, 153, 154, 158, 162, 164, 169, 185, 186, 197, 198, 200
Burney, C. F., 97, 217
Busch, F., 290

Cadoux, C. J., 188, 200
Campbell, J. Y., 158, 163
Cassirer, E., 33
Chrysostom, 289
Collingwood, R. G., 58
Conzelmann, H., 222, 223, 265, 266

Croce, B., 15
Cullmann, O., 55, 166, 175, 179, 180, 181, 182, 195, 197, 227, 231, 235, 241, 243, 244, 258, 263, 264, 265, 266, 267, 268, 271, 273, 275, 285, 290, 291, 294, 299, 305, 308, 311
Curtis, W. A., 163

Daube, D., 206, 301
Davey, F. N., 147
Davies, J. G., 223, 224, 226
Davies, W. D., 206, 301
Dehn, G., 268
Deissmann, A., 151
Denney, J., 211
Dibelius, M., 52, 268, 298
Diem, H., 72
Dodd, C. H., 142, 157, 158, 159, 175, 190, 191, 192, 209, 211, 212, 263, 282, 291, 292
Doresse, J., 178
Duncan, G. S., 163, 284

Eissfeldt, A., 61
Engnell, I., 36, 98, 118

Farrer, A. M., 42, 43, 44, 155, 303
Feuerbach, 57
Fison, J. E., 295, 302, 303, 311
Frame, J. E., 298
Fuchs, E., 72
Fuller, R. H., 55, 158, 160, 164, 167, 169, 200, 201, 202, 203, 204

Galling, K., 93
Glasson, T. F., 284, 285, 287, 296, 308
Grant, R. M., 178
Grether, O., 63
Gunkel, H., 113

Haldar, A., 60

Hanson, A. T., 190, 304, 305
Harnack, A. von, 68, 69, 70, 169
Harris, J. R., 174
Headlam, A. C., 208
Hebert, A. G., 252
Hegel, 15
Heidegger, M., 70, 71
Heim, K., 39, 83, 222, 245, 249
Hempel, J., 114
Héring, J., 180, 181
Herodotus, 14
Heschel, A., 64
Higgins, A. J. B., 203
Hodgson, L., 211
Holland, B., 292
Hooke, S. H., 36, 98
Hoskyns, E., 147, 151, 175, 177
Hoyle, F., 34
Hügel, F. von, 292
Hunter, A. M., 55

Irenaeus, 214

Jacob, E., 115, 120, 123, 129
Jepsen, 62, 63, 64
Jeremias, J., 55, 203, 204, 211, 241,
    259, 260, 261, 262, 263, 264,
    282, 284, 287, 288, 289, 291
Johnson, A. R., 36, 37, 61, 98, 110,
    118, 123, 259
Jones, G. V., 47

Käsemann, E., 72
Kiddle, M., 303
Kittel, G., 157, 241, 252
Kierkegaard, S., 89
Klausner, J., 77
Kleinknecht, H., 157, 241
Köhler, L., 97, 98, 100, 107, 109,
    115
Kuhn, K. G., 157, 241
Kümmel, W. G., 55, 158, 159, 160,
    161, 165, 262, 280, 281, 282,
    287, 291,

Lake, K., 77, 80
Leivestad, R., 212, 214, 217, 218,
    298, 302, 303

Lietzmann, H., 140, 141
Lindblom, J., 62, 63
Lods, A., 61
Lohmeyer, E., 180
Luther, M., 106

McIntyre, J., 154
Manson, T. W., 55, 56, 128, 157,
    161, 165, 188, 202, 267, 280,
    281, 282, 284, 287, 288, 292,
    295
Manson, W., 169
Marsh, J., 151, 152, 231, 237
Marx, K., 15, 57
Messel, 128
Michaelis, W., 290
Minear, P., 286
Moffatt, J., 307
Moore, G. F., 130
Morgenstern, J., 112
Morrison, C. D., 268, 269, 270, 275,
    276
Mowinckel, S., 27, 36, 37, 62, 63,
    64, 98, 110, 112, 114, 118, 129,
    164, 165, 166, 167
Munck, J., 264, 265, 266
Murray, G., 140

Niebuhr, Reinhold, 40, 41, 43, 44
Niebuhr, R. R., 81, 82
North, C. R., 121
Noth, M., 61, 97, 101

Ogden, S., 72
Oman, J., 303
Origen, 270
Otto, R., 125, 159, 163, 279

Pedersen, J., 233
Philo, 149, 175, 179, 180
Phythian-Adams, W. J. T. P., 261
Plato, 136, 138, 233, 301
Pliny the Elder, 139
Porphyry, 270
Preiss, T., 287
Pritchard, J. B., 60

Quick, O. C., 78

Rad, G. von, 15, 16, 52, 157, 241
Ramsey, A. M., 79, 80, 223, 228
Ramseyer, J.-Ph., 257
Rashdall, H., 201
Reid, J. K. S., 156
Reitzenstein, R., 179
Richardson, A., 83, 163, 194, 219, 220, 223, 237, 246, 255
Robinson, H. W., 62, 93, 114, 231, 233
Robinson, J. A. T., 254, 255, 284, 295, 296
Robinson, J. M., 53, 72
Robinson, T. H., 62
Rowley, H. H., 61, 64, 93, 95, 96, 97, 119, 121, 128, 155, 156
Rust, E., 37, 59, 86, 115, 165, 231

Sanday, W., 208
Schmidt, K. L., 157, 241, 252, 282
Schniewind, J., 282, 290, 291
Schweitzer, A., 53, 69, 70, 157, 278, 280, 291
Schweizer, E., 37, 164, 166
Scott, C. A. A., 214, 215, 217
Scott, E. F., 52, 192, 193, 303, 309
Seneca, 138
Skinner, J., 64
Socrates, 51
Spengler, 15
Stauffer, E., 82, 166, 221, 228
Strachan, R. H., 267
Streeter, B. H., 80
Swete, H. B., 289

Tasker, R. V. G., 211
Tarn, W. W., 138
Taylor, V., 52, 55, 165, 172, 201, 202, 203, 211, 217, 289, 291
Thielicke, H., 71
Thornton, L. S., 155, 253, 254
Thucydides, 14
Tillich, P., 31, 43, 88
Toynbee, A., 15
Trocmé, E., 239

Unnik, W. C. van, 178
Urban, W. M., 33

Valla, L., 52
Vico, 58
Virgil, 140
Vischer, W., 155, 224
Voltaire, 36
Vriezen, Th. C., 111, 113, 114, 115, 124

Weiss, J., 69, 184, 295, 309
Welch, A. C., 16
Wellhausen, J., 68, 202
Werner, M., 278, 288
Windisch, H., 301
Wingren, G., 214
Wolf, E., 268
Wrede, W., 68
Wright, G. E., 15, 118, 119

Zeno, 138
Zimmerli, W., 211

INDEX OF PASSAGES CITED

I. OLD TESTAMENT REFERENCES

GENESIS
1 ......25, 28, 37, 41, 59, 174
1:26 181
1:27 179
2 ......29, 37, 120
2:7 179
3 ....29, 199
9:8-17 31
12:2 99
18:18 99
21:33 233
26:4 99
28:14 99

EXODUS
4:10 122
4:22-23 168
6:6 122
6:7 96
9:1 102
12 212
14:21 50
14:31 122
15:13 121
15:15 94
15:16 94
19:4-6 251
24:1-8 212
24:8 ....122, 203
25:17 209
29:18 212
29:25 212
32:11 122
34:5 285

LEVITICUS
1:9 212
1:13 212
15:20 ff. 212

NUMBERS
11:11 122
12:7 122
21:29 94
23:7-10 99
23:18-24 99
24:3-9 99
24:9 99

DEUTERONOMY
3:24 122
4:1 100
4:9 100
4:10 122
4:15 100
4:20 104
5:23 100
6:2 100
7:6-7 94
7:7-8 93
7:12 122
9:4-5 93
9:10 249
9:18-20 122
10:15 93
14:1 ......94, 250
26:5-9 15
27:26 216
30:4 284
32:6 94
32:8 267
33:13-17 99
33:25-29 99
34:5 122

JOSHUA
24 ....97, 105
24:17-18 15

JUDGES
9:3 113

1 SAMUEL
9:9 61
10:5 61
10:10 61
19:18 61

2 SAMUEL
7:12 117

1 KINGS
8:27 224
18:25-29 60
19:8 101
22:1-28 61

2 KINGS
2:3 61
2:5 61
4:38 61

PSALMS
2:7 ......162, 168
11 131
18:11 285
22 131
42 131
43 131
74:2 94
89:39 123
90:2 233
98:2 205
102:26 ff. 233
103:17 234
104:3 234
106:47 284
110 226
110:1-2 226
110:4 226
145:13 234
147:15-18 25

PROVERBS
8 173

ISAIAH
1:2 100
1:2-3 115
1:25 ff. 115
2:2-4 ....116, 121
3:14 251
4:5 121
5:1-7 251
6 118
6:3 109
8:12-16 131
8:16 ff. 116
9:3 113
9:6 119
9:7 119
10:26 113
11:1 ff. 119
11:6 ff. 113
11:6-9 120
11:9 .....113, 121
11:11 284
14:1 94
14:32 116
19:1 285
24-27 ....124, 308
26:4 234
26:6-7 261
27:1 113
27:12 284
28:16 116
30:19-26 120
32:15 120
35 120
40-55 52
40:4 251
40:8 234
40:11 121
41:18-20 120
42:1 162
42:1-4 121
42:6 .....203, 261
43:10 94
43:25 100
43:27 100
44:22 100
49:1 ff. 123

49:1-6 121
49:6 .122, 123, 261
49:12 261
50:1 100
50:4-9 121
51:9 113
51:9-10 121
51:9-11 154
51:11 120
52:12 121
52:13 123
52:13—53:12 .121
52:15 261
53 ......122, 144
53:3 201
53:5 100
53:7 211
53:8 100
53:10 ....201, 211
53:11 201
53:11-12 183
53:12 123
55:10-11 25
56:1 205
56:7 261
57:15 233
61:1 162
63:1 305
63:3 194
63:10 106
65:17 127
65:20 ....120, 232
66:22 127

JEREMIAH
2:21 251
2:29 100
7 116
12:10 251
14:14 65
21:8 65
23:5-6 119
23:13 ff. 65
23:17 65
23:18 65
23:21 65
23:22 .....64, 65
23:30 64
23:32 65

24:4 ff. 117
26 116
29:21 ff. 65
31:31-34 .117, 203
31:33 ....110, 111
42:10-22 117
48:7 94

EZEKIEL
1 285
11:19 117
11:23 116
15:1-6 251
16:8 93
19:10-14 251
28:13 120
31:3 120
34:1-19 251
34:23 251
36:27 117
36:28 111
37:27 116
38-39 297
39:27 284
43:2 116
45:35 116
47:1-12 ..116, 120

DANIEL
7:9 233
7:13 .233, 261, 284
7:21 128
7:21-27 297
7:22 233
7:27 128
9:27 282
10:13 267
10:20-21 267
11:36 297
12:1 267

HOSEA
1:10 250
2 120
2:23 251
5:3 94
5:14 304
5:15 107

6:2 202
8:1-2 100
11:1 ....101, 168
11:8-9 108
14:1 108
14:4 108

JOEL
2:28 ff. 117
3 125
3:20 232

AMOS
1 121
2 121
2:4 100
2:6 100
3:1-2 100
3:2 ....94, 95
3:12 115
4:4 ....**100**

5:3 115
5:12 100
5:18 109
5:20 109
9:3 113
9:11 119

MICAH
3:5 65
3:11 65
3:12 116
4:1-3 ...116, 121
5:2-4 119
5:4 251

HABAKKUK
3:2 107
3:6 233

ZEPHANIAH
3:9 121

HAGGAI
2:23 119

ZECHARIAH
2:6 284
3:8 119
6:12 119
8:4 120
8:21 117
9:9-10 119
9:14 124
13:7 250
14 125
14:2 ff. 297
14:7 232
14:8-9 116
14:16-17 117

MALACHI
1:2 124
1:14 109
3:16 131
4:1-3 131

II. NEW TESTAMENT REFERENCES

MATTHEW
5:3 287
5:21 ff. 187
5:22-23 287
6:2 ff. 190
7:3 ff. 287
7:17 ff. 183
8:5-13 260
8:11 306
8:11-12 261
8:20 ....**165**
8:29 236
10:5-6 259
10:7-11 158
10:15 260
10:16 250
10:23 ...164, 165,
                290, 291

10:32-33 285
10:40 ff. 259
11:2-3 160
11:19 ...165, 182
11:27 168
12:32 238
13:16-17 159
13:37 164
13:41 164
15:24 260
18:35 287
19:28 164
20:1-16 183
22:1-14 306
23:8 287
23:15 259
23:39 282
24 ......295, 296

24:3 286
24:14 ...262, 263
24:27 286
24:37 286
24:39 ...164, 286
24:43-44 280
24:44 165
25 178
25:1-2 280
25:31 ...164, 165
25:31-32 261
25:31 ff. .188, 260
25:31-46 187
25:32 288
25:40 287
25:40 ff. 188
25:45 287
26:18 236

26:45 236
28:2-15 78
28:13-15 77
28:16 ff. 81
28:18 ff. 227
28:19 77
28:20 256

MARK
1:10-11 162
1:15 158
2:10 .....164, 165
2:17 182
2:28 .....164, 165
3:33-34 287
6:7-13 259
6:30 259
7:2 ff. 183
7:20-23 183
7:24 260
7:24 ff. 260
7:31 260
8:31 .162, 164, 202
8:38 ....164, 165,
      167, 187, 284,
      285, 286, 287
9:1 ......158, 200,
      289, 290
9:9 164
9:31 .....162, 164
9:42 190
9:43-48 187
10:33 164
10:34 162
10:45 .....164, 201
11:15 ff. 190
11:17 261
12:1 ff. 291
12:1-9 168
12:10 261
12:25 306
12:27 306
13 ......188, 277,
      280, 281, 283,
      284, 295, 296
13:2 188
13:3 281
13:6 283
13:7 .....281, 283

13:8 281
13:10 ....259, 262,
      263, 264, 282
13:12 281
13:14 188
13:14-20 281
13:17-18 188
13:21 283
13:22 ....283, 297
13:24-27 .281, 283,
      284
13:26 ....164, 284
13:27 285
13:30 290
13:32 ....168, 280
13:32-33 283
13:33 242
13:33-37 286
13:35 280
14:9 .259, 262, 263
14:21 164
14:24 202
14:25 204
14:27-28 250
14:36 204
14:41 164
14:57-58 188
14:58 261
14:62 ....164, 227,
      284, 291
16:9-20 222
16:19 222

LUKE
5:32 182
6:40 291
7:18-20 160
7:20-22 194
7:34 164
7:34 ff. 182
9:1 ff. 259
9:55 260
9:58 164
10:9 .....158, 259
10:12 260
10:12-15 288
10:14 260

10:16 259
10:22 ff. 168
10:23-24 159
10:25-37 260
11:20 159
11:30 164
11:31-32 .260, 288
11:31 ff. 187
11:38 183
11:42 ff. 190
12:8 .....187, 287
12:10 164
12:32 250
12:39 286
12:40 164
13:1-5 ...260, 281
13:28 261
13:28-29 288
13:32-33 202
13:34-35 189
14:15-24 .288, 306
14:16-24 183
15:11-32 183
17:20-21 280
17:21 160
17:22 164
17:22-37 286
17:23-30 .187, 286,
      287
17:24 ....164, 165
17:26 ....164, 286
17:30 164
17:31-32 188
17:34 ff. 188
18:8 164
18:9-14 183
19:10 164
19:41-44 282
20:34-36 306
20:36 306
21:20 ff. 188
22:15-18 203
22:18 204
22:24 ff. 201
22:29-30 306
22:69 285
23:28 ff. 282
24:13-52 222
24:26 217

24:30 ff. 81
24:37 83
24:50-51 222
24:51 222

JOHN
1:1-14 227
1:9 176
1:9-10 176
1:11-13 176
1:14 .....173, 176
1:18 .....173, 176
1:29 211
1:36 211
2:14-16 190
3:5-8 247
3:13 179
3:13-15 178
3:14 217
3:16 .....173, 178
3:18 .....173, 178
3:18-19 191
3:18-20 191
3:29 145
3:34 174
3:36 191
5:19 ff. 174
5:19-23 173
5:21-29 178
5:24 178
5:26 173
5:28-29 ..147, 190,
               215
6:15 161
6:27 179
6:39-40 247
6:44 247
6:47 247
6:54 247
6:62 179
6:63 ......26, 247
7:6 236
7:8 236
7:17 23
7:39 225
7:56 164
8:28 .178, 207, 217
8:31 26

8:34 195
8:45 174
8:47 174
8:58 ....173, 174
9:39 191
10:11 ff. 251
10:16 251
10:30 173
11:50 207
12:23 236
12:28 ff. 178
12:31 ....191, 199,
                215
12:31-32 218
12:32 207
12:32-33 217
12:34 207
12:44-45 173
12:47 178
12:48 ....147, 192
13:1 236
13:2 217
14:1-3 308
14:6 174
14:9 178
14:9 ff. 173
14:14 248
14:16-17 248
14:20 246
14:23 246
14:26 ....246, 247,
                256
14:30 ....199, 215
15:1-5 251
15:1-9 179
15:1-10 246
15:24 174
15:26 ....246, 247
16:11 ....199, 215
16:13 ....246, 247,
                256
16:28 226
17 213
17:1 236
17:15 199
17:17 174
17:17-19 213
17:23-24 246
18:36 301

20:17 .....83, 225
20:19 ff. 225
20:20 ff. 81
20:22-23 267
20:27 83
21:12 ff. 81

ACTS
1:7 242
1:9-11 222
2 247
2:1-3 222
2:14-36 143
2:16-17 238
2:16-21 144
2:17 237
2:24 .....220, 221
2:32 220
2:32-33 225
2:33 144
2:34 226
2:36 .....143, 172
2:38 144
2:44-47 248
3:12-26 143
3:13 143
3:19 144
3:20 143
3:21 144
3:24-25 144
3:26 .....143, 144
4:8-12 143
4:25 ff. 272
4:26 143
4:27 143
4:30 143
5:29 274
5:31 226
7:55 226
7:56 164
10:13 273
10:34-43 143
10:36 172
10:38 162
10:42 144
13:16-41 143
13:47 143
14:16-17 30
17:22-34 30

20:30 297
24:25 235

ROMANS
1 ....31, 106
1:2-5 142
1:3 ......143, 172
1:4 ......159, 172,
            221, 246
1:7 253
1:16 ff. 205
1:18 .....190, 192
1:18 ff. 176
1:18-21 30
1:18-32 191
1:21-22 191
1:21 ff. ...32, 140
1:24 .....190, 198
1:26 190
1:32 198
2:5 189
2:6 ......189, 191
2:8-9 191
2:14-15 30
2:16 .....189, 300
3:6 189
3:9-18 191
3:10 184
3:19 189
3:20 196
3:21-26 ..209, 210
3:23 184
4:22-25 221
4:24-25 142
4:25 .....144, 220,
            244
5:1 205
5:10-11 206
5:12 .....184, 195,
            198
5:12 ff. 197
5:12-21 ..228, 245,
            257, 361
5:13-19 210
5:17 258
5:18 210
5:19 210
5:19 ff. 184
5:21 195

6 246
6:4 220
6:9 220
6:10 216
6:13-14 186
6:20 195
6:21 .....198, 240
6:23 .....191, 198
7:5 198
7:5-9 196
7:9-11 198
7:12 196
7:13 196
7:14 .....195, 246
7:19 184
7:21-23 186
7:24 198
7:25 246
8 274
8:1 192
8:3 ......177, 208,
            215
8:4 185
8:7 185
8:9 256
8:11 308
8:12-17 248
8:14 .....145, 256
8:15 248
8:16 256
8:17-23 222
8:18-39 299
8:19-23 191
8:23 246
8:26-27 256
8:31-34 142
8:32 208
8:33-34 228
8:34 ....225, 226,
            227, 228
9-11 .....250, 264
10 264
10:8-9 142
10:12 172
10:14 264
11 264
11:13 264
11:15 282
11:25-26 282

11:32 310
12 253
12:5 253
13:1 269
13:1 ff. ..269, 270,
            275
13:1-7 271
13:4 185
13:4-5 191
13:7 273
13:8-11 237
13:11-14 299
14:10 189
16:4 252
16:20 199
16:23 252

1 CORINTHIANS
1:2 252
1:18 257
1:20 17
1:23 143
1:24 173
1:28 309
2:1 21
2:1-9 22
2:2-6 143
2:4 ......22, 256,
            257
2:5 22
2:6 ......214, 309
2:6-7 216
2:8 ......195, 199,
            268, 272
2:10 22
3:10 143
3:13-15 300
3:15 189
3:16-17 248
3:21 258
4:5 ......189, 300
4:8 ......227, 310
4:9 189
5:5 189
5:7 211
6:1 ff. ...268, 275
6:2-3 ....257, 310
6:3 267
6:9-10 241

6:20 214
7:17 252
7:23 214
7:29 299
9:16 264
9:27 189
10:1-4 252
10:1-5 145
10:1-13 155
10:4 .....155, 173
10:11 146
10:32 252
11:23-25 202
11:29 192
11:30 191
12:4-11 253
14:23 252
14:33 252
15 .....76, 77, 80,
       226, 307, 310
15:3 144
15:3 ff. 142
15:4 ....76, 77
15:6 77
15:12 143
15:12-19 221
15:15 220
15:17 221
15:20 238
15:21 245
15:21-22 .184, 197
15:23 238
15:23-24 241
15:24-25 273
15:24 ff. ..227, 301
15:24 ff. 227, 301
15:24-28 309
15:25 226
15:26 ...198, 220
15:28 309
15:42 ff. 221
15:44 307
15:45 ...220, 245
15:45 ff. 180
15:49 307
15:50 307
15:51-52 .299, 307
15:52 308
15:56 195

16:1 253

2 CORINTHIANS
1:1 252
1:17 185
3:6 256
3:13-16 145
3:14-18 256
3:18 .....246, 308
4:4 ......173, 180,
              199
4:5 172
4:5-6 220
4:12 299
4:16 ff. 307
5:1-4 306
5:5 308
5:8 308
5:10 ....189, 191,
              300
5:14 213
5:16 185
5:17 .....220, 247
5:18 205
5:20 264
5:21 192
6:2 237
8:18 252
9:1 253
9:12 253
10:2-3 185
10:3 185
10:5 210
11:2 145
11:3 199
11:28 252
13:4 221
13:14 256

GALATIANS
1:3-4 142
1:4 .....208, 238
2:20 185
3:7-16 250
3:9 250
3:10 216
3:13 ....214, 216
3:22 195
3:28 247

4:4 ......135, 177,
              215
4:4-5 216
4:5 .....145, 216
4:6 .....248, 250
4:6-7 248
4:7 248
4:19 310
4:23 185
5:16 185
5:16-23 185
5:18 256
5:19 185
5:21 241
5:22 256
5:24 185
5:26 256
6:15 247
6:16 145

EPHESIANS
1:4-5 244
1:5 241
1:9-10 ....22, 310
1:10 173
1:20 ....225, 226
1:20 ff. 227
1:21 ....238, 269
2:2 ......199, 238
2:3 191
2:5 300
2:5-6 274
2:6 ......227, 239
2:11-16 247
2:14 257
2:22 248
3:1 264
3:4 244
3:10 .....267, 269
3:10 ff. 309
3:16 246
4:3 256
4:3-4 248
4:9-10 225
4:15-16 254
4:22-24 246
5:2 212
5:5 241
5:6 237

5:22-33 145
5:23 253
6:12 269

PHILIPPIANS
1:1 253
1:22 185
1:23 307
2:1 248
2:1-2 256
2:5-11 ...145, 167,
          180
2:7 216
2:7-8 177
2:8 210
2:9 ......225, 226
2:9 ff. 224
2:9-11 173
2:10 273
3:3 ......145, 250
3:9-11 220
3:11 306
3:20-21 299
3:21 307

COLOSSIANS
1:1-17 173
1:2 ......252, 253
1:13 241
1:15 ....173, 180
1:15-20 ..145, 173
1:16 ....269, 271
1:16 ff. 273
1:16-20 227
1:20 ....210, 310
1:22-29 264
1:26 252
1:26-27 ...22, 253
1:27 ....240, 299
2:9 ......172, 310
2:10 ....269, 271,
          274
2:12-13 300
2:15 ....214, 216,
          269, 273
2:10 254
2:20 274
3:1 ......226, 227,
          257

3:1-3 274
3:4 299
3:10-11 247
3:18—4:1 300
3:25 189
4:5 237

1 THESSALONIANS
1:9-10 142
1:10 ....144, 192
4:1—5:11 296
4:14 ff. 308
4:17 180
5:2 242
5:9 192

2 THESSALONIANS
1:5 241
1:6—2:10 297
1:9 300
2:3 297
2:6-7 266
3:3 199

1 TIMOTHY
2:1 ff. 273
3:16 225

2 TIMOTHY
1:7 256
2:9 257
2:11-12 258
3:1 237

TITUS
2:12 239
2:14 251
3:1 269

HEBREWS
1:1 ......174, 206
1:2-3 227
1:2 ff. 145
1:3 ......226, 227
2:8-9 227
2:10 145
2:13 145

3:1 207
3:7 ff. 237
3:14-15 206
4:14-16 228
4:15 215
4:16 207
6:4-5 207
6:5 238
6:20 ....207, 227
7:23 206
7:24-28 207
7:25-26 228
8:1 ......207, 226
8:2 206
8:2 ff. 207
8:5 206
9:5 209
9:6-8 206
9:11 ....207, 301
9:11-12 206
9:13-14 210
9:14 211
9:15 145
9:22 210
9:24 207
10:5-10 210
10:10 211
10:12 226
10:12-13 227
10:20 207
10:25 301
11 251
12:22 251
12:24 145
12:26 ff. 301
13:20 220

JAMES
2:14-26 189

1 PETER
1:2 212
1:3 220
1:11 236
1:14-15 244
1:18-19 212
1:18-21 220
1:21 220

2:6-7 145
2:8 257
2:9 ......220, 227
2:9-10 ...145, 257
2:9 ff. 251
2:10 251
2:17 273
2:21-24 ..144, 212
2:25 145
3:18 246
3:21-22 225
3:22 ....145, 226,
      227, 269, 273
4:14 246
4:17 238

1 JOHN
1:1 24
1:1 ff. 145
1:7 209
1:8 184
1:10 184
2:13 199
2:22 298
3:8 ......199, 218
3:16 212
4:2-3 298

4:10 .....208, 209,
            212
4:14 208
4:17 192
5:7 246
5:19 199

REVELATION
1:5 ......212, 218
1:6 .....227, 251,
            258
1:9 257
1:18 218
1:19 256
2:10 258
3:21 .....226, 227,
            258
5 193
5:5 216
5:5 ff. 219, 304
5:6 226
5:9 212
5:9 ff. 219
5:10 .227, 251, 258
6:1-11 305
6:8 ......199, 218
6:9-11 308

6:15-17 304
6:16 193
8:1 303
10:6-7 303
11:15 241
11:15 ff. 303
12 218
12:5 193
14:6-7 305
14:14 227
14:14 ff. 193
14:19-20 193
18:8 244
19:1-8 309
19:11 ff. 193
19:13 193
19:13 ff. ..304, 305
19:15 193
20:2 ff. 310
20:6 ....251, 311
20:14 ....199, 218
21:1 222
21:2 145
21:9 145
22 309
22:16 216
22:17 145

III. REFERENCES TO THE
APOCRYPHA AND PSEUDEPIGRAPHA

2 ESDRAS
5:6 297
13 129

THE WISDOM OF
SOLOMON
7:22-30 173
9:9 ff. 173

ECCLESIASTICUS
24 173

ASCENSION OF
ISAIAH
2 297
4:2-4 297

1 ENOCH
37-70 128
49:4 129
61:8 129
62:2 ff. 129
62:13-14 129
63:1-4 129
63:11 129
89:59-60 267

THE TESTAMENTS
OF THE TWELVE
PATRIARCHS
Judah
  25 297

THE SIBYLLINE
ORACLES
3:63-74 297

THE SYRIAC APOC-
ALYPSE OF
BARUCH
39 297

IV. REFERENCES TO RABBINICAL LITERATURE

THE BABYLONIAN
TALMUD
　Sanhedrin
　　f. 43a 51
　　97b 299

THE MISHNAH
　Berakoth
　　V, 5 259
　Pirke Aboth
　　6:10 176